DOING
ANTI-OPPRESSIVE
PRACTICE

DOING
ANTI-OPPRESSIVE
PRACTICE

SOCIAL JUSTICE SOCIAL WORK

2nd Edition

edited by DONNA BAINES

Fernwood Publishing • Halifax & Winnipeg

*To all those fighting injustice and inequity in its many forms
and on its many fronts, large and small.*

Editing: Judith Kearns & Brian Turner
Text design: Brenda Conroy
Cover design: John van der Woude
Printed and bound in Canada by Hignell Book Printing

Published in Canada by Fernwood Publishing
32 Oceanvista Lane
Black Point, Nova Scotia, B0J 1B0
and 748 Broadway Avenue, Winnipeg, Manitoba, R3G 0X3
www.fernwoodpublishing.ca

Fernwood Publishing Company Limited gratefully acknowledges the financial support of the
Government of Canada through the Canada Book Fund, the Canada Council for the Arts, the
Nova Scotia Department of Tourism and Culture and the Province of Manitoba, through the Book
Publishing Tax Credit, for our publishing program.

Library and Archives Canada Cataloguing in Publication

Doing anti-oppressive practice: social justice social work /
edited by Donna Baines. — 2nd ed.

Includes bibliographical references and index.
ISBN 978-1-55266-428-5 (bound).—ISBN 978-1-55266-410-0 (pbk.)

1. Social service. 2. Social service—Political aspects. 3. Social justice.
I. Baines, Donna, 1960-

HV40.D64 2011   361.3   C2010-908035-1

Contents

Section Three: Resistance 249

About the Authors

DONNA BAINES Donna Baines is a professor of labour studies and social work at McMaster University. Her research focuses on restructuring social services work; paid and unpaid care work; race, class, and gender in everyday social services work; and anti-oppressive/social justice-oriented social work practice. Baines is currently leading a four-country comparative study of restructured work in the non-profit social services.

LISA BARNOFF teaches social work at Ryerson University. Her most recent research focuses on the implementation of anti-oppression practices in social work agencies and on processes of anti-oppression organizational change.

MICHELLE BATES is a practising school social worker at Hamilton-Wentworth School district, gathering practice-based evidence and exercising her perennial curiosity in "what works." She is keen to explore the tensions around evidence-based practice and does so in her practice, research, and teaching activities.

AKUA BENJAMIN teaches and is Director of the School of Social Work at Ryerson University. Her research and community work focus on anti-oppression, anti-racism, feminism, immigrant issues, criminal justice, and the intersectionality of race, class, gender, and other social locations. Akua is also involved in international community development in Trinidad, W.I.

CATRINA BROWN teaches social work and is cross-appointed to gender and women's studies at Dalhousie University. Her work focuses on women's health and mental health issues, including eating "disorders," substance use problems, and depression trauma and post-trauma, within a feminist post-modern/anti-oppressive lens.

LORI CHAMBERS, M.S.W., has been involved in a number of community-based research projects, including the Research Action Alliance on the Consequence of Work Injury (RAACWI), the Health and Housing research project at Fife House Organization, and the Families, HIV and Housing research project at McMaster University. She is currently working as a Research Coordinator at the Ontario HIV Treatment Network, an organization that supports community-based initiatives in HIV-related research.

GARY DUMBRILL is Associate Professor at McMaster University School of Social Work. Gary previously worked as a child protection worker in Canada and the U.K. Gary's research examines anti-oppressive practice, child welfare service users' perspectives, and ways to work in partnership with parents receiving child protection intervention.

JEANNE FAY has been a welfare rights advocate and activist in both Canada and the U.S. She served as a community legal worker at Dalhousie Legal Aid Service in Halifax, becoming an expert in poverty law and representing hundreds of people on social assistance. She taught community practice and social policy at the Dalhousie School of Social Work. Now semi-retired, she continues her work for social justice and equality as the coordinator of Women's Centres Connect, the Nova Scotia Association of Women's Centres.

BONNIE FREEMAN is Algonquin/Mohawk from the Six Nations of the Grand River Territory. She is a Ph.D. candidate in Social Work at Wilfrid Laurier University and on faculty at McMaster University in the School of Social Work under an Aboriginal

Pre-Doctoral Fellowship. Her doctoral work focuses on the cultural-based activism of Aboriginal youth for justice for Aboriginal people. Bonnie is also interested in the areas of self-determination in Aboriginal communities and public policy development; traditional Aboriginal cultural interventions in social work practice; Aboriginal collective and community healing approaches; Aboriginal perspectives on anti-oppressive practices; and indigenous health and wellness.

SAARA GREENE is an assistant professor in the School of Social Work at McMaster University. Her commitment to engaging in community-based research (CBR) projects requires community-based collaboration and leadership at all stages of the research process. Her most recent CBR project is aimed at exploring the experiences and needs of HIV-positive mothers in Ontario throughout their first year of mothering.

MARTHA KUWEE KUMSA teaches social work at Wilfrid Laurier University. Her interests in research, pedagogy, and practice include engaging the macro-micro rift; reflexive practice; interdisciplinary knowledge; spirituality; the paradox of nationalism and transnationalism; and issues of identity, home(land), and belonging.

NOTISHA MASSAQUOI is currently the Executive Director of Women's Health at Women's Hands Community Health Centre. Her research and publications have focused on health equity, Black women, and HIV/AIDS as well as anti-oppressive service delivery. She is completing a PhD in Sociology and Equity Studies at OISE/University of Toronto. She has taught at the faculties of social work at Ryerson University and Dalhousie University.

NORMA JEAN PROFITT is Associate Professor in the School of Social Work, St. Thomas University. She has maintained a relationship with social workers in San Ramón and the Career of Social Work, University of Costa Rica, for many years, along with her passion for feminisms and, in particular, the issue of violence against women.

MEAGHAN ROSS recently completed a Master of Arts in Globalization Studies from the Institute of Globalization and the Human Condition at McMaster University. Her studies were influenced by her previous participation in the Labour Studies and Social Work degree programs, also at McMaster. She has worked in mental health, community development, and research, and she continues to be employed in social work, aiming to implement the lessons she has learned about activism into her own practice, as well as her community activism and labour organizing.

KRISTIN SMITH is a PhD candidate in the Department of Sociology and Equity Studies in Education at OISE/University of Toronto. She was recently appointed to a faculty position at the School of Social Work at University of Victoria. Her research interests include neoliberal restructuring of social and health services; critical analysis of social work practice; and the politics of resistance. Kristin's interest in these areas is informed by over eighteen years of work experience in front-line social, health, and women's services.

SAMANTHA WEHBI'S practice has focused on international social work and activism, including community practice on queer issues, disability rights and feminist organizing. Her research interests also include anti-colonial explorations of Arab experiences and contexts. She is currently Associate Professor at Ryerson University School of Social Work in Canada.

Chapter 1

An Overview of Anti-Oppressive Practice

Roots, Theory, Tensions

Donna Baines

This introduction explores the historical roots of anti-oppressive social work, the theory it draws on, and on-going tensions in both theory and practice. In addition, it discusses ten core insights that have stood the test of social justice social work practice.

As you read this introduction, ask yourself the following:
1. What are the roots of anti-oppressive practice (AOP) and social justice approaches, and how can we draw on these roots today?
2. What are some of the gaps in the historical and current writings on AOP and its predecessors? What are some of the points of agreement?
3. What is the difference between more mainstream approaches and AOP?

An Indigenous social work student spends her week comforting neighbours traumatized by events on the barricade at Caledonia, Ontario. She asks for extensions on her final papers, wondering whether her professors will see the links between anti-oppressive theory and her involvement in the frontlines of activism.

Initially full of enthusiasm, a student doing a placement in a child welfare agency soon becomes disillusioned. She feels that she does little more than fill out forms and complete computerized assessments. She never has time to challenge oppressive practices, or even think about them. Workers in her agency are sympathetic, but tell her to get used to it because "there's no room for theory in the real world."

An anti-oppressive therapist who doesn't use the title "social worker" is told that she will lose her job at a family counselling centre because she hasn't registered with the Social Work College. Primarily providing services to very poor women of colour, many of whom are survivors of abuse and torture, she wonders whose needs are being served by the College.

Oppression

Oppression takes place when a person acts or a policy is enacted unjustly against an individual (or group) because of their affiliation to a specific group. This includes depriving people of a way to make a fair living, to participate in all aspects of social life, or to experience basic freedoms and human rights. It also includes imposing belief systems, values, laws, and ways of life on other groups through peaceful or violent means. Oppression can be external, as in the examples above, or internal, when groups start to believe and act as if the dominant belief system, values, and life way are the best and exclusive reality. Internal oppression often involves self-hate, self-censorship, shame, and the disowning of individual and cultural realities.

Charity and Band Aids versus
Social Justice and Transformation

The vignettes above describe real-life conflicts and tensions that social work students and practitioners experience in everyday frontline practice. Although details have been changed to protect confidentiality, these vignettes are based on real events and people. They highlight the complexity of struggles in the world of social work practice, the need for models that advance social justice at multiple levels, and the kinds of struggles in which social workers find themselves. Social work is a unique field in many ways. It contains a number of distinct approaches and philosophies regarding care, what constitutes care, and how to stop or slow the social problems that generate the need for care. Social work is generally thought to have first emerged from charitable roots (for example, Carniol 2010; Mullaly 2002; Abramovitz 1988). Employed by groups such as the Charitable Organizations Society, Victorian-era social workers frequently provided the poor with enthusiastic lectures on morality and hygiene, as well as infrequent but much-needed food baskets or clothing boxes (Abramovitz 1988). These interventions did little more than place leaky band aids on deeply rooted social problems, failing to challenge systems that exploited the poor and sustained the wealthy (Carniol 2005; Withorn 1984). This tradition continues today in social work in the form of interventions aimed at providing a subsistence level of support to clients while leaving social systems that generate such problems untouched.

Fortunately, more social justice-oriented approaches to social work also exist. Throughout the history of social work, workers, clients, and average people have asked, what are the causes of social problems and, crucially, what can we do to address those causes and prevent social problems rather than merely treating the victims? These questions have been central to the development of a strand of social work emerging from social movements and aimed at fundamentally transforming the political, economic, social, and cultural

Social Movements

Social movements are one of the major roots of politicized, transformative social work. Social movements are groups of people who come together to enact change on specific political, economic, cultural, or social issues. While they are normally thought of as progressive in nature, they can also be regressive and work to halt or revoke social reforms and transformative policies. The authors in this book use the term social movements to refer to the collective action of individuals with reform and transformative agendas of social justice, equity, and fairness.

factors underlying and generating inequality and injustice. Groups such as the Rank and File Movement, the Settlement House Movement, and the Canadian League for Social Reconstruction called on social work to serve those in need, while simultaneously working to fundamentally reorganize society (Hick 2002; Withorn 1984; Reynolds 1963, 1951, 1946). In other words, politicized, transformative approaches to social work have a long history. Within the field of social work, social justice-oriented practice happens in a number of ways, including education and consciousness-raising among clients and co-workers; the development of social justice-based therapies such as feminist therapy and First Nations interventions; community development and organizing; political activism and workplace resistance; and broad-based organizing around policy changes, world peace, international equity, and the development of social systems based on fairness and social justice.

Transformation

In this book, transformation refers to ways of relieving people's emotional pain and immediate difficulties while simultaneously working to change the larger forces that generate inequity, unfairness, and social injustice. These forces include racism, sexism, colonialism, capitalism, ableism, ageism, and other hierarchical, authoritarian relations. With somewhat different emphases, these forces are often referred to interchangeably as social relations, social forces, social systems, social structures, and social factors. These social relations are shaped by and shape the social, political, economic, and cultural norms, structures, systems, discourses, forces, policies, organizations, and practices of our everyday lives and societies. Anti-oppressive practice and other social justice-oriented social workers seek to transform these larger social relations through direct practices that incorporate liberatory approaches within specific interventions and interactions, as well as through larger actions aimed at structural or macro-level change such as activism, scholarly work, resistance, advocacy, collective organizing, mass actions, and long- and short-term mobilization of individuals, groups, and societies.

Anti-oppressive practice (AOP), which will be discussed in greater detail later in this and the following chapter, is one of the main forms of social justice-oriented social work theory and practice today. It is a promising and exciting approach to the complexity of today's social problems, operating in the context of multiple oppressions and the growing need for fundamental reorganization of all levels of society. Anti-oppressive practice attempts to integrate the search and struggle for social change directly into the social work experience. This can take the form of new practices, new sources for and ways of understanding and building knowledge and practice, and new ways of building activism and opposition. Rather than a single approach, AOP is an umbrella term for a number of social justice-oriented approaches to social work, including feminist, Marxist, postmodernist, Indigenous, poststructuralist, critical constructionist, anti-colonial, and anti-racist. These approaches draw on social activism and collective organizing as well as a sense that social services can and should be provided in ways that integrate liberatory understandings of social problems and human behaviour. As part of larger movements for social change, AOP is constantly refining its theory and practice to address new tensions and social problems as well as underlying structural factors.

Broadly speaking, anti-oppressive social workers try to provide service to people seeking it, but also they help clients, communities, and themselves to understand that their problems are linked to social inequality — to understand why they are oppressed and how to fight for change. AOP does not claim to be an exclusive and authoritative model containing every answer to every social problem. Instead, consistent with its emancipatory heritage, AOP is a set of politicized practices that continually evolve to analyze and address constantly changing social conditions and challenges.

Core Themes

While a number of social justice-oriented frameworks exist and disagreements continue at the level of theory, there are ten common themes or core insights that stand the test of frontline practice in terms of promoting social justice at the level of everyday frontline social work.

1. Macro- and micro-social relations generate oppression.

Social relationships are enacted by human beings and generate the ongoing oppression of many groups and individuals. That they are enacted by people means that these oppressive relationships can be changed by people. Macro-level social relations are also known as social structures, social forces and social processes, or the so-called larger forces in society, such as capitalism; governments and their economic, social, financial, and international polices; religious and cultural institutions; and international trade and financial bodies. Micro-level social relations include social norms, everyday practices, workplace-specific policies and processes, values, identities, and so-called common sense. Using the term "social relations" highlights that these relations are organized and operated by people and can be halted or reorganized by them as well; they are wholly *social* processes, not inevitable conditions of modern life or ones that we cannot change.

2. Everyday experience is shaped by multiple oppressions.

Macro- and micro-social relations shape, perpetuate, and promote social ideas, values, and processes that are oppressively organized around notions of superiority, inferiority, and various positions between these two polar opposites. These multiple oppressions, including gender, class, disability, sexual orientation, and race, do not just lie quietly alongside one another, rarely compounding one another or interacting (Collins 2000; Baines 2002; Anthias and Yuval-Davis 1992). Instead, multiple oppressions overlap, contest, undermine, and/or reinforce one another in ways that depend on a variety of factors in the immediate and global environment.

3. Social work is a contested and highly political practice.

"Politicize" and "politics" refer to small "p" politics — everyday struggles over meaning, resources, survival, and well-being. Using this definition, everything is political despite the relatively widespread sentiment that most of everyday life is completely apolitical. Small "p" politics is different from big "P" politics, which assumes that politics occurs mainly during elections in which parties and individuals run for the right to govern. From the big "P" political perspective, only a very few issues are thought to be political. For example, social problems are conventionally understood to be the result of individual difficulties and poor decision-making rather than unequal distribution of power, resources, and affirming identities. People holding the big "P" politics perspective seek solutions by tinkering with the existing social system, applying managerial techniques to most or all social questions, or encouraging individuals to seek medical or psychological intervention for the problems they experience.

In contrast, people holding the small "p" politics viewpoint see social problems and their solutions as shaped by one's access to power and resources, as well as by one's ability to use and expand this access in ways that are socially just and promote equity. In order to determine whether we have power in any given situation, we can begin by asking what we would like to see changed, who else would like this change, and whether we can make the change happen. Our answers to these questions usually show us how much power we have and can access, what the available means and strategies are by which we can wield power, who else holds power, and how such people can wield, barter, extend, or redistribute their power. As we try to bridge practice and social activism, it is important to ask who benefits from the way things operate at any given point in time, who can help make the changes we want, how we can help ourselves

5

and others see the many ways in which issues are political, and how multiple strands of power are operating in any given scenario.

To politicize something or someone is to introduce the idea that everything has political elements; that is, to introduce the idea that nothing is neutral, and everything involves an overt or covert struggle over power, resources, and affirming identities. This struggle may be very calm and easily negotiated between two people in banal, everyday conversation, or it may bubble more explicitly to the surface as people challenge the way they are spoken to or about by others, the opportunities provided to or denied them, and the ways they can access and experience the positive aspects of life such as employment, arts, social involvement, and so forth. When an issue is politicized rather than just thought of as an unfortunate social problem or individual shortcoming, individuals and groups can more easily analyze and act upon it. At the very core of social work's existence are conflicts between competing social-political groups and forces over defining needs and how to interpret and meet needs. These groups can be comprised of communities, classes, cultures, age groups, a certain sector of the workforce or those excluded from the workforce, and so forth. These competing groups represent a wide range of political perspectives and strategies for change. Social workers differ deeply over whether to support the status quo, what political perspective to adopt, whether strategies for change are justified, and if so, which ones and to what degree.

4. Social work is not a neutral, caring profession, but an active political process.
There is no "politics-free-zone" (London-Edinburgh Weekend Return Group 1980), nor are there ways to avoid power and politics in social work, especially when we are trying to meet client needs in the context of an increasingly pro-market, corporatized society that supports and benefits from war, colonialism, poverty, and injustice at the local level and worldwide (see Chapter 2 and Akua Benjamin's Afterword). Every action we undertake is political and ultimately about power, resources, and who has the right and opportunity to feel positive about themselves, their identities, and their futures.

5. Social justice-oriented social work assists individuals while simultaneously seeking to transform society.
Rather than an exclusive emphasis on changing individuals, social justice-oriented social work assists individuals in meeting their needs, whenever possible, in participatory and transformative ways, and simultaneously focuses on challenging and transforming those forces within society that benefit from and perpetuate inequity and oppression.

6. Social work needs to build allies and work with social causes and movements.

Social workers cannot resolve larger social, economic, and political problems on their own. Social work must join with other groups to organize and mobilize people to make larger-scale, transformative changes. Social movements and activist organizations offer some of the best options for building lasting social change and provide the best "fit" with social work values and ethics (see Baines' Chapter Six in this book).

7. Social work's theoretical and practical development must be based on the struggles and needs of those who are oppressed and marginalized.

As Bertha Reynolds (1946) noted, "Social work exists to serve people in need. If it serves other classes who have other purposes, it becomes too dishonest to be capable of either theoretical or practical development." Social work knowledge and practice need to be grounded in the lives of those we serve, assessed in relation to critical approaches in order to ensure that we are building lasting change and not unintentionally reproducing various kinds of oppression.

8. Participatory approaches are necessary between practitioners and "clients."

Clients are not just victims, but can and need to be active in their own liberation and that of others. Their experience is also a key starting point in the development of new theory and knowledge, as well as political strategies and resistance. Their voices must be part of every program, policy, planning effort, and evaluation. Participatory forms of helping tend to be those that offer the most dignity as well as far-reaching and lasting impact (Moreau 1981; Reynolds 1963, 1946, 1951).

9. Self-reflexive practice and ongoing social analysis are essential components of AOP.

Social workers should constructively criticize their own participation in and link to social processes (de Montigny 2005; Miehls and Moffatt 2000). We lose an invaluable source of information when we fail to use our own insights, frustrations, disappointments, and successes as entry points into improving theory and practice (see the Chapters Twelve and Fifteen by Massaquoi and Kumsa, respectively, in this book).

10. A blended, heterodox social justice perspective provides the best potential for politicized, transformative social work practice.

Rather than claiming any single social justice-oriented model as the complete truth, a heterodox approach, involving and incorporating the strengths of a variety of critical approaches, provides the greatest vibrancy and potential to deliver emancipatory theory and practice. Rather than locking itself into defending the boundaries of a particular perspective, this approach provides the greatest potential for ongoing development and refinement of theory and practice. The authors in this book discuss, use, and clarify a healthy spectrum of overlapping, though sometimes contesting, perspectives (including feminist, Marxist, postmodernist, Indigenous, poststructuralist, critical constructionist, anti-colonial, and anti-racist).

The Roots of Anti-Oppressive Practice

As noted earlier, is it commonly thought that social work emerged first as a profession among groups providing charity (Carniol 2005; Mullaly 2002; Abramovitz 1988), such as the Charitable Organizations Society in the Victorian era. The interventions of these early professionals did little more than place leaky band aids on social problems, failing to challenge systems that exploited the poor and sustained the wealthy (Carniol 2010; Withorn 1984). This tradition continues today in social work in the form of interventions aimed at providing subsistence to clients while leaving social systems that generate such problems untouched. For example, employment services push unemployed people to accept any job regardless of wages, working conditions, or match with skills and life goals. The wages on most of these jobs are too low to support an individual, let alone a family, and are usually short-term — in short order throwing people back into a depressed and unstable job market. These solutions fail to address deep problems in an economy that simply does not create enough jobs for everyone and benefits from low wages and desperate job-seekers. It also fails to look at possible long-term correlations between race, gender, dis/ability, or region and access to or systematic exclusion from better jobs.

Fortunately, more social justice-oriented approaches to social work also emerged at the same time, reflecting the conflicts that rocked Victorian society, namely struggles between those who work for a living (or would if employment was available to them) and those who live off the wealth produced through the labour of others. By the late-1880s social workers participated in and led social justice-directed organizations such as the Rank and File Movement, the Settlement House Movement, and the Canadian League for Social Reconstruction (Hick 2002; Withorn 1984; Reynolds 1963, 1946). An early social justice social worker and educator, Bertha Reynolds (1946, 1951, 1963), was a member of the Rank and File as well as an active socialist and communist who wrote several pivotal books describing egalitarian approaches to social work. Like those who take anti-oppressive approaches today, Reynolds and these groups called on social work to serve people in need, while simultaneously working to fundamentally reorganize society.

Though social justice-oriented social workers continued to develop their practice knowledge, academic publishing was fairly limited prior to the 1970s. Work from England during this time, such as Bailey and Brake's *Radical Social*

Work (1975) and *Radical Social Work and Practice* (Brake and Bailey 1980) and Corrigan and Leonard's *Social Work Practice under Capitalism: A Marxist Approach* (1978), was rooted in Marxist models of class struggle, while the U.S. version of radicalism is reflected in Galper's *The Politics of Social Services* (1975). Works emerging in the late- and middle-1980s reflected a broadening of class analysis to include other key bases of oppression, particularly race and gender, as exemplified in *Feminist Social Work* by Dominelli and MacLeod (1989; see also *Anti-racist Social Work*, Dominelli 1988 and *Serving the People: Social Service and Social Change*, Withorn 1984 in the United States). A number of important feminist social work writings emerged through the 1980s and 1990s, including *Gender Reclaimed: Women in Social Work* (Marchant and Wearing 1986a); *Social Change and Social Welfare Practice* (Petruchenia and Thorpe 1990) in Australia; and *Social Work and the Women's Movement* (Gilroy 1990) and *The Personal is Political: Feminism and the Helping Professions* (Levine 1982) in Canada. In Canada, early versions of a multiple-oppression analysis emerged as "structural social work," emphasizing the way that everyday problems are social in nature; that is, they are shaped by social structures and relations interacting with individuals, their personalities, families, and communities, which are also social in nature. These social structures include patriarchy, racism, capitalism, heterosexism, ageism, and ableism. The structural approach is epitomized by the work of Moreau (1993, 1981, 1979) and Mullaly (1993). In his social work classic, *Case Critical*, Carniol (1987; now on its 6th edition) analyzed social work practice from a similarly structural perspective. Fook (1993) and Rees (1992) used social justice-oriented social work framing to undertake similar work in Australia. By the mid- to late-1990s much of the multiple voice, multiple oppression focus had turned to postmodernism and poststructuralism, as seen in works by Pease and Fook (1999), Leonard (1997), and the Canadian collection by Chambon and Irving (1994). In the 1990s and into the new millennium, social justice-oriented work shifted anti-oppressive or critical social work, exploring a blending of critical postmodernism and intersectionist, class analysis (Mullaly 2002, 2007; Allan, Pease and Briskman 2003; Lundy 2004; Dominelli 2004; Carniol 2010; Hick, Fook and Pozzuto 2005). Although this blending of theories is often less than straightforward and many debates continue, it produced new generations of social justice-oriented practitioners and academics (for detailed summaries and analyses of these theoretical perspectives and debates see McDonald, 2006; Dominelli 2004, 2002; Allan, Pease and Briskman 2003; Fook 2002; Pease and Fook 1999). Postmodernism and poststructuralism offered ways of understanding multiple oppressions such as identity, social location, voice, diversity, borders, anti-essentialism, inclusion, exclusion, and difference, while simultaneously emphasizing the importance of everyday experience (definitions for many of these terms are included in various chapters as well as listed in the index at the end of the book). Some argue that the use of postmodernist and poststructuralist concepts represent a decisive break with older theories such as feminism, Marxism, anti-imperialism, and anti-racism. For example, the older theories contain a clear sense of who the oppressed and oppressor groups are in society while postmodernism challenges the notion of oppression, who is oppressed, and the multiple ways that oppression may or may not be sustained and reproduced. Others argue that postmodernist concepts are extensions of issues tackled by the older models and add useful complexity to debates that have raged through the years. For example, some argue that older theories failed to discuss overlapping oppressions, difference, diversity, or identity. However, starting in the early 1980s, Heidi Hartman (1981) and others working from a Marxist-feminist or socialist-feminist perspective produced pivotal articles exploring overlapping oppressions. Similarly, Black feminists such as Angela Davis (1981) and Patricia Hill Collins (1986, 1989, 1990) were addressing class, race, and gender before postmodernism promoted the notion of multiple identities. Rather than the exclusive domain of postmodernism and poststructuralism, context and everyday practice were an early focal point for theorizing by feminists such as Dorothy Smith and others (1987; Smith and David 1975; with Burstyn 1985). While real differences exist (see, for example, discussions in Pease and Fook 1999 or Hick, Fook and Puzzuto 2005), significant similarities predominate in the work of most anti-oppressive scholars. For example, both the older and the newer frameworks explore the individual and his/her place in the world recognizing, for example, that one's identity is shaped by their class, race, gender, etc. — in short, that we all have multiple and socially constructed identities. The older and newer frameworks also recognize that the ways that we interpret our identities and experiences are also buffered and shaped by class, race, gender, etc.

While real differences exist (see, for example, discussions in Pease and Fook 1999 or Hick, Fook and Puzzuto 2005), significant similarities predominate in the work of most anti-oppressive scholars. For example, both the older perspectives such as Marxism and feminism and the newer theoretical schools such as critical postmodernism and poststructuralism argue for ongoing refinement of theory in response to changing social conditions; versions of each type of theory have struggled with the complexity of multiple axes of oppression and all are concerned with power. As Steve Hick and Richard Puzzuto (2005) note, the mingling of postmodern and critical theories is debated across many fields, cannot be rigidly defined, and is a necessary aspect of theorizing today's world of social work.

It is not just theoretical progression that underlies the development of AOP. Global capitalism, neoliberalism, and managerialism generate practice environments in which social workers encounter new kinds of challenges and issues. To address these challenges AOP social workers find themselves asking many questions, some the same as those asked by workers during much earlier periods. These questions include:

- How do we provide resources to and act in solidarity with exploited groups?
- How do we nurture local leadership and encourage social justice initiatives?
- How do we sustain ourselves and analysis in alienating and sterile environments?

In the new contexts of practice, social work practitioners also find themselves asking questions such as:

- How do we understand and work across multiple and intersecting differences (intersecting and interlocking oppressions; see Hulko 2010; Baines 2002)?
- In building oppositional analyses and resistance, how do we draw on the voices of marginalized people and their everyday knowledge as well as practice knowledge, research, and theory?
- How can resistance strategies promote a clear political program of change while remaining open, fluid, and inclusive (that is, embrace both certainty and uncertainty; see Adams, Dominelli and Payne 2009; Stepney 2009; Mullaly 2007)?

Attempting to engage with these and other questions, recent writing on AOP reflects a new phase in its history. Rather than establishing itself and drawing on its links with other types of social work, such as feminist or structural, AOP is sufficiently established that much of its writing focuses on taking AOP into new practice areas, analyzing the changing context of AOP, and extending and refining AOP theory. One of the most challenging tasks is the translation of theory into frontline practice, and fortunately there is a great deal of new writing in this area. Given that much of social work practice is particular to the distinct area in which it operates, summarizing these developments is difficult. However, in broad strokes, this work highlights clients' strengths while being keenly aware of the ways that their experiences and life chances have been limited and shaped by larger, inequitable social forces. While addressing service users' concerns in the most robust and respectful way possible, it links individual problems and individuals to others in the same situation, drawing links between personal pain, political inequities, social policies, and economic forces. In terms of new writings on AOP: Carniol and Del Valle (2007) provide practice insights into AOP with immigrant women; Danso (2009) does the same for de-valued, skilled immigrants; Fish (2008) provides a theoretical foundation for AOP with lesbian, gay, and bi-sexual people; Pollack (2010, 2004) delves in AOP with women in prison; Parrott (2009) extends understandings of AOP in the context of cultural diversity; MacDonald (2008) discusses AOP with chronic pain sufferers and people with disablities; Brown and Augusta-Scott (2006) critically engage with narrative therapy to produce more empowering outcomes for clients; Aronson and Smith (2009) explore resistance among social justice-oriented managers and supervisors; and Todd and Coholic (2007) analyze the challenges of teaching AOP to diverse and resistive students, including Christian fundamentalists.

The impact of new global management models and social policy frameworks has also been analyzed from an AOP perspective, helping practitioners understand and take creative actions against the further integration of neoliberal work practices and forms of organization. As discussed in Chapter One, neoliberalism is a global system that emphasizes individual responsibility and the private purchase of services rather than shared social responsibility and public services. These philosophies are introduced in the workplace in the form of standardized, alienating work practices such as New Public Management (NPM) and other performance management models or as so-called scientific approaches such as evidence-based practice that provide tight prescriptions for social work practice, replacing workers' discretion with pre-allotted amounts and types of interventions (see Bates' chapter in this book). Analyzing and theorizing the operation and impacts of managerialism as well as specific policy and funding reforms, Garrett (2009, 2008) writes convincingly of restructuring in child protection in Ireland and the U.K.; Baines (2010a, 2010b) provides an analysis of similar changes in non-profit social service work; Carey (2009b, 2007, 2006) discusses changing labour process for public sector social workers under policies that claim to challenge social exclusion but seemingly only perpetuate it; and McDonald (2006) analyzes the context and possible futures for social work in the context of constraint, a heavy emphasis on self-regulation, individualized and competitive professionalism, and NPM.

Finally, numerous authors have taken on theoretical refinement of social justice-oriented practice. Much of this writing focuses on specific and thorny questions that continually arise in social work aimed at liberation. Many of these questions pivot on the issue of power, what it is, how and when it is used, and what are more equitable and fair ways of conceiving of and using power in society at large and social work in particular. Some important discussions include Adams, Dominelli and Payne (2009) on complexity and uncertainty; Gilbert and Powell (2010) on knowledge and power; Mullaly (2007) on oppression; Tew (2006) on power and powerlessness; and Sakamoto and Pitner (2005) on critical consciousness.

Ongoing Tensions and Gaps

There is never a one-to-one direct translation of theory into practice in any situation, and the rapidly changing, multi-level world of AOP is no different. At the level of frontline practice, an amalgam of theories and practices generally works quite well, opening up and guiding possibilities for new ways to understand and act upon social problems and keeping theories growing, constantly expanding, or turning in new directions and fluid. At the level of theory, this amalgam is not always quite so happy (Tester 2003; Rossiter 1996). There are a number of tensions.

Epistemology

As a heterodox, umbrella term, AOP borrows bits and pieces from the various theories mentioned earlier in this chapter. These theories each have a somewhat different epistemological base or basis on which they can claim that their knowledge is credible, or in more simple terms they can claim that they know what they know. Structural, feminist, anti-racist, and Marxist social work draw on (modernist) epistemologies emphasizing the existence of social structures that shape, but do not determine, everyday experience. These structures, even something as seemingly concrete as the private market, are a series of social relations that have been put together and can be dismantled and rebuilt by human beings.

Moral or normative knowledge and projects contain a ballast or central tenet that assists in distinguishing better from worse or right from wrong. Structural, feminist, anti-racist, and Marxist theories all identify a key oppressed group or groups (e.g., women, racialized groups, working class, and poor people) who require liberation through the fundamental reorganization of social relations (i.e., social structures). This central tenet provides the moral-political project of each of these theories, or ways of knowing right from wrong and how to proceed with liberatory practice. In more everyday terms, this central tenet provides a moral compass for those using these theories and a set of projects or values that need to be pursued in order to create a more just and ethical way of being in the world.

In contrast, postmodernism *is* an epistemological theory about ways of knowing and how language and discourse exercise power — not, as Fook (2002) notes, a moral theory for political action. In other words, postmodernism does not have a moral project or group of people it is trying to liberate. Instead, it is a project aimed at gaining a deeper understanding of knowledge itself and how power operates through the words we and others use and the ways that language is used in professional and technical practice to define problems and in the process limit more complex and dynamic ways of understanding and acting

---

Epistemology

Epistemology is the theory or study of knowledge itself. It asks questions such as what is knowledge and therefore what is not, how do we know what we know, how is knowledge acquired, and, given the answers to the first three questions, what do people actually know? Epistemology is important in evaluating whether our claims about something are credible and something on which we feel we can base actions and interventions.

> ## Ontology
> Ontology is the study of being, existence, or reality. Our sense of reality shapes the ways we understand and act on the world. Some social work theories such as Marxism, feminism, and most of AOP believe that there is a real world that we can change in positive ways. Other theories, such as some versions of social construction-ism, postmodernism, and poststructuralism, are ambivalent about how and whether positive change can be enacted. They argue that because we can only draw on existing constructions and discourses to build new ones, there is little hope of building social relations free of oppressive discourses and social constructions.

on them. In order to avoid constructing oppressive discourses, postmodernism avoids moral projects, preferring to deconstruct and reveal the operation of oppressive uses of language and knowledge rather than developing roadmaps for liberation. Mullaly (2007) argues that despite this epistemological disagreement between these approaches in terms of what knowledge is and what it is for, critical postmodernism, Marxist, feminist, and other social justice-oriented approaches can be jointly mobilized to develop social theory and address social problems.

Stepney (2009) is less optimistic about this melding project, pointing out that the ontologies that underlie each framework draws are very different and largely incompatible. He and others (Pease 2007; Fook 2002) have advanced a perspective known as critical realism within social work. Critical realism embraces Marxism, feminism, and anti-racism's recognition of the existence and impacts of social structures (and hence its moral project and capacity to judge better from worse practices and processes), as well as postmodernism's sensitivity to the social construction of knowledge and the "multiple realities of subjective experience" (the idea that all knowledge is created socially, that is, by people, in order to serve a particular purpose or many purposes, and the recognition of the many social and individual perspectives and interests that make up individual and social experience). It does this without the "abyss of relativism" that accompanies projects that lack moral or normative bases (Stepney 2009: 18). (As noted above, lacking a moral project or group to liberate, postmodernism and poststructuralism tend to view all issues and viewpoints as valid and each solution as legitimate as the next, making it nearly impossible to develop social justice strategies and interventions.) Drawing on the strengths provided by structuralism and critical postmodernism, Stepney argues that critical realism offers a viable basis for social justice-oriented social work.

At the level of everyday practice, it is doubtful that critical realists do anything differently than an anti-oppressive practitioner, and using their own arguments it would seem that globalization and managerialism are more likely impediments to emancipatory practice than minor ontological differences between postmodernism and the more structural-based critical theories. The

> ## Social Construction
> The theory of social construction asserts that all knowledge, includ-ing taken-for-granted common sense, and all concepts, such as oppression and social change, are socially constructed by human beings on the basis of shared, though frequently changing, social understandings. Critical social constructionists believe there is a reality on which we can act; pure social constructionists argue that the concept of reality itself is a constructed social convention.

lively debate that critical realism has introduced to social work helps to expand and refine both theory and practice, and as such it is a welcome addition to the multiple perspectives informing social justice-oriented approaches. In short, AOP and critical realism seem to cover the same ground and can draw usefully on each other's contributions.

None of the disagreements discussed above are unique to AOP or particularly new to struggles for social justice. Disagreement is part of the landscape when the stakes are high, as they are in the case of social work practice. Fortunately, it is not necessary to have complete agreement on all aspects of theory and practice in order to move ahead with agendas for social justice (Mullaly 2001, 2007). Indeed, the kinds of conflicts mentioned above are best worked out in frontline practice and within the struggle for social justice, with social move-ments and marginalized groups acting as the final arbitrator of the strengths and weaknesses of any given approach.

The State

Mullaly (2007: 25) notes that in order to deal with the current crises facing the world, social workers need to understand the state (elected government, civil service, policy apparatus, funded services, and so forth) and social work's relation to it. That is, social work needs to theorize its connection and operation within, against, and in support of the state. Many social workers are employed directly by governments (such as welfare employees, workers' compensation services, employment services, housing, school boards, policy analysts and so forth). A large portion also work in government-funded and mandated services such as health care and child welfare. A third very large group works in the non-profit or voluntary sector, which receives most of its funding from government and must therefore meet government-required reporting standards (such as outcome and performance measure), accreditation standards (how many employees require professional accreditation, what kind of credentials, etc.) and other contract requirements. Social workers are employed in the larger state apparatus and by implication work *for* the state; many also organize lobby briefs, policy analysis, activist groups, and protests *against* the state, while others rally *in support* of government policies and direction. Of course, social workers often occupy more than one, or even all, of these roles simultaneously — employed by one arm of the state, protesting cuts in another, and rallying in defense of politicians trying to make a difference. This makes the state a very complex but important set of relations for social workers to understand and theorize.

Most people think of the state as an arm of government that develops policies and programs in more or less neutral ways, trying to reflect the interests of the many groups that make up society. A more structural analysis argues that the government and the state reflect and extend the interests of dominant groups while attempting to appear neutral and even-handed. For example, governments claim that tax cuts benefit everyone though they tend to benefit the rich far more. Also, by reducing the amount of tax dollars coming into government coffers, cuts reduce the amount available to spend on social programs aimed at alleviating inequality and poverty, relegating these programs to the back burner of government and social priorities.

Given their claim that power is diffuse (that is, power does not operate against people but simultaneously through, against, in support of, and alongside them, as well as other possible variations), postmodernists and poststructuralists have not developed a comprehensive theory of the state per se and do not tend to view the state as having a pivotal or central role in social life. Instead, various forms of power (discourses or debates/discussions of social issues, professional bodies of knowledge and practice, and language itself) operate through individuals, such as social workers, who work within, against, and in support of the state. This very open-ended understanding of power reminds us that power is complex and contradictory, but it also makes action or the development of strategies for social justice difficult: if power always simultaneously oppresses and resists oppression, one may find it hard to believe that any social change effort or strategy will help more than it harms, and that these kinds of social change will improve things rather than just recreating existing injustices in new ways. This means that on the frontlines of practice, or when social workers are trying to develop new social policies and programs, it is not possible to know with any confidence that new strategies will empower or liberate people; and when the implementation of such strategies leads only to the status quo, or when it makes things worse, hope for improvement will be diminished. These issues become particularly acute in discussions over whether the state, which employs or funds most social work services in most industrial countries, helps its citizens, reflects the interests of dominant groups, or simply reproduces inequities/resistance in an endless circle.

In contrast, more structural approaches to power — Marxist, feminist, and anti-racist — assert that power is something that individuals and institutions can use to promote their own and others' interests and that these interests can be oppressive, productive, or both. Within a Marxist, feminist, or structuralist analysis the state is seen a set of *processes* that *can* assist oppressed population interests and even remove the cause of their maltreatment. This does not mean that the state always or even often does promote social justice through its policies, because at the same time that it can reduce oppression, the state *can* and *often does* sustain and extend oppressive relations reflecting the interests of dominant socio-economic groups (London-Edinburgh Weekend Return Group 1980). For example, major state programs such as welfare in Canada may appear to be helping those receiving payments, but a growing body of evidence suggests that the strongly negative stigma associated with and the bare subsistence rates of these programs ensures a supply of desperate people compelled to take any job regardless of its rate of pay, permanence, workplace safety, and so forth (Lightman, Herd, and Mitchell 2010; 2009). In short, rather than addressing the poverty caused by a system that is driven by profit and needs a pool of low-cost workers, most state-sponsored welfare programs meet the needs of the business sector by ensuring an endless supply of cheap labour.

Rather than being neutral or non-aligned, the state reflects an unstable equilibrium of struggles between those who benefit from inequity and those who strive to eradicate or reduce it (Wetherly 2008; Sassen 2003; Panitch and Leys 1999). The state also reflects the intended and unintended consequences of policies developed in response to the aforementioned struggles as well as the individual priorities of influential politicians, civil servants, and intellectuals (Wetherly 2008). This dynamic but grounded formulation of the state permits AOP social workers to see that, as employees within a larger state or state-funded system, they often inadvertently play a part in legitimizing, perpetuating, and benefiting from ongoing injustice. On the other hand, though they are part of the state machinery (that is, the state provides funding to most social services and mandates parts of it as well), social workers work within complex sets of policies that reflect not just the interests of dominant groups but also those which progressive forces have been able to stake out. As noted earlier, social workers often challenge or protest these policies while simultaneously employed within them to provide services to those in need. Many social justice social workers also build new services and ways of understanding social problems that may operate outside of government, or they cautiously draw on government funding, ever aware of the ways that this funding may compromise (or enhance) the services. Social workers of all political stripes are also active in elections and new policy development.

Most structural approaches (Marxist, feminist, anti-racist, etc.) assert that the state reflects the interests of dominant groups, making it a partriarchal, racialized, classist force in society. However, this assertion can make it seem that little can be done to change the state, that our only recourse is to capture it. The notion of the state as a constantly changing, unstable equilibrium of struggles and counter-struggles permits AOP social workers to recognize that there are spaces in this instability in which to resist oppression and to build new practices, relations, and solidarity with others doing likewise. Indeed, many of the most cutting-edge, innovative, politicized social services carefully adhere to the accreditation and documentation requirements of state funders even as they simultaneously push back the boundaries of how to engage with highly marginalized client groups, draw them in to receive and participate in services, integrate their insights into practice models into front-line approaches, and build new kinds of social relations and structures in the process of service development, delivery, and evaluation.

A few years ago, one of my students was involved in developing an anti-racist, feminist collective to address the needs of recently arrived immigrant women experiencing violence from a male partner, often their sponsor for immigration. The collective carefully and thoughtfully developed ways of working and of organizing services in order to draw in the community, share knowledge, challenge racism and sexism, and deliver services respectful of both service users and providers. Though funding was difficult to get and the state funders' reporting requirements were challenging, the collective continued to operate differently from more established hierarchical, bureaucratic agencies and to defend their more politicized and liberatory practices and methods of service delivery, on the grounds that these approaches provided users with respectful, engaged staff and a constructive, rewarding work environment.

Managing and Supervising Social Work

Managerial and supervisory issues are largely underdeveloped in the social justice-oriented social work literature. Frontline social work supervision used to be characterized by learning and development and included practices such as support, trouble-shooting, problem-solving, brainstorming, and case-by-case review. Liz Beddoe (2010: 1280) argues that under managerialism there is increasing pressure to use supervision as an opportunity to micro-manage practitioners and their "outcomes" in order to minimize risk to the agency and transfer responsibility for potential problems to frontline staff. Beddoe observes that this shift in supervisory practice is an aspect of the "risk society" that promotes increased surveillance of many groups and practices, including professional practices, not with an eye to strengthening social justice mandates but in order to exercise greater control of practice (by reducing professional discretion and standardizing) and to minimize costs.

It is not surprising, given this context, that many social justice-oriented social workers tend to avoid managerial positions, perhaps assuming that managerial power is exclusively an oppressive form of power. This means that these positions and skills often end up in the hands of more conservative workers. Rather than simply avoiding these positions, social workers need to remake and re-theorize this level of practice (incorporating politicized and transformative values and knowledge), and ultimately the positions need to be filled by critical, activist social workers. Particularly given the current popularity of business-based management models, anti-oppressive social work needs to seriously examine management practices and to promote alternative models that share workplace power, drawing on the expert knowledge of practitioners and services users while simultaneously providing leadership, protection, and support to the staff, service users, the wider community served by the agency and joining in shared activist campaigns to defend and expand human rights and social programs (see Aronson and Smith 2009 for an example of this). As Healy (2002) notes, while tensions have increased between social justice mandates and new management techniques, opportunities for liberatory practices still exist.

Indigenous Knowledge, Practice, and Theory

A notable gap in AOP is the question of the role for Indigenous knowledge and practice. As a "post-colonial" country, non-Indigenous Canada continues to have an oppressive relationship with Indigenous people at the levels of policy and everyday practice (Brant 1990; Morrissette et al. 1993; Navigon and Mawhiney 1996; Duran et al. 1998). First Nations social work, as discussed in Bonnie Freeman's chapter in this book, directly addresses the challenges facing Native people, drawing on Native knowledge and traditions. What are and what should be the connections between anti-oppressive and Indigenous social work practice? What are the similarities and differences? What role should First Nations knowledge play in AOP theory and practice and vice-versa? Currently, the two forms of practice have been developing alongside each other but with less interaction than most AOP practitioners think is appropriate. What are the best ways to go about developing a lively dialogue and constructive critique between the two bodies with an eye to strengthening both?

Differences from Mainstream Practice

On the surface, it is sometimes difficult to discern good mainstream social work practice from AOP. Skilled practitioners from both traditions use respectful and consultative approaches with service users, and both include advocacy and policy critique in their repertoire of good practices. However, mainstream social work draws on a number of theories that see social and economic systems as politically neutral (Payne 2000) and that fail to recognize the serious inequities in our society or the way these injustices are embedded in the profit-model of patriarchal, racialized, homophobic, colonial capitalism. Though many social workers mix mainstream, AOP, and other perspectives in their everyday work, the term "mainstream" is used in this book as a general term; it refers to approaches that may, to some extent, ease people's suffering or difficulties, but that depoliticize social problems and fail to see the larger dynamics shaping social work practice or to imagine alternative solutions that can be undertaken with and for our clients.

> ### *Mainstream Social Work*
> Although often claiming the opposite, mainstream social work tends to view social problems in a depoliticized way that emphasizes individual shortcomings, pathology, and inadequacy. Interventions are aimed largely at the individual, with little or no analysis of or intent to challenge power, structures, social relations, culture, or economic forces. Mainstream approaches such as the ecological, psychoanalytic, and systems approaches emphasize professionalism, career advancement, and the authority of experts, often having little or no space for the struggles of clients, communities, and larger social justice causes.

AOP differs from mainstream social work in a number of ways. Child welfare and hospital social work are often referred to as mainstream practice sites. However, mainstream social work is not a type of workplace or a series of places in which social work is practiced; it is a way of looking at social problems and their solutions. A comparison of AOP to mainstream social work practice highlights some important differences. Though they may not agree entirely with a particular approach, mainstream social work does tend to accept existing narrow, individually focused interventions as the best that can be done at this point in time. In contrast, social justice-oriented social workers attempt to keep in mind the bigger picture of oppressive policies, practice, and social relations even as they address immediate crises and emotional pain. For example, anti-oppressive practitioners argue that what we call "clinical depression" cannot be fully addressed separate from the poverty, sexism, racism, social alienation, and other oppressive forces experienced by many people bearing this label (see Catrina Brown's chapter in this book). Temporary relief may be provided in the form of medications and verbal therapies, but the social problems and struggles experienced by many sufferers of clinical depression must also be analyzed and addressed through actions such as critical consciousness-raising, advocacy, radical therapies, mobilizing for policy and economic change, and broader reorganization of society and social relations.

Secondly, while mainstream approaches usually accept the status quo, AOP tries to repoliticize issues and to understand the problems that clients experience as emanating not only from individual choices but also from socially conditioned, limited choices and the interplay of social, political, cultural, and economic factors over which service users generally have little awareness or control. For example, it is not uncommon in child welfare and pediatric social work for families to be labeled "dysfunctional," a label that fails to recognize the strengths that have kept such families afloat during difficult circumstances and the ways that overlapping layers of class, gendered, and often cultural, racialized, and regionalized systems have worked against their success in life, leaving them marginal, excluded, and with few resources to draw on.

Labelling the family as dysfunctional places the blame on them and makes them seem almost exclusively responsible for making changes in their lives. It also depoliticizes the situation by obscuring the complex web of inequities that have shaped their opportunities and disadvantage. If something is hidden from view, it is very difficult for social workers to discuss with co-workers and others — much less act on. *Depoliticization* refers to processes that take politics and political awareness out of issues in order to control these issues and those seeking social change. In our society, access to power, resources, and affirming identities are unevenly distributed along the lines of class, race, gender, ability, and so forth; and this maldistribution is fiercely defended, legitimized, and normalized through social, cultural, political, and economic practices. As noted in the example above, in many social work situations, social problems resulting from maldistribution are generally depoliticized; they are seen as the failings or shortcomings of individuals rather than what they are: the consequences of attempts to cope with difficult situations generated by society.

Another common way that social problems are individualized and depoliticized is by giving them medical or psychiatric diagnoses, or criminal labels. While mainstream social work tends to accept medical and criminal labels, often uncritically embracing the power to diagnose and define others, social justice-oriented perspectives recognize the power of language to shape identities and opportunities (Hick, Fook and Puzzuto 2005; Mullaly 2007). They remain skeptical of diagnoses and labels and try to use these designations in strategic and critical ways. For example, many people were harmed for many years when queer sexualities were labeled as criminal or a form of psychiatric illness. Once a largely unquestioned professional norm (Morrow and Messinger, 2006), this labelling, as well as social work's role in perpetuating the oppression such labelling caused, are now seen as deeply wrong and destructive.

Thoughtful critique and skepticism are important reflexive practices to employ when addressing any of the social problems on which social workers act. Social justice-oriented social workers may choose to use medical or psychiatric diagnoses to describe a set of problems encountered by an individual or group, while simultaneously maintaining an awareness of the ways that medical and psychiatric labels shape, oppress, and marginalize people. However, if housing, social assistance, child care supports, or counseling are available to individuals based on a given diagnosis and will be denied to them otherwise, AOP social workers may encourage people to use their diagnosis strategically to improve their lives and access needed resources.

Another way that social work has been depoliticized and remade as a neutral profession is by taking struggle out of practice, remaking it as an apolitical, technical form of professional work undertaken by well-educated and kindly people. In actuality, social work is a series of acute, ongoing, political struggles over what services and resources will be provided, to whom, by whom, in what amount, and to what end. Linked to this, mainstream social work tends to pro-mote the idea that social work is a united, apolitical body of expert knowledge. In reality, social work is a number of distinct, disparate, and intensely political *bodies* of knowledge which have a long history of conflict based on real-life struggles within our everyday worlds.

In workplaces that are closer to state power and coercion, such as the correctional system, welfare provision and child welfare services, and many for-profit settings, the deployment of a full AOP model may seem nearly impossible. Indeed, sometimes a practice setting is so narrow, conservative, and limiting that it is difficult to do more than enact the beginning phases of anti-oppressive practice. However, even within these settings it is possible to promote ideas, ask questions that encourage critical thought, draw co-workers together to share concerns and experience, and approach work in a more holistic and critical matter that expands the space for AOP thought and practice (see for example, Gary Dumbrill's chapter on child welfare, Michelle Bates' chapter on evidence-based practice, or Kristin Smith's chapter on mental health practice). The chapters of this book highlight the diversity and richness of contemporary social justice-oriented social work practice, the kinds of possibilities that can be exploited, as well as the kinds of practice dilemmas encountered by progressive social work practitioners, leading us to conclude that it is possible to practice social justice-oriented social work, in some form, in any organization.

Names and Labels

Language is always a force in political struggles, and the struggle for First Nations self-determination has used language and labels in strategic ways to name "prob-lems" and their "solutions," reclaim sovereignty in the lives of First Nations people, and gain public awareness. Recently, Taiaike Alfred (2005) advanced an argument concerning "aboriginalization" or processes that continue and deepen colonialization, assimilation, and integration. While Alfred's argument focuses on processes of domination rather than advocating particular word choices, his arguments reaffirm the power of language to perpetrate harm. In solidarity with this struggle, terms used interchangeably in this book include First Nations, Native, Indigenous, Aboriginal, and words in indigenous languages.

Respecting a similar politics of language issue, a lively debate recently oc-curred in social work journals, particularly in the UK, concerning the terms used for people who make use of social work services (Carey 2009a; McLauglin 2009; Scourfield 2007; Hefferman 2006). Though seemingly "constructive and altruistic" (Carey 2009: 179), these terms are not neutral; rather, they label individuals and are part of a process of constituting identities, possibilities, and power differentials. Most of the authors involved in this debate also note that these terms reflect changing relationships among service users, governments, and markets, emphasizing individual rather than social or governmental responsibility and management of one's own services (if entitled) and difficulties (if not). These new self-managed models work best if service users are entrepreneurial (Scourfield 2005) and tied closely to agendas of New Public Management (Heffernan 2006: 139). Alternative, non-oppressive terms are not readily available, hence the chapters in this book use terms such as "client," "community member," "women," and "service user," with no particular discourse or intended set of power relations attached to any. While some may claim that this diversity of terminology lacks rigour, it may also reflect the strength of heterodox methods and the authors' thoughtful and respectful approaches to naming and categorizing people. The diversity of terms used in this book also highlight the authors' ties to social movements and the messy but constantly changing way that language gets challenged and mutates within these struggles.

Does It Always Work?

AOP is not a formula or a prescription that works every time in every situation. Like social problems, AOP is a messy, uneven process that requires ongoing critical reflection, debate, and refinement. AOP practitioners will find themselves struggling in rapidly changing contexts with social problems that are not easy to address and for which there is very little social support and fewer resources. However, there are also many rewards and successes possible with an AOP approach, among which the foremost are that we can contribute to social care and the greater social good rather than regretfully but passively accepting injustice and oppression. Rather than approaching AOP as something that has all the answers, we ought to approach social justice as a lens through which to view the world and ask questions about who is benefitting from this problem or issue, who is harmed, who may be on the same side or provide support for a particular struggle or solution. AOP social workers also need to remain open to new ideas and to continue to evolve their practice in the nitty-gritty of frontline practice as contexts change and new challenges arise. Building and sustaining respectful, supportive relationships with service users, their allies, and others active in social justice is key to high quality AOP. Of equal importance is the capacity to endlessly question and learn more about the social world we wish to emancipate.

A Radical Agenda

Radical means to be rational and direct in the search for social peace; it means to go to the roots of a problem and not just deal with symptoms … in the struggle against injustice one cannot be moderate. That's why (we need) a radical agenda, in the deepest, most humanist and most committed sense of the word. (Alejandro Bendana 1995: 5)

Social work operates at the nexus of social structures and human pain. If we are genuinely to assist people with the kinds of problems they encounter in today's neoliberal, globalized world, radicalism is a necessity. It is not enough to be highly skilled and professional, dealing efficiently with immediate problems, as compelling as they may seem. We should be passionate about the need for social justice and work continuously to provide a full range of caring interventions; continuously develop new, radical, liberatory therapies; draw on alternative knowledge bases that dislodge oppression; and at the same time, advocate, agitate, and organize in order to fundamentally challenge the forces that generate and benefit from the pain and oppression we address every day in social work practice. As Bendana notes above, we cannot afford to be moderate; we need to go to the roots of the problem and to be active and direct in the search for social peace.

It is also important to remember that social workers who want to build a better world are not alone. As Ben Carniol (2010: 141) notes, "They have allies everywhere in the movement for social justice, both locally and globally," including clients, anti-poverty activists, unions, the women's movement, anti-racist groups, Indigenous organizations, and anti-globalization activists. Carniol also notes that social workers have professional allies in other occupations facing similar conditions, such as nurses, teachers, child care workers, and academics as well as policy analysts, community development workers, public officials, and those working in progressive think-tanks and research institutes (see also Baines 2007d: 195). The struggle for social justice has always been global, but now more than ever we need global strategies and inter-connections. Often the developed world thinks it has provided and will provide all the solutions to today's problems. However, we can gain a great deal by looking to "Third World" and Indigenous experiments in participatory democracy, participatory budget and policy making, and new forms of collective social support. Some of our best hopes for social justice lie in finding common ground and internationalizing our struggles — that is, in finding ways of supporting and working in solidarity with the struggles for self-determination, peace, and sustainable development taking place around the world.

At the end of our careers, I am betting that few of us will remember how many ticky box assessment forms we completed or how often we got our statistics in on time. But I am absolutely positive that we will remember the times we advocated for and with clients and found a way to improve things, the times we helped build campaigns to resist cutbacks, the participatory processes we helped to develop for program evaluations, and the many times we marched, advocated, petitioned, sang, laughed, cried, and dreamed about a better future with our clients, co-workers, and fellow activists. As social justice-oriented social workers we can humanize ourselves, our work practices, and our communities, liberate and politicize our workplaces, and transform and dignify our existence through the creative, collective, and ongoing pursuit of peace, equity, and social justice.

Chapter 2

An Overview of Anti-Oppressive Social Work Practice

Neoliberalism, Inequality, and Change

Donna Baines

This chapter looks at forces shaping social work practice and workplaces, including globalization, neoliberalism, and managerialism. It explores how these changes impact the labour force and front-line social work practice. Finally, this chapter draws on a study of the changing context of practice to highlight ways that social workers continue to resist injustice, envision a better future, and build better, more emancipatory practice.

As you read through this chapter, ask yourself the following:
- What are some of the ways that globalization and neo-liberalism are experienced in front-line practice?
- How do managerialism and standardization restrict social workers' opportunities for social justice-oriented practice?
- Have twenty years of restructuring reduced or removed social workers' commitment to and capacity for social justice practice?

If you ask five social workers what social work is, it is likely that you will get five different answers. This is partly because social work is such a hybrid, diverse field, and partly because the field is deeply split among those pursuing conventional, professional goals; those seeking to change the world along more democratic, participatory and egalitarian lines; and those pursuing many variations in-between. Unlike many professions, social work draws on a number of knowledge and theoretical sources, remaking some to fit the demands of everyday, front-line practice and adopting others wholesale for their capacity to shed light on the complexities of the social problems that social work addresses. The main source of social work's intellectual integrity and potential for theoretical development (Reynolds 1946) is its connection to people's everyday struggles for dignity and well-being, its ability to alleviate their pain and to address the deep roots of inequity and injustice that generate their distress. Social justice-

> **Egalitarian**
> Processes and practices based on the belief that all people are equal and deserve equal rights and opportunities, including social, political, and economic ones.

oriented approaches to social work have a long history and an important place in the contemporary world of social work (see Introduction Part 1 for more discussion of history).

Anti-oppressive practice (AOP) is a social justice-oriented practice model currently taught in a number of schools of social work around the world and embraced by a wide swath of social workers in clinical, community, and policy settings (Adams, Dominelli, and Payne 2009; McLaughlin 2005; Mullaly 2002). Its strength grows primarily from its compassionate embrace of humanity in all its diversity and adversity, and its whole-hearted commitment to social justice in the immediate and the long-term. Rather than a single approach, AOP is an integrated model drawing on a number of social justice-oriented approaches to social work, including feminist, Marxist, critical, postmodernist, Indigenous, poststructuralist, critical constructionist, anti-colonial, and anti-racist perspectives. It attempts to analyze how power works to oppress and marginalize people as well as how power can be used to liberate and empower them across a wide range of social settings, relations, environments, and systems.

A commitment to developing socially just ways of practicing social work is found in social work bodies around the globe. For example, the International Association of Schools of Social Work (IASSW) and the International Federation of Social Workers have made an explicit commitment to social justice approaches by defining social work in this way:

> The social work profession promotes social change, problem solving in human relationships, and the empowerment and liberation of people to enhance well-being. Utilizing theories of human behaviour and social systems, social work intervenes at the point at which people interact with their environments. Principles of human rights and social justice are fundamental to social work. (IASSW website)

While many would argue that most approaches to social work adopt a depoliticizing approach and fail to live up to the profession's commitment to social justice, social work is nevertheless unique among professional groups in having such a commitment. This commitment provides a useful basis for debate, exchange, theoretical and practical development, and provides a space for the growth of critical approaches such as AOP.

A book like this tries to walk a razor's edge, encouraging and energizing those wanting to work in more creative and empowering ways while simultaneously justifying the need for anti-oppressive practice by outlining the massive threats humankind faces in the form of growing global inequity and oppression. The latter runs the risk of overwhelming those who simply want to help the clients who appear in their doorways. Without a larger understanding of how oppression operates, however, there is little likelihood that "help" can be more than a temporary, band-aid measure. Global capitalism may seem a distant issue to most social workers, but in a myriad of ways it shapes our work and the way we are able to think about, generate, and attempt to enact emancipatory social work.

Given the huge demand for services and support, some social workers may ask if it is really necessary to understand more than the immediate and pressing problems facing service users and their communities. However, in order to remove the source of many of these problems, it is important to understand the interconnection of larger systems and everyday problems. The connections between globalization and the client seeking mental health supports may seem few, but after an initial conversation and social work assessment, you may discover that your very resilient client is female, Aboriginal, works part-time in a fast-food venue even though she has a university degree, and provides support to her extended family. Finding respectful and robust ways to support this client involves developing an understanding of her strengths and challenges in the context of the services your agency provides, services and supports that should be provided either by your agency or somewhere else in the community but may no longer be available, and anti-Aboriginal racism. Though many social workers will ask why you bother, high-quality social work practice also involves being attuned to and finding ways to address the ongoing negative impacts of European colonization of Canada, and understanding that anti-colonial struggles for social justice are rarely tackled with enthusiasm or full commitment either in Canada or in the many other places in the world where land and wealth has been stolen from people.

Much of the wealth in the First World was acquired through colonization of the Third World and theft of land from indigenous peoples. For the most part, the incredible wealth in industrialized countries and among ruling elites in third-world countries first came from the exploitation of the planet and from the labour of working and poor people. This exploitation was and is stratified by race, gender, class, region, and indigeneity (indigenous peoples); that is, people who are white, male, heterosexual, and able-bodied, and who live close to centres of wealth and power, hold the more influential and well-paid jobs and positions in society, while those farther away from this centre-point fare increasingly worse. This set of relationships has shaped the poverty of countries in the Global South and ensured that their economies remain dependent on trade with the First World, providing disproportionate benefits to the First World and deprivation to the majority in the Third World.

In terms of indigenous people, Canada exists on land extracted from First Nations peoples through trickery, unequal treaties, and violent conflict (Carniol

2010). Though rarely discussed in polite circles or most academic work, unre-solved Aboriginal issues are part of the Canadian reality and must be central to struggles for social justice. Canada's situation is not unique. Moreover, unre-solved colonial issues around the planet are exacerbated by globalization, as rich populations within rich countries get richer and poor and racialized populations around the globe become poorer and more excluded. For social work, these unresolved and difficult to resolve problems underscore how important it is to our collective struggle for social justice that all countries and cultures learn to build real equity and fairness, work across cultures and difference, and celebrate resistance and the contributions of those on the margins. These unresolved is-sues also highlight the importance of looking beyond the immediate problem presented by service users to the larger context of the community and culture, to the economy, and to racial and gender inequities; such a perspective reveals how service users have been socially positioned and conditioned by all these forces to end up where they are. Finally, since these kinds of problems shape the everyday experience of service users, it enhances the quality and integrity of our practice to educate ourselves on these issues and use whatever power and privilege we have to reduce and address inequity and injustice in its many forms — even if that involves only treating our clients consistently with deep respect and providing them with the opportunity to talk and think about how these forces shape their lives and what we might all do about it collectively.

In short, while it is important for social workers to be very clear where they are placed on a multi-level continuum of privilege and oppression, it is equally important to understand, critique, and improve how they use that privilege to challenge oppression in everyday life (Baines 2007c: 25). Each chapter in this book provides concrete insights into how this process works and reflects on the author's experience with putting these theories into practice.

The Changing Context of Practice: Neoliberalism, Globalization, and Workplace Restructuring

> *Emancipatory*
> To free someone from oppressive restrictions and conventions. In the case of AOP, emancipation is thought to be a mutual process in which people contribute to their own and each other's liberation.

Promoting social justice within the field of social work has never been easy, but today it faces more serious challenges than ever. Some background is needed in order to understand the current context in which social work operates. The welfare state (government policies and programs providing social supports and services) was set up following the Second World War to compensate for the failure of capitalist markets to meet social needs; that is, our economic system

> ## Welfare State
> A series of social programs and policies aimed at reducing inequity through redistribution of goods and services and correcting for the inadequacy of the private market to provide sufficient good employment.

could not prevent recession or provide all citizens with employment or enough income on which to live (Stanford 2008; Teeple 1995). Although one of the original concepts of the welfare state was universality, or making programs and services (such as Medicare in Canada) available to everyone regardless of income, most services are now targeted to particular populations (for example, people with problem drinking, dependent children, people with disabilities, etc.) who often have to prove repeatedly that they meet the criteria for service, in order to receive services that are minimal and tightly quantified (Lightman 2002). These changes in service models reflect a shift from more liberal and social-democratic values to neoliberal pro-market values.

Neoliberal governments promote policies that expand opportunities for businesses and corporations to increase their profits while simultaneously shrinking the funds available for human services (Harvey 2005; Cohen 1997). Though some argue that neoliberalism is brand new, others argue that it is an unfortunate but logical outgrowth of a capitalist system based on maximizing individual wealth rather than overall social well being (Stanford 2008; Harvey

> ## Universality
> Having the quality of being applicable and available for everyone. In the case of welfare states, social programs are universal when all citizens are entitled to them regardless of their income or social location. Universal programs are provided by the government, funded through taxes. They have lower administration costs since service users tend to have to apply only once. Canada's remaining example of a universal program is Medicare.

> ## Targeted
> Targeted social programs are available only to those who meet certain criteria (e.g., age, income level, type and level of disability). Service users usually have to prove repeatedly that they meet program criteria, making such programs costly to administer and intrusive for service users. Services are often funded by government and contracted out to for-profit and non-profit organizations, though some, like social assistance, continue to be operated by government. Other examples of targeted social programs include addictions services, employment services for the unemployed, and services for people with mental health problems.

2000). In the area of social policy, neoliberalism discourages government programs and support, encouraging people to purchase care from private providers or turn to their families (Wiseman 1996; Teeple 1995). Naturally, this strategy is possible for the well-off, while the less-fortunate find themselves with very little. Neoliberal governments also encourage cuts in social service funding and privatization of services, with the result that the welfare state has been drastically reduced from that which developed after the Second World War and up to the mid-1980s (Mullaly 2007; Leonard 1997).

Overlapping with the introduction of neoliberalism was a series of processes that have come to be known as globalization. Globalization refers to the closer integration of economic, social, political, environmental, and legal policies across nations. Globalization has the potential to promote social justice agendas: uniting nations, eradicating inequality and exploitation, preserving the global environment, and ensuring mutual sustainability and peace. However, it has tended to do just the opposite, promoting policies that increase poverty, environmental degradation, and economic and political insecurity for many, while amassing

> ### Neoliberalism
> An approach to social, political, and economic life that discourages collective or government services, instead encouraging reliance on the private market and individual skill to meet social needs. In the social welfare arena, this approach has resulted in reduced funding for social programs, new service user groups, and workplaces with fewer resources and increased surveillance, management control, and caseload size. World-wide it has resulted in a growth of poverty, decrease in democracy, and increased social and environmental devastation.

wealth and privilege for corporations, their higher-level employees, and investors. Anti-oppressive social work has become harder to do because of the increasingly aggressive nature of globalization and neoliberal governments' response to it in the form of policies and practices. In particular, the gap between rich and poor has widened under globalization, generating new populations of impoverished and marginalized people in need of social support at a time when neoliberal policies have ensured that social support is increasingly difficult to find.

Most front-line social workers experience globalization in two ways: first in the form of changing client needs and populations, and second in the changing organization of their work and workplaces. We are often told that globalization makes it easier for people, goods, and capital (that is, technology, equipment, investments) to move around the planet in rapid and unprecedented ways. While some of the movement of people is voluntary — individuals making choices they hope will improve their lives — much of this human migration is compelled by wars, persecution, natural disasters, and poverty. As noted above,

> ### Globalization
> A process of knitting together economic, political, and social systems across nations. This process could produce greater equality, social participation, and democracy but has instead resulted in the effects of neoliberalism noted above as well as a concentration of economic, political, and social power in the hands of international corporations and those who benefit from the commercialization of everyday life.

a growing worldwide gap between rich and poor has become characteristic of global capitalism (Harvey 2005; Teeple 1995). The 2010 earthquake in Haiti demonstrates one of the consequences of this gap: many countries find it nearly impossible to deal with natural disasters, disease pandemics, and the displacement and disruption of wars in their own or bordering countries. These conditions generate groups of refugees who are forced to leave their homes. Voluntary immigrants follow in their wake as unstable conditions make migration a more appealing option than remaining in place.

The global movement of people requires new approaches and skills from social workers. In some cases these skills focus on developing new counselling approaches for survivors of torture and trauma; in others, on provisioning, such as locating the goods and services necessary to survival (Hayes 2009). In still other cases, social work skills have melded with analysis to produce finely tuned anti-racist, post-colonial, and ethno-specific approaches in specific as well as general settings (Baines 2008; Dominelli 1999).

The growth in poverty, nationally and internationally, is a major factor adding to the complexity and intensity of clients' problems. When wages are kept low and large pools of unemployed people are available to draw into the workforce at will, corporations and businesses keep profits high, a key feature of neoliberalism. Solutions to radically reduce poverty are not difficult to develop or enact in policy. For example, boosting the minimum wage (as recommended by anti-poverty activists) would provide a significant and badly needed increase in take-home pay for over two million low-income workers in Canada. And it would allow single people, working full-time and year-round, to finally reach the poverty line (although workers with dependents would still be left below the poverty line). In an era in which policy-makers are complaining about a looming "labour shortage," a higher minimum wage would actually pull more potential workers into the labour force (some people quit looking for work because wages are seen to be too low) — contrary to the dire warnings of business lobbyists that higher minimum wages destroy jobs.

New populations that social workers see growing are groups of poor people including the working poor (those who are employed but whose wages leave them below the poverty line); people experiencing long-term homelessness; immigrants and refugees with foreign credentials who have difficulty getting these credentials recognized or entering the labour market; and workfare participants who are kept interminably poor. By reducing services that support them and lowering the levels of financial and social assistance available, government polices and practices have made these groups increasingly marginal and desperate. Taking advantage of the climate created by funding cuts, political and media commentary vilifies the poor, making them appear greedy, lazy, and unmotivated (Martin 2002; Mosher 2000). As seen in Jeanne Faye's chapter in this book, this situation often frustrates the best efforts of social workers to advocate for and with people who are impoverished, or to assist them in meeting their needs.

Managerialism, New Public Management, and the Social Work Workplace

The second way most front-line social workers experience neoliberalism and globalization is in the form of rapid, and often ongoing, reorganization of their workplaces and various restrictions put on the use of social justice skills and interventions. Restructuring, as this reorganization is often called, is particularly advanced in most child welfare and public sector social work jobs, and found in lesser forms in the non-profit sector. As will be discussed in more detail below, these new forms of workplace organization are often called "managerialism" because of their tendency to view all aspects of the social work endeavour as issues requiring pro-market, business-like management solutions, rather than non-market initiatives stressing social connection, equality, and a public service ethos (McDonald 2006; Clarke and Newman 1997; Fabricant and Burghardt 1992). The market is a term commonly used to refer to services and goods that are sold to make a profit. This includes goods we need, such as food and clothing, luxury items like high-end cars and houses, as well as services people want such as house cleaning or IT support, and services they need such as private home or nursing care, private counselling services, or private mental health supports. Services are non-market when they are provided as a right of citizenship and do not charge a fee or require private insurance from those using their services. These services do not make a profit and used to be run on an ethos of public good, social justice, equity, care, or a combination of these themes. Increasingly,

Pro-Market, Non-Market

Human services of all types are increasingly used to legitimize the private market and encourage public support of private solutions to social problems (pro-market). Though they work alongside and extend and support the private market, sectors like the social services remain nominally non-market in that, for the most part, they do not turn a profit and thus remain just outside commercial relations.

> ### Public Sector Ethos
> The sense that governments should provide respectful and sup-
> portive public services to their citizens and take measures to
> reduce inequities and improve social well-being.

however, even non-market services are starting to look and behave like market services, adopting management models, institutional values, and work cultures that legitimize business approaches rather than care-based approaches. Such changes make it harder, though not impossible, to do AOP and other social justice-oriented forms of social work practice.

Some social service workplaces, particularly in the non-profit sector, have managed to avoid many of these changes and still find significant space for anti-oppressive and social justice work (Barnoff and Moffatt 2007; Carniol and Del Valle 2007: Barnoff and Coleman 2007). Those working closer to or within the state, however, find their working conditions deteriorating and their space to develop alternative practices restrained. AOP social workers often turn to social justice non-profit agencies to learn new practices or refine existing ones, but they also learn from the resistance practiced by those working in the more constrained circumstances of managerialized worksites.

Many social workers never give a second thought to the way they are managed at work until their jobs are cut or their caseloads doubled. A clear idea of what is going on at the level of agency ideology and management models is nonetheless necessary in order to keep oneself and others safer in the workplace and to protect the rights of service users. Understanding how the logics and practices of neoliberal management operate gives AOP social workers a much better chance of avoiding or at least challenging practices that can harm service workers and social workers. Neoliberal managerial models, such as "New Public Management," embrace the notion that waste and inefficiency can be removed by standardizing work practices and skills (Baines 2004b). While currently promoted as a form of "performance management," best practice or professional competency models tend to standardize social work by breaking practices down into their smallest possible features, documenting and promoting them as the most economical and effective way to practice (see Braverman 1974, for the classic description and analysis of these processes).

For example, rather than viewing an initial meeting and assessment with a client or community group as an open-ended, reciprocal process of relationship building, current social work intakes often make use of standardized paper- or computer-based assessment tools. The goal of these forms is speed and accuracy: more work can get done in a shorter period of time. As discussed below and in Kristin Smith's chapter in this book, these tick-box forms focus on very narrow and particular aspects of people's problems, leaving out most of the larger context and excluding other ways to tell and interpret the client's story; as a result, the forms develop a very small snapshot of the complexity of people's lives and the problems they experience. Rather than undertaking ongoing relationship building and interactive case-plan building, the worker adds up scores on tick-box forms. Each score dictates the kinds of solutions that will be presented to the clients and pursued by the worker. Deviations from the tick-box form and other types of so-called best practices are discouraged on the basis that they will involve unnecessary risk, cost, and waste. Standardization of this kind deskills and routinizes work, limiting both the kinds of actions that are seen as efficient and effective and the ways that social workers feel entitled to think about social problems and generate innovative and untried interventions.

In addition, standardized work processes such as assessment or intake forms remove or reduce opportunities to think outside the box, or in this case, the "tick–box." There is little or no space on these forms for referrals to social action groups or to link clients with advocacy centres, to attend meetings with them to challenge injustice or to co-write complaints about problems in the various systems in which poor people's lives are enmeshed. Though the new processes do not entirely remove these options, they make it very difficult for workers to find the time to generate creative ideas, to find the resources and the referrals necessary to make them a reality, and to build the kind of caring, trusting relationship with a client that is needed for them to want to take risks such as joining an advocacy group or launching an appeal. As Kristin Smith (2007) notes, many anti-oppressive practices have had to go "underground" (160) and workers have had to develop new ways to elude the restrictions imposed on their work practices, often by coming in "under the radar" rather than undertaking social justice practices openly as they may have done in the past (164).

Related to this is the way that standardization restricts the use of discretion and decision-making. Prior to restructuring, social workers had a "fair degree of discretion in their work" (Dominelli and Hoogvelt 1996: 56); they could decide how to undertake intake assessments and often kept these assessments ongoing and open-ended, constructing case plans and locating resources as decided in conjunction with the service user. Though still possible in some social work settings, rather than standardized assessments or computerized case plan programs, public sector workers were encouraged to build open-ended, caring relationships with service users through activities such as expressing an interest in the clients' struggles and dilemmas; listening to clients' problems; suggesting alternative solutions and resources; providing hands-on support, counselling, and active intervention; developing short- and long-term case plans; and referring clients to and helping to organize services and activist groups undertaking actions beyond the workers' capacity to provide on their own (Carniol 2010; Lundy 2004; Baines 2004a). Though such an approach is still possible in some social work settings, under NPM many social workers are restricted in the amount of time they can spend with each client and required to complete "tick-box" forms that determine the length and amount of service to which each client is entitled as well as the content of that service and timelines for the worker's completion of each task. This model of work is intensely frustrating to most workers as indicated by a front-line social worker in Nova Scotia:

> The identifying issue might be the same but every person and family is different. We can't treat them all like little chocolates on an assembly line. Each person needs a different level of care and I, as a social worker, should get to decide that level in conjunction with the client rather than a stupid form telling me how I have to work with each person. (Baines 2004a)

Consistent with findings in other care professions, NPM has dramatically increased the amount of paperwork required of social workers (Cunningham 2008; McDonald 2006; Baines 2004a). Some estimate that social workers in fields such as child welfare spend up to 70 percent of their time doing paperwork — completing standardized forms of every type, keeping statistics, returning calls, and attending meetings with other professionals — with very little time left for interaction with clients or communities (Ontario Association of Children's Aid Societies 2001).

In order to save costs even further, neoliberal management models encourage "flexible" workforces. Rather than full-time, permanent, unionized jobs, new forms of flexible private sector work organization are characterized by the following features: "thin" staffing such as solo shifts; lean shifts (one or two workers per site, sometimes with cell phone access to workers or supervisors at other sites); split shifts (wherein staff work an hour or two in the morning and return in the evening for a few more hours of work); part-time, contract, casual, on-call, and other forms of temporary work; and expanded reliance on volunteer work (Baines 2004b, 2004d; Aronson and Sammon 2000). The standardization of work practices common under NPM makes it easier to supervise part-time and impermanent workers or to replace them with less costly workers (or volunteers) with less training and fewer credentials (Baines 2004a, 2004c).

In a recent study of the developmental services, more than two-thirds of the jobs were found to be casual, part-time, or contract (Baines 2005). All the agencies involved in the study used thin shifts, casual workers, temporary workers, and contract workers, and all made extensive use of volunteers. All agencies had high rates of client violence against workers; constant changes in staffing disrupted clients' capacity to cope, and impermanent staff had few opportunities to learn routines that might provide reassurance rather than aggravation to stressed-out clients or to develop techniques that might identify and diffuse tensions before they reached the breaking point (Baines 2005). Studies in other social service agencies show a similar story of rising workplace violence and abuse, exacerbated by managerial forms of work organization

(Baines, Cunningham, and Fraser 2010; Baines and Cunningham forthcoming; Mcdonald and Sirotech 2001). In short, within flexible work models, social workers experience increased job insecurity, decreased income, few or no benefits, increased workplace violence and added pressure on home life in the constant struggle to juggle home and work demands, while agencies save costs.

Social work, like other types of care work, is also highly gendered, with women forming the majority of the providers, clients, and volunteers. Jobs involving caring labour are commonly assumed to be merely an extension of what women do "naturally" rather than a distinct set of sophisticated skills, knowledge, and creativity (Baines, Evans and Neysmith 1998; Ehrenreich 2003; Herd and Meyer 2002). This assumption has meant that social workers continue to rank among the low-pay, low-status professions (Abbott and Wallace 1999; Cohen and Wagner 1982). Care work is also racialized, with people of colour only recently gaining access to many of the better jobs in social work (Bernard, Lucas-White, and Moore 1993) or often finding themselves employed in ethno-specific programs and projects aimed at specific groups such as Chinese and Asian elderly or urban Aboriginal youth. These marginal locations and the heavy client demand associated with them has meant that many Aboriginal social workers and social workers of colour have developed unique skill sets that can differ significantly from those of their white counterparts. Thus, while ignoring difference and oppression at the level of managerial models, neoliberalism has increased many of the differences between and among white social workers and social workers of colour (including Indigenous social workers) (Baines 2008).

"If You Could Change One Thing": Lessons from a Study on Restructuring, Social Workers, and Social Justice Practice

Faced with reduced social funding, neoliberalism, and global capitalism (discussed above and in Chapter One), many social workers question whether human needs can still be met with fairness and dignity. Practitioners, activists, and social policy analysts in Canada and elsewhere are searching for new models to meet diverse needs, expand social justice, and counter growing inequalities. Several troubling questions arise. Have increased workloads and stress-filled working conditions eliminated much of the practice wisdom and social justice ethic that strongly influenced social work practice in previous decades? Have more than twenty years of neoliberal restructuring constrained the thinking and practice of front-line practitioners to the point where they have been absorbed into bureaucratic agendas and pro-market solutions? What would front-line workers and supervisors reply if asked what changes they would like to see in contemporary social services? Highlighting the impacts of restructuring, neoliberalism, and new corporate-like managerial models, this section explores the experience of a group of front-line social service workers. This section also underscores the importance of asking new questions, developing new knowledge, and continuing to expand our resistance and social justice-oriented practice.

In a recent multi-year, three-province study of social service restructuring in Canada, my research team and I asked front-line practitioners about their everyday work experience in the context of ongoing cuts to funding, new philosophies of service, and new forms of work organization.[1] They were also asked *what they would alter about the system if they had the power to enact one change.* Their answers to the latter question provide a useful way to launch a broader discussion of the constraints and possibilities for anti-oppressive and other liberatory forms of social work practice. Indeed, their responses not only highlight the dilemmas under which social services currently operate in many parts of the world, but also reveal the indomitability of worker resistance and the social justice ethic that underlies anti-oppressive and other radical/social justice approaches to social work practice, demonstrating that new, liberatory practices can continue to develop even in the face of cutbacks and constraints.

Much of the discussion in this section is based on two sets of interviews with social workers.[2] Initially, eight-three front-line social service workers and a small number of managers, supervisors, policy-makers, and advocates working in British Columbia (twenty-nine), Alberta (twenty-eight), and Nova Scotia (twenty-six) were interviewed. Two years later, a second round of interviews was undertaken with the B.C. group (twenty-two additional interviews).[3] In B.C., the election of a strongly neoliberal government had resulted in a rapid and massive overhaul of services in what had, up to that point, been the province with the highest levels of human service funding in English Canada.

B.C. is one of the more industrialized regions in Canada. It has a relatively strong working-class culture, a high rate of unionization and (until 2001) a social democratic government that tried to implement moderate fiscal and social policies. In 2001, an explicitly anti-welfare-state, neoliberal government was elected, one that was proposing and implementing the deepest cuts to social programs in Canada. The twenty-two follow-up interviews we conducted in 2003 provided an opportunity to explore the impacts of welfare-state restructuring almost as the process unfolded. While these workers are not necessarily representative of the larger population of social workers in Canada or elsewhere, their responses allow us to explore the durability of the social justice and social care orientation in social work practice.

Resistance and Radical Practices

Given the constraints under which social workers practice during the current era of restructuring and cutbacks, what is the likelihood that the opinions of front-line practitioners will differ from popular and managerial opinions supporting private-sector-like restructuring of the social services? As discussed below, one question in our second round of interviews proved to be exceptionally useful in understanding social work practice: "If there was one big thing you could change in social services, what would it be?"

Lost Our Vision

In our initial interviews, workers lamented the loss of relationship with clients that accompanied the standardization of work and the use of flexible staffing patterns. Two years later, those who participated in follow-up interviews went further. They lamented the "loss of our vision of what social work is supposed to be and who it is supposed to serve," and they suggested that "we forget what social services should be about" and "we forget why we are here in the first place and get caught up in other directions." Reflecting the sentiments of many, one senior advocate decried the tight-fisted, punitive aspects of the current system: "We are called on to be mean in our jobs, and this not what any of us went into social work for." Invoking the sense that social work has lost its social vision, other workers reflected negatively on the preoccupation with "business goals" such as cost saving, lean work organization, and competitiveness, rather than goals of social justice, mutual obligation, and care.

Preventive and Pro-active

While the social services system in general was described as lacking vision, there were many ideas for how to renew and rebuild systems of social caring. Particularly emphasized was the need for pro-active and preventive approaches. Reflecting social justice goals, a long-time clinician asserted, "I would turn the whole thing (system) on its head. I would put all the money into prevention so that we head troubles off long before they get to the point where they are social work problems." A welfare worker promoted an AOP perspective when she argued, "we need a different way of providing services — supporting families and communities at the ground level so that neighbourhoods are safe and caring places, and people have local places to go if they need help — that don't really feel like heavy intervention, just like support and taking care of each other."

The social workers always emphasized the need to tie pro-active and preventive approaches to increased funding. Across the board, workers noted that the lack of resources constrained their capacity to find services for clients and to provide them with the things they need. Emphasizing social justice values and concerns about the growth of poverty and violence, a veteran child welfare worker made this recommendation: "I would take all the money they've cut back from everywhere and dump it into early childhood services — really good preschool, well-subsidized child care, services that really strengthen the family, the child, and the community for everyone. Not for a particular group, but for everyone. And I'd make sure the jobs were unionized."

The social workers also highlighted the need for preventive services to be provided from within a wider system of "public care," emphasizing a mixed economy of government and non-profit services in which the government does not act merely as a "broker, contracting out services and washing their hands of them," but as a facilitator and guarantor of "high quality, accessible services" emphasizing community involvement, public funding, and secure jobs for social workers.

Holism

It was commonly felt that the current system of fragmented and residual services has resulted in a patchwork of subsistence services in which people "fall through the cracks." Clients who find their way into the system often have their needs met in ways that can be punitive and socially controlling. Workers emphasized the need for comprehensive, integrated services in which community members avoid the stigma associated with being a social work "client" or workfare participant, and instead receive a range of everyday activities and programs that strengthen relationships, individuals, and social support systems. The implementation of so-called accountability measures in most social service agencies has meant that workers' time is dominated by statistics-keeping and other forms of documentation. Research participants expressed frustration at the way these tasks dominated their work days, sharply curtailing interactions with clients. Some workers questioned the current model of performance evaluation in which evaluation measures are established by managers and highly paid consultants, rather than by service users and communities.

Dovetailing with these concerns and highlighting the need to involve clients and communities in social policy and social service decisions, many workers expressed acute discomfort with the lack of a meaningful voice for clients at any level of policy or program delivery. An inner-city addictions counselor reflected the needs of many when she asked, "whose needs are being served by this obsession with accountability? — it sure isn't the clients', and it sure isn't [those of] the workers or any of the rest of the average people out there."

Residual
This term refers to minimal services that are available only to those who meet a means test. A residual state is one that provides services only to those who lack other options. Residual services in Canada include welfare, public housing, and food banks. In contrast, universal services avoid the deterrence and humiliation of means testing by providing quality services to all. Universal services in Canada include public education, health care, and old age support.

Fragmentation
Services are fragmented when they address only a portion of the problems people experience and fail to integrate services either within agencies or between and among agencies.

Emphasizing holistic services with full *community* participation and ac-countability, research participants favoured the removal of standardized job performance, replacing it with collaborative forms of intervention in which the workers' expertise and resources are mobilized to assist service users in meeting mutually agreed-upon goals. In this context, accountability would shift from "funders and taxpayers to service users and communities."

Participatory Democracy

In Canada and other countries, unresponsive governments have caused peo-ple to look for new forms of democracy and social participation. These new ideas were very strong in the responses of research participants. Ranging from critiques of accountability and evaluation measures to calls for a complete overhaul of the existing electoral system in Canada, these responses indicated that the new participatory democracy models pursued in Brazil, Argentina, parts of India, and elsewhere were in the thoughts of the B.C. social service workers. At the level of the workplace, most workers felt that new forms of management have closed down ways in which employees used to have input into the priorities and organization of their agencies. While few social service workers identified a specific link to the new forms of democracy emerging in the Third World, many called for increased worker input, more forums for discussion, and more avenues for shared worker control. Integrating this with more choices for clients, research participants asserted that formal channels must be developed for client input or the insertion of clients' voices into service priorities and directions. Indeed, one veteran child welfare worker presented a strong case for inverting the system so that evaluation, continuation, and development of programs could be placed entirely in the hands of service users and the communities in which they live. A community worker agreed, speaking of the need to "turn democracy upside down" by empowering the disenfranchised to change their worlds through policy planning and devel-opment processes similar to those used by the poor and marginalized in the Third World. Clinicians and settlement workers, working with disempowered communities in downtown east-side Vancouver,[4] asserted that social workers should insist on "as many mass meetings as necessary" to involve dispossessed people in determining how to address their own complicated, deep-rooted social problems and to collectively build strong, inclusive communities. Like the preventive and pro-active services discussed earlier, changes in policy mak-ing were coupled with the need for new resources and levels of funding that can "actually produce change."

Did Place of Work Count?

Most of the critiques and visions of social work practitioners described above echo global resistance themes of participatory decision-making and social caring. However, the new forms of social work organization also seemed to limit the responses of some research participants. In particular, waves of downsizing and layoffs in B.C. meant that *some* social service workers were reluctant to speak openly. A couple of participants asked to speak "off the record," while others asked to have certain portions of their interviews erased.

Fears of this kind were more prevalent, although not uniformly, among those employed in large government bureaucracies and among racialized populations who had only recently gained access to public-sector jobs. Research participants employed within large government bureaucracies were more likely to provide answers that narrowly addressed dilemmas in their own workplaces and client groups. By contrast, workers in less-bureaucratic, less-managerialized, non-profit agencies were likely to have broader, cross-sector visions of what could be changed — almost as if working in the non-profit sector in and of itself increased one's capacity to imagine social change and to believe that social change can happen. Narrow visions were also found among those who had management, rather than social work, training. These individuals tended to provide responses that echoed popular, right-wing discourse vilifying so-called lazy, unmotivated clients and displayed little or no empathy for clients, and no macro-analysis. In contrast, those employed in storefront, community-activist, non-profit services provided the most politically aware, internationally attuned, and socially comprehensive analyses and solutions (even though some of these workers supplemented their incomes with construction work and babysitting). Exceptions to these trends included veteran child welfare workers who favoured Brazilian-style participatory democracy and a hospital-based clinician who advocated local control and service provision through community-based, non-hierarchical, feminist collectives. These exceptions speak to the ways that new managerial strategies may standardize work pace, content, and tasks, and that restricted labour markets may make workers cautious about speaking out. However, front-line practitioners have not been wholly absorbed by neoliberal agendas. They continue to find ways to think "outside the box," to pursue notions of social justice and fairness, and to practise anti-oppressive social work. Interestingly, in this predominantly female sector, gender did not emerge as a predictor for any of these trends — except insofar as social workers generally demonstrate a willingness to take on large quantities of unpaid work and to resist agendas of social meanness.

From Macro to Micro: Impacts on Social Work Practice

While numerous authors have commented on the changing realities of social work practice, few explore the way that macro-forces (structural, socio-economic and political) and meso-forces (workplace and organizational) shape and constrain how social work practitioners think about and perform their work (micro). As noted earlier in this chapter, public sectors across the industrialized world have been downsized and restructured, in large part, to make it easier for corporate and pro-business organizations to dominate all areas of life (Stanford 2004; Panitch and Gindin 2004; Esping-Andersen 1996). The globalization of corporate power has been accompanied by a narrowing of alternative visions of human service provision (Wiseman 1998: 69) as public provision has been replaced by "contracting-out, privatization and the empowerment of business and quasi-business actors" (Considine 2000: 74). This reorganization of social services has been criticized for fragmenting services, decreasing service quality, reducing accessibility, and contributing to the growing gap between rich and poor (Dominelli 2004; Lundy 2004; Wiseman 1998; Mullaly 1997).

The impact of constraints on the work of social workers has been compounded by the effect of these constraints on the larger community. The lives of clients have been made more difficult and often more impoverished, which has, in turn, made social work even more challenging. While social workers seem to feel these constraints most in everyday frontline practice, they have operated at three distinct and often overlapping levels: the structural or macro-level; the policy and organizational or meso-level; and the level of interpersonal or micro-practice.

Reduced Welfare State (Macro-Constraint)

Local impacts of globalization and neoliberalism include a reduced welfare state and the domination of labour markets by insecure, short-term forms of employment, lower wages, and few benefits. This contingent labour market (Broad 2000; Campbell and Brosnan 1999) serves to keep workers in their jobs regardless of working conditions and makes it less likely that they will speak out against unfavourable developments in services or practice. Cutbacks in the welfare state mean that fewer supports such as unemployment insurance, skill training, and welfare are available to workers should they lose their employment, a prospect that also makes workers less likely to take risks that might result in job loss and more likely to comply with their employers' directives, even those directives that they feel are counter to social justice and social care.

Private-Sector Forms of Work Organization/Restricted Labour Markets (Macro- and Meso-Constraints)

The findings of this study confirmed claims made earlier in this chapter regarding the impacts of globalization and restructuring on frontline working conditions. As is occurring in global labour markets, so too in the social services sector are full-time, permanent, unionized jobs being rapidly replaced by part-time, contract, casual, on-call, and other forms of temporary, insecure work (Baines 2004b; Aronson and Sammon 2000). Under these new forms of work organization, individual workers are unlikely to be able to determine the process of completing tasks, the order of tasks, or the tasks themselves. Assessment tools, intake forms, case notes, and even supervision are increasingly standardized, often taking the form of step-by-step "best practice" flow sheets and computerized case management packages.

> ### Best Practice
> Currently, most social service agencies try to document the prac-
> tices seen as the most effective and efficient. Workers are coached
> to use these practices to improve the quality of service. Efficiency
> and effectiveness tend to be measured by criteria developed by
> managers and professionals and to focus largely on cost savings,
> rather than by criteria developed by clients and communities,
> which are more likely to focus on social caring or capacity to make
> real changes in people's lives. Hence, best practices often narrow
> what is viewed as good practice and eliminate skills and actions
> aimed at long-term assistance to clients or structural and policy
> change, since these tend not to result in immediate changes or
> cost savings.

New forms of work organization also include the widespread use of check box forms in which interactions among players in the social work endeavour are tightly scripted (Baines 2004b). Increased standardization means that work can be sped up and readily assumed by part-time, temporary, and contract employees. Clearly, it is no idle threat that professionals may be replaced by less skilled and lower-paid employees, or even volunteers. Coupled with the decrease in job opportunities across the sector, this threat could constrain workers' willingness to protest such unfair circumstances in their workplaces as cutbacks to client services and eroded working conditions for themselves.

Gender (Macro-Constraint)
Welfare state downsizing has had a disproportionate impact on women, as it has reduced the number of better-paid, full-time jobs available to them, replacing such positions with temporary, part-time, and insecure employment as well as expanding the role of unpaid familial and voluntary care (Cohen 1997). Moreover, skills such as listening, empathy, counseling, problem-solving, multitasking, and facilitation are thought to be extensions of the skills all women have by virtue of their gender; thus predominantly female job categories such as social work remain low-status and lower-paying than many other professions (Baines 2004c; Neysmith 2000; Marchant and Wearing 1986b).

Race (Macro-Constraints)
In some areas of the Canadian social services, equity programs and requirements from funders have compelled employers to hire a more diverse workforce and provide more inclusive services. As noted earlier, just as Native workers and workers of colour gained access to better public sector jobs, standardization decreased the satisfactions of the work and funding cuts reduced the number of staff. Currently, most jobs in equity programs and departments are contract positions or other forms of temporary work that rarely provide benefits and contain little in the way of job security. As discussed earlier in this chapter,

many First Nations workers and workers of colour in Canada have been in the unique position of going against the deskilling trend seen in many of the helping professions. Due to the complexity of client issues and of the tasks facing workers in equity programs, Indigenous workers and workers of colour are generally expected to come to a job with a higher level of skill and then to develop a more diverse range of skills on the job than is expected of their white counterparts. Most of the Indigenous workers and workers of colour involved in this study have developed new ways of conceptualizing all levels of social work practice (Baines 2008).

Loss of Practice-Knowledge and the Narrowing of Skills (Meso-Constraints)

As discussed earlier in this chapter, under new, private-sector-like models of work organization, skills are no longer recognized as a complex synergy of formal, informal, individual, and collective knowledge that develops incrementally through social interactions (Darrah 1997; Manwearing and Wood 1984). Those skills that do not contribute to cost savings are often eliminated from workers' prescribed routines, while standardization further reduces the range and complexity of skills used in the social services. Flexible and thin staffing makes it less possible to establish the kinds of relationships with co-workers in which the practice skills of more experienced workers can be exchanged and intermingle with the new ideas of new staff; eventually, much of this practice knowledge is lost (Baines 2004c). In short, complex skills and knowledge become casualties of restructured, ostensibly improved, social services.

Constraints on Social Workers

Macro-Constraints	Meso-Constraints	Micro-Constraints
Reduced welfare state	Workplace organization: • loss of practice skills • heavy workload • standardization • lack of resources • no voice for workers or clients	Meanness
Restricted labour market & private sector work organization		Loss of vision
Gender		
Race		
Restricted democratic processes		

Restricted Democratic Process
Many of these constraints have been strengthened under governments that have assisted those with power to acquire more, even as those without power have been increasingly marginalized. International trade agreements and organizations now have the capacity to direct local policies in many areas. These trends have acted as a spark, igniting long-standing disenchantment with current models of electoral democracy that limit people's opportunities for input into the decisions that frame their everyday lives (Gindin and Stanford 2003; Rebick 2000; Wiseman 1998). Social work's commitment to provide voice and self-determination to clients (Canadian Association of Social Workers 2005a) is compatible with community experiments aimed at turning power structures on their heads so that those previously silenced are given voice, resources and collective power.

Further Thoughts from This Study
Despite the multi-level constraints discussed above, social service workers continue — at least in their talk and their dreams — to resist dominant discourses that discourage social caring and resistance. At the micro-level, social service workers chaffed at the loss of social vision within the current system, the social "meanness" under which they operated, and the lack of preventive, pro-active, holistic services. Instead of parroting government and employers' excuses for cutbacks and anti-client stories, workers described changes that addressed meso- and macro-constraints. In the face of narrow and miserly approaches to social care, social service workers showed that a commitment to social justice has survived pro-market restructuring. They enacted their commitments in a myriad of ways, from organizing for expanded democratic control of social services to working unpaid overtime in order to meet the needs of clients and communities. They also regularly undertook workplace advocacy, grassroots organizing around client issues, and working with their unions to prevent further erosion of services (Baines 2004b). As discussed above, workers recommended policy and practice changes aimed at creating democratic, holistic, participatory services. Arguably, the impact of many of these actions on the global tidal wave of neoliberalism is limited. However, they certainly create space for further resistance and rebuilding. Notwithstanding their somewhat limited impact, these actions are crucial tactics in the battle for people's hearts and minds in an era characterized by the growing polarization of rich and poor and the uniculture promoted by corporatism and consumerism. Indeed, many see this as a time when a battle of ideas is being fought over if and how societies will provide care for those suffering from the impacts of global capitalism.

As noted throughout this book, anti-oppressive practice is part of an overall struggle to bring about fundamental change to our social systems, so that the conditions that generate and benefit from inequities are replaced by systems that foster equity, fairness, and the healthy development of all. The findings of this study show that despite restructuring and years of neoliberalism, social work resistance and visions for a better world continue. This is something to celebrate and build on in the front lines of everyday transformative, politicized social work practice.

Building Transformative Social Work

In addition to exploring the "doing" of anti-oppressive practice, this book also focuses on building transformative, politicized social work. Transformative refers to working simultaneously at two levels, that is, working to relieve people's emotional pain and immediate difficulties while simultaneously working to change the larger forces that generate inequity, unfairness, and social injustice (Mullaly 2002). Politicized refers to putting understandings of power into our every interaction and endeavour in social work (Tew 2006). This includes remaining aware of how power can be both damaging and productive (Tew 2006), as well as of the ways that people's everyday struggles for survival and dignity are intensely politicized struggles over the power to define problems and their solutions; it includes both the capacity to access resources (cultural, social, economic, and political) and the capacity to link these issues to other struggles for social justice, fairness, and equity, locally and on a global level.

It is commonly said that during this period of history, when right-wing thinking is on the rise and governments are retreating from social responsibility, much of the struggle for social justice is a struggle over ideas. Interestingly, the authors in this collection go farther than ideas — they suggest ways to be reflexive and undertake social analysis as well as concrete ways to act within the complicated and demanding field of contemporary social work. Drawing on a wide range of practice examples that reflect the diversity of Canada today, this collection invites readers to reflect critically on ways to do transformative, politicized, anti-oppressive social work practice, and then armed with this critical thought, go out and build a better world.

Notes

1. Funding from the Social Sciences and Humanities Research Fund (Canada) is gratefully acknowledged, as are the contributions of the research coordinators, Candace Bernard, Linda Kreitzer, and Shannon Steele, the twenty-five research assistants and the 122 research participants. This chapter draws extensively on an article originally published in *Australian Social Work* (see Baines 2006a).
2. Research participants worked in the public or non-profit sector for an average of eight-and-a-half years. Similar to the broader social services workforce, the sample was roughly 80 percent female. Research participants included roughly equal numbers of those with professional education and credentials (B.S.W., M.S.W.) and those without. Interviewees were asked to comment broadly on the changes they experienced in their paid and unpaid work over the past five years.

3. Three of the Native social workers originally interviewed could not be located, so three Native workers doing similar types of jobs were substituted.
4. Downtown east-side Vancouver has experienced numerous problems associated with long-term poverty and structural injustices. Among other challenges, it has the highest rate of heroin use in Canada and a large population of homeless, hard-to-house, and semi-housed citizens.

Section One

TYPES OF PRACTICE

Introduction

Donna Baines

Social Work students often ask how AOP differs from good, high-quality, generalist social work practice. The two traditions have many skills and practices in common: communication, intake, interviewing, assessment, support, planning, and referral. However, AOP is also likely to include advocacy, reflexivity, social analysis and an awareness of larger social dynamics, and various forms of activism and community building.

Though some argue that they are not professional practice skills, social justice practitioners also see the following as pivotal to liberatory practice: a skepticism about organizational processes and categories that may harm or limit our understanding of social processes that bring people to social work services and make it hard for them to change the conditions of their lives; a commitment to seeing the problems that service users experience as part of larger systems of inequity and injustice; an awareness of the social worker's own social location as a professional within an institution and of the kinds of power that title and position entail, as well as a commitment to using that power for and with oppressed groups; an ongoing respect for differences, grounded in a celebration of human diversity; and a sense that as a social worker one always has one foot within the state and social service bureaucracies and one foot outside, building resistance and the capacity of individuals and communities for social analysis and activism. Basically, AOP comes down to social workers having to deal with class, race, gender, sexual orientation, and other forms of oppression in everyday life, using a unique lens or framework through which to understand, question, and improve practice.

This first section of the book focuses on AOP in a number of different practice settings, drawing on case scenarios and practice wisdom from those with frontline experience or/and research studies. The section provides concrete suggestions, practice wisdom, and theory to help those struggling to use AOP in their everyday social work.

Chapter 3

Doing Anti-Oppressive Child Protection Casework

Gary Dumbrill

This chapter takes the position that anti-oppressive child protection practice requires workers to have investigative forensic skills and the ability to use authority effectively, combined with an array of casework skills that engage parents in a process of change. It examines the casework skills needed in this process, but does so within the context of the forensic and authority-based roles that child protection workers also need to employ. The central message of the chapter is that anti-oppressive child protection practice begins with the worker trying to understand the perspective of the parent receiving intervention. This focus on parents is not because their perspective is more important than children's, but because wherever possible, the best way to serve and protect children is by engaging their parents in a process of change, and because in social work, change begins by understanding the perspective of the person with which one is working.

As you read this chapter, ask yourself the following:
1.   Why do I need to understand a parent's perspective in child protection work?
2.   Once I understand the parent's perspective, what do I do if I disagree with it?
3.   What if I need to investigate parents and take their children away — isn't that oppressive?
4.   Are there attitudes and values I need to embrace to do child protection work?
5.   What about bigger structural societal issues — where do they fit in?

After knocking a third time I hear bolts being undone. The door opens slightly to jolt against a security chain. The eyes of a tired-looking parent peer through the gap, and in the background a child cries.

"Who are you and what do you want?" the parent asks.

I pause, wondering how to tell them that I am a child protection worker and that I have come to conduct a child abuse investigation.

Doing anti-oppressive practice (AOP) begins by understanding what is occurring at this door — not only in understanding life outside the door and the tasks the worker must perform, but also in understanding life on the inside of the door from the perspective of the parents and children who live there. It involves grasping what sociologists call "Verstehen" and anthropologists refer to as an "emic" perspective, both referring to ascertaining another person's definition of a situation from an inside understanding of their life world (Schwandt 1994: 118).

Understanding the perspectives of those we serve has always been the beginning point of social work. Pilsecker says that to start in this place, social workers must

> Understand from our clients' point of view, the troubles and frustrations that bring them to us, what gives them hope, the resources that sustain them, the perceived limitations that distress them. But we must not stop there. We must strive to comprehend fully their inner stirrings and their external world, listen carefully, and keenly observe their nonverbal signals. In so doing, we build a picture of the person-in-context. (Pilsecker 1994: 447)

When Pilsecker said that we must "understand from our clients' point of view, the troubles and frustrations that bring them to us," (1994: 447) he was probably not thinking about parents receiving child protection intervention. Such parents do not usually have problems that bring them to us; instead, their problems bring us to them. We usually arrive at their door unannounced, often with armed police and always with concerns about the way they are raising their children. Parents who open their door to child protection workers will almost certainly be facing some form of investigation or assessment that questions whether they have abused or neglected their children. They may face arrest, and they risk losing their children — perhaps forever. Consequently, the first problem the child protection worker needs to understand from the parents' perspective is that a child protection worker knocking at their door is likely to be a problem for them. Before we try to imagine what this event is like from a parent's perspective, however, it is important to explore why we need to develop this understanding.

The Dual Roles of Investigation and Helping

In Canada during the late 1990s, it was emphasized that child protection social workers needed to develop a more forensic and police-like manner that paid little attention to the perspective of parents (Dumbrill 2006; Parada 2004).

> ### Forensic
> Forensic refers to a process of scientifically gathering evidence for legal purposes. The focus of forensic social work is uncovering facts through investigation and presenting these to court.

It is of course true that child protection work must, at times, be investigative and policing of parents; that it must, on occasion, remove children from their homes despite a parent's views or wishes. If a child protection worker fails to operate in these ways when necessary to protect a child, they will ultimately fail the children they serve, and failing to protect a child who was relying on a social worker to protect them from harm has to be considered oppressive. It is equally true, however, that if a worker resorts to policing parents or removing children in instances where casework skill could have resolved the issues that brought the social worker to a parent's door, this fails to protect the integrity and dignity of the family. That also has to be considered oppressive, because dismantling a family that could have been kept intact with appropriate support is an inappropriate use of state power. Anti-oppressive child protection work, therefore, requires workers to have forensic skills combined with the ability to use authority effectively, along with an array of casework skills that engage parents in a process of change. This is often described as the "dual roles" of child protection work (Trotter 2002).

There are, of course, situations where starting intervention by understanding a parent's perspective or initiating a casework process is completely inappropriate. In cases where children have suffered horrific injuries, or where there is imminent danger to a child, the starting point of intervention is removing that child to a place of safety. Most cases, however, are less dramatic than this and do not require children to be removed. The 2003 Canadian Incidence Study of Child Abuse and Neglect (Trocmé et al. 2005) describes the typical situations workers encounter in Canada (excluding Québec where data was not gathered in the study). In most investigations (53 percent) there are either no protection concerns or not enough evidence of concern for social workers to intervene against a parent's wishes. Indeed, in 40 percent of investigations the protection concerns that caused workers to investigate prove unsubstantiated. In 13 percent of investigations, workers will leave suspecting that some form of abuse or neglect has occurred but will have insufficient evidence to act on these suspicions. In the remaining 47 percent of investigations, concerns are substantiated; of those, 30 percent involve neglect, 28 percent exposure to domestic violence, 24 percent physical abuse, 15 percent emotional maltreatment, and 3 percent sexual abuse. Serious physical injury is relatively rare even in these substantiated cases: in 90 percent of substantiated maltreatment cases, there is no physical injury to a child at all, in 7 percent, harm not requiring medical treatment, and in 3 percent, harm severe enough to require medical attention. In other words, the archetypal battered child that often comes to mind when visualizing child protection work occurs only in about 3 percent of substantiated abuse cases, about 1.5 percent of all cases investigated by child protection services.

The above figures are not meant to downplay the seriousness of child abuse and neglect; indeed, the impact of abuse is often not measured in physical injury but the profound emotional and psychological damage it causes to children (Corby 2000). The point is, however, that because most cases do not involve extremes of abuse where children have to be immediately removed, workers are most often responsible for protecting children who could safely remain in their own homes. The success of this process hinges on the worker engaging the child's parents in a process that promotes protective change — and that process begins, as observed by Pilsecker (1994), with the worker understanding the parent's perspective.

Starting with the Client's Perspective

The importance of understanding the parent's perspective is derived from its being a part of the engagement process required to produce worker-client alliance. The terms "engagement" and "alliance" can be confusing because the concepts have no universally agreed-upon definition and at times they are used interchangeably. I use Altman's definition of engagement as "an interactional, interpersonal process, beginning when workers establish communication with a potential client and ending when there is preliminary agreement to work together" (Altman 2008: 43). I use Kelly's definition of alliance as "the therapeutic bond between the client and therapist and their agreement on the goals and tasks of therapy" (Kelly and Yuan 2009: 194). Consequently, engagement is the process of a worker's establishing an agreement with a parent to work together toward a shared purpose, and alliance is the interpersonal bond through which worker and parent work toward that purpose. In reality, engagement does not end where alliance begins, and the two processes are much more interwoven, yet temporarily separating them helps explain how these concepts operate.

It is difficult to underestimate the importance of alliance. Dumbrill and Lo (2009) refer to it as the most powerful intervention tool available in child protection work, and Marziali (1988) contends that it is "the glue" that cements a constructive casework relationship (cited in Dumbrill and Lo 2009: 129). It has long been established that alliance is essential in any effective helping process. Following a meta-analysis of alliance research, Horvath and Greenberg (1989) concluded that the quality of the working alliance is predictive of a significant proportion of therapeutic outcomes. Marziali and Alexander (1991) conducted a similar review and concluded that regardless of the therapeutic approach used, alliance is one of the best predictors of outcome. These findings are confirmed by Dore and Alexander (1996), whose review of twenty years of alliance research led them to conclude that "across a broad range of therapeutic technologies…

> ## Meta-Analysis
> Meta-analysis is a research process that combines the results of several studies that have examined a specific issue. Meta-analysis does not simply summarize these studies, but using various statistical and analytic methods, draws out core variables and conclusions with more certainty than each of the individual studies being examined could do alone.

alliance measures have proven to be one of the most promising within-treatment predictors of favorable treatment outcome" (352). More recently, Roth and Fonagy (2005) undertook a review of psychotherapy research and concluded that without alliance, "no therapy would succeed" (cited in Platt 2008: 313).

For alliance to form, the worker must not only understand their client, but the client must perceive their worker as "a person who is able to understand their thoughts and feelings" (Marziali 1988: 27). Understanding the client's feelings is sometimes referred to as empathy, which entails that one attempt to understand what a client feels (cognitive empathy), feel what a client feels (affective empathy), and somehow communicate to the client that this level of understanding has been achieved (Gladstein 1970; Orlinsky, Grawe, and Parks 1994). The key to alliance, therefore, is not to just build an understanding of the parent's perspective, but to use the process of gaining this understanding to communicate a genuine caring for the parent, and through this to build engagement and alliance. It is both the understanding the worker has gained of the client's world and the relationship this has helped forge that provide the basis for engagement and alliance, which in turn become the elements of casework most associated with change (Davis 2001; Hollis and Woods 1981; Lee and Ayon 2004; Platt 2008; Radmilovic 2005; Searing 2003; Trevithick 2003).

Developing the Worker's Perspective

The child protection worker attempts to understand the parents not only to engage them in an alliance, but to also develop a clearer understanding of the child abuse and neglect issues that are occurring so that the worker can determine viable ways to address these issues. For example, imagine an infant with fingers blistered from a hot stove and a worker whose investigation has established that this injury was caused by the child's parent (let's assume a father) deliberately holding the child's hand on the stove. To protect the child, the worker must understand, from the parent's perspective, the issues that led to this event. One potential explanation is that the father burnt the child's fingers because he wanted to teach her not to play with things that are hot. Another explanation is that he burnt her fingers because he gains psychological pleasure from seeing a child in pain. Knowing which one of these (or other) possible explanations motivated the father has a profound impact on intervention. Burning fingers to teach a lesson would be considered a misguided attempt at education, and a viable intervention plan might include child management classes geared toward enabling the father to distinguish appropriate from inappropriate ways of guiding the child. Burning a child's fingers to gain pleasure, however, would be indicative of the father's having a deeper personality or psychiatric problem which child management intervention would not be able to address (Bowdry 1990). For the child protection worker, therefore, gaining an insider understanding of the parent's world not only sets the stage for the process of building a possible alliance, it also helps the worker identify the viability of various intervention strategies available to her or him.

When developing potential intervention plans, it is important that the worker not only understand the parents' personal troubles that lead to the child abuse and neglect in question, but also understand the social issues that may have caused or compounded those problems (Dumbrill 2003). If unemployment, poor housing, lack of daycare, poverty, or some other issue has compounded the parents' troubles, leaving them unable to handle the daily challenge of meeting their children's needs, or meeting them in an appropriate manner, these issues need to be understood by the worker. Indeed, the relevance of these broader societal issues to the worker's efforts to help a parent is central to an anti-oppressive perspective (Dumbrill and Lo 2009).

Building Congruence Between Worker and Parent Perspectives

Once a worker has developed an understanding of the events and issues that brought him or her to the parent's door, the worker begins to look for "congruence," which is an overlapping and alignment of key aspects within the worker and parent perspectives. Figure 3.1 illustrates this process. The worker's and client's views are shown as shaded circles. The process of pulling the circles into an overlapping position is engagement. Congruence — the extent to which overlap is achieved — provides the basis for an alliance which allows worker and parent to work together toward an agreed-upon goal, which in turn becomes an opportunity for change. Alliance thus represents a bond developed between the worker and parent that enables them to strive toward a shared goal. This goal will usually entail multiple shared objectives that address a combination of factors at an individual, family, community, and at times political level which have contributed to the concerns that brought the worker to that parent's door.

Establishing congruence is difficult. Maluccio (1979) examined voluntary clients attending a family service agency in the north-eastern United States. In two-thirds of cases, he found ongoing negotiations between clients and workers produced and maintained complimentarity (his term for congruence) that led to an alliance that produced treatment outcomes with which workers and clients were satisfied. In the remaining one-third of cases, unwillingness or inability on the part of clients and/or workers to share their different expectations resulted

Figure 3.1 Social Worker-Client Alliance

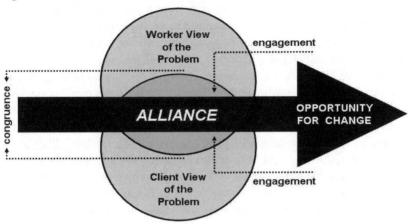

in considerable mutual frustration; the majority of these clients withdrew. If it is difficult for social workers to establish the congruence necessary to build a helping alliance when clients voluntarily come to them for help, how much harder is it in child protection cases, where clients are often non-voluntary and may not want help? Indeed, in child protection work, "the parents' perspective must be understood but not necessarily accepted ... social workers often have to help parents face up to some painful realities about themselves and their child" (Searing 2003: 341). Congruence, in other words, can be achieved not by avoiding difficult issues with parents, but through raising them while employing attitudes and values that are conducive to engagement.

The Golden Rule of Engagement

To some extent, one can intuitively understand the worker values and attitudes that promote engagement by doing what was suggested at the beginning of this chapter: imagining the intervention process from the perspective of parents. Try it for yourself. Imagine that there is a knock at your door, you set this book aside, open the door, and you are confronted by a child protection worker who is investigating allegations that you have abused or neglected your children. If you do not have children, try to get into the spirit of this exercise by imagining that you do, or by imagining that this process is happening to you in relation to children that you are somehow responsible for, such as younger siblings or nieces and nephews who are in your care. You are given little choice — you can go through this interview now, or your children will be removed, and you can go through it later. Take a deep breath and write down the emotions you are feeling and the thoughts running through your mind. Next, write down how you hope the worker will treat you, and make a list of the personal qualities and skills you hope she or he will employ.

I have been using variations of this exercise for about fifteen years, and approximately 3500 workers or students have participated. Responses vary widely, but some core answers consistently emerge: participants say that they feel apprehensive or scared, and they hope that their worker will be a good listener, caring, understanding, non-judgmental, respectful, genuine, open, honest, and collaborative. Your list probably contains these or very similar items. If it does, just like the participants who have previously engaged in this exercise, you have intuitively listed a number of the worker attributes that research shows help develop engagement and are linked to protective outcomes for children (see for instance, Akin and Gregoire 1997; Lee and Ayon 2004; Lo 2007; Platt 2008; Trotter 2002, 2004). At the heart of this list is a common denominator, treating a client in a "human" manner — a manner that preserves one's dignity and conveys respect. If your list looks like this, your task is clear: the way to begin child protection intervention is to treat your clients in the way that you would want to be treated if you were in their position. Sometimes called "the golden rule," this ethic of reciprocity, many believe, is the foundation of ensuring justice for others and the essence of humanity itself. This essence, however, lies not in the feeling and attitude alone, but in action. Social justice and anti-oppression are meaningless if they stop at empathy and treating people politely. The golden rule becomes meaningful when we develop an insider understanding of the changes another person wants in his or her life and needs in the world and when we act on personal and political levels to make those things happen.

The Importance of Tentative Knowing

The exercise above has its limits: even though it anticipates what a parent may feel, one cannot wholly pre-determine the emic view of a person one has not yet met. Even when face-to-face and interacting with another person, the "golden rule" is problematic. It has been criticized in medicine, for example, because it has led physicians to do to patients what they would have wanted done if they were patients, without appreciating that this might not be what their patients themselves wanted (Kothari and Kirschner 2006). Such critiques, however, misunderstand the rule. The point is not to merely do what one would want done to oneself if standing in another's shoes, but to take this further by looking

---

Other

Other refers to another person, but the term carries with it a deeper meaning developed in exploring the struggle a person or group of people have when understanding or relating to persons or people different to themselves. Some authors build on these philosophical debates by using the term other sometimes capitalized as Other to make the usage clear to refer to a person or group marginalized and oppressed by the dominant group within society.

Alterity and the Same

Alterity is a term used in philosophical writings to refer to the recognition that another person's or group's perspectives are different to one's own. In this context, the term "same" refers to oneself or one's own perspective.

through that person's eyes, feeling with his feelings, and experiencing events in the light of his histories, his values, and his beliefs, and ultimately to offer help based on this emic understanding of their life world.

Attaining such a complete understanding is impossible, but striving for it nevertheless is the essence of humanity which underpins a social worker's responsibility to care for another. The philosopher Emmanuel Levinas claims that any person who believes that he or she truly understands another person has absorbed that other person's "alterity" (differences and idiosyncrasies) into "the same" (his or her own world view and consciousness), in essence destroying the other person's unique existence. Levinas further explains that in doing so, this person has made his or her own thoughts and ways of being the only form of recognized existence in the universe (Levinas cited in Hand 1989). In a metaphysical sense, therefore, each of us can only have being (a separate existence and place in the world) in the face of the incomprehensible other who refuses to be absorbed into the totality of one's own thoughts and universe. Since it is through the other that our own place in the universe comes into being, Levinas claims that we are responsible for the other: "In the face of the other man [sic] I am inescapably responsible and consequently the unique and chosen one" (Levinas cited in Hand 1989: 84). In more simplified terms, Levinas says that people who think that they fully understand another person have essentially forced the other person's existence into their own conceptual frame, which renders their own view the only view that counts. Sadly, such people can then never gain insight into their own being or uniqueness, because by not acknowledging the uniqueness of others, they are consumed by their own egocentricity.

Guarding Against Oppression

The philosophy of Levinas may seem far removed from the day-to-day realities of child protection work, but it offers an important lesson for the anti-oppressive practitioner. Indeed, the profoundly egocentric view of the world Levinas cautions against was exactly the perspective employed by the founders of residential schools who tried to eradicate the unique languages and cultures of indigenous children and impose their own white ways of being on these children. It was also exactly the perspective employed by the nineteenth-century founders of child protection agencies when they tried to "save" children of the mostly poor and immigrant inner-city families they claimed to serve by imposing their own white middle-class conservative values. These class-and race-based ethnocentric practices are often used as examples of how social work has colluded with and perpetuated oppression in order to maintain the power of society's dominant classes (Chen 2005; Gordon 1988; Murdoch 2006; Swift 1995). Practices that preserve existing "ruling relations," such as these, fit Levinas' reflection on the outcomes produced by a disregard for the alterity of other:

> My being-in-the world or my 'place in the sun,' my being at home, have these not also been the usurpation of spaces belonging to the other man [sic] who I have already oppressed or starved, or driven into a third world; are they not acts of repulsing, excluding, exiling, stripping, killing? Pascal's 'my place in the sun' marks the beginning of the image of the usurpation of the whole earth. (Levinas cited in Hand 1989: 82)

I mention the history above so that its lessons can help us guard against oppression in the present. Child protection services continue to force upon the lives of clients conceptual frames which reduce the realities, struggles, and problems clients face to the categories decided upon by middle-class policy-makers and administrators. Indeed, the size of child protection caseloads rarely gives workers the time needed to properly ascertain parents' perspectives; the time workers do have is spent fitting everything they learn about a parent into the parameters and language of risk assessment or some other standardized framework required by their agency. These agency-based frameworks are important because they help workers identify issues that place children in jeopardy. However, they also make it very difficult for workers to develop and maintain a picture of the parent's perspective. For instance, in Ontario, an African refugee mother who left her infant daughter alone in a crib, because she thought it abusive to take her to the store in Canada's biting winter, became a mother who caused (potential) harm by omission through inadequate supervision. Another mother was unable to obtain help for her unstable mentally ill teenage son, and forced the system to admit him to a treatment resource by leaving him in the reception area of a Children's Aid Society; she became an abandoning parent. An aboriginal father who bruised his thirteen-year-old daughter's arm by dragging her into his car and driving her home, after finding her skipping school and drinking in a bar with adult men, was jailed for assault and became an abusing father who caused physical harm by commission.

Classification is not always a bad thing; indeed, it can aid in understanding and communicating otherwise complex issues and phenomena. Consider, for example, the case discussed above of the father who burned his daughter's fingers; determining whether this resulted from a misguided attempt to educate the child or an attempt to gain personal pleasure from seeing the child in pain is a valuable form of classification used in child welfare to determine viable intervention (Bowdry 1990). That particular classification, however, emerged from the worker's understanding the perspective of the father. Responses to the other cases — the aboriginal father, the refugee mother, and the mother with a son who had mental health problems — demonstrate shallow attempts to classify which stripped away the emic understanding the workers were trying to achieve and destroyed their ability to work with the parents' perspectives. In such circumstances, not only will workers fail to understand whether efforts to bring protective change are viable, but they will also fail to understand enough of the parent's perspective to establish the engagement, congruence, and alliance required to bring such change.

The Gentle Art of Merging Perspectives

Recognizing the need to work with parents' perspectives, child protection workers and supervisors will often do their utmost not to lose sight of parents' stories. Nevertheless, with file audits and assessment frameworks geared toward documenting a standardized version of events, the perspective and concerns of parents are sometimes inadvertently lost. As well, although assessment frameworks contain several ways workers can formulate the personal troubles parents face, they provide few ways of articulating or addressing the social issues that cause or compound these troubles. Thus the nuances and meanings of parents' lives are absorbed into a case designation routinely applied to the type of event occurring in the family, on the level of personal problems. As a result, parents are often offered the same pre-packaged solutions, even if these make little sense in the world these parents occupy or if they fail to address the child protection risks posed by the larger structural inequalities the family faces. And, indeed, there are often unintended negative consequences to this approach (even if they are immediately obvious to the worker). For example, I asked the Aboriginal father referred to above how he dealt with his daughter now, after his arrest. "I don't," he replied. He explained that he was now too scared to say anything to correct her. I asked if his worries about his daughter's behaviour were acknowledged or taken up by his worker. "No," he replied. The worker, in other words, may have protected this child from being harmed by her father, but by failing to recognize and respond to the father's very real struggles with his daughter, the worker left her vulnerable to other significant dangers in the community.

The worker's perspective in the case above was of course correct — it is inappropriate for a parent to assault a child. The worker, however, needed a way to articulate that principle in a manner that complemented the father's perspective. The worker might have attempted to do this by agreeing with the father that some form of urgent action was needed when he found his daughter in a bar, and by suggesting that she or he work together with the father to find a way to deal with such incidents in the future in a manner that does not lead to his daughter being injured and him being rearrested and again in trouble with child protection services. In a similar manner, a worker might agree with the refugee mother that Canada's winters are biting and that it is important that her daughter stay warm, and then suggest that they look for ways to ensure her daughter stays warm but is not left alone unsupervised at such a young age. A worker might also agree with the mother who left her son at a Children's Aid Society office that this showed ingenuity in getting her son's treatment needs met, and then discuss with the mother ways to avoid this or something similar happening in the future; the worker might also suggest working with the mother at a political level to prevent other parents from being left in a similar position regarding treatment choices.

The reality of casework, however, is never quite this simple. Parents (and sometimes workers) bring their own emotional issues to the casework relationship; as these play out, it can be hard to achieve the logical and rational conversations described above. The process is further complicated by the fact that workers are never really sure that a parent is being honest with them or that their understanding of the case is accurate. What if the father above has a habit of assaulting his daughter and it just so happened that this latest incident occurred after he found her in a bar? What if the mental health problems that caused the mother to leave her son at a CAS office were his reactions to serious issues of abuse and neglect issues in the home? What if the mother who worried about taking her infant daughter out in the cold agreed to never leave her home alone again, but then continued to do so in an apartment where there was a substantial fire risk? The worker has to consider such possibilities. Indeed, a consistent mistake that has been shown to be linked to the death of children receiving child protection intervention, is the belief on the part of workers that they understood the nature of a case and their subsequent failure to look for evidence that their assessment of risk might be inaccurate or that dangers to the children were shifting or were greater than originally perceived (Munro 1996). Workers, therefore, need to question the explanations given by parents. For example, the worker must ask the daughter with the bruised arm and the father, in separate interviews, whether similar incidents have occurred in which the daughter or other children in the family have been injured. The worker must ascertain whether the daughter feels safe with the father. Does the father have a partner? If so, does she or he also get into conflict with the father? Are there ever injuries from these conflicts? Such questions are extremely intrusive, yet until such possibilities are addressed, the worker will not have sufficient understanding of the case to provide children with the protection they need and parents with a viable opportunity to bring change.

"Emic" and AOP

Child protection workers require considerable casework skills to undertake the intervention described above effectively. This work begins by developing an inside understanding of the parents' world along with their personal troubles and the social issues that gave rise to child protection intervention. The worker has to simultaneously formulate his or her independent views about the issues that caused child abuse and neglect to occur and develop viable remedies. The worker then needs to engage the parent in a process that establishes enough congruence between views to develop an alliance that enables them to work together to address these problems. For the child protection workers there is no shortcut to alliance by avoiding tensions between their views and those of the parents; instead the workers rely on the values and attitudes toward the parent epitomized by the golden rule, along with an array of casework skills and the ability to use forensic approaches and authority effectively, to open the possibility that engagement and alliance may begin. If workers fail in these endeavours, they leave a child at risk of harm or they tear apart a family that could have been safely kept together. Both of these potential failures oppress. As shown above, the best opportunity for the worker to navigate around these potential failures is to begin intervention by developing an emic insider understanding of the parents' life world.

Chapter 4

Let Us Work Together

Welfare Rights and Anti-Oppressive Practice

Jeanne Fay

If you have come to help me, you are wasting your time. If you have come because your liberation is bound up with mine, then let us work together.
—Aboriginal activist group, Australia[1]

Drawing on a case study involving a single mom who has been cut off welfare for failing to ask her abusive boyfriend for child support, this chapter discusses ways of working collaboratively and strategically with people living in poverty. The chapter also compares traditional, modern, and anti-oppressive approaches in order to highlight the importance of working with individuals and the community to challenge poverty, inequity, and injustice.

As you read through this chapter ask yourself the following:
1. How does the worker work collaboratively with Audrey to reinstate her welfare?
2. Who in society benefits from poverty and low-waged work?
3. How is the liberation of people in poverty tied to our own emancipation and the empowerment of other oppressed groups?

Social assistance programs enshrine and reproduce the stigma of being poor. During the 1960s, in the United States and in Canada a bit later, welfare rights groups organized to fight for adequate financial assistance and respectful treatment. The U.S. groups were composed primarily of single mothers of African descent inspired by the Civil Rights movement (Piven and Cloward 1979). In Canada, the early groups tended to be led by disabled white men with families, but the inspiration was the same (Fay 1997).

It was in Pittsburgh, Pennsylvania in 1969 that I learned my first lessons in what has come to be known as anti-oppressive practice (AOP), lessons that have stood the test of time and the theoretical evolution from Marxism to

> ### Welfare Rights
> This is a term coined by African American single mothers to make claims for adequate income assistance in the mid-late 1960s. The U.S. National Welfare Rights Organization grew out of the Civil Rights Movement and from local groups of single mothers who advocated for each other at welfare offices.

structuralism to feminism to critical postmodern thought. The women of the Welfare Rights Organization of Allegheny County (WROAC) in Pittsburgh were empowered by collectively challenging a system that degraded and punished both them and their children for being impoverished African American women. Strong, eloquent, and savvy as these women were, there was never any question that anyone but them would determine the issues and the actions of the organization; that anyone but them would be delegated to speak when confronting welfare officials. The women and their counterparts across the U.S. placed themselves and their situation in the centre of analysis and made welfare claims as mothers and citizens. WROAC's advocacy — for individuals and to change the system — became the touchstone of the welfare rights movement. Welfare was a right, not a charity. These women would beg no more.

Audrey's story is a fairly typical case study involving a single mother and the many systems that worked together to keep her poor and powerless. In Audrey's case, we worked together to advocate for her entitlements and to make social change in her life. Moreover, her case illustrates anti-oppressive practices embedded in welfare rights advocacy that have been clear to me from more than thirty years of doing this work.[2] Many of these practices are not new, especially those used to relate to and work with individuals. For example, good practice requires listening actively to the client as she describes her situation, whether one is helping or empowering. And the theory behind these practices can be found in many traditional theoretical frameworks. Systems theory, for example, posits that individuals are affected by the social systems that enmesh their lives (Pincus and Minahan 1973). However, without a critical analysis of these systems to guide one's interaction with traditional institutions and individual cases, social work practice become a charade that does nothing to advance social justice or equality.

> ### Systems Theory
> This theory posits that larger social systems, such as family, education, justice, and the market, affect people in ways that cause them problems. Systems theory identifies, defines, and addresses these problems as "social functioning" issues on the part of individuals. The goal is to work with people to change their interaction with the systems.

Audrey

Audrey, a thirty-five-year-old African Nova Scotian woman and single mother, called Dalhousie Legal Aid[3] early one cold December in a panic: her electrical power had been disconnected and she and her newborn baby girl were freezing in their two bedroom apartment, an old converted store front. It had started snowing, and the snow was blowing around the door and piling up under the door when I got there. The baby coughed deeply and fussed. Social assistance had cut off Audrey's benefits because she refused to take the baby's father to court for child support. He gave her money from time to time and bought formula for the baby. And Audrey did not want to piss him off; he had a history of threatening her every time another letter from her social assistance caseworker arrived. Audrey had never told her worker that her boyfriend threatened to beat her or why she did not want to contact him for support, and her social assistance worker never bothered to build enough trust with Audrey to bring these kinds of issues out. Instead, her worker just cut her off assistance, leaving Audrey in the situation where she could not pay her rent or other bills. Even though the place she lived was barely habitable and needed repairs, she was afraid of being evicted. The only food she had in the house was Kraft Dinner and baby formula. The baby needed medication, but when Audrey asked for her help, her social assistance worker said no and sarcastically told Audrey to ask her boyfriend to buy the prescription.

When I called Audrey's worker to advocate for emergency assistance, she responded with a litany of the rules Audrey had violated and how rude she was when she called. In particular, the worker remarked that Audrey was a drain on the system because she kept having babies. The worker's position signaled that she held Audrey personally responsible for her alleged transgressions, including the fact that the apartment Audrey lived in was substandard. The worker informed me that the social assistance system would not respond until Audrey initiated court action against her boyfriend. If she failed to do this, the worker indicated that she would assume he was living with Audrey, which would ensure that Audrey would get no more assistance. The worker did authorize payment for the baby's medication.

If You Have Come to Help Me…

Before reading further, stop and conjure up Audrey in your mind. What is her demeanor, her attitude toward and analysis of her situation? Is she a victim? A villain? Depressed? Despairing? What narratives about single mothers on social assistance are you invited to reproduce in thinking about this scenario? Blaming the victim is one of the dominant narratives casting Audrey as ungrateful and unworthy. Another renders Audrey powerless — her ability to speak and act has been compromised by a system that takes few prisoners. Still another discourse casts her as a hero of her own life (Gordon 1988) — a single mother struggling against all odds. These narratives recreate hierarchical relations of power that help maintain the socio-economic status quo and keep single mothers in their place. Whether as victims, villains, or heroines, single mothers are constructed by social assistance narratives as lacking sufficient agency to make changes for themselves; instead, they need someone to act for them. To garner support, single mothers often feel compelled to make their stories as heart-rending as possible so as to fit the "poor, unfortunate mother" construction. For poor women, one of the most difficult aspects of constructing convincing stories about themselves is to make clear that they are poor through no fault of their own. If a woman feels she cannot construct a story in which she is entirely or largely without fault, she may opt instead to make herself look pitiful and deserving of sympathy and support.

Our society has many narratives about poor women. These narratives create expectations and reproduce assumptions that shape our view of clients and what they need or deserve. We often find that we consciously or subconsciously expect single mothers to be and act like poverty-stricken victims, to be desperate, and, ultimately, although we do not admit it, we expect them to be grateful. Audrey, however, as desperate as her situation, did not act like a victim. She did not weep; she did not grovel. She rejected out of hand my early suggestion that she make an application for child support so her assistance could be reinstated. My next suggestion — that she charge her boyfriend with uttering death threats — angered her. "What are you trying to do," she said, "get me killed?" Ultimately, when it came time to take her case to a social assistance appeal board, she agreed to let me cast her as a victim using what I have come to call the Kraft Dinner argument. "Look at this pitiful woman: Christmas is coming and the only food in her place is Kraft Dinner." Audrey played her part admirably, but the rest of the time she absolutely refused to look or act pitiful. Not for her the powerless victim role.

Some Analysis: The Blame Game

Audrey's situation is an all-too-familiar example of how social assistance systems punish and humiliate single mothers for being without men to support them and their children. When women have boyfriends or a relationship with ex-husbands or common law partners, the system suspects them of living with the men and receiving financial support from them, both of which are expressly forbidden. The fear of being cut off assistance haunts single mothers, and when it happens, it terrorizes them. The scenario in Audrey's case delineates the layers of issues created by living on the financial edge: any disruption creates a domino effect as one problem exacerbates another. Holding individuals responsible for their poverty arises from a classical liberal analysis of our economic system postulating that anyone can succeed by working hard. If one is poor, it must be because one is lazy and will not work. In this view, people are the authors of their own misfortune and the system was correct to terminate Audrey's assistance. After all, she was responsible for her situation: she had a child out of wedlock and she refused to sue the father for child support.

A structural analysis turns this view inside out and examines the causes of Audrey's situation from a systemic perspective. Rather than being the author of her own misfortune, placing Audrey's experience at the centre of analysis uncovers the sexism, racism, poor-bashing, and elitism that underpins most kinds of oppression. Social assistance policies replicate the sexist hegemony that forces women to seek financial support from men. As an African Nova Scotian and single mother, Audrey also faced racist stereotypes casting black women as Jezebels for their alleged sexual exploits (Collins 2000) and as scary because of their anger. The entire social assistance system encourages poor-bashing. For example, the wholly inadequate financial rates of assistance ensure that the lazy feel "the whip of privation" (Fay 1997: 88). The principle of less eligibility — that public assistance should always be lower than the lowest paid work, mere subsistence — was the centrepiece of the New Poor Law introduced in England in 1815, designed, in part, to address the alleged vagrancy of soldiers returning from the Napoleonic wars (Polanyi 1944: 100). This policy arose from a capitalist economic system that needs a pool of people in poverty forced to work for low wages (Lightman 2003).

> ### Structural Perspective
> The structural perspective identifies oppression and inequality built (structured) into relations between individuals and the socio-economic systems that govern their lives. It looks for underlying causes of poverty and other social ills in these structures rather than individuals. The goal is to change these oppressive structures. The welfare rights movement is a good example of what can emerge from a structural perspective.

A critical analysis can help examine the unequal power relations inherent in our socio-economic and cultural institutions; it asks the question, who benefits from the imbalances of power and resources described above? In the case of social assistance programs based on the principle of less eligibility, there are many who benefit financially, but recipients are not amongst them. Those who benefit from the social assistance system do so directly and indirectly, including box stores and other businesses that rake in larger profits because they can employ low-waged, part-time workers; landlords who feel they can charge high rents for substandard properties because their tenants, like Audrey, have nowhere else to go; social agencies that sub-contract with governments to provide employment services to unemployed people, often ushering them into temporary, dangerous and marginally paid jobs; well-intentioned social work graduates who need work; and the rich and very rich who make and inherit billions of tax-free or nominally taxed dollars. Tax cuts and low rates of taxation may not appear to have an immediate connection to poverty and inadequate social assistance, but when tax rates are low, governments do not have the money to put into social care programs (Stanford 2008). Similarly, low wages and low taxes benefit those who own or invest in businesses and already have some form of wealth, at the same time producing people who are likely to work for any wage just to survive. Ironically, even social justice-oriented social workers can and do benefit from systems that create high rates of poverty, because dealing with people in poverty is increasingly seen to require professional training and standing (Hebert Boyd 2007), producing long-term employment for those seen to have expertise in the field. The impact of these power imbalances on the recipient, however, is immediate, direct and ongoing. The personal faults a recipient brings to the system cannot compare with the hunger, cold, dark, illness, and potential homelessness that poverty engenders.

Critical analysis requires social workers to examine their own power and privilege (Benjamin 2007). Deciding how to use it is a central component of anti-oppressive practice. Social workers have power conferred on them by their status in the hierarchy of the institution where they work, their professional status, and, in the case of social assistance workers, power conferred by the state. Professional standing also creates power and confers privilege; social workers have advanced education and, often, membership in a provincial, professional association. One's socio-economic position in the matrix of domination (Collins 2000) confers power and privilege in direct relation to the number of dominant positions one holds. White, Anglo, middle-class, heterosexual, able-bodied people have a lot of power and privilege that is largely invisible to them and gets taken for granted (Yee 2005; McIntosh 1989). The social assistance worker in Audrey's case, for example, abused her institutional and professional power by refusing to grant emergency assistance and by belittling Audrey and her boyfriend. She reproduced the sexism inherent in the social assistance program by terminating a single mother's assistance for failing to seek support from the father of her child. Finally, the worker used a racist stereotype of African Nova Scotian women to imply that Audrey was a loose woman because she had babies out of wedlock.

Professional Standing

Professional standing is the status conferred by holding academic degrees, having membership in professional associations, and being employed in positions of power and privilege in government and private institutions, such as schools of social work, public income assistance programs, hospitals, and courts.

Let Us Work Together...

A critical analysis can help uncover the operation of unjust power structures, but our practice cannot end at simply identifying injustice (Carniol 2005). AOP in the welfare rights field differs from traditional and modern interventions (for a summary, see Table 4.1) by its emphasis on acting in solidarity with the client (Baines 2008). This does not mean supporting or approving of everything she says and does; rather, it means taking her side, becoming her ally (Bishop 2002). More than pleading her case as an advocate, solidarity means standing with her against an unjust institution, its policies and processes, with a simple, but seldom easy, pro-client intervention.

Acting in solidarity addresses some of the immediate effects of unjust power imbalances in social services systems. In the first instance it gives legitimacy to the client's own view of her circumstances. Accepting Audrey's version of events opened up a space in the system's institutional processes for her voice to be heard, as did resisting the worker's invitation to buy into the social assistance system's narrative of blame and unworthiness. Dominant narratives such as this are seductive. They are reproduced *ad infinitum* in the media, in government, in education and justice systems, and in the beliefs of our families and communities.

Secondly, solidarity with the client, in the scenario described above, miti-

Table 4.1 Comparison of Practice Models Table

Model	Traditional	Modern	Anti-Oppressive
View of power*	Power over	Power within	Power with
View of the social order	Hierarchical	Egalitarian	Unjust
Institutional processes	Paternalism	Individualism	Solidarity
Nature of relationship	Pedagogical	Neutral and Professionally distant	Mutual and dialogic
Nature of intervention	Corrective; punitive	Counseling and personal support; self-help; Information and referral	Advocacy; organizing and political action
Examples	Child welfare, Social Assistance	Sexual assault centres, Addictions counselling	Grassroots, anti-poverty groups

* Anne Bishop (2002) cites Starhawk's analysis of power. "Power over" is hierarchical, "power within" is inner strength, and "power with" is collaborative and collective.

gates the power imbalance between the social assistance worker and client. As a representative of Dalhousie Legal Aid, a legal advocacy organization in Halifax, I was a powerful ally in Audrey's struggle for justice, but anyone with professional standing could help to balance the scales. Thirdly, practicing solidarity means using one's privilege to ease the material deprivation people on social assistance face as a matter of course. For example, rather than make an appointment for Audrey to walk or take a bus to come and see me at my office, I offered to go to her (in my car) that snowy December afternoon.

Acting in solidarity with people from different socio-economic and cultural backgrounds requires an understanding not only of one's own place in the matrix of domination, but also how race, class, gender, ability, sexual orientation, and ethnic origin affect those in different places. Social workers inevitably work with people who are oppressed in some way, and it is our responsibility to educate ourselves about those oppressions. Depending on people in poverty, people of colour, gay/lesbian/bi/trans people, and people with (dis)abilities to educate us reproduces their oppression. Depending on cultural sensitivity training sessions is rarely enough. AOP compels us to recognize and un-learn the everyday practices, assumptions, approaches, and methods that help maintain the status quo. In addition and often before learning about cultural diversity, we need first to learn about how the dominant culture (of which most of us are a part in one way or another) reproduces oppression and how we benefit from it. In order to act in solidarity with people of colour, white people, for example, must understand how racism operates — often almost invisibly — from the structural level-down to taken-for-granted personal interactions (Carniol 2010; Yee 2005; McIntosh 1989).

Working with Audrey exposed some of my racist ignorance. African Nova Scotian women often feel caught between a rock and a hard place when it comes to domestic violence. Calling the police on a black man exposes him to a racist system that will treat him more severely than white men. Little wonder that Audrey responded negatively when I suggested she do this. Race and class solidarity often trump gender (Douclos 1990). Women who are oppressed by race and class may choose to act in solidarity with their men rather than buy into strategies for ending domestic violence developed by white, middle-class society, with little thought to the ways these strategies impact differently on different groups. Even though I had knowledge about the treatment of black men in the justice system and other injustices faced by people of colour, I inadvertently failed to understand Audrey's quandary because I did not make the connection between the statistics about people of colour, the legal system, and the reality she lived. When viewed from her perspective, my suggestion that she call the police on her boyfriend was unthinking and insensitive. The fact that I acted this way is a regrettable outcome of being white in a racist society. When learning about how our privilege reproduces oppression, the learning curve can be steep and uncomfortable, as it was for me in this case. Regardless, social workers have an ethical duty, it seems to me, to learn as much as possible about the historical and current experiences and analyses of groups who are oppressed. For social workers who want to practice in solidarity with their clients, this is essential learning.

Anti-oppressive practice changes the relationship between worker and client. Rather than as teacher and student, which is a "power over" relationship where knowledge is passed from subject to object, from knower to known, worker and client engage in a mutual dialogue to uncover, name, and articulate the politics of the client's situation. Discomforting for the worker as this may be, this dialogue must, by virtue of its nature, examine the existing relationship between worker and client. "Dialogue implies talk between two subjects, not the speech of subject and object. It is a humanizing speech, one that challenges and resists domination" (hooks 1989: 131). Engaging in dialogue means naming and giving voice to experiences of oppression. For people who are oppressed, this is an act of resistance, a speaking of truth to power that can threaten even those who are allies. "When we dare to speak in a liberatory voice, we threaten even those who may initially claim to want our words" (hooks 1989: 18).

In what way might Audrey's words and reactions have been threatening to me, for example? When she rejected out of hand my suggestion that she take her boyfriend to court and continued this stand unabated throughout our relationship, she challenged my ability to resolve her situation. From experience I knew that the social assistance supervisor and district manager were unlikely to overturn the decision to terminate her assistance. For the same reason, I doubted that it would be possible to obtain emergency assistance except, perhaps, the medicine for the baby, which turned out to be the case. By continuing a stand against taking her boyfriend to court, Audrey exposed case advocacy for the house of cards it is. Rather than something concrete that clients can expect to work fairly and transparently, individual welfare rights are ephemeral. Social assistance law and regulation contain so much discretionary power (that is, power for the worker and supervisor and district manager to make unilateral decisions) that rights can be denied with impunity. The section of the Nova Scotia Family Benefits Regulations requiring social assistance applicants and recipients to pursue child support through the courts, for example, tends to be strictly enforced as it was in Audrey's case. Another equally important regulation, which allowed for the waiver of this requirement under certain conditions, was seldom, if ever, invoked.

Audrey's stand against taking her boyfriend to court for child support also threatened me in some ways and exposed my self-interest — my need to win my case; to get as much as possible from the system despite the roadblocks. Like the poverty lawyer in "Practicing Law for Poor People" (Wexler 1970), I, too, wake up in the night screaming, "I know we can win this one because I am an expert in poverty law, I know the system and how it works, I know how to construct an appeal argument that will achieve results."

Dialogue requires mutuality: "all who are involved help each other, growing together in a common effort to understand the reality which they seek to transform" (Freire, quoted in hooks 1989: 118). Both worker and client have information, knowledge, and experience to bring to the dialogue. Both have the capacity to analyze the situation, develop a strategy, and carry out action. Both have what academics call "agency." Shaking off the "poor, unfortunate, powerless" narrative and treating a service user like an ally opens up space for her voice and her actions to play a crucial role in the advocacy process. Audrey knew, better than I did, the injustices inherent in the social assistance system. For her, the injustice of this policy came not only from her own critical analysis of a flawed system, but also from her experience of the physical pain of hunger, cold, illness; the emotional pain of abuse and anger; the social pain of isolation and the political pain of degradation and de-humanization (hooks 1989: 4). These were all lessons that were important for me to remember and remain sensitive to throughout our work together.

Advocating up the line to the social assistance director failed to produce a satisfactory resolution to Audrey's financial crisis, as I had predicted. The social assistance system essentially refused to budge, except to pay the power bill arrears so her electricity could be restored. This payment was called an overpayment and would be recovered from any future assistance Audrey received. Audrey and I then appealed the denial of emergency assistance and sought an emergency appeal hearing. As I explained to Audrey, winning an appeal was the only way I knew to make the system respond positively to her.

The social assistance appeal system is a highly flawed process within an institution founded on profound power imbalances. The actual appeal process plays fast and loose with the rights of appellants to fairness and due process. Cross-examination, for example, is an anathema. The chairs of appeal boards have declared this type of questioning unfair to social assistance workers. At the same time, appellants are questioned not only by the worker, but also by the chair. Even the courts have criticized appeal boards for failing to adhere to basic principles of fairness. The department has redrafted the appeal decision form more than once in an attempt to guide board chairs to make findings of fact and to tie decisions to the relevant regulations and policy.

Let Us Work Together... Collective Action

All of the welfare rights advocates working full-time cannot address the injustices faced by people in poverty (Wexler 1970) because the roots of these injustices are systemic, not individual. As Audrey's case demonstrates, justice for individuals remains elusive in a system based on stigma and unequal relations of power. AOP has the potential to transform these relations, but not as long as frontline social work eschews collective action as a relevant and necessary intervention. The literature contains examples of shifts in meaning that emerge when people resist, subvert, and/or challenge the categories, labels, and roles to which they have been consigned and the institutional practices to which they are subjected (Piven and Cloward 1979; Wexler 1970). People will act together to resist and change those systems that do not meet their needs (Jenson 1993).

With that potential, why cannot child welfare workers organize parents' rights groups? Why cannot social assistance workers form alliances with anti-poverty groups? In the first instance, the answer is obvious: as a result of the shrinking of the welfare state over the past twenty years, workers have been overwhelmed with casework. Even where social activism is still part of the job — an increasingly rare situation — collective action competes with individual casework; the immediate and compelling suffering of individual clients demands individual interventions, rarely leaving any time or energy for thinking about, let alone undertaking collective action. Secondly, collective action challenges to unjust systems demand change. Few social agencies are willing to expose themselves to these kinds of demands; they fear that their funding will be jeopardized if they are cast in a negative light by their own workers and clients. Finally, fewer and fewer workers have any skills or experience in the area of community organizing, and it would not occur to them to initiate these activi-ties, if their jobs allowed it, or even to join in should other workers or clients launch a social justice initiative.

Despite this bleak scenario, collective action continues to empower people who are oppressed. As noted above, empowered clients are more likely to disrupt individual practice and the procedural systems that make institutions func-tion smoothly. Empowered clients are also more likely to reject solutions that undercut their political stances against injustice. For example, Audrey refused to compromise her stand for race solidarity even though it meant losing the social assistance appeal. She adopted this position because she felt it challenged fundamental injustices in the system and larger society. It was only under the duress of hunger and the real potential of homelessness that Audrey chose what she considered the lesser of two evils. Rather than risk his violence, she disclosed, in a letter I wrote to her worker, that her boyfriend verbally abused her and threatened to kill her if she took him to court for child support. With this admission, the system restored her financial assistance and waived her ob-ligation to seek child support. This admission cost Audrey some of her power: a loss of pride and a breach of solidarity with her man and all black people.

Empowerment has the potential to move people from fatalism to critical consciousness. Fatalism immobilizes people and inures them to the status quo because they believe nothing can or will change. Critical consciousness that develops as people examine their situation together and take action to change it has the potential to empower. This process of action/reflection/action is called

> ### Mothers United for Metro Shelter (MUMS)
> MUMS started as a group of women in Bryony House — a transition house for battered women — in the early 1980s in Halifax. Their common experience was landlord discrimination against single mothers and lack of affordable housing.
>
> Their first collective action was to write to the premier and the minister of housing because MUMS believed the problem was that the politicians did not know about the problems single mothers were having finding decent housing. MUMS believed that once the politicians knew about the problems they would take the appropriate action.
>
> MUMS received form letters from the politicians. Clearly, they had not "heard" the women. The leader of the group said this was a transformative experience for her. She never looked at politics and the power structure in the same way again. It became clear to her and the other members of the group that they would have to make some noise and be more confrontational to get their message across.
>
> MUMS spent the next few years demonstrating loudly, gathering allies, speaking at every opportunity. Eventually a housing crisis was declared in the city, more money was freed up for low-cost housing, and the Human Rights Code was amended to protect family status.

praxis (Freire 2003). Praxis begins with people meeting together to name the injustices they face and to talk about what is happening to them as a result. Naming can be done in an individual setting, but the power of people doing this together cannot be over-stated. Naming poverty as the result of an unjust system rather than individual failings helps to liberate people from the tyranny of stigmatizing, oppressive systems. Groups can then analyze these unjust systems using their common experiences and questions to guide their inquiry: What is happening to us? Why is it happening? Political analyses often lead into strategies for action focusing on the question, what can we do about it? Once the group takes action, the process often seems to begin all over again. The group engages in analyses of what happened as a result of the actions they took and why they think this happened. As the process spirals,[4] the political analysis usually deepens and the actions tend to become more radical.

Audrey did not join an anti-poverty group, but women and men like her did and do all the time. I have had the privilege of working with several of these organizations. From Operation Family Rights (OFR) in Toronto, to Canso and Area Welfare Rights (CAWR), to the Anti-poverty Network (APN), People on Welfare for Equal Rights (POWER), Humans Against Resource Deprivation (HARD), and Community Advocates Network (CAN) in metro Halifax. All named their own issues and developed and executed strategies intended to achieve positive change in social assistance systems and to educate the public and politicians about living in poverty. Each group's composition reflects the divisions among people in poverty created by a system that categorizes people based on their cause of need. OFR was single mothers. The Canso group and CAN included primarily persons with disabilities. POWER and HARD were made up of unemployed single men and women. APN was one of the few groups that contained a mix of single mothers and persons with disabilities.

A range of options can bring people together. For example, OFR started as a group of women who used a neighborhood centre, the Canso group was organized by a social worker who brought his clients together, MUMS came out of a shelter for battered women, POWER developed from a conference on poverty, and the Community Advocates Network emerged from a workshop on changes to the social assistance system. The APN's genesis differs in that it did not arise from people coming into contact with one another through community-based organizations and events. Instead, it was a group of community agency workers that had been organized by a local food bank with the intent of lobbying for increased food and shelter allowances. The strategy adopted by this group was to foreground the voices of people with direct experience of living in poverty. Each of the community workers was asked to bring a person on social assistance to a meeting. A dozen or so showed up and the Anti-Poverty Network was born.

Although letter-writing and briefs to government bodies dominated these group's actions, they also engaged in creative, oppositional actions. For example, the APN made the front page of the main newspaper in Nova Scotia by presenting "briefs" to Lloyd Axworthy's hearings in the early 1990s. This process by the Federal Government preceded the gutting of the Canada Assistance Plan, which we knew was coming. The group was reluctant to participate because they felt the policies had already been decided. At the same time, however, we were keen to use the opportunity to once more raise the reality of living in poverty. As the group debated this, one of the members said "I always thought briefs were men's underwear." We laughed and laughed and then pulled together a plan of action: three members of the group went to a local church's clothing bank and stocked up on underwear of all kinds. After brainstorming slogans to go on the "briefs" we wrote them on the underwear with markers. The day of the hearing, we walked as a group into the hotel hearing room with a plastic laundry basket and dumped it on the table in front of the Honourable Mr. Axworthy. One of the members made a short statement and we left. The media loved it, and the woman who proposed the strategy had her picture in the paper holding up a pair of men's underwear. Besides being creative and fun, this action honoured one of the cardinal rules of organizing: stay within the experience of the people (Alinsky 1972). Because clothing banks and laundry were part of the members' experience, they felt great about turning the brief writing around to make it their own.

Because Your Liberation Is Bound Up with Mine...

"We will not be free until the humble women speak."[5] This line from a Canadian social justice song articulates the connection between a society and its poorest members. We are bound together in a skein of oppression and privilege that only unravels when people who are oppressed are empowered to speak, when people with privilege practice humility and listen, listen, listen times ten (Bishop 2002). Just as violence against women will not end until men stop beating women and racism will not end until white people stop perpetuating it, poverty will be with us until the financially comfortable majority shifts from acts of charity to acts of solidarity. Charity without a critique of the socio-economic system that keeps people impoverished makes the donor feel good while it perpetuates the problem. Imagine if everyone who gave to a food bank wrote a letter to the Prime Minister calling for social justice. Imagine if every time a social worker helped an individual, she or he raised systemic issues of injustice. A top bureaucrat in the Nova Scotia Department of Community Services told me once that anti-poverty groups raising issues publicly on the outside gave allies on the inside the impetus they needed to work for change.

AOP demands this commitment to justice and social action. It challenges social workers to defend clients against institutional oppression in the systems in which we work. It means questioning the rules and processes that perpetuate injustice, which may make colleagues and managers defensive. It means becoming an active participant in the struggle for social justice — during work, as a volunteer, through a union or professional association. The existence of poverty in Canada diminishes us all. The futility of addressing it through individual casework confronts social workers daily. Joining with people living in poverty to fight for justice empowers us to take a stand against oppression and liberates us from the fatalism of these neoliberal times. Anti-poverty organizing inspires hope in people who have suffered alone and in silence. Even if the measurable changes are few and far between, we win every time people are empowered to speak their truth — in the words of the Anti-Poverty Network's slogan, "poverty sucks" — every time people are empowered to work together for social justice.

Notes

1. Words used by **Lilla Watson**, Aboriginal elder, activist and educator from Queensland, Australia. <lillanetwork.wordpress.com/about/>
2. The author worked as a welfare rights/anti-poverty advocate and activist in the U.S. and Canada beginning in 1969.
3. Dalhousie Legal Aid Service is a clinical program for third-year law students at Dalhousie Law School. The author worked there as a community legal worker from 1985-2005. Dalhousie Legal Aid was the first poverty law clinic in Canada and the first legal aid office in Nova Scotia.
4. The Spiral Model of Social Analysis and Action expands the action/reflection dyad

of praxis to delineate the process more concretely. The questions posed in the text are spiral model questions. See Bishop2004.

5. This is a line from "Freedom Has Beckoned," written by Delvina Bernard and recorded by *Four the Moment* in 1993 on a disc entitled *Four the Moment — Live* (JAM Productions).

Chapter 5

Bridging the Practice-Activism Divide in Mainstream Social Work

Advocacy, Organizing, and Social Movements

Donna Baines

This chapter uses examples from frontline social work practice and schools of social work to highlight ways to integrate activism into everyday social work practice. It also discusses social work interventions that, in my experience in the South Bronx, expanded opportunities for anti-oppressive practice and those that were not helpful. Lastly, it provides six principles for safe, effective activist social work practice.

As you read this chapter, ask yourself the following:
1. Why were some practices unhelpful in the context of the South Bronx and why were some helpful?
2. What is the overlap between good social work practice and activist social work practice?
3. Which of the activist skills discussed in the section on six principles do you already have and which would you like to expand?

Social justice organizing and advocacy is not something that a person undertakes once or twice and then puts aside for the rest of one's life. The anti-oppressive perspective (AOP) encourages students to think of collective social change and individual advocacy as central to one's career as well as integrated into everyday life (Lundy 2004; Carniol 2005; Mullaly 2002). The responsibility to make social change becomes one of the lenses through which we view the world and evaluate it. Instead of seeing social problems and shaking our heads at the apparent neglect of governments and fellow citizens, AOP practitioners think of solutions and actions, big and small, needed to change these conditions. Given other constraints and demands on their time and energy, they may not take action immediately, but they reflect on what can be done and how to do it.

Social activism tends to ebb and flow in people's lives in relation to the number of people for whom they provide care and other compelling tasks in their lives. This is particularly true for women, who make up the majority of the social work labour force (Baines 2004c). For example, parents of young children, particularly mothers, are the least likely to have the time to undertake social activism. Likewise, women with elder care responsibilities often lack the energy or time to advocate for clients and communities. This does not mean that these groups never take on social justice work; in fact, many do. The child care movement, for example, would be nowhere without the involvement of many parents with young children and endless demands on their time. However, while there are times when people can afford to be directly involved in activist work, at others they just analyze problems, often seething in silence, and wait until they have enough time and energy to become involved in social justice.

A drive for social justice prompted the development of a number of theory and practice models in social work, and it is also a central plank in our *Code of Ethics* (Canadian Association of Social Workers 2005a). For decades academics and practitioners have debated the complexities of how to approach and pursue our mandate for social justice. Social action and organizing are two forms of social work practice that are very effective in the struggle for social justice. There are many ways to undertake social action and organizing, and many ways to incorporate activism into everyday frontline practice. Drawing on examples from my past practice as a hospital social worker, my current practice as an educator, activist, and researcher, this chapter will discuss some ways to (re) politicize frontline practice so that social justice and activism become part of our everyday practices.

> ### Politicize
> To politicize something or someone is to introduce the idea that everything has political elements; that is, nothing is neutral, everything involves struggle over power, resources, and affirming identities. When an issue is politicized, individuals and groups can more easily analyze and act upon it, rather than thinking of it as just an unfortunate social problem or individual shortcoming.

Activism In Frontline Clinical Practice

Some years ago, I worked in a large, public hospital in the South Bronx.[1] For many, the name South Bronx instantly conjures up dramatic images of a tough neighbourhood characterized by poverty, neglect, and despair; and in many ways, those negative associations proved entirely true of the South Bronx I knew as a social worker. Yet it was also full of the richness of everyday life: warmth and kindness, ambivalence, bureaucracy, and strong instincts for survival. In short, like most communities in which social workers are employed, it was complicated.

I was a newly minted M.S.W. and wanted to practise from the structural-

Activism
Activism refers to taking action in pursuit of social justice. Activism can involve organizing, educating, and mobilizing people in pursuit of a single or multiple end goals. It involves skills and knowledge, but can be practised by anyone.

feminist approach I had just learned in university. I worked on the baby ward and the Pediatric Intensive Care Unit. A quick look at the issues for which I was responsible gives a flavour of the desperate living conditions in the South Bronx: lack of income (not low income); lack of housing (not poor housing); diagnosis of severe or terminal injury or illness; possible child abuse; violence on the ward; gunshot wounds; hit-and-run car accidents; and the then-overlapping epidemics of tuberculosis, measles, and AIDS. Although not described as such, my work was always crisis work and was never long-term therapy, family or case work. I discovered that many of the techniques I had been taught in university were little or no help in my work, while others seemed to make matters worse.

What Worked and What Did Not

Practices that did not work well in this particular setting were those rooted in white, middle-class experiences — practices like individuation, encouraging women to express their anger, and equalizing power in the therapeutic relationship (see Figure 5.1).

Although these practices were drawn from feminist therapy, which is generally a very constructive approach, they did not work in a setting in which racial, ethnic and class disparities were acute. This is not to say that they would not work well in therapy in other contexts with other people, but these practices did

Figure 5.1: Feminist Social Work Practices: What Worked, What Didn't

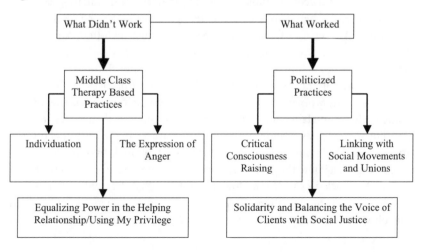

Reciprocity

Reciprocity is a relationship between people involving an exchange of goods, services, obligations, and privileges. It involves mutuality or give and take, rather than a relationship in which something is provided by one party and received by another.

Critical Consciousness-Raising (CCR)

With roots in feminism and most left-of-centre traditions, CCR refers to a process popularized by Paulo Freire (1973), in which groups of people learn to understand and take action in their lives through critical reflection, action, and more reflection, or conscientization and praxis. CCR usually starts with discussions of people's everyday worlds and helps them to understand how their worlds are organized, who holds power, and how power can be used to make social change.

not transfer easily to the multi-racial, low-income realities of the South Bronx. On the other hand, practices that did work well had their roots in the *activism* of feminism: practices such as reciprocity, critical consciousness-raising, and linking with social movements and unions. These practices encouraged and nurtured action and resistance on the part of the social worker and the client. They did not obscure domination or oppression; instead, they helped to reveal its existence and operation and directed energy at changing things, even if this meant that we adopted complicated or seemingly contradictory strategies.

What Did Not Work: Depoliticized Practices

Individuation

Individuation assumes that women spend a lot of time taking care of other people's needs, particularly those of family members. Individuation assumes that in order to feel better and operate better in the world, women need to focus on themselves as separate from their husbands, partners, children, parents, and others demanding care. An individuated person is assumed to be autonomous and have a series of voluntary rather than obligatory responsibilities (Brown and Augusta-Scott 2007b; Perry 1993; Eichenbaum and Orbach 1983; Greenspan 1983). For many women, this concept is likely very helpful; it lets them focus on themselves and claim some psychic space and time for themselves amid an unending sea of demands and responsibilities. However, in the context of poverty and material deprivation, a focus on individuation can make it more difficult to recognize and facilitate the interdependence that is necessary for survival (Evans et al. 2005; Stack 1974). It also downplays the reality of extended family and kinship ties and the part these ties play in sustaining women and children in difficult situations (though these ties can also be oppressive and restrictive; see

> ### Individuation
> Individuation is the process or act of making a person separate and distinct from others. In most western psychology it is thought to be an important developmental stage. This concept has been critiqued, however, for its failure to recognize that social life is based on a series of relationships between and among people and institutions, and that developmental stages are historically, culturally and contextually specific. Individuation can be seen to be a social process that meets the needs of capitalism for competitive, entrepreneurial, self-absorbed individuals, rather than nurturing the development of the people who are connected to others and concerned about their needs and hopes.

Baker 2001, 2006) and the important role these networks play in basic survival. For most of my clients, the realities of inner-city life and urban decay had destroyed or displaced their support networks. Most were autonomous to the point of despair and alienation. They wanted nothing more than to find people with whom they could build lifelong relationships and share their worries, fears, and care responsibilities. Many yearned to learn how to facilitate and nurture the positive aspects of these multi-layered ties. Further individuation was a frightening and insulting notion to them and a concept that I quickly discarded.

The Expression of Anger

According to mainstream feminist therapy, most women turn their anger inward to present a feminine, compliant, and agreeable face to the world (Brown and Augusta-Scott 2007b; Evans et al. 2005; Burstow 1992; Goldhor-Lerner 1989; Greenspan 1983). Repressed anger can result in depression and other emotional difficulties, while its constructive release can assist in problem solving, enhancing confidence in one's capacity to navigate oppressive situations, and staking emotional and psychic space in relationships of all types. It instantly became apparent to me that expressing direct anger was not a problem for many of my clients in the South Bronx. The ability to deliver a quick, direct, intimidating blast of in-your-face anger was an important survival skill for the many women and their children living in the massive, impersonal, and high-stress environments of shelters for homeless people and on the tough streets of the South Bronx. Rather than encouraging women to express their anger, I was often called upon to deal with mothers or grandmothers who, fearing that their child was not getting adequate care, had just "cursed out" — that is, verbally abused and intimidated — the physician, leaving the doctor shaken and reluctant, or even fearful, to return to the patient's room.

Rather than admonish the women, a reaction that would further assault their sense of security in the hospital setting, I tried to figure out how to help them thread their way more effectively through middle-class bureaucracies without undertaking actions that had the potential to scare off their care providers. Part of this involved ways of getting the physicians (most of whom were also people of colour) on their side and developing a sense of when and whom to "curse out" in the many contexts of their lives.

Using a practice known as reciprocity or mutuality (Moreau 1981; Reynolds 1946, 1951, 1963), wherein the social worker and the client learn from each other, we developed an exchange. My clients taught me their near-poetic capacity to curse people out or to intertwine outrageous and lengthy strings of curses and I taught them what I knew about how to get the doctors and nurses to pay more attention to their babies and respond to their medical needs. This meant that I had to develop a very keen sense of what made doctors and nurses pay more attention to families on the ward (which I observed to be polite, subdued, and sometimes even obsequious, middle-class behaviour). I also had to communicate my knowledge to the women in a way that made them believe these behaviours were worth learning. The women seemed to find my suggestions easier to accept if I made it clear that these middle-class ways of behaving were advocacy strategies *specific* to bureaucratic settings like hospitals and welfare offices, rather than strategies for remaking themselves totally in all areas of their lives. In other words, when it was useful they should feel free to continue to express anger quickly and loudly. However, in more middle-class environments like hospitals and schools, a more subdued, formal approach would likely prove much more effective for themselves and their children.

Equalizing Power in the Helping Relationship/Using My Privilege

Mainstream therapy has been roundly critiqued for the ways that therapists control the sessions and, in the process, make service users feel controlled and even oppressed. Feminist and other social justice-oriented therapies have emphasized the importance of encouraging service users to set the goals, pace, and direction of therapy, as well as building in a process of joint evaluation and reflection on how therapy is going and whether it is doing what it should (Evans et al. 2005). Some refer to this as demystifying the helping endeavour — taking the mystery out of the process and thus reducing the power it commands (Brown and Augusta-Scott 2007b; Greenspan 1983). These processes of reflection and cooperation are most important in longer-term therapy. However, as mentioned earlier, my hospital practice, which was supposed to be clinical and hence contained the possibility of being longer-term, was almost always very short-term crisis work. The clients on the wards I serviced were not interested in understanding the therapeutic process. They needed solutions and they needed them quickly, without any clinical "babble," as one woman termed it. Another client told me to "cut to the main business" rather than spend time talking about process, while yet another told me that my focus on process might make me feel like I was important in her life, but it was not helping her or her children. Needless to say, I quickly adopted ways of intervening that may not have demystified the helping process but did redistribute much-needed resources and produce much-needed immediate results.

In a different kind of scenario, service users encouraged me to use my privilege strategically in order to enact desired changes in their lives. Throughout my social work education, I had been taught to assist clients in finding their own voice and advocating for themselves. In the South Bronx, many of my clients knew how to advocate, and most of them also knew that the racialized, classed system in which we lived responded much more quickly to white, well-educated, middle-class voices than to their own. Many of my clients knew that using their voices would produce bureaucratic stalls and little in the way of solutions. Hence, rather than finding their own voices, many of my clients wanted to strategically use mine.

In one scenario, a seriously ill baby had been discharged home with life-sustaining equipment. A fire in the apartment next door meant that electricity had been shut off to the building and the baby's equipment was no longer working. When the mother phoned me for help, I tried to develop a strategy that would put the mother in the central role of advocate. The mother was tearful but adamant. To the bureaucracies of New York City, she was "just another lazy, no-good Black mom who deserves what she gets." She pointed out that with my well-educated, Canadian accent I sounded like a white lawyer, particularly on the telephone. She asked me to use my "big words" and medical-sounding threats, act like I was connected to a lot of powerful people, and "scare them" into turning the power back on. Though somewhat dubious, I followed her directions and after a few hours of high drama in which I energetically played the role of white girl lawyer/social worker, the power was turned back on and the baby got to stay home. In this case, following the advice of the client, who knew her environment and its power dynamics far better than I, permitted a successful outcome in a situation in which time was everything.

Self-Disclosure

Self-disclosure is another technique used in feminist and anti-oppressive therapies to demystify counselling, lessen isolation, and help service users see that many people, including professionals like social workers, experience similar kinds of problems (Brown and Augusta-Scott 2007b; Greenspan 1983). However, the highly classed and racialized differences between me and my clients in the South Bronx meant that we shared few problems. Even when I found problems that I thought were similar, self-disclosure turned out to be an ineffective technique. For example, one young woman spoke to me about the crushing disappointment she felt in the face of her mother's frequent outbursts of anger and violent behaviour. While I didn't have a violent or angry mother, I had felt disappointed in her from time to time, and I shared this carefully. The client rolled her eyes, sighed deeply, and asked if my mother was armed. I quickly abandoned the technique of self-disclosure in favour of more listening and more concrete results.

What Worked — Politicized Practices

Some practices used by social justice-oriented social workers re-politicize client problems and social work struggles. These practice stories are rarely discussed in dry and disinterested ways; indeed, social workers who tell stories involving them often get excited and energized (Baines 2000). I present these practices here in hopes that they will prove useful to readers. They include critical consciousness-raising, solidarity and balancing the voice of clients with social justice, and linking with social movements and unions.

The Personal is Political/Critical Consciousness-Raising

Critical consciousness-raising is central to any number of models of social work practice, community development, and liberatory education. CCR is a participatory education process aimed at developing an understanding of how everyday personal experiences are part of larger political, economic, cultural, and social structures — or in other words, developing an understanding of how "the personal is political" (Keefe 1981). Many see Paulo Freire (1974) as the "father" of CCR, although women's groups throughout the world have been using similar techniques dating back to at least the nineteenth century and most likely long before (Burstow 1992; Levine 1982). Friere argues that liberatory practices such as CCR are not gifts that can be given to someone, nor is liberation an individual achievement, as liberal political theory asserts. Instead, it is a shared process between social activists and those who are oppressed.

Social workers often feel hesitant to raise political issues with clients or link clients' problems to larger social forces. Sometimes they fear that it may upset clients. They worry that they lack a far-reaching understanding of the issues or that they are missing out on important details. The beauty of CCR is that social activists need not have all the answers or analysis at their fingertips. What they require is a critical, questioning lens on the world and a willingness to work with clients and others to find far-reaching understandings and to develop critical ways to engage in change efforts around these understandings. The mutuality, or shared process, of CCR leaves social workers feeling less cynical and alienated about their work, while providing ways for clients and workers to join together in action on issues. In the process, we all can begin to see ourselves and our places in social life in new ways.

A mutual or reciprocal CCR process was used in my story of South Bronx women learning where and when to express anger directly as well as where and when to adopt more formalized, middle-class ways of communicating concerns about their children. The women not only taught me how to improve my cursing — which was the source of shared laughter and provided an irreverent way to connect across differences (Lourde 1990) — they also taught me about the realities of living in shelters for the homeless and on the streets of the South Bronx. They helped me understand how race, class, and gender played out in their lives and my own, and how to be a more effective activist and ally.

I hope I taught them about bureaucracies — about how to negotiate them, how to avoid alienating potential care givers, how to use anger strategically. If I had simply admonished the women when the doctors asked me to intervene with mothers who had just "cursed" them out, we would have missed the opportunity to participate in a critical analysis of hospitals and other bureaucracies, as well as how the professional power of groups like doctors and nurses play out in bureaucratic settings, what behaviours are valued in these settings, and how to strategically adopt a variety of behaviours in order to get one's needs met. Also important to the whole scenario was the simple fact that it was energizing and humanizing to be involved in a shared CCR process in a large, overextended, alienating, and dehumanizing environment.

Solidarity and Balancing the Voice of Clients with Social Justice

Anti-oppressive social work asserts that while social workers may have more formal education and knowledge as well as more legitimacy in the professional world, each client has greater knowledge or expertise in the day-to-day experience of living with the relations of domination and subordination unique to his or her position. Mutual input is required in order to arrive at a full understanding of the problems facing clients and to draw the links to social problems and struggles for social justice. This is not to say that clients' analyses should never be questioned or reconstructed. Their analytic frame generally comes from the same right-wing, oppressive sources the rest of society draws on. They may blame themselves for their problems, or they may blame other groups that have little or nothing to do with the problem. For example, it is quite common to hear children or women state that they deserved to be hit because of something they did or failed to do. This kind of analysis needs to be reworked rather than taken at face value. As one clinical social worker told me, there is no such thing as pure experience; we need to understand all experiences as shaped and interpreted by the structures and relations around us. She noted further that when we talk about our experience we usually reconstruct it in ideological ways that quite frankly are not always in our own or others' best interests. Another social worker once told me, "People who have been oppressed for a long time may duplicate that oppression in any number of ways. This is not okay." In other words, while service users' understandings of their own experience is key to developing good AOP, their understandings are shaped and often limited by the kinds of stories larger society tells about who is a credible and legitimate person in our society and who is less valued and valuable.

This worker and others argued that stories of personal experience need to be balanced and sometimes re-storied through the interpretive lens of social justice. Rather than absolute notions of social justice, principles need to reflect local conditions and experience and be sufficiently fluid to change when such change is warranted.

Linking with Social Movements and Unions

My research also showed that social work agencies that maintained reciprocal ties with social movements were more in touch with emerging political debates and less likely to find themselves behind the times in terms of changing social conditions and struggles. They tended to be agencies in which advocacy and activism were an expected part of every social work job (Baines 2002; Baines 2000). Agencies with these ties to social movements are often feminist agencies, some of the store-front agencies serving "street people," and providers of more politicized services such as food politics agencies or grassroots services for people with HIV.

While some agencies, such as many women's services, grew out of social movements and have little difficulty linking back to them, other services grew out of the welfare state or charitable and religious roots (Carniol 2005). These agencies have never had ties to social movements, making it harder to establish appropriate ties and linkages. It is hard, for example, to imagine how to link child welfare agencies to mass movements. Workers in many of these more formalized state-run or state-mandated agencies (as well as many of the less formal, more politicized services) find their most likely ally to be the union movement. The majority of social workers in Canada are unionized, most with the Canadian Union of Public Employees or provincial public-sector unions (such as the Ontario Public Service Employees Union, the Alberta Union of Public Employees, the British Columbia Government Employees Union and the Nova Scotia Government Employees Union) and increasingly with private sector unions such as the CAW (Canadian Auto Workers). Unions can provide important resources and credibility to social change projects. For example, clients are often very pleased when unions join a social action initiative, feeling that the union's size, legitimacy, resources, and access to broader audiences give social justice projects expanded possibility and scope. In addition, the collective bargaining process legally mandated to unions has been an important way that social workers have been able to reduce caseload sizes, improve the quality of service, address workplace stress and violence, as well as develop much-needed workplace services such as on-site child care and social support services (Lundy 2004; Carniol 2005).

Unfortunately, unions can be quite bureaucratic; it can sometimes seem daunting to get involved. A quick email or phone message to the local union office should produce a link to the local union president or shop steward. Almost all unions have websites which a social worker can check out to make an initial contact. Making these links can be one of the most important steps to expanding one's repertoire of social activist skills and resources.

Six Principles for the Activist Practitioner

Based on my experience through the years, I have identified at least six principles for effective activism that social workers can use to stay safe, productive, and energized. Social justice workers do not gain much if they burn out and lose most of their friends in the process of organizing around social issues. To be effective, social workers simply need to develop skills and practices of advocacy, social organizing, and resistance in the same way they develop social work skills such as listening, assessment, case management, and policy analysis. Many books exist on activist skills, workshops are available in many communities, the internet is an excellent resource, and shadowing or being mentored by a social justice activist in a project one admires is always a reliable (and enjoyable) way to build skills. In every place I have ever worked, there were social workers who resisted. They bent and stretched rules to get clients everything to which they were entitled and more; they also coached clients on how to appeal and how to agitate for better services even when these efforts led the client to lay a complaint again the worker herself. Other workers refused to document things that might jeopardize clients, grieved increased workloads through their unions, leaked documents to the media regarding agency cuts to service, built new services from the ground up, and organized or attended actions against cuts to human service funding.

Though valuable, micro-resistance, like the tactics detailed above, tends to slow down or temporarily sidetrack right-wing agendas rather than fundamentally reorganize the systems that generate oppression and exploitation. However, tactics like these generally foster more resistance and foster debate and interest, and, as Jesse Jackson notes, they "keep hope alive." Hope is one of the strongest tools for those of us who choose resistance over compliance with oppressive and exploitive systems.

Figure 5.2 displays six principles for activist practice that will be discussed in greater detail below.

Be Likeable! Be Charming! Be Human!

One of the reasons that many social workers are tentative about advocacy and activism is that these actions are sometimes associated with conflict, hostility, and other highly charged and uncomfortable emotions that social workers prefer to dissipate rather than instigate. If you want to become more activist and you are already comfortable with confrontation, there is no need to change; but I would argue that the same is true if you are someone who likes to be liked. You don't have to change your personality or personal style. Humour and courtesy have opened a lot of doors in the struggles with which I have been associated. What's more, being a likeable human being makes the whole process of activism a lot less intimidating and closer to my normal way of doing things.

During my years as a student at one of Canada's most beloved schools of social work, I had occasion to try to arrange a meeting with one of the university's senior administrators. The opposing group in our struggle had the ear of this person, and we had already been told that he would never agree to meet with us. Assigned the responsibility for finding a way to make the meeting happen,

Figure 5.2: Six Principles for the Activist Social Work Practitioner

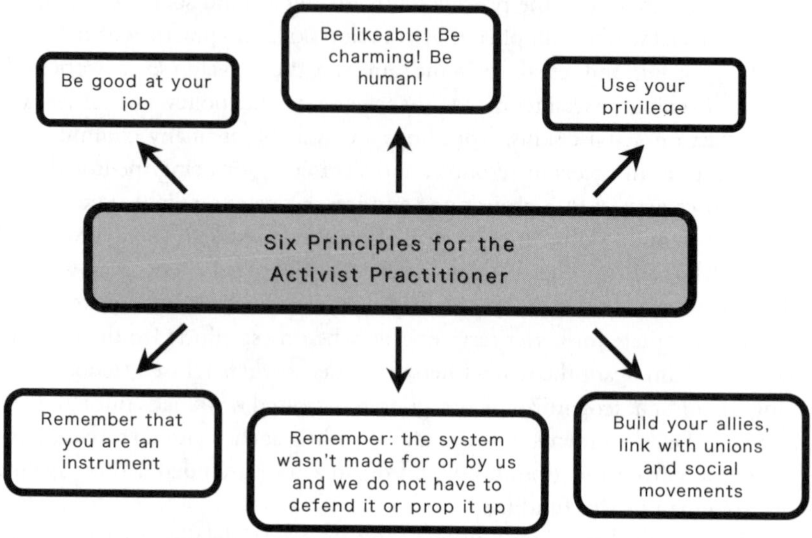

I took it upon myself to charm his secretary. She, an overworked and under-recognized member of the support staff, very quickly warmed up to us and found a tiny space in the senior administrator's busy calendar. In part because we were being presented in the larger university community as outrageous and unreasonable, we decided to throw everyone off guard by being charming and terribly polite while in the company of "the great man." He was clearly taken aback by our sincerity and courtesy. I could see him looking at us covertly, as if at any moment we might suddenly whip off and set fire to our bras or other pieces of intimate apparel, then transform into the shrill and hysterical harridans we were rumoured to be. When this did not happen, he became intrigued by our arguments, to the point of accidentally aiding us once or twice in the meeting (which, to give him credit, he continued to do publicly). Two or three years later we out-and-out won what we had been assured was a totally hopeless battle. In this case, courtesy, warmth, and humour were conscious tactics — ones that paid off well for our struggle.

Be Good at Your Job

Many authors note that the most effective advocates tend to be those who are "good at their jobs"; in other words, effective advocates and activists tend to meet or exceed the expectations outlined in their job descriptions, not only earning the respect of clients, supervisors, and co-workers but also increasing their willingness to listen to ideas and concerns (for example, see Sherman and Wenocur 1983). This may be an interestingly virtuous circle. People who do a good job are often in a position to see what could be improved in their work-places. Engaging in social change makes them more energized and likely to do an even better job. Doing a good job also protects a person should management or some other group feel the need for retaliation or discipline. Unions can more easily defend those who are doing a good job, while co-workers are more likely to stand up for people who are known to be hard-working and likeable.

In another NYC hospital in which I was employed a year or two after the first hospital in the South Bronx, I became known as someone who kept up with her casework and offered successful programs to clients and families beyond my job description. I was also constantly suggesting policy changes even though my job was described as clinical. Eventually one of my supervisors, who had an interest in social policy, decided to start a social policy committee that could systematically review our own and the larger policies impacting on clients. She invited me to join. In addition to my clinical work, which was seen as solid and well done, I was soon asked to sit on hospital and community social policy committees, organize forums, and start campaigns aimed at introducing a Canadian style of universal medical insurance in New York. While obviously the campaign has yet to be successful, the work was important, not to mention fun, and a welcome respite from the frustrations of my clinical work. It was quite clear that my credibility as a clinical social worker was key to having people take my policy advocacy seriously and to giving me broad latitude in pursuing these agendas.

Use Your Privilege

Resources like skills, knowledge, and networks are unfairly distributed in society according to class, race, gender, ability, age, and regional privilege. In social justice terms, using your privilege means using whatever advantages, power, and resources you have to the advantage of the marginalized and oppressed. In the example of the baby in the South Bronx apartment with no electricity in her apartment, I used my white, middle-class privilege in the form of my lawyer-like advocacy skills to promote the interests of the baby and the family. At times, in that scenario, it felt almost as though I was play-acting myself, performing as a privileged white person who knew how systems really worked and wasn't afraid to wade into deep waters in order to get the job done. Most social workers will likely encounter less theatrical examples, but the principles remain the same. We should use our skills and insider knowledge to make more space and resources for clients.

Remember That You Are an Instrument

I used to say, remember that you are a tool. But since the word "tool" has taken on a whole new slang meaning that makes my class crack up for at least twenty minutes every time I say it, I now encourage students to think of themselves as instruments. Charles Novogrodsky (1996) also uses this concept, arguing that one needs to remember that one is not just representing one's own pet peeves, frustrations, and agendas. Instead, we are part of a much bigger struggle and a long-term effort towards society-wide anti-oppressive change. In our society, it is often hard to get people to put aside their particular concerns to join with others on broader and shared interests. Many groups and individuals fear that their concerns will be lost within wider agendas, so that cooperation across issues can be very difficult to build and sustain. When you find an issue on which you want to be active, think of it and approach it as a long-term project. A longitudinal view often helps people overlook minor setbacks and disappointments and look for common cause with others, while persisting with the issues that seem uniquely their own. In activism, advocacy, and organizing, it is crucial to remember that despite little setbacks, roadblocks, and frustrations, you are part of a much bigger and longer-term effort towards society-wide social justice. You are an instrument of social change.

Build Your Allies: Link with Unions and Social Movements

As mentioned above, workplace advocacy, social movement activism, and organizing need to be part of a larger struggle for social justice. So build supports for yourself and your ethics within and beyond the workplace. As Bob Mullaly (1997) would say, "build allies" (also Bishop 1994). Turn to your friends inside and outside of the workplace, as well as to your union (encourage your shop steward and union structure to be in tune with your concerns and those of your colleagues).

Having a support network or group of allies already in existence means that when a bombshell drops on your desk, you can act immediately rather than having to carefully assess who might be on-side and who might get cold feet or provide opposition. When I worked in the overcrowded, underfunded public hospital in the South Bronx, a group of us initially got together just for lunch and coffee. This group moved quickly from idle gossip to venting frustrations over the insanity of providing health care in the decaying context of the South Bronx to taking small actions in the name of rebalancing the scales of social justice. My co-workers and I began to call ourselves "The Conspiracy" because of the little acts of rebellion and rule-bending in which we participated with and on behalf of patients. When a big issue came along (and it always does), the members of "The Conspiracy" were ready to act; indeed, we moved seamlessly and decisively into the spotlight, with each person knowing that passionate and humane backup existed. We knew that we were not alone in this struggle. We were part of a group of co-workers committed to social justice and itching for a bigger way to make a difference.

Remember the System Wasn't Made For or By Us and We Do Not Have to Prop It Up

The social services system has a lot of strengths, but like the broader society it serves, it has a lot of serious problems too. Neither system was made for or by social workers, our clients, or other marginalized, exploited populations. We have no ethical obligation to defend or legitimize a system that we know oppresses most people in our city, province, country, and in fact, the whole world. This system pushes us and our clients around, and we need to push back, to disrupt its seamlessness, and to reorganize it in whatever ways we can. As the London Edinburgh Weekend Return Group (1980) says, "one thing we cannot ask for is new relations, these we have to make ourselves."

The following is an example of pushing back an existing system and reorganizing it in small ways. Some time ago I was asked to sit on an appeal committee in order to hear the case of a social work student who had failed her core courses because of alleged racism. It was clear from the beginning that racism existed on multiple levels in the case and the appeal process. The appeal hearing was a very formal, quasi-legalized ritual in which the student was made to feel like the accused in a criminal case, while we highly ethical social work professors sat about like Supreme Court judges wisely calling upon witnesses and dispensing our learned decisions. The system was organized in a way that reflected privilege: it was congruent with white, middle-class professionalism and process. Uncomfortable with this, I proposed a few changes that would shift power and reflect processes more in tune with the student and her community. During a very strained discussion, the chair of the committee refused to let me finish a single sentence, greeting each of my sentences with exclamations like "that's insane," "I can't believe I'm hearing this," and "you clearly have no idea what you are talking about."

Later that night I wrote a memo outlining my concerns and proposal for a new process. I then copied this memo to everyone (and their dog). In some ways this felt risky: it made my challenge to the system more public. Yet, as I have learned over the years, it's often smart in activist work to move discussions out of a two-person debate, in which power can be exerted downward on you, and into the public arena, where disciplinary action will have an avid audience and wider ramifications. This alone is usually enough to prevent most people from taking rash measures. It also can build allies and promote your cause.

The director of my school, to whom I had copied the memo, was swayed by my arguments, where the chair of the committee had not been. With her support, we introduced an appeal process that was somewhat more user-friendly, including letting the student take the lead on how many of her elders she wished to accompany her during the appeal meetings, as well as what role community elders and others should play in an appeal process. We also managed to downplay the heavy-handed legalistic feel of the whole event. While I did not feel that the changes went far enough, we did reorganize key parts of the process, and not coincidentally, the appeal committee decided in favour of an excellent and courageous student.

Conclusion

In summary, frontline social work can be fully connected to a larger agenda of social justice. Using our privilege, critical consciousness-raising, and organizing with unions, social movements, and like-minded people inside and outside our workplaces are crucial parts of social justice-oriented social work practice. Certain workplaces lend themselves more easily to these activities, so don't lose focus if things seem more difficult in your place of employment. Even in narrow, under-resourced, clinical settings, advocacy, organizing, and activism keep us grounded in the real struggles of our communities and provide ethical and humane links between us and our clients.

Note

1. Much of the social work experience discussed here is taken from Baines 1997.

Chapter 6

Reconceptualizing Feminist Therapy

Violence, Problem Drinking, and Re-storying Women's Lives

Catrina Brown

This chapter discusses an important anti-oppressive approach to therapy known as feminist therapy. Therapy helps people understand and deal with emotional pain and difficulties by talking them through life experiences and analyzing them. The author argues that feminist therapy needs to take a critical view of the stories people tell about their experiences in life and of the ideas that women (and men) hold about how they should behave and think in everyday life. This approach ensures that we do not unintentionally reproduce oppression through the therapy process. Blending modernist and post-modernist theory, the author analyzes three related trends in therapy: essentialism, subjectivism, and reification of dominant social discourse. Case material and therapeutic questions are provided to explore how these processes work in clinical interactions.

As you read through this chapter ask yourself the following:
1. How can anti-oppressive feminist therapy focus on women's voices and treat their stories with respect, while at the same time "unpacking" stories that are unhelpful?
2. How can a feminist therapy help women create less oppressive stories without relying on the idea that if we peel back layers of oppression we can discover the "real self"?
3. How can feminist therapist avoid "essentializing" women or treating them in ways that unintentionally recreate stereotypes and oppression?

We live storied lives. People organize and give meaning to their experiences and ultimately to their lives through the storying of experience (White and Epston 1990). When people seek help from social workers or therapists, they usually

> ### Feminist Therapy
> Feminist therapy is a form of helping in which the therapist (usually a woman) helps a client (usually a woman) explore emotional pain and difficulties through therapeutic conversations that situate the problems women are experiencing within the social context and political context of their lives. Women's stories often reveal dominant discourse; that is, women often tell unhelpful stories about their own lives that reflect dominant notions about what it means to be a good woman in this society. By unpacking women's stories or taking them apart to reveal oppressive norms and values, feminist therapy can help to uncover new kinds of stories that may be less oppressive. Within a narrative approach to feminist therapy, stories are externalized, placing the problem stories outside of the women themselves.

begin by telling their story, their version of the events that led to their current situation. Stories are at the centre of social work practice, particularly in clinical practice. Yet our stories do not simply represent or reflect lived experiences like a mirror. The process of putting our life stories into a narrative organizes, structures, and gives meaning to events in our lives. Our stories do not exist outside of culture or power; they are not simply made up inside the minds of individuals but arise within larger cultural contexts of meaning. When narratives are seen not only as structures of meaning but as structures of power, there are no neutral stories (Bruner 1986: 144). An anti-oppressive feminist therapy approach to stories or narratives deconstructs problem stories and the negative identity constructed within them. Since stories reveal both dominant and subjugated or marginalized knowledge, anti-oppressive feminist therapy needs to explore how stories both consolidate and challenge dominant social ideas. This allows us to avoid reproducing stories that have been unhelpful or directly oppressive to women. From this perspective therapy is a political activity that can challenge the normalizing truths that constitute people's lives (Foucault 1980a).

> ### Dominant Social Ideas
> Creating distance from problem-saturated stories allows women to see things in new ways and enables other stories to emerge. Rather than focusing on individual deficit or pathology, this approach involves unpacking stories to see how they have been organized over time and how alternative stories have been made invisible. No story can communicate the full richness of women's lives. Stories about experience reveal gaps, contradictions, and uncertainty. Feminist therapists can help women see how their selective and interpretive processes work, as well as what is left in and taken out of women's stories. In order to develop alternative more helpful stories, women's stories about themselves need to be told, retold and re-authored.

Historical Context

Historical context refers to an analysis of a situation or idea in relation to its position in time and the other events surrounding it. This allows one to see that ideas change over time and that they are not neutral or apolitical, as well as to perceive the active role of individuals and groups in making history. For example, placing eating disorders in historical context reveals that this problem grew dramatically during the 1970s, largely in western society, among economically advantaged and young women, at a time when acute struggles were taking place over gender roles, gender violence, and the larger gender order. An historical analysis makes it possible to view eating disorders as an expression or "symptom" of women's struggles during a particular time period rather than as a new kind of illness or individual pathology.

The Therapy Relationship:
Acknowledging Knowledge and Power

Within the feminist approach advocated in this chapter, both therapist and client contribute partial knowledge to the therapeutic conversation. They work together to unpack experience and rewrite stories. While maximizing the client's power in therapy and society, the therapist also acknowledges her own knowledge, authority, and power instead of fearing them or forcing them underground. Unlike in other forms of therapy, the therapist does not seek to be neutral or detached. Instead, feminist therapists adopt a nuanced stance toward power, whereby power is seen to have the potential to oppress and hold people back while simultaneously helping to build them up and to act upon their own choices (Foucault 1980a, 1980b). In this way power can be both constraining and creative. The client's power and agency (the capacity to take action) is also understood as complex and the client's potential for action is acknowledged alongside her victimization and oppression. The social justice orientation within feminist therapy emphasizes that women are not simply products of society. They are actors able to both reject and accept social expectations. Individual power and agency co-exist with the harmful effects of social power such as social norms, values, and legal constraints. Individual power is not considered to be simply a matter of free will or independent thinking. Instead all choices are understood to be constrained by norms, laws, practices, values, and the stories

Agency

Agency refers to the capacity of individuals to take action in order to make things happen. In this chapter, agency refers to the way that people participate in constructing their lives and society. They are not passive, nor are their lives determined by society; rather, people use their energies, knowledge, power, and privilege to make their worlds and those of others.

we tell (Butler 1993). Feminist therapists, like all therapists, need to be aware of the potential constraining, controlling, regulating, and normalizing effects of therapy itself.

Creating Alternative Stories

Feminist therapy emerged as a critique of androcentric or patriarchal approaches that construct women's experiences and problems as diseases and pathology. By emphasizing women's empowerment and social change, feminist therapy has offered a valuable alternative to women who are struggling with issues in their lives. Feminist therapy has attempted to translate feminist understandings of women's issues into women-centred counselling practice by challenging the dominance of psychiatry and traditional notions of mental illness. Instead of focusing on symptoms it stresses the importance of understanding the meaning of women's experiences in the context of their lives. From this view, feminist therapy explores what makes sense about women's experiences and interprets their coping strategies as creative.

Despite the major contributions of feminist therapy, it also has had a

Essentialism

Essentialism is a way of thinking about identities that assumes that factors such as gender, race, and class have natural, intrinsic, unchanging qualities that determine what a person can be in the world. This means that groups of people are thought to be naturally good or bad at certain things; for instance, women are thought to be better at caring for small children or white men at running large corporations. Contrasting points of view argue that identity is socially constructed and always changing as social conditions and social meanings change.

Subjectivism

Subjectivism is a process in which the individual and his or her actions, choices, thoughts, and behaviours are treated as if they were completely separate from the influences of larger society and the operation of power and politics. Subjectivism in therapy operates on the assumption that an internal private life, untouched by social forces, exists for every individual. Within a subjectivist framing, the role of mainstream therapy is to help individuals discover this true self (Brown and Augusta-Scott 2007a; White 2001). In contrast, feminist and other social justice-oriented therapies encourage people to understand themselves and their choices as shaped by society, as well as to recognize the capacity they have for resistance and change, and the value in exploring and re-authoring life stories.

Reification of Dominant Stories

Reification of dominant stories refers to processes in which dominant ideas and storylines are made real in the talk and actions of individuals, groups, and institutions. As a central part of talk and actions, these ideas shape other ways of thinking about and acting in the world. These stories have no life of their own until individuals and groups make them real in various ways. For example, when governments cut funding to daycare centres and right-wing groups promote stories that children are harmed if they are not cared for at home by their own mothers, this sets up the conditions under which mothers have few choices but to stay at home with small children or feel guilty and worried if they do not. These overlapping processes reify dominant stories about mothers (women) being uniquely suited to the care of small children.

Postmodernism

Postmodernism gained popularity in the last thirty years. It contends that all truths and realities are constructed by individuals, groups, and organizations rather than existing independently of social forces. It favours methods such as deconstruction (unpacking) to explore the ideas and power relations (discourses) underlying a particular truth or claim.

number of limitations. Roughly thirty years after the emergence of feminist therapy, we are well-positioned to re-examine some of its basic assumptions. Audre Lourde (1984) famously said, the "master's tools will never dismantle the master's house," suggesting that we must question the effect of using dominant social ideas when we want to disrupt, challenge, or change society. There are three central limitations within mainstream feminist therapy: essentialism, subjectivism, and reification of dominant stories.

If practitioners using feminist therapy wish to unpack dominant social stories that are not helpful to women they must also challenge some of the taken-for-granted ways in which we often think of women's experience. In order to help women create more helpful stories I will argue for a blend of modernist and postmodernist approaches. I recommend that feminist therapy abandon modernist ideas about experience and the self that have the effect of simply reproducing dominant oppressive social stories. In contrast, parts of postmodernism are useful to feminist therapy because they help to unpack how we understand the construction of women's lives and recognize that the idea of "women" as a social group is itself socially constructed. This helps the anti-oppressive feminist therapist avoid treating traits often associated with women as though they were natural and common to all women. Instead, this approach emphasizes the diversity among women and the way that our behaviour, values, norms, and stories are shaped and limited by social forces. A major limitation associated with postmodern theory, however, is its inability to take a political position for which it is accountable. In its emphasis on difference and diversity and rejection of ideas of complete truth and objectivity, postmodernism adopts a view from everywhere, rather than adopting a view on behalf of a particular marginalized group or groups. Hence it is hard to advocate for social justice using a postmodern approach (Bordo 1990; Haraway 1990). Feminist therapy has always stood apart from mainstream therapy because it does take a position, a position on the side of women. Therefore, in order to remain politically positioned on the side of women, while also not assuming that characteristics associated with women are "natural" or common to all women and recognizing that women's experiences reflect the social worlds in which they arise, I adopt a blended modernist/postmodernist feminist therapy. This approach allows for a feminist therapy practice that seeks to challenge rather than reinforce oppressive social discourses and that helps women to re-story their lives.

Problem One: Essentialism
Central to my critique of the modernist limitations of feminist therapy is the idea that most of what we take to be true in day-to-day life is socially constructed, that is, created by individuals and groups. Most of our truths wouldn't exist if people hadn't developed and made use of them. While dominant stories about social life are not inherently true or real, they are often treated in day-to-day life as though they are the *complete and only truth*. Dominant cultural expectations such as the norms and values concerning gender expectations can still be seen in any school yard. Girls continue to be rewarded for being nice and taking care of others, and boys continue to be rewarded for independence and competition. These behaviours and rewards result from social ideas, but they are treated as facts, as though they are inherently real or true parts of the natural way of things. It can be very difficult to question or challenge these ideas when they are treated as facts, or as though they are the only possible way to view reality. Essentialism occurs when gender traits are treated as though they were natural and not socially constructed. When gender traits are treated as inevitable, they limit and define what woman can be and other possibilities are shut off. Women and girls, men and boys, get tied to these traits, and they often subsequently define and value themselves accordingly. In short, sex-role stereotyping that presumes women are one way and men are another is essentialist. In feminist therapy, when we generalize or universalize women, talking about women as though they were all the same, or when we treat gender as though it were natural and unquestionable, our position is essentialist.

In feminist therapy, essentialism limits the creation of alternative stories for women. For example, if it is assumed that women are passive and gentle, those who do not fit this description are "othered." Stereotypes like this presume that there is one kind of female experience and all other experiences are deviant and problematic. Other assumptions about women — for example, that they

> ### Diversity
> Diversity refers to processes aimed at involving a variety of individuals or social groups. This stands in contrast to processes — often political, social, cultural, and economic — that exclude, marginalize, and oppress certain individuals and social groups, while privileging the involvement and benefit of others.

are never violent — make it difficult to establish helpful conversations about women's violence in relationships with their children or male or female partners. If feminist therapy is to help women create alternative stories, it cannot start with assumptions about women that limit their choices, and it cannot act as though our knowledge about women is somehow outside the influence of dominant society and other forms of oppression.

By the early 1990s feminist therapy had begun to recognize that women's experiences were diverse and were influenced by ethnicity, race, sexual orientation, age, and life experience (Brown and Root 1990). Feminists began to critique modernist feminist therapy and feminist psychology for falsely generalizing women's experience and treating all women as if they were the same (Brown 1994; Butler 1992, 1993; Nicholson 1990; Riley 1988, 1992; Scott 1992). Feminist critics argued that although feminist therapy advanced a politics for women based on the value of women's experience, ironically, it also continued to keep many women's experiences invisible. A common response to this critique was to shift the focus from the idea that all women have the same or similar experiences, to the idea that women have many or multiple standpoints. This emphasis on multiple standpoints was subsequently criticized for its tendency to over-generalize within groups. For example, all lesbian women or all aboriginal women were characterized as the same although they were considered different from women with disabilities or older women. This problem can also be found in anti-oppressive social work. Although the focus in radical practice today is on difference *between* social groups there is a tendency to emphasize the idea that everyone *within* oppressed groups shares the same ideas, reality, and experience. Like the focus on sameness, the focus on difference has failed to recognize that both similarities and differences exist *between and among* social groups. An emphasis on rigid differences between groups tends to fossilize those differences as if they were inherently real and never change. The resulting problem is once again essentialism, which locks people into traits and qualities as though they were innate to people rather than created within societies. This leads to real problems for people whose experiences, hopes, dreams, and behaviours differ from these rigid norms.

Problem Two: Subjectivism

A major contribution of feminist therapy care has been the idea that women do not exist in a vacuum, that is, women become who they are through their lived experiences in the world. They are at all moments shaped by the social world. Despite this view, feminist therapy sometimes slips into what is called *subjectivism or a subjectivist focus*. While feminist therapy focuses on validating women's experiences, which are often made invisible within traditional mental health services, this can result in an overly individual focus that decontextualizes, or takes the context out of, the story of each woman's life. In other words, therapy gets stuck at the level of affirming every aspect of a woman's experience as she tells it, rather than challenging hurtful constructions and linking them to larger social, economic, historical, and political forces. Paradoxically, those committed to anti-oppressive practices such as feminist therapy understand that individual struggles are linked to the social context of oppression. Yet, in the desire to validate women's gendered experiences, we may take both gender and experience at face value rather than unpack their meanings. When gendered experience is treated as though it is not influenced and framed by social forces, as if it exists somehow outside the social, we lose the history of its construction, we lose sight of how it was put together, how it was socially and politically organized.

As I will illustrate using Cary's story, bringing women's voices into view and uncovering unheard stories require treating experiences as social, not simply as individual truth or subjective reality. This means asking a series of overlapping questions about the stories told by women that seem to reinforce dominant social stories and taken-for-granted everyday discourses. Seeking out "thicker" descriptions (bigger stories with more detail and nuance) means exploring not only the gaps and contradictions in stories, but what has been left out or kept invisible. Instead of taking up stories of experience as though they were "truth" rather than interpretations, feminist therapy needs to explore the ways that experience has been put together within the social context in which it occurs.

Thick Description

Thick descriptions refers to providing alternative accounts of people's stories by exploring the history of the problem, the influence of the problem on people's lives, aspects of experiences that have been left out, and the force of larger social relations. In contrast, thin descriptions typically present a single storyline, are often pathologizing, support negative identity conclusions ("I'm bad," "I am unworthy," "I am unlovable"), and fail to show how life stories are put together over time. Thicker accounts are generally less limiting and less pathologizing; they can reveal alternative and less oppressive ways of interpreting life events, as well as the spaces available for resistance and growth.

This allows one to both value experience and challenge unhelpful aspects of stories that continue to foster oppression.

Problem Three: The Notion of the Natural Self

Taken together, essentialism and subjectivism result in the view that the "self" is entirely natural. Treating the self as natural means that dominant social constructions of the self remain unquestioned. Uncovering, encouraging, and validating the suppressed voices of the oppressed are key assumptions of most anti-oppressive based practice, including feminist therapy. Often, this "uncovering" is thought to reveal the non-oppressed or true self. This view suggests that there is an authentic self that can be freed or liberated from oppressive structures and narratives simply through expression of a suppressed voice. All we have to do is peel back the layers of oppression and the authentic real self will be discovered, which will presumably put an end to the emotional pain and confusion of clients. This view suggests that the self is somehow independent of the social world and that the discovery of it provides a major solution to social problems, although in actuality nothing is independent of the social world. In others words, no one can live outside of social norms, values, stories, and ideas. We are all shaped by them in one way or another, even if we resist or try to live apart from them. Most psychological approaches to "the self" reinforce dominant social ideas that separate the individual from society or social context and, therefore, politics. Thus, they reinforce the notion that there is little people can do to change themselves or each other (that is, you can't teach an old dog new tricks). Dominant culture relies on this unchanging concept of the self, for if we can't teach old dogs new tricks, we have little hope of changing social values, norms, stories, or ideas, let alone oppressive systems and structures.

Anti-Oppressive Feminist Therapy

In some interpretations of experience, the self is presented as separate from power, that is, from the social construction and practice of power (White 2001). When feminist therapy essentializes women by treating experience and the self as though they were inherently "true," it often results in a subjectivist or psychological approach rather than a socio-political approach to clinical care. It also reinforces dominant and oppressive notions about gender, identity, experience, emotion, and the self. Everyone draws upon available social stories, or the stories and common sense that exist all around us and are used everywhere to describe, explain, and analyze everyday life. Available stories consist of subjugated and dominant knowledges, that is, they consist of mainstream and alternative knowledge, values, norms, and stories. Just as our lived experiences exist within a field or web of power and knowledge, no story exists outside of webs of power and various forms of knowledge (White and Epston 1990). No telling or hearing of a story is outside the social construction of meaning and, therefore, neutrality is not possible (White 1989c). If we understand the social world as socially constructed we also need to adopt a constructionist approach to the self, subjectivity, and experience. Experience and the self can then be understood to be socially constructed, historically located, and interpretive. From this perspective, stories we tell about ourselves are not inherently truer than other stories. They need to be unpacked and questioned just like stories in the media about governments, wars, and social struggles or stories from neighbors about lazy teenagers, recent immigrants, or misbehaving children.

Anti-oppressive feminist therapy must explore the less obvious as well as the obvious ways power operates (Brown 2007a, b, c, d; Fook 2002). Essentialism, subjectivism, and the reification of dominant discourse are examples of less obvious practices of power (Brown 2007a). If we recognize that power can be exercised in unintended ways, we can begin to see the subtleties of power that occur when individuals act against themselves in the stories they tell about themselves. Individuals often participate, albeit unwittingly, in their own powerlessness, described by Mullaly (1993) as a process of internalized oppression. We can see this clearly in the way people internalize dominant social discourses as their own, when these stories contribute not to greater power and agency but less (Brown 2003; Hare-Mustin 1994; Sanders 1998; White 2007; White and Epston 1990). Popular examples of internalized dominant discourses include the notions that poverty is caused by individual failure, that alcoholism is a disease, that eating disorders are caused by genetics, and that "good women should always be nice." Feminist therapy unintentionally reinforces dominant social ideas when it accepts women's stories about themselves that emphasize being victims or being powerless and pays no attention to ways in which their lives are much more complex, including the ways in which they have also been "survivors" and exercised power. Ignoring this power does little to help women address pain and struggle in their lives or point them towards ways to live better lives.

Disease Model

Disease models are often contrasted with sociological models to explain people's behaviours and problems. From a disease model, alcoholism is viewed as a chronic, primary disease, and the focus is on individual pathology rather than on the social context in which people's problems emerge and on the social meaning those problems hold. The disease model has been described as a way to blame the individual for problems that arise from within society. Feminist therapy typically rejects the disease model, which often focuses on managing or changing behaviours, stressing instead the need to understand the meaning of people's problems and to adopt an approach to change that starts from where people are and what is realistically possible for them.

Rethinking power includes unpacking ways that both feminist therapists and clients keep oppressive stories alive. If we want to avoid solidifying dominant and oppressive cultural stories, we need to unpack and *reconstruct* clients' stories rather than leave them intact. "Reframing" in feminist therapy shifts unhelpful stories and enables the creation of alternative or preferred stories. It is also important to explore the question of women's agency or action, and the possibility for resistance and action outside of dominant stories. Using these approaches, feminist therapy can acknowledge and support women's self-determination, agency, and power.

Working with Cary

Cary, age twenty-eight, is a white working-class woman originally from a small rural community. She is currently living in a small city, has limited formal education, and is unemployed. She has struggled with an alcohol use problem since she was eighteen and is in treatment at a women's "addiction" centre. She describes feeling powerless and out of control over her drinking. Cary also describes herself as an alcoholic, reporting that she is afraid to have even one drink as this often results in a drinking binge, which she feels unable to stop. She reports emotional, physical, sexual abuse during childhood and adolescence as well as subsequent abuse in adulthood including battery and rape. Cary connects the ongoing abuse she has experienced to a lifetime history of depression, believing that she drinks in order to numb or minimize her depression. She is currently abstaining from alcohol use and using anti-depressants prescribed by her doctor to help deal with her depression. Cary describes herself as having an addictive personality and "ocd" (obsessive-compulsive disorder); when she is not binge-drinking, she reports that she binge-eats to deal with her depression. Throughout her life Cary has had very few positive relationships, and she describes very few material (financial) or emotional supports. She reports that her life experiences have left her with very low feelings of self-esteem or self-worth and few expectations for greater satisfaction in her life. Cary's story reveals that she believes appropriate behaviour for herself as a woman involves not expecting or demanding too much for herself and avoiding conflict with others.

Unpacking Dominant Stories

Cary appears to weave dominant cultural ideas into her story of self in an effort to make sense of her struggles. Arguably, these ideas also result in negative identity conclusions. Feminist therapy that leaves these dominant social constructions intact reinforces conservative and often oppressive cultural notions of the individual and society. It also leaves Cary in emotional pain and distress. Efforts at understanding her struggles need to go beyond taken-for-granted assumptions about being "an alcoholic," being ocd, having an addictive personality, and understanding what constitutes a good woman. These assumptions all need to be unpacked rather than simply taken up as-is. Unpacking or taking apart stories is a practice of asking a series of overlapping questions aimed at helping people see how their story has been put together over time and how alternative interpretations are possible. Through unpacking the thin descriptions of these labels, thicker or richer descriptions of her struggles become possible. These thicker stories allow Cary to connect her behaviours to the context of her life and acknowledge how her behaviours are ways — and not necessarily the best ways — of coping with her pain. Cary's narrative appears to reflect the belief she is not entitled to her experiences of anger and pain. Underneath her struggles with body image, depression, alcohol use, and her experiences of violence are her internalized ideas about how to be a good woman, ideas in which she always sees herself as failing to achieve.

Overall, Cary's story about herself is that she is "no good." Her belief that she is no good is confirmed in her mind by dominant cultural stories that emphasize individual deficit. Taking these stories up as presented risks unintentionally reinforcing her negative ideas about herself. The re-authoring of a preferred or better story for Cary needs to confront the unhelpful and oppressive stories that encourage her to believe that she is no good. The re-storying needs to unpack how Cary has put this story together over time, as few people arrive at instantaneously negative conclusions about themselves. Through unpacking Cary's story that she is an alcoholic and that she is "no good," feminist therapy can help facilitate Cary's re-authoring of unhelpful stories by avoiding essentialism, subjectivism, and reification.

Unpacking Essentialism
In feminist therapy, women are invited to explore the effects of essentialist ideas on the "problem" story and on the negative stories they often believe about themselves. Questions such as the following help to explore the totalizing and limiting idea that Cary is an "alcoholic" who has no power over her drinking. These questions help to challenge the way her identity is reduced exclusively to that of alcoholic.

- What effect does the idea that you have no control over drinking have on your use of alcohol?
- Have you ever felt that you were making a choice to drink?
- Have there ever been times when you felt that you did have control over drinking?
- What was different about these times?
- What does it say about you that you were able to have this control?
- How has the idea that you have no control over drinking prevented you from taking control over yourself?
- Are binge-drinking and binge-eating ways of coping for you?
- How do they help you cope?

- You have described yourself as "no good." Where did you first learn this idea?
- How does your drinking problem make you feel you are no good?

Responding to these questions, Cary says that when she thinks she has no control over her alcohol use she doesn't need to examine how she often makes a choice to drink. For example, she says that she plans a drinking binge when she knows she will get her unemployment benefit cheque. She knows what liquor store she is going to, what she is going to buy, how much it is going to cost, where she wants to drink, and who she wants to drink with. When we unpack this it is pretty clear to Cary that she makes more choices about drinking than she has been aware of. She also notices that there are times when she is more in control of her drinking. For instance, she describes how she will not drink if she is around her mother and how she will limit the amount she drinks if a very good friend of hers comes to town and they go out. She doesn't want either her mother or this friend to think she has a drinking problem. Times like these are different for Cary because she cares how such people see her. These occasions provide her with actual evidence that she is able to control how much she drinks; she tells me that they show she can make choices about drinking. Cary also describes how she was always sober at work and that she mostly drinks only in the evening. In short, she is able to control her drinking around certain people and at certain times. From these questions, then, Cary is able to see greater possibility for a different story about her relationship to drinking. She is able to see that she hasn't wanted to take control over her binge-drinking or binge-eating because they have provided her with a way to deal with difficult feelings, but when she chooses to control her drinking she often can.

Cary describes how her history of trauma and abuse resulted in her feeling as though she was no good. She blamed herself, feeling that there must have been something about her that deserved to be treated like this. The binge-drinking and binge-eating were able to take Cary temporarily away from her painful experiences and her feeling that she was no good. She notices that the bingeing is only temporary and doesn't really change anything in the long term. She describes how feeling out of control about binge-drinking and -eating just made her feel worse about herself. She observes that her story that she is "no good" was reinforced over and over again and rarely challenged.

These kinds of questions move the focus away from Cary as the problem, challenging the idea that she is either inherently an alcoholic or no good by suggesting not only that she may have more power and control than the disease model of alcoholism maintains, but that there are other ways to interpret her experiences. The focus shifts away from her self-limiting stories and begins to look at binge-eating and binge-drinking not exclusively as problems, but as coping strategies that simultaneously work for her and cause problems.

Unpacking Subjectivism

One of the main problems with subjectivism is that political and social problems such as women's alcohol use problems get turned into problems of individual deficit, disease, and disorder. The effects of the disease model approach to alcohol use reinforces the idea that individuals have no control, power, or agency over their drinking, while it simultaneously prevents feminist therapists and their clients from developing a better understanding of the ways that women's alcohol use can make sense in the context of their lives. The disease model focuses primarily on behaviour and behavioural change, while a feminist approach is also interested in the meaning and history of such behaviours. When Cary tells the story of her childhood abuse and of abuse again later as an adult woman, and when she shares the struggles she has had with depression, one begins to get a pretty clear sense that she uses alcohol to self-soothe. Many women use alcohol, drugs, food, exercise, and overwork in a similar attempt to relieve and subdue feelings of pain and frustration. Recognizing the context of abuse and depression provides the grounds for a very different model for understanding Cary's alcohol use. Cary's story of being an alcoholic relies on a subjectivist understanding of her problem drinking rather than the feminist therapy idea that the "personal is political."

The subjectivist undercurrents of Cary's story centre on the idea that the problem is with Cary. Her story asserts that her alcohol problem is based on individual pathology or disease. She believes she has a disease that is genetic, evidenced by her report that everyone in her family is a "drunk." This story is inherently limiting. It closes off possibilities for providing a thicker description of how Cary developed a problem with drinking and why it may make sense for her to use alcohol as a way to deal with psychological distress and pain, even as it causes other kinds of problems for her. While feminist therapy is interested in encouraging Cary's voice and her story, it is also determined to understand her story in a social context. Instead of a disease model, which reinforces the idea of individual deficiency and powerlessness, feminist therapy shows how other experiences in her life have contributed to her alcohol use and how she came to see herself as "an alcoholic" and as "no good." In helping to explore a thicker description of her life, feminist therapy will look at the meaning of depression, binge-eating, and trauma in Cary's life and help her develop ways of coping that make her feel less unhappy and anti-social.

This framing of Cary's problems opens up the possibility for her to begin to develop stories of herself that allow her to acknowledge and confront her history of trauma and the pain it has caused her. Cary's dominant story, "I am no good," is challenged by exploring ways that her drinking makes sense in the oppressive and painful context in which she has lived. It encourages self-compassion and acknowledges that she is entitled to her anger and pain.

When asked about her reasons for drinking, Cary says, "I don't need an excuse to drink. I am an alcoholic. I will drink for any reason." The following questions help to unpack the idea that reasons for drinking are just excuses, rather than explanations of painful life experiences. These questions try to open up the possibility for Cary to explore how a context of trauma and depression are related to her drinking rather than focusing on individual pathology. This line of questioning allows her to move out of subjectivist self-limiting descriptions toward more self-compassionate and more positive re-descriptions of her self.

- You have told me about struggling with depression through your life. Do you ever drink or eat to deal with depression?
- How does drinking or eating help your depression?
- What other ways do you cope with your depression?
- You told me that your depression is related to how painful your childhood was. Do you think that your alcohol use may be a way to deal with all of that stuff?
- How does your depression add to your story that you are "no good"?
- Does alcohol use or eating ever help you numb your feelings? Tell me about this.
- What does it say about you that you have been able to cope as well as you have?
- Have there been times when you haven't struggled with depression?
- What is different about these times?
- How much strength has it taken to be able to deal with all of this pain?

Through these questions Cary begins to look a little more closely at her experiences of depression. In particular, she connects depression to her trauma history and then to her subsequent use of alcohol and food as coping strategies. This unpacking helps Cary to stop judging herself for her bingeing, to see how these coping efforts make sense and how they tell a story about her struggles. Cary tells me that she uses drinking and eating as a way to numb, avoid, or escape depression and how she feels about herself. When Cary is depressed, her belief that she is no good has a very strong hold on her. Cary recalls that, as a teenager, she did not always feel depressed — especially when she was doing well in school and had lots of friends. She felt good about herself at these times. She notices that when things are not going well she is more depressed, feels badly about herself, and binge-drinks and binge-eats more. While Cary began to feel she was "no good" through her emotional and physical childhood experiences, this story has carried over into adulthood. She says that being treated badly as a child and adult made her think she actually was bad, not a good person. As she continues to unpack her negative beliefs about herself, her history of abuse, and her binge-drinking and binge-eating, she also feels stronger, more in control of her life, and more positive about her future. She begins to consider going back to school, and she has some friends that she met through her therapy group. Overall, she describes a sense of feeling more hopeful and less depressed.

The kinds of questions posed above helped to move Cary toward descriptions that acknowledged her pain and suffering rather than keeping it invisible. As she explores how her drinking behaviour makes sense, she may begin to make room for other explanations of her drinking problem, ones that move away from individual deficit, instead honouring her capacity to cope. By exploring parts of Cary's experience that haven't made it into her story that she is no good, the groundwork is established to help her re-story her life. Asking questions that link binge-drinking and binge-eating as possible interchangeable coping strategies may have the effect of further separating Cary from the problem story she tells about herself.

Unpacking the Naturalized Self

By challenging both essentialism and subjectivism the social worker or therapist is more likely to avoid reinforcing the social myth of the "natural self" or the real self hiding somewhere deep within each person's inner being. The goal of feminist therapy is not to discover "the real self" underneath pain and oppression. Instead, the focus is on building less oppressive or preferred stories of the self. New or re-authored stories are not any more "real" or "true" than oppressive dominant stories. Their goal is to be less oppressive and empowering, but they are still stories that we tell ourselves about ourselves. Rather than calling them the truth, these new understandings of the self are called preferred stories. Feminist therapy can help women develop stories about the kind of self they wish to live with. By challenging the story of being "no good," feminist therapy can help women like Cary develop more positive identity conclusions. While we may explore the strength it has taken for Cary to deal with the traumatizing and abusive events in her life and the consequences of her alcohol use itself, we must also be cautious not to turn this story into the new "real" self. A rigid story of strength also has its limitations and will prove to be troublesome to Cary. Instead, it is important to explore a story line that allows Cary to be both vulnerable and strong. Questions such as those listed below could be helpful in this process.

- Does it take more courage to explore your pain or to avoid it?
- What difference will it make to your life if you keep on dealing with this pain straight on?
- What does it say about you that you are looking at how hard all of the abuse has been for you?
- Does it make sense to you that you would use alcohol as a way to numb your pain?

When Cary describes the struggles she is having and the pain she has when she thinks about her past, it is clear that facing these emotions is very hard. When asked, she is able to say that it takes lots of courage to face pain and that it is easier to avoid. But she also notices that avoiding the pain seems only to make it a bigger problem in the long term. Cary says that if she keeps dealing with the pain straight-on there is more chance it will stop having so much influence over her life.

Restorying Preferred Stories

Cary's story can be re-storied in ways that reduce her pain and open new possibilities for living. Anti-oppressive feminist therapy moves beyond limiting binary, either/or constructions by acknowledging that Cary is both strong and vulnerable, a victim and a survivor, and that she has been violent in her life and has experienced tremendous trauma. This both/and approach allows therapy to develop richer, thicker stories. Underneath her struggles with binge-eating, alcohol use, depression, and experiences of violence are her internalized ideas about what constitutes a good woman. A feminist therapy approach to Cary's story explores ways she has more power/agency and ways she has less power/agency. By not pathologizing her experience or treating her stories as if they were the complete truth, therapy can explore how her understanding of alcohol use, binge-eating, depression, and trauma make sense in the context of her life. While exploring how these stories make sense, Cary can also begin to see how the story she tells about herself reinforces her powerlessness and fails to acknowledge her capacity to take action and resist. Unpacking her totalizing and negative identity conclusions means that alternative identity stories become possible. The development of alternative identity stories changes the focus from individual deficit to an appreciation of Cary's creativity, vulnerability, and strength in her efforts at coping. From this blended approach, feminist therapy can explore what is and isn't helpful about Cary's efforts at coping. The creation of alternative stories that challenge negative and oppressive identity conclusions helps to foster alternative ways of living.

Restorying Essentialism, Subjectivism and the Natural Self

By re-authoring Cary's negative identity that she is an "alcoholic" who is "no good," the new story shifts the focus from Cary as the problem to the social context and circumstances that influenced the problem and the power she has had within this limited context. Unpacking Cary's dominant story emphasizes the influence her problem has had on her, while re-storying involves looking at how she has influence over the problem. Questions such as those listed below aid in this process.

- How did the abuse you experienced make you think you are "no good"?
- How does being depressed make you feel like you are "no good"?
- How does feeling like you have no control over drinking make you feel like you are "no good"?

- What are some of the ways you are now challenging the idea that you are "no good"?
- Are there other ways that you might cope with life than binge-drinking and binge-eating?
- Do you feel you could learn to have more control over choosing binge-drinking and binge-eating?

Cary continues to unpack how her experiences of abuse made her think she was not good. She describes how, as a child, she thought that she must be doing something to cause people to treat her badly and that she wasn't good enough. She believed that if she could be better and cause less trouble she wouldn't be hurt by people. As an adult Cary can now see how she has carried this story around with her; she realizes that she was not responsible for the abuse that occurred to her as a child and also recognizes how her adult experiences of battery and sexual assault reinforced her childhood story that she had no worth. Through conversations about her abuse she sees how her feelings of being uncared for, vulnerable, hopeless, and powerless often made her feel depressed. Feelings of depression compounded the story of worthlessness that resulted from her history of trauma and abuse.

By questioning her story, Cary realizes that her experiences of abuse and depression do not mean that she is "no good." She tells me that her current treatment program, the women in her group, and her new aspirations to go back to school are making her feel more hopeful and that she has worth. In this way they challenge her story that she is "no good." She reports that she is more aware of making choices about binge-drinking and binge-eating and that she thinks she can learn to exert greater control over these choices in her treatment program. She believes it is important to continue to deal with the painful effects of her trauma history on her sense of self and to try to do so without relying on alcohol or food to soothe her. Cary is hopeful that her new friendships will be an important form of coping support for her.

In the process of re-authoring her identity Cary tells more positive stories about herself while learning to let go of the story that she is no good. The following questions begin to help thicken her new story that she has worth and value.

- What are some of the things you value most about yourself?
- Who knows these things about you?
- What will your future look like if you continue to challenge the idea that you are "no good" and deal with the painful feelings you often have to face?

Questions like these encourage Cary to notice what she values and how she would prefer to live her life. She says that she values her compassion and caring for others and believes that being compassionate and caring say that she is a good person. The women in her therapy group help thicken this new story through their appreciation of her in the group. Cary thinks that if she can stop thinking that she is "no good," she has a better shot at feeling better about herself and her life.

Reconstructing and Re-authoring Cary's Story

The deconstructive process emphasizes how Cary sometimes has both power and agency and sometimes she has less or little. By not pathologizing her efforts at coping through alcohol use and binge-eating or her experiences of depression and trauma, and by exploring how these make sense in the context of her life, Cary can begin to see how alternative stories to the totalizing negative stories she tells about herself are possible. The re-storying of thin descriptions of alcoholism and helplessness over drinking; the shift in focus from herself as the problem to the social circumstances that influenced the problem; the letting go of the story that she is no good; the thickening of the story that she has value and worth: all these constitute elements in reconstructing Cary's story. The creation of alternative stories that challenge negative, oppressive, and totalizing identity conclusion help to encourage the reconstruction of alternative, more affirming ways of life. The process of deconstruction and reconstruction is not linear, as deconstruction or unpacking is ongoing.

In the re-authoring process the focus shifts from the influence the problem has had on the person in the past and continues to have in the present to the influence the person has on the problem in the past, present, and future. This, of course, not only emphasizes agency and power, but allows people to build on those events in their lives that did not support the dominant or unhelpful story. The new or preferred story has a life outside of the problem.

Drawing on White's narrative work, reconstruction involves tracing unique outcomes over time. This means listening for times that Cary's experiences fall outside the dominant or problem-saturated story that she is not good enough. These unique outcomes are the entry points for the living of a preferred story. So unique outcomes refer to parts of experience that "fall outside the dominant story" and are therefore not oppressed by the problem (Goffman 1961; White and Epston 1990: 15). For Cary this will mean times that she has felt good enough or when others have communicated positive things to her. These moments are important building blocks in the development of her re-authoring story. Because we develop our stories of identity not in a vacuum but through social interaction, experience, and a prevailing culture of meaning and value, the development of a new story necessarily means building an audience for the new or preferred story. This can mean giving less value or power to some people's influence and more to others. We do know that alternative stories of identity are co-created and maintained. Seeking out an audience helps to support and reinforce a new preferred story. Thickening the new story and making it the new reality also involves exploring how the new story might impact on her future life.

- Who else knows that you are a good person?
- What do they know about you that makes them think this?
- Who else should know this?
- How will your new story that you are a good person make a difference in the future?
- As you continue to build the idea that you are a good person, how might others in your life respond?

Cary sees not only that she is entitled to the pain she feels but that her use of alcohol and eating as a way to deal with it make sense, since she didn't know any other way cope. She also recognizes that she does not need to see herself as weak or no good or to put herself down because she has coped the way she has. She is starting to get a sense of how much strength and courage it has taken to deal with what she's been through and that she is not a bad person. Cary believes that the women in her therapy group and those in her treatment program understand what she has been going through and consider her a good person. Through this experience she sees that she is often kind and caring about other's pain, and that she often has good things to say in support of others. Cary reports that the other women know these things about her. These other people have become an audience for Cary's new story about herself. She feels that if she continues to build the story that she does have worth she can be more hopeful and less depressed about her future.

Within a feminist anti-oppressive practice, both the practitioner and Cary will work together to unpack her unhelpful stories of self and reconstruct a preferred identity. This collaborative approach can get Cary closer to what she prefers and allow her to see more clearly the direction she wants her life to go.

Anti-Oppressive Feminist Therapy

In this chapter I have argued that a blended approach to feminist therapy (combining modernist and postmodern feminism) can avoid essentialism, subjectivism and reification of dominant discourses. This blended approach remains political and self-reflexive. It is grounded in the everyday world as well as the social and individual stories we tell ourselves about ourselves. A blended approach to feminist therapy challenges the dominant social storylines embedded in the stories women tell about themselves and makes space for aspects of women's experiences that have been suppressed and marginalized within these dominant storylines. While women's experiences remain central to therapy, experience is not essentialized. Women's voices are encouraged and challenged. Rather than representing the whole, complete, and unchanging truth, women's experiences are seen to be multiple, complex and changing, socially constructed, interpretive, contestable, and political.

The self within this approach is seen as fully social, that is, there can be no discovery of the "real self" as the self is created through stories we tell ourselves about ourselves within the social world in which we live. Women's stories need to be situated within the larger social context that shapes them. Alternative, more helpful stories can be co-authored in the anti-oppressive feminist therapy process emphasizing women's action, agency, and resistance.

Chapter 7

Indigenous Pathways to Anti-Oppressive Practice

Bonnie Freeman

D rawing on Indigenous knowledge and cultural practices
(Haudenosaunee or Iroquoian), the author discusses the
need for anti-oppressive practices that address the multiple
and compounded layers of trauma experienced by Indigenous
people as a product of colonization and its continuing aftermath. Arguing that understanding historical and contemporary
contexts are important forms of practice, the author explores
social work practices she and others have developed to assist
Native people in their everyday struggles for well-being and
cultural survival.

As you read this chapter, ask yourself the following:
1. What are some of the events and factors that form the
    context of Indigenous people's lives in Canada?
2. What are some of the practices that the author has used
    to assist First Nations students and community members?
3. Why does the author believe that practices that draw on
    Native knowledge are more likely to be helpful in work
    with Native people?

This chapter will explore an Indigenous perspective on anti-oppressive practice. Understanding anti-oppressive practice from this perspective involves
a process of integrating cultural knowledge, drawing on practices that exist
within the customs, traditions, and language of Indigenous peoples. This
understanding may also include explorations of the history of the particular
Indigenous group with whom you are working. It may be useful for anti-
oppressive practitioners to integrate various social justice approaches in their
work with Indigenous populations.

I am Algonquin and Mohawk from the Six Nations in Ontario, Canada.
The anti-oppressive practices I share, from an Indigenous perspective, draw on
my lived experience and understanding of the Haudenosaunee (People of the
Longhouse/Iroquois) culture. I will incorporate aspects of my language, culture,
traditions, and stories to demonstrate that Indigenous anti-oppressive practice

> ### Haudenosaunee
> Haudenosaunee refers to the People of the Longhouse or Iroquois people of North America. Prior to European contact, Haudenosaunee people lived in areas now known as New York, Ohio, Pennsylvania, Québec, and Ontario. Composed of five tribes, the Haudenosaunee also call themselves the League of Peace. The Haudenosaunee operate under the oldest continuous form of democratic and participatory government in North America, a form known as the Grand Council of the Haudenosaunee Confederacy.

acknowledges, and can be helpful to, not only Indigenous peoples, but all human beings.

Many of you may have heard and used the terms First Nations people, Aboriginal people, and Native people to refer to the many Indigenous nations who originate from and live upon the North American continent. Among the Haudenosaunee, we acknowledge ourselves and our ancestors in the languages of our people, referring to ourselves as Onkwehonwe — the original people of North America. In other nations of Indigenous people, the words used to describe themselves and other Indigenous people will be different, reflecting their various languages. However, in all Indigenous languages, the words used to describe Indigenous peoples acknowledge the connection of the people to the land they live upon. As a Haudenosaunee person, I believe it is important to incorporate the words we use for ourselves because these words possess and reflect the culture, spirituality, and Indigenous knowledge of the Haudenosaunee people. Much of this content and context is lost when we use the English or other European words to describe ourselves.

As an anti-oppressive practitioner, I still use terms such as First Nations, Aboriginal, and Native people interchangeably, depending on the context in which I am speaking or writing. However, it is important to understand what these terms really mean to Indigenous peoples of North America. For example, the term "Aboriginal" is widely used in Canada to refer to the ancestors of the original people who first occupied the North American continent. It is also used as a general term for three distinct groups of Indigenous peoples within Canada: the First Nations, Métis, and Inuit. The First Nations people represent over 500 different Indigenous groups who are diverse from one another in language and

> ### Onkwehonwe
> Onkwehonwe is a Haudenosaunee word for the original people of North America. Among other nations of Indigenous people, the words used to describe themselves and other Indigenous people will be different, reflecting their various languages. However, in all the languages, the words used to describe Indigenous peoples acknowledge the connection of the people to the land they live upon.

culture. The Métis are similarly defined through various regions, languages, and cultures across Canada. The Inuit are a distinct people whose culture is tied to the ice, snow, and land of northern Canada. In the United States, Indigenous peoples are referred to as Native Americans or Native people. Highlighting the arbitrariness of the Canada-US boarder, many First Nations people refer to themselves as Native people on either side of the boarder. These are general, informal, public practices. In more formal or Indigenous contexts, Native people will identify themselves by citing their nation, clan, and Onkwehonwe name. By using a variation of this in Indigenous anti-oppressive practice, I am tapping into a powerful set of traditions and reclaiming the power to name ourselves and our realities.

Many of us interchangeably use the terms listed above when referring to Onkwehonwe people. We don't realize the oppression that we are perpetuating by generalizing, by using such terms to refer to many different Indigenous groups. Although many of us have been taught that it is politically and socially correct to refer to Onkwehonwe people in such a manner, these are not neutral terms. Taiaiake Alfred (2005: 23) eloquently articulates this position by stating:

> Onkwehonwe are manipulated by colonial myths into a submissive position and are told that by emulating white people they can gain acceptance and possibly even fulfillment within mainstream society. Many Onkwehonwe today embrace the label of "Aboriginal," but this identity is a legal and social construction of the state, and it is disciplined by racialized violence and economic oppression to serve an agenda of silent surrender. The acceptance of being Aboriginal is as powerful an assault on Onkwehonwe existences as any force of arms brought upon us by the Settler society. The integrationist and unchallenged Aboriginal vision is designed to lead us to oblivion, as individual successes in assimilating to the mainstream are celebrated, and our survival is redefined strictly in the terms of capitalist dogma and practical minded individualist consumerism and complacency.

Words have political as well as everyday meanings and have the power to create and recreate power relations among people. The words we use signal the kinds of relationships we want to promote. By changing the words we use, we can help to shift popular perceptions, spark debate, and repoliticize situations and struggles. Becoming aware of and changing the language we use begins to put into practice the anti-oppressive perspective that we are striving to accomplish in our work.

This has become an important factor for me in the work that I do with Onkwehonwe people. My interest in anti-oppressive practice grows from my personal and family experience with oppression, discrimination, and colonization as an Algonquin and Mohawk woman. I have worked in the field of social work with Onkwehonwe people for many years and have tried to understand the deeper issues and problems that affect them. I have come to understand that many of these problems are not of our making. They are structured within the white colonial Canadian society and thus can be changed. All is not hopeless. Structures support the beliefs and values of people within Canadian society. These beliefs and values in turn recreate the structure and systems of oppression. Practicing from an anti-oppressive perspective, we can slowly restructure our society to honour and acknowledge Native people rather than continuing colonial oppression.

As social workers, we need to understand the perspectives of the people we work with. Often these perspectives will be extremely new and will differ from the views, perspectives, and behaviours we bring to our work. This chapter will provide examples of anti-oppressive practice that incorporate an Indigenous perspective on ways to work with Onkwehonwe people.

Contextual Understanding as Practice

Through my personal and professional experiences, I understand the impact that generations of traumatic experiences have had on Onkwehonwe people. I have witnessed the results of alcoholism, addictions, family violence, suicides, deaths, mental illness, and poverty in my family and within my community of Six Nations. This experience led me to wonder how Haudenosaunee culture helped our people prior to European contact. I wondered if Haudenosaunee practices could help to overcome the emotional and psychological pain, grief, and loss associated with the experiences listed above.

As a professional, I felt that my personal experiences as a Native person were inextricably linked to a shared understanding of how to work with Native people; yet I felt inadequate at times because I did not grow up on a reservation, nor do I speak an Onkwehonwe language. However, I am learning. From my work at McMaster University, I learned that having an understanding of Indigenous cultural practices, languages, and ceremonies, as well as sustaining a connection to the family and land, play important roles in maintaining good health and well-being among Onkwehonwe students. Through my work with these students, I learned a lot about the foundation of cultural knowledge and practices of Haudenosaunee people. This again led me to wonder about the importance of cultural practices in recovering from generations of trauma.

Soup Days

In my early attempts to assist Onkwehonwe students I tried to approach my practice from a cultural perspective and began to incorporate ways of helping and connecting to Native people that had been part of my growing-up. For example, at McMaster, I implemented a cultural practice I had seen my grandparents use. For my grandparents, it was an honour to have people talk and visit and they treated each guest with respect and warmth. Every morning they would prepare a big pot of homemade soup and fresh baked bread for people who would drop by to share news or catch up on community events. As a child I would hear the conversations, stories, and laughter in the kitchen. When I looked back on this experience I realized that I had witnessed something very powerful — yet so simple. Whether my grandparents realized it or not, their generosity and caring contributed to promoting the good health and well-being of those who came to visit, as well as of my family.

Starting in 2001, I brought this concept to McMaster by creating "Soup Days." I would make a big pot of homemade soup and bring along sandwich fixings, a variety of fruit, and some cookies. I invited everyone (Native and non-Native) to drop by. This initiative was very successful among the students. Afterwards, I found out that many of the students would eat when they were at school so they could save what little money they had to pay their bills or feed their children. This small intervention not only built relationships and community for Onkwehonwe students at McMaster, it extended their financial resources and eased their stress. This made me wonder how other traditional Onkwehonwe practices could be implemented into social care and social work practice, as well as how other Haudenosaunee social workers, counselors, and traditional helping practitioners were integrating cultural knowledge and practices into their work.

Storytelling

Stories can be very important in anti-oppressive practice with Native people. They are affirming, providing people with a connection and cultural grounding in an often hostile and difficult world. For many generations, the history of the Haudenosaunee has been shared through an oral tradition. This ancient forum of recording and passing down history through stories has been very important in building and maintaining relationships among the Haudenosaunee people. In more recent times, the stories have been preserved in books for future generations (Mitchell 1984; Parker 1990; Barreiro and Cornelius 1991; Schoolcraft 1992; Thomas 1994; George-Kanentiio 1995; Wallace 1997). The history of the Haudenosaunee explains many phenomena such as the creation of the earth, reciprocal roles and relationship with natural environments, and spiritual beliefs and cultural values. This history also teaches lessons about the challenges of life. For the Haudenosaunee, historical stories are very real and tangible.

Vital to Indigenous epistemology is the question of how information is shared within cultures. For Native people, the use of storytelling, narration, and/or life experiences when explaining or sharing imperative moments allows the listener (or reader) and the teller to connect to the material in a way that is relevant and non-intrusive to all.

In research I conducted for my Master's thesis, an interviewee shared the importance of learning lessons from the history and stories of the Haudenosaunee. To convey the importance of understanding people's behaviour and the practices of anti-oppressive helping, this practitioner shared the cultural story of the Peacemaker and Tadodaho. The story, a very important one to the Haudenosaunee, provides the foundation for understanding the establishment of governing structures of the Haudenosaunee Confederacy under the Great Law of Peace (Lyons 1984; Mohawk 1986). The story also demonstrates to practitioners the importance of cultural beliefs, values, and practices in anti-oppressive practice with Indigenous peoples.

The story of Tadodaho is very long and detailed; what was shared by the practitioner in my study highlights the level of understanding that a practitioner needs to strive for when working with a service user. This part of the story tells of when the Peacemaker left the north shore of Lake Ontario and travelled across the water to the area we know as Syracuse, New York, to deliver the Great Law of Peace to the Haudenosaunee. The first person the Peacemaker meets is the Onondaga man known as Tadodaho. At a young age, Tadodaho became known for his great powers that could hurt or kill people, and that scared many people around him. This fear led his family to abandon him on a hilltop, which is where the Peacemaker met him. By the time they met, Tadodaho had become physically deformed with snakes in his hair. The story, as summarized by my interviewee, is filled with information about human behaviour and responses to difficult experiences:

> His [Tadodaho's] mind was not good because as a young boy he was a healer and he helped people. He had this gift at a very young age... he worked with his gifts and people would come and see him. His community and mother got frighten[ed] of his gifts and so they had taken him way up on a hill and they left him there, all by himself as a young boy. He had so much abandonment and so much grief that this is what make his back have crooks ... and have the snakes in his hair because he didn't have a good mind. Anyone that has that amount of abandonment and grief, would be that way ... They say in the story, how they could hear him crying out his evil words in his voice and that was pain, it was pain that Tadodaho was crying out ... It wasn't until the Peacemaker said, when we (collective group of chiefs) go to him, you will show him nothing but love. I want you all to look at him with love in your eyes and in your heart. When all of those chiefs from each nation and Jogosaha, our first clan mother, had gone to Tadodaho, they had so much love in their hearts that the crooks were removed, and the snakes started to fall out of his hair ... they removed all that stuff from him. (J. Burning in Freeman 2004)

Tadodaho faced abandonment and isolation from his family and community, which resulted in the deep grief, anger, and mental and emotional anguish that transformed him physically. The Peacemaker saw beyond the physical, mental, and emotional distress Tadodaho was encountering and healed his wounded spirit through the collective love and compassion of the chiefs, the clan mother, and the Peacemaker.

This story illustrates to practitioners the depth and effect that relationships have on all peoples' lives. The existence and survival of Native people depends on the unity of family and community. The Haudenosaunee philosophy extends to the health and well-being of individuals, family, and community. The "collective self-esteem" of Native people was referred to by another interviewee who also highlighted how being a part of a group contributes to an individual's self-perception. Self-esteem for Native people is developed through belonging to a caring community that is proud of their heritage and has placed meaning in their world through sharing and love.

Affirming Identities

Displacing negative images of Onkwehonwe people with affirming identities and pride in our social and political achievements is another way to perform social caring and healing through anti-oppressive work. Rather than "backward savages," Onkwehonwe people were in many cases much more democratic and egalitarian than the European invaders, ruled as they were by authoritarian monarchies. It is said that the Haudenosaunee possess one of the world's oldest democracies, known as the Haudenosaunee Confederacy (Johansen 1995). The Confederacy is a spiritual and traditional governing and social structure based on the Great Law. The Peacemaker brought the Great Law at a time when many Native people were not getting along, and were even at war with each other. The Great Law was meant to provide a structure that would unify and "use the mind to create peace, power and righteousness" (Mohawk 1986: xvii) among nations of people. The Confederacy primarily consists of the five nations: the *Mohawk, Oneida, Onondaga, Cayuga,* and *Seneca.* It also includes the *Tuscarora, Tutelo,* and *Delaware* nations who have not completed their acceptance into this structure. The ambition of the Confederacy is to carry out the tenets of the Peacemaker; the "goal of society which the Peacemaker envisioned was one in which human beings are loving and caring and interacting in a positive way on the emotional level and in which collective rational behaviour and thinking was possible and desirable" (Mohawk 1986: xvii).

The Peacemaker recognized that our minds may at times become clouded by emotional pain, rage, and despair. One story tells of how the Peacemaker helped the Onondaga leader, Hiawatha, through the grief and pain he experienced at the death of his beloved daughters (Mohawk 1986). It is said that

Hiawatha would wander through the forest weeping. Meeting him at a small lake, the Peacemaker soothed Hiawatha's anguish:

> speaking directly to Hiawatha's despair and his hopelessness, the Peacemaker uses soothing words and sincere caring to wipe away the tears from his eyes and remove the lump from his throat. He unplugs the ears and restores Hiawatha to a whole man, so that he can see, talk and use his mind. (Mohawk 1986: xviii)

As a result of this compassion and love for another, the condolence ceremony was created to help people through the grieving process when a chief dies and a new chief is put in place within the Confederacy. It serves as a model to help our people transcend the grief and despair we may experience from great losses.

Neither the stories nor the literature about them identify when these events may have happened. This is not to say that the oral tradition of story-recording among Native people was not a valid way to keep and share our historical accounts. The opposite is true. Storytelling establishes and maintains connections and relationships among people, and offers hope, strength, and vision. Interestingly, it seems that spiritual phenomena often occurred at times when the Haudenosaunee people were enduring painful and traumatic incidents. During these difficult times the Haudenosaunee are reminded to seek strength from their culture.

For practitioners who are working from an anti-oppressive framework with Indigenous people, stories such as these lift people out of themselves to see how others would deal with a situation that may be similar to theirs. An example is the coming of the Peacemaker. Born at a time when the lifestyle of the Haudenosaunee people was very destructive, the Peacemaker brought the teachings of the Great Law to show the Haudenosaunee that it was more meaningful to live peacefully. Another example occurs when Hiawatha came to a spiritual understanding of the teachings and showed people how they could deal with painful losses and grief through the condolence ceremony. Further spiritual phenomena were said to occur when Handsome Lake received the dreams and visions of Gaiwiio (how the Haudenosaunee are to live according to their ancient teachings and customs) at a time when the collective values of the Haudenosaunee were weakening from the impact of colonialism and wars. Like storytelling and soup-making, natural or spiritual phenomena reveal different forms of resistance, resiliency, and social cohesion at a spiritual and cultural level that can offer strength and hope to Haudenosaunee people. Like any other social work technique, storytelling can be used in a number of contexts ranging from informal conversations to more formal counseling sessions, meetings, or workshops. Stories can be told in their entirety or in smaller pieces as is appropriate to the setting and participants.

These pivotal stories and practices are the larger context that has helped

Haudenosaunee people endure and survive a difficult history. Social work interventions have been developed within this context to help Onkwehonwe people. In particular, culturally-based interventions have been developed to address the impact of trauma in relation to Onkwehonwe culture and Onkwehonwe lives.

Building Better Practices: Aboriginal and Non-Aboriginal

A great deal has been written in the counselling field about Onkwehonwe people as clients. Most of it, however, has been written from a Eurocentric perspective (Heinrich et al. 1990; Herring 1992; Thomason 1991). There is little that integrates traditional Onkwehonwe practices into social work counselling. The main focus of earlier writing was to provide information to non-Native practitioners about differences between Onkwehonwe and mainstream culture (Heinrich et al. 1990; Thomason 1991; Paniagua 1994; Wade 1995). Information about cultural values (such as respect for the environment, non-competitiveness, non-interference, little or no eye contact) and beliefs (collectiveness, importance of children, traditional ceremonies, etc.) was provided to assist non-Native practitioners help Onkwehonwe people through the problems and issues they face in their daily lives (poverty, alcoholism, poor housing, lack of employment, depression, and so on). This information encouraged non-Native practitioners to understand Onkwehonwe people better and expand their skills as counselors.

Yet as one author argued, "current counseling paradigms do not include the necessary skills for effective results with Native American clients" (Herring 1992: 35). Some interventions recommended to non-Native practitioners have included the following: involving family (group/family counselling, go to client's home); building and/or drawing on resources from the community (elders, traditional healers, community organizations, etc.); and understanding the use of culture practices (sweat lodges, smudging, vision quests, etc.). Herring (1992) suggests that if non-Native practitioners are to work successfully with Native people they need to establish linkages within the Native community, emphasize Native values, recognize and reflect nonverbal behaviours, develop nonverbal communication skills, incorporate family and group techniques and humour.

Non-Indigenous practitioners who use the suggested social work interventions but lack cultural awareness and sensitivity to Native people, however, may be perpetuating colonialism and oppression. The success of such interventions may be limited because there is no understanding of the struggle Aboriginal people face when their history, cultural values, and beliefs are denied on a broader level. Such a practitioner is treating only the symptoms and not the deep psychological wounds experienced over generations of oppression (Morrissette et al. 1993; Duran et al. 1998). Drug and alcohol treatment programs, for example, often fail to incorporate an understanding of Indigenous history, cultural values, beliefs, and social dynamics. Without a historical understanding of the generations of trauma and grief, practitioners cannot address the underlying issues of shame, lack of identity and belonging that stem from continued oppression and marginalization over generations. By establishing links and alliances with Native communities, the anti-oppressive practitioner will learn that the history, culture, and causes of oppression affect Native people on a deep level.

Onkwehonwe-Appropriate Interventions

In the last ten-to-fifteen years, more Onkwehonwe academics and professionals have entered the social work field and have produced culturally appropriate interventions drawn from Onkwehonwe knowledge, practices, and perspectives (Brant 1990; Morrissette et al. 1993; Nabigon and Mawhiney 1996; Duran et al. 1998). "Programs that have succeeded are programs that have utilized Indigenous epistemology as the root metaphor for theoretical and clinical implementation" (Duran et al. 1998). As Morrissette et al. (1993: 101) note, "While culturally sensitive services advance awareness of issues in the Aboriginal community in the context of involvement with ethnic minority, culturally appropriate service integrates core Aboriginal values, beliefs and healing practices in program delivery".

First Nations practitioners are wise to draw on the rich knowledge and cultural practices of their communities. First Nations people have survived for many generations without "social work" by providing help to each other using their own knowledge and healing practices. Though officially banned in most of Canada, cultural and healing practices were maintained by elders and/or people who dedicated their lives to learning and sharing cultural knowledge and healing practices in order to help the community. In some instances, Onkwehonwe people practiced ceremonies such as the pot latch, sun dance, and sweat lodges in secret. It was not until the late 1970s that Onkwehonwe people were allowed to carry out ceremonies openly without punishment. In many Onkwehonwe communities, seers or visionaries are important people who possess the gift of visions and/or dreams to help guide Onkwehonwe people to find purpose through their cultural knowledge and practices. Visionaries such as Handsome Lake (a Haudenosaunee prophet) encouraged "cultural revitalization as a way of counteracting the devastation of colonialism and its effects" (Duran et al. 1998). In the past several years, many effective therapies and interventions have been developed by integrating and reviving traditional cultural teachings in social work practice with Native people (Duran et al. 1998).

The Medicine Wheel

One helping practice in anti-oppressive practice is the medicine wheel teaching. This teaching is based on a circle divided into four sections and four colours (white, yellow, black, and red) (Morrissette et al. 1993; Nabigon and Mawhiney 1996; Grey and Nye 2001).

The medicine wheel in Figure 7.1 is drawn from Anishnaabe teachings, which are based on a continuous process of restoring balance and harmony within one's life. The four different colours represent the four colours of races in this world and the harmony and respect we can achieve in living with one another. Following the lines up and down and left and right in the medicine wheel conveys the four directions (north and south, east and west). The four quadrants represent the process of human development and child-centred society — children, young adults, adults and older people — as well as the cycle of seasons — spring, summer, fall and winter. Most First Nations teachings are based on the natural cycles of the environment. There are slight variances in the medicine wheel teaching depending on its First Nations origin. For example, in the Cree First Nations' medicine wheel, the different sizes of circles overlap within each other to represent interconnectedness (Nabigon and Mawhiney 1996, see Figure 7.2). This medicine wheel highlights the social structures and the importance of relationships within an Aboriginal community. Aboriginal communities are child-centred, recognizing that children represent the future and hope of the community. The next circle out from the centre represents the elders, who hold the cultural knowledge and teachings of the people. Placing the elders and the children close to one another means that cultural knowledge and language can be shared with the children. The next circle would represent the women, highly respected within Native communities for their strength and role of producing life. The outer circle represents the men, providers for and protectors of the community.

Haudenosaunee teachings would resemble the Cree and Anishnaabe models, representing a child-centred society. A Haudenosaunee model may also include connected circles that form a larger circle (see Figure 7.3). The Haudenosaunee model creates a cycle that gratefully acknowledges the connection of all things and the responsibility each has to another. An example of this acknowledgement would be the Gonahónyohk (Words Before All Else, otherwise known as the Thanksgiving Address). In these words we offer greetings to all the people, Mother Earth, the waters, fish, plant life, natural medicines, insects, natural

Figure 7-1: Medicine Wheel

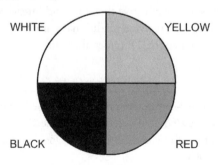

Figure 7.2: Cree Medicine Wheel

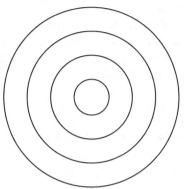

foods, fruits and berries, animals, birds, trees, winds, thunders, moon, sun, stars, Handsome Lake, the four beings, and the Creator. Speaking these words brings everyone's mind together in a good place, as one mind.

The medicine wheel can be used in a variety of specific ways to help Onkwehonwe individuals, families, and communities. What unites these varying processes in anti-oppressive practice is the fact that they honour an Onkwehonwe worldview and can be used to work through the impact of colonialism and its resultant problems and issues (Morrissette et al. 1993). In all the helping forms, though, drawing on the clients' experience is of the utmost importance to assist them through the process of healing and recovery. From the medicine wheel model, the anti-oppressive practitioner can develop questions or activities to help the client respond and heal from the effects of colonization and oppression. Activities for the client may involve attending ceremonies, participating in cultural practices, and/or forms of questioning that help them develop a narrative to assist in releasing thoughts and emotions associated with the trauma and grief. The medicine wheel framework is a flexible and holistic process, an empowering tool that encourages self-reflection as an element in

Figure 7.3: Haudenosaunee Model

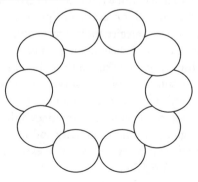

change and that emphasizes the interconnectedness between the client and the issue or problem experienced.

A new generation of Onkwehonwe practitioners have gone beyond the dominant paradigms of social work to create interventions that will better assist Aboriginal people (Morrissette et al. 1993). One such intervention is called "resistance knowledges." This therapy is

> based on a recognition of the spontaneous resistance of Aboriginal persons to the various forms of oppression they have experienced …. Therapists may conceal or suppress this resistance by encouraging victims to view themselves as persons with various psychological problems … or reclaim this history of personal resistance. (Wade 1995: 168)

The anti-oppressive social worker and the Onkwehonwe client identify the parallels and connections between personal traumas and resistance to the historical oppression they have experienced. The social worker becomes an ally with the client while simultaneously illustrating expertise and authority through anti-oppressive methods of questioning and storytelling (Wade 1995).

While this approach may work with many Onkwehonwe people, it may not be a solution for all. If it is not used properly or if the individual is not ready to face his or her issues, the approach may continue to restrain and oppress. I would like to offer a note of caution for the anti-oppressive practitioner in working with Aboriginal communities; it is important to start where the individual, family or community is "at." If a Native family practices Christianity, the medicine wheel or other cultural practices/teachings may have very little relevance to their lives. If the basic needs of a family or community, such as clean water, food, or housing are not met, then cultural teachings and medicine wheels are not top priority. Measures must be taken by the anti-oppressive practitioner to work with and alongside their clients to address basic needs first.

Historical Trauma and Resiliency

Peter Elsass (1992) notes that cultural resiliency can grow from values and practices promoted within a cultural context that helps members adapt to reactions of trauma. He explores the strategies Indigenous cultures have developed for cultural survival despite the overwhelming impact of modernization, industrialization, and capitalism. Commenting on the cultural survival of Indigenous people, he notes that a culture's ability to survive is contingent on being able to develop a shared body of knowledge, a matrix, or a web of individual relations. The basis for a matrix of survival is the shared development of a body of knowledge, which gives a form of solidarity and inertia to the group. This shared knowledge binds the strong forces which exist in larger groups into a shared concept (Elsass 1992: 176).

An example of a survival matrix is the Lakota's "Mending the Sacred Hoop Ride." The Lakota experienced cultural genocide at the 1890 Massacre at Wounded Knee. Lakota elders say that on December 29, 1890, the hoop of the Lakota nation was broken. If we take an anti-oppressive perspective, recognizing that Native worldviews are represented within medicine wheel models, we can begin to understand how this expression conveys the loss of cultural knowledge and practices. Brave Heart-Jordan (1995) defines this traumatic event, along with the horrible experiences of residential schools, as historical trauma and unresolved historical grief. The Lakota, like many Native people, have not had the opportunity to grieve and heal from the oppression and marginalization they have experienced. The "Mending the Sacred Hoop Ride" offers that opportunity. It is a Lakota ceremonial journey on horseback that retraces the experience that led to the 1890 Massacre at Wounded Knee and develops solidarity among the Lakota people based on their own cultural knowledge and practices.

There is very little research about historical trauma, particularly the trauma experienced by the Onkwehonwe people of North America. At the point of European contact, Onkwehonwe peoples were judged negatively for their view of life (Hill, Antone and Myers 1980; Churchill 1995; Duran and Duran 1995; Gagné 1996; Manson et al. 1996; Robin et al. 1996; Ball 1998). Shortly after contact, Onkwehonwe people were intentionally relocated onto reservations and even killed to gain access to their land and resources. Settlers, traders, missionaries, religious organizations, and governments provoked wars, massacres, colonization, and genocide. Traditional ceremonies were prohibited and children sent to residential schools, while alcohol, disease, imprisonment, and violent abuse took a further toll (Hill, Antone and Myers 1980; Brave Heart-Jordon 1995; Duran and Duran 1995; Ball 1998). These events generated multiple and compounded layers of pain, grief, and loss and contributed to underlying psychological wounds that have been passed on from one generation to the next (Brave Heart-Jordan 1995).

As Brant (1990: 535) notes, "Forty-four percent of the Native people who consulted a psychiatrist… were suffering from a grief reaction of one kind or another." Research conducted by Maria Yellow Horse Brave Heart-Jordan, a Lakota social worker, identified similar percentages of Native people seeking

Historical Trauma
Historical trauma refers to the multiple and compounded layers of pain, grief, and loss experienced by Indigenous people since European contact through genocidal, assimilationist, and racist policies and practices. These compounded layers of grief and trauma contribute to the underlying psychological wounding of Indigenous people passed on from one generation to the next. Like all trauma, it must be addressed directly and supportively in order to heal individuals and communities.

professional help. She used the term "historical unresolved grief" to describe the emotional, psychological, and spiritual loss among Onkwehonwe people:

> The mourning resolution is incomplete and the grief is manifested in various symptoms which may include prolonged signs of acute grief, depression, substance abuse, and somatization ... Lakota unsettled bereavement is prominent, significant, and results from generations of devastating losses that have been disenfranchised through the prohibition of Indigenous ceremonies as well as through the larger society's denial of the magnitude of genocide against American Indians. (Brave Heart-Jordan 1995: 5)

Moreover, this grief exists in the context of "historical trauma," a concept that "emphasizes that the trauma is multi-generational and is not limited to one life span." It is cumulative trauma, "collective and compounding emotional and psychic wounding over time, both over the life span and across generations" (Brave Heart-Jordan 1995: 6). Brave Heart-Jordan developed a culturally responsive model, which I describe below, to incorporate these concepts. This model provides a framework to assist Indigenous people in revitalizing, restoring, and rebuilding their individual psychological well-being as well as that of their families and communities.

Brave Heart-Jordan's Indigenous anti-oppressive practice draws on her research into traumatic events such as the 1890 massacre at Wounded Knee, the relocation to reservations, and the effect of residential schools. The social work intervention she developed is based on the traditional practices and knowledges of the Lakota. The first intervention took place in an area sacred to the Lakota known as the Black Hills of South Dakota. For the Lakota people, connection to the land and the natural environment is an important aspect of the healing process. The intervention, an intense and stimulating process, combines Lakota cultural methods and ceremonies such as smudging, sweat lodge, the "releasing the spirit" ceremony, and a "feast for the dead." The results indicated that "100% found that the intervention helped them with their grief resolution ... Ninety-seven percent felt they could now make a constructive commitment to the memory of their ancestors ... All respondents felt better about themselves after the intervention" (Duran et al. 1998). These results support the fundamental importance of using Onkwehonwe cultural knowledge and methods as a foundation in anti-oppressive social work practice for Onkwehonwe people. It also demonstrates the resiliency that exists within the Onkwehonwe culture and the capacity of cultural practices to provide solace and support.

While Brave Heart-Jordan is a Native practitioner whose interventions were very successful for the Native participants involved, I would caution non-Native practitioners considering an anti-oppressive initiative such as this. Because Native people's experiences with cultural and historical trauma, oppression, and marginalization have been at the hands of white colonial people, it is important to respect the boundaries of helping so that Native people are not restricted or halted the process of recovering and healing. This includes knowing when to step back and defer to those Native people or communities that possess the cultural knowledge to heal deep wounds. It is important for anti-oppressive practitioners to gain knowledge, understanding, and sensitivity in working with Aboriginal people, as well as to learn where to find resources and assistance when working with delicate and complex issues such as these.

In many ways, Native people have been very accommodating to Eurocentric society and culture. One of the products of this cooperation and accommodation has been the creation of a shared culture in many institutions such as social services, universities, and community centres. Partnerships with Onkwehonwe people and communities mean that these programs can provide understanding and sensitivity to Native history and culture from and Indigenous perspective.

Conclusion

This chapter has described and analyzed some of the issues and problems faced by Onkwehonwe people. A commitment to anti-oppressive social justice provides an important impetus to explore oppressive structures and practices and to nurture and support new practices. This chapter suggested some practical ways for Native people and their allies to incorporate anti-oppressive practice into their work with Indigenous and non-Indigenous people. An analysis of the underlying emotional, social, and mental issues of trauma endured by Native people shows that they have had very little opportunity to recover from generations of hurt, loss, grief, and anger associated with the long history of wars, massacres, residential schools, governments policies, the Indian Act, relocation to reservations, oppression, racial discrimination, and so forth. Unfortunately, this unresolved grief and trauma continues to have a dramatic impact on Aboriginal communities, as can be seen in the high rates of depression, mental illness, suicide, family violence, child and woman abuse, sexual abuse, alcoholism, addiction, accidents, and violent deaths. Native practitioners are developing innovative strategies that incorporate Indigenous cultural knowledge, language, teaching, and practices into their work with Native clients. Doing so contributes to the cultural revitalization and resiliency of Onkwehonwe people. Non-Native practitioners have also contributed to this effort and continue to develop sensitivities and understanding from their work with First Nations clients. It is from these new practices and the regeneration of cultural knowledge and language that Native/Indigenous social work will find its focus and strength.

Chapter 8

Anti-Oppression Community Organizing

Lessons from Disability Rights Activism

Samantha Wehbi

Focusing on disability rights activism in Lebanon, this chapter discusses social work community practice. The discussion focuses on people with disabilities not as recipients of care but as activists. I argue that anti-oppression practice has much to learn from the resistance and struggles of those in the South. Through practice examples, I highlight four interconnected principles of anti-oppression community organizing: being reflexive about positionality; working with (not for) a community; recognizing power dynamics; and linking to other struggles.

As you read this chapter, ask yourself the following:
1. As you read the theoretical framework section of this chapter, think of the last time you came across a depiction of a person with disability in the media or in the social work scholarship. How did that depiction reflect, reinforce, or challenge a medicalizing discourse?
2. Reflecting on our responsibility as social workers to engage in anti-colonial resistance, how do you anticipate being able to do so in your future practice, and what might this concretely look like?
3. Being reflexive about your positionality, how are you situated in relation to the community where you practice and how has this impacted your work?

In this chapter, I draw on experiences from Lebanon to discuss social work community practice with a focus on people with disabilities not as recipients of care but as allies and activists. Though most formal social work knowledge has been developed in the North and exported to the Global South, anti-oppression practice has much to learn from the struggles of those in the South, including Lebanon. Through examples from my practice in Lebanon with disability rights organizations, I highlight several key principles of anti-oppression community organizing that could guide social work practice in Canada and most other places. Over the past decade, I have worked with disability rights groups on issues involving marginalization and exploitation. Like other disability rights groups and movements throughout the world, our areas of focus have included accessible environments, education, employment, and civic rights (e.g., Barnes and Oliver 1995; Bérubé 2003; Bricout and Bentley 2000; Chimedza and Peters 1999; Cooper 1999; Ghai 2001; Hayashi and Okuhira 2001; Kjellberg 2002; Lavia 2007; Lordan 2000).

One Day at the Ministry

My years of work have been marked by triumphs and by losses, by victories and by setbacks, sometimes all on the same day. This example will illustrate. A few years ago, my colleague and I left the offices of the Ministry of Social Affairs in Lebanon with a triumphant feeling that was soon deflated. My colleague, the prominent Executive Director of a disability rights organization described by Coleridge (1993) as a pioneer in Lebanon, had been invited by the Ministry to participate in discussions about funding criteria for institutions housing people with disabilities. Having stated a desire to shift the emphasis of governmental funding from exclusionary institutions to inclusive practices and measures, the Ministry had invited representatives of these institutions to engage in what proved to be a very heated discussion. My colleague and I were the only two participants to represent a disability rights organization, and we were, to put it mildly, not the most popular people in the room. It appeared that our type of organization posed a threat to a fundamental understanding of social services for people with disabilities; in other words, by calling for inclusionary practices and policies, we were proposing a perspective that would automatically reduce funding to exclusionary institutions. Despite our unpopularity, we felt the meeting to be a success for several reasons. First, we were able to represent the voice of a disability rights organization in the midst of the cacophony of institutional representative voices calling for the safeguarding of the status quo, such as maintaining funding for exclusionary care institutions to house people with disabilities. Second, our organization was the only grassroots civil society organization that had been invited, and our presence at the meeting further affirmed the rightful place of that organization at the negotiations table, its role in setting the state agenda with regards to funding social services for people with disabilities. Finally, we were able to secure a promise of a state shift in terms of funding — regrettably, a promise that has yet to be realized and that we continue to fight for.

We were excited as we came down in the elevator and exited the stuffy building into the open space of the boulevard. Our discussion of the successes of the meeting was punctured by an insistent question from a passerby about the mobility aid used by my colleague, "Where did you get her wheelchair?" I turned around to see a woman who proceeded to ignore my learned colleague completely and address her question exclusively to me, explaining that her sister had recently acquired an impairment and that she did not know where to go to get her sister a wheelchair. After recovering from my shock I replied, "She knows how to speak for herself; you can ask her." It is ironic that, in recognition of her untiring work as a social activist, civil society organizations had recently voted this colleague one of the most powerful women in Lebanon. One simple question from a stranger minimized my colleague's voice, confirming society's perception of people with disabilities as incompetent and incapable. However, this passerby's question also reminded me of the need to continue to work to lobby for better services and greater availability of information for people with disabilities and their families.

Working on disability rights in Lebanon has taught me to understand the issues facing people with disabilities as experiences of oppression. I also learned the importance of South-to-North knowledge-sharing. Echoing the concerns of social work scholars such as Caragata and Sanchez (2002), Heron (2007) and Razack (2000, 2002), most knowledge-sharing has happened as "transfer of knowledge" from North to South. Indeed, M. Gray (2005) cautions us not to engage in perpetuating social work imperialism by imposing our practice models on those in the South. These scholars have argued that the profession must adopt an anti-colonial stance in recognition of historical and contemporary North/South power imbalances that continue to shape social work practice.

Alongside the push to internationalize social work practice and education, several authors, including myself, have argued for a recognition of social work's role in perpetuating neocolonial discourses and practices (Abram, Slosar, and Wells 2005; Askeland and Payne 2006; Razack 2000; Sewpaul, 2006; Wehbi, 2008, 2009). Razack (2002: 253) notes that social work must play a role in countering North/South power relations if it is to stay true to its social change mission; thus far, social work has paid little attention to a critical examination of North/South relations, a neglect that has contributed to "benevolent imperialism." Askeland and Payne (2006) further argue that social work education has a role to play in promoting an anti-colonial mes-

> ## Anti-Colonial
> Anti-colonial refers to historical and contemporary resistance to practices and discourses that explicitly or implicitly position the Global North as superior. This term acknowledges the continued struggle against new forms of colonialism (neo-colonialism) such as the agendas and practices of multinational corporations, international financial institutions such as the International Monetary Fund and World Bank, and international development agencies such as the Canadian International Development Agency and the United States Agency for International Development.

sage and in better equipping future social workers to practice within a global context of North/South power relations. Considering that Arab contexts have been theorized within neo-colonial discourses as repressive and oppressive, highlighting the resistance efforts of local activists offers insights to challenge these ethnocentric misconceptions (Bush 2006; Barsamian and Said 2003; Said 1978, 1997), and informs international social work practice and education. This opportunity is especially relevant in a globalized world characterized by increased migration, where social workers in countries such as Canada are called upon to work with diverse communities (Healey 2001; Lyons, Manion, and Carlsen 2006).

Anti-Oppression Theoretical Framework for Disability Issues

A few years ago, I assisted a disability rights organization in Lebanon to develop a five-year strategic plan to direct their advocacy and research work. This process included engaging in a visioning exercise with the members of the organization. Throughout the exercise, the activists discussed the issues facing them and others as people with disabilities in Lebanese society. By the end of the day-long meeting, the theoretical underpinnings of the organization's vision emerged. Specifically, the activists discussed the issues facing them as manifestations of oppression and located their broader purpose as achieving social justice. These activists saw an anti-oppression framework not as solely a theoretical vision but as central to redefining the problems facing them and to creating radical solutions.

This kind of framework is important because social work has often been charged with contributing to a disabling view of people with disabilities, framing them as "in need of [either] treatment, cure or regulation" (Meekosha and

Medicalizing Discourse

The medical model with regard to people with disabilities uses the lens of a medical diagnosis or notion of impairment. This understanding posits disability as a deficit that needs to be remedied, and seeks solutions in medical interventions. These discourses have been linked to institutionalization, experimentation, forced sterilization, and charity conceptions of people with disabilities.

Social Model

Within the social model, there is an understanding that the impairment that a person may have is not in itself the disability. Instead, the social model of disability asserts that social attitudes, norms, practices, discourses, and systemic barriers such as policies lead to disabling environments and dictate how people with disabilities are constructed and perceived in society, including by social workers.

Dowse 2007: 170) and by adopting a medicalizing discourse (Carey 2003; Dossa 2009). In an anti-oppression approach to disability issues, it is understood that people with disabilities face barriers to inclusion in society not because of their own individual "deficits" but because of their social location in a society fraught with conflictual relations (see Burton and Kagan 2006; Leslie, Leslie and Murphy 2003; Sargent 2005; Sin and Yan 2003; Morris 2001; Scherer 2005). People with disabilities experience these conditions as oppressive, but do so differently depending on overlapping social locations such as gender, race, class, and sexual orientation (Humphrey 1999; Peterson 2006; Watson et al. 2004). For example, feminist analyses have been undertaken of the intersection of gender and disability (Dossa, 2009; Fawcett 2000; Hillyer 1993). My own work in Lebanon has illustrated how normative constructions of women's roles impact on perceptions of women with disabilities in terms of sexualized violence (Wehbi 2002). Other factors are also important in analyzing disability oppression. For example, in Lebanon, like many other nations in the Global South, a history of sectarian and regional conflicts fed by colonial and neo-colonial interventions (Faour 2007) makes religious sectarian background and geographic realities (e.g., rural versus urban areas) important elements — an example is how funding for social services for people with disabilities is often allocated by sect.

Those who adopt an anti-oppression framework to understanding disability issues define social inclusion not merely as the act of "integrating" people with disabilities into an already pre-built society, but as a process of "changing" society so that it becomes more accessible for all (Morris 2001; Sin and Yan 2003). In working towards inclusion, the adoption of a social instead of a medical model helps us see people with disabilities as more than a sum of their health or abilities. Rather than considering the barriers that face people with disabilities to be products of their individual condition, the social model of disability locates such barriers within a larger "disabling society" permeated by multiple oppressive power relations (Corker and French 2002; Dossa 2006; Leslie, Leslie, and Murphy 2003; Race, Boxall, and Carson 2005; Sargent 2005; Sin and Yan 2003; Watson et al. 2004). For example, social policies that reinforce institutionalization of people with disabilities contribute to marginalization and exclusion, and hence to an environment that further reinforces oppressive "disablement."

However, Watson and his colleagues (2004) argue that the social model has its own limitations, specifically, its overemphasis on the social at the expense of the bodily/emotional experience of disability at the level of the individual. By relying on an anti-oppression approach to social work, it is possible to overcome this limitation by understanding the links between the social context and the lived experience of individuals. For example, as my research has shown, the low employment rates of people with disabilities in Lebanon can be attributed not to their lack of capacity to work as individuals, but to systemically ableist perceptions and practices within the labour market (Wehbi and El-Lahib 2007a).

Moreover, although the social model is useful in clarifying how societal power relations construct "disability," it fails to consider how North/South power relations shape "disabling" societies (Stubbs 1999). Holden and Beresford (2002: 194) argue that although the majority of people with disabilities live in the South, Northern conceptions of disability have been applied to their lives without regard to "their particular histories, cultures, traditions, circumstances or preferences." The example of Lebanon adds detail and nuance to the understanding of societal power relations and the importance of context; my current research explores how the long history of war has occasioned setbacks as well as offered opportunities for advancing disability rights.

Another important concept inherent in an anti-oppression framework is that of resistance to (disability) oppression. It is important for social workers to locate sites of resistance and work with those engaged in ending their own oppression (Shragge 2003). Authors such as Batavia (2001) have reacted vehemently against seeing people with disabilities as members of an oppressed social group; part of his argument rests on a desire not to further disempower people with disabilities by exclusively relegating them to the status of "oppressed." However, by acknowledging that people are not passive "victims" of oppression, we can, as Shragge suggests, recognize and support their acts of resistance.

Practice Principles of Anti-Oppression Community Organizing

What does it mean concretely to practice community organizing from an anti-oppression perspective? How do we examine disability issues by focusing on resistance? It is especially important to answer these questions for at least two reasons. First, as anti-oppressive practitioners, we are often faced with the critique (from colleagues, for example) that anti-oppression theories do not easily translate into practice. As the contributions in this book and the previous edition have demonstrated, however, this is far from accurate. In a situation where apathy may carry the day, as practitioners we all have a responsibility to share stories of practice interventions that have applied an anti-oppression framework to counteract hopelessness (Murphy 1999). In other words, not only is applying an anti-oppression framework to practice possible, it is also a responsibility that has been undertaken by practitioners the world over. In my experience, the key to applying this framework has been its concretization in four interconnected practice principles.

Four Interconnected Principles:
AOP and Disability Rights Activism
1. Being reflexive about positionality
2. Working with (not for) a community
3. Recognizing power dynamics
4. Linking to other struggles

Principle 1: Being Reflexive about Positionality
The first principle translates into an ongoing exploration of self in relation to practice. As a social worker, I am charged with the task of continually asking myself questions related to who I am in relation to the community I am working with: Am I an insider, outsider, expert? Do I own my privilege? Do I understand the complexity of my social location and its impact on my work? How did I come to this work? We need to move beyond simplistic dichotomies in answering these questions (Abu-Lughod 1991; Absolon and Herbert 1997; Narayan 2003). Specifically, we need to recognize the complexity of our social locations and how these position us within particular contexts. Therefore, instead of seeing ourselves as insiders or outsiders, experts or novices, the authors argue for the need to see that we are always "in relation." We must, in other words, explore how we are situated in relation to a particular community and how this then impacts our practice. Sometimes, the principle of being reflexive about positionality is understood as simply reflecting on one's own social location. Being reflexive, however, moves beyond a mere description of our social l ocation attributes to seeing how they connect to and impact our practice.

It is equally important to recognize the shifting nature of our positionality. While I am of Lebanese origin, I have been a resident of Canada since 1987. This background challenges the insider/outsider dichotomy, as I am neither just an insider nor just an outsider; instead, I am both at the same time. I regularly think about how my status as a Lebanese "*mughtaribih*," or emigrant, impacts my practice. Joseph (1993), a Lebanese-American ethnographer, notes how this status makes her Lebanese and yet potentially treated with suspicion by local residents in Lebanon.

Having been displaced by the lengthy civil war, I have been given access to foreign education and credentials by status as a *mughtaribih*, which yet keeps me firmly rooted in Lebanese cultural origins. Within a context such as Lebanon, shaped greatly by colonial and neo-colonial influences, my positionality has opened several doors in terms of practice situations, while it has also closed others. In terms of the former, I have been treated as more knowledgeable by foreign donors and organizations operating in Lebanon because of my Canadian educational credentials. Having become aware of this impact, I have been able to use this treatment to the advantage of my partner organizations and colleagues in Lebanon. For example, while I rarely discuss my educational credentials with my activist colleagues, I often present myself as having a doctorate when meeting with government officials, since I have been told this lends credibility to my partner organizations.

On the other hand, my status as a *mughtaribih* has also meant being treated with suspicion and a degree of mistrust in some practice circles or some communities, where I may be seen as wishing to impose a neo-colonial agenda due to my affiliations with the North. For example, I have repeatedly been asked

> ## NGOs
> Non-governmental organizations (NGOs) are organizations that are not officially part of the state apparatus, even if they can at times be sponsored by the state or work under its auspices. NGOs are quite diverse and could include international development organizations, local community groups, and grassroots groups.

by colleagues about the sources of my research funding and the purpose of my findings. I respect that these types of questions are possibly ways of ensuring that my work does not support or will not promote detrimental and ethnocentric perceptions of Arabs and Arab contexts.

It is important to be aware that multiple themes may be operating simultaneously during any meeting or encounter. People may trust me both more and less because of my education and credentials, and though it is difficult to keep both these thoughts at the forefront of one's mind during any given encounter, they often shape the kinds of conversations we have, the options that open up or close to us, and the way others may choose to develop helpful relationships with us or avoid them.

It is also important to understand that our positionality is shifting, not static. When I first began to practise with disability rights organizations, I was one of a handful of workers without a disability in a grassroots organization created and run by people with disabilities. I needed to learn to be an ally and to explore what my status as able-bodied meant in terms of practice. For example, I was often aware that I was treated, by those in mainstream organizations (international and local non-government organizations, or NGOs), as being more capable or more knowledgeable than my colleagues with disabilities. This treatment occurred even though my colleagues had much lengthier practice histories. Flower and Wirz (2000) confirm that people with disabilities are often seen as incapable of being active contributors. Cameron (2007) also argues that, as social service providers, we tend to see people with disabilities as less capable than others.

A few years ago, my health/ability status changed and I had to relearn my work. I became a member, not just an ally, in grassroots disability organizations. Although this is not the place to elaborate on this shift, it is important to note it to emphasize the importance of continued reflexivity on our shifting positionalities and what they mean for practice. I had to reflect on my own assumptions about the community and its needs and how we come to this work. For example, I have explored how my research agenda can evolve to serve the practice needs of community as defined by its members and not only to suit my academic pursuits. In doing so, I have found it important to observe a second practice principle, that of working with (not for) a community.

Principle 2: Working With (not For) a Community

At a recent workshop held by a disability rights organization, I listened to a social worker explain that she appreciated working in a grassroots organization because she believed in its "members' social cause." The reaction following her statement was vehement: while well-intentioned, her statement reflected a sense that she saw herself working for, not with, the organization and its members. One of the few workers currently without a disability, she had unwittingly reinforced the sense of difference between "us" and "them," between herself and those members who have disabilities. She also unintentionally reinforced the distinction between professionals (social workers) and members. Indeed, many members commented that they felt her statement reinforced a view of people with disabilities as clients or recipients of care, not as colleagues and activists. In social work practice, we have the opportunity to challenge this perception of people with disabilities, especially in our work alongside communities.

As noted by Shragge (2003), when working with community members, we have the responsibility of not taking their role. Concretely, this means understanding and believing that we are working alongside (or with) communities, not for them. In their discussion of anti-poverty work focusing on people with disabilities, Yeo and Moore (2003) echo the familiar cry in disability rights activism — "nothing about us without us" — as a reflection of histories of exclusion in terms of decision-making. At times, the principle of "not taking their role" is easier said than done: indeed, it can appear much less complicated to accept the belief that as social workers, we are the professionals and the experts, and as such, we know what is best for the community and its members. However, while this may sometimes work in the short term, the long-term implications are counter-productive for several reasons. First, community trust will not be so easily gained, thereby impeding our work. Second, if we leave when our particular job or task is done, the community loses an important resource; in other words, "doing for" the community does not reinforce and strengthen its own existing resources. Third, the sense of community ownership of a particular project or initiative is not fostered if we choose to work for a community and not alongside or in solidarity with its members. Finally, our own sense of ourselves as co-activists contributing to an anti-oppressive vision of society is not reinforced.

Making a commitment to work *with* communities, not *for* them, requires first and foremost a shift in our perception and understanding of people with disabilities. We need to challenge our own misconceptions and limitations in working with these population groups, learning to perceive people with disabilities not primarily as service users or "care recipients," but as potential resources and allies. Starting from this point, we can work with people with disabilities to understand their needs in terms of capacity-building and alliances. Working with and not for people with disabilities also requires us to acknowledge and locate sites of resistance to oppression, so that we can be allies. My own practice experience has shown me how it is easy to fall into the trap of doing for and how beneficial it is to make the shift to working with communities.

A few years ago, one of the disability rights organizations I have been partnered with asked me to set up, launch, and head a vocational training and social service centre in a rural area. This meant hiring staff, organizing the first few events, and planning for the continuation of the centre. The original funding proposal had included several resume-writing training workshops aimed at building the capacities of people with disabilities and enhancing their job opportunities. As acting director of the centre, I oversaw these workshops and was quite surprised at the turnout. It was very poor, in contrast to the high attendance at the literacy training programs, which were attended not only by people with disabilities but also by so many of their neighbours or family members that we actually had to add seats! The centre's social workers met informally to ask a few of the people frequenting the centre about the poor turnout at the resume workshops. The answer was simple: no one had asked them if they required these types of workshops. They explained that in a small rural community, resumes were not relied upon to gain access to employment opportunities, so what use would a writing workshop be? Indeed, the original idea for resume-writing workshops had been transplanted from the disability rights organization's work in Beirut, a large urban centre, without consultation with the local community in the rural area. Raised in a city and having most of my social work experience in urban centres, I also did not question the original proposed workshops. This practice example clearly demonstrates the importance of being aware of the particularities of context in developing our interventions. This example also makes clear how crucial it is to work with the community to understand its members' needs, as opposed to believing that as professionals, we know what's best.

At one point in my practice, I had the opportunity of being involved with a team of social workers, vocational therapists, parents, and grassroots disability rights activists on a national project aimed at fostering inclusion for people with disabilities in Lebanese society. I was asked to work as a "social development specialist" on the project. The first phase attempted to assess the current state of inclusion in mainstream education, employment and social environments, noting successful inclusion attempts and identifying service gaps. The second phase would build a community development plan to implement the findings of the first phase; I have written more amply about this project (Wehbi 2006). During our initial assessment planning, we quickly identified children with disabilities as an important group to consult with regarding issues of educational inclusion. Our reasoning was that if we were to propose a community development plan targeting these children, then they needed to be part of its planning, not only its recipients. To our surprise, we discovered that it was the first time any professionals working on social inclusion had consulted children themselves; typically, only their parents, guardians, or teachers had been consulted. We also consulted parents and teachers, but clearly felt it important to consult children themselves about their own experiences. However, it is understandable why children would not have been consulted in the first place: given the power dynamics in a patriarchal society where children and youth are typically marginalized, it is understandable (though not excusable) that children would not be seen as valuable resource-persons on their own lives. This example ties directly to the third practice principle — understanding power dynamics in order to enhance our interventions.

Principle 3: Understanding Power Dynamics
An essential element of any anti-oppression framework is being aware of power dynamics and their interplay with our practice (Ristock and Pennel 1996). In terms of community practice, it is important to recognize power dynamics operating both within and between communities. In other words, it is important to recognize the heterogeneity of communities (differences within and between them), as well as how these same communities are located within a broader web of power relations. As with the example of the resume-writing workshops discussed earlier, we cannot assume that the needs of all people with disabilities are the same. Working with community members, we can begin to understand their differing needs from their own perspectives. Social differences between large urban centres and small rural centres translated into job opportunities that needed to be accessed differently, and hence differing needs in terms of capacity-building. Considering the history of marginalization of rural regions within the broader Lebanese societal context, we can begin to understand how an idea such as "resume-writing," even if well-meant, can be experienced as an imposition.

The intersections of gender, rural context, class, and disability also lead to differing experiences (Abu-Habib 1997; Wehbi and El-Lahib 2007a) in terms of needs, voice, leadership, decision-making, and participation, as can been seen in another example involving employment opportunities and accessibility. The social workers at the employment centre found out early on in their work that for many of their women clients, the biggest barriers to gaining employment were not external market conditions and employer discrimination, but pressures exerted by the women's families (particularly parents and male siblings) to observe particular societal norms surrounding gendered roles. Moreover, considering the impact of ableism, many of these women experienced the perception within their families that they were "incapable" of performing any meaningful labour, despite the high levels of domestic labour they performed in their own homes. For the social workers at the centre, whenever an employment opportunity arose for one of their women clients, it was important to work with the family members to raise awareness about the capacities of women with disabilities and the benefits of paid employment for the individual woman and her family. Equally important was their work with the women themselves to raise their awareness about their own capacities and potential.

A final example comes from the civic rights campaign spearheaded by two disability-rights organizations during the Lebanese parliamentary elections in 2005 (see Wehbi and El-Lahib 2007b). The campaign highlighted the rights of people with disabilities to exercise their civic responsibilities to vote and run for office. During this campaign, the focus for community organizers was raising societal awareness of these rights while simultaneously counteracting a history of marginalization and exclusion. It was also equally important to work with people with disabilities themselves to raise awareness of their rights to vote freely and to participate without undue influence from their families.

Work on this campaign confirmed the importance of understanding that people are not politicized by virtue of having a disability. Histories and contemporary practices of marginalization within Lebanese society have made people with disabilities quasi-invisible and have limited their opportunities to develop leadership skills and capacities to be involved in the political realm. The campaign sought to change this by equipping people with disabilities with a political analysis and an awareness of their constitutional rights. This type of awareness is important not only for becoming disability rights activists in our own personal lives but also for developing a broader vision of a society free of oppression. In this regard, for many of the disability rights activists I have encountered, and indeed as enshrined in their organizational mission state-ments, the key to their success in challenging exclusionary power relations is their ability to work as allies in other struggles.

Principle 4: Linking to Other Struggles
Working with disability rights activists, I learned firsthand what it means to have a commitment to a vision of a society free of oppression. As Barnoff and Moffatt (2007) argue, oppressions need to be seen as intersecting; ranking them on a scale of which is more or less harmful is both misleading and counterproductive. Starting from an understanding that all forms of oppression are interconnected, the disability rights activists I have worked with have sought to work as allies with members of other activist organizations, including those working against sexism, homophobia, classism, and sectarianism and on social issues such as war, violence against women, worker exploitation, state corruption, and the mistreatment of prisoners of conscience.

A powerful example happened recently. In May 2008, disability rights activists made world-wide headlines with their public protest against the civil strife and political wrangling of Lebanon's leaders, feared by many to be driving the country to the brink of a new civil war (Daragahi 2008). Organized by a disability rights organization, the protest saw activists with disabilities and their allies demonstrate on the road to the airport where the political leaders were getting ready to leave for Qatar, where peace talks were taking place. The activists held placards saying, "if you don't agree, don't come back." This public action on issues related to peace was not narrowly focused on disability issues. Instead, it reinforced the message that people with disabilities exist and are active members of society who can provide important leadership on all kinds of critical social issues. Working on other struggles thus provides an opportunity to make links between disability issues and rights and broader social concerns. Indeed, a few days after an agreement was reached between feuding political leaders, the newly-elected Lebanese President referred in his inauguration speech to the impact of war on people developing impairments (BBC Monitoring Newsfile 2008).

Similarly, in another example from the civic rights campaign, disability rights community organizers worked with members of other civil society organizations on greater democracy in elections. By allying with other civil society actors, the disability rights organizations had the opportunity to raise awareness among these other organizations about the needs and rights of people with disabilities. No longer were we the only ones on the ground during election day to monitor rights violations against people with disabilities. By attending meetings and working with representatives of other organizations, the disability rights community organizers provided these representatives with the tools necessary to monitor violations. We won an important victory when the first point in the official report issued by the United Nations election observers focused on rights violations against people with disabilities. In short, allying with others provided us with the opportunity to learn about how we can support each other in building a society where all are included.

We Are Not "Burdens of Care"

The four principles of an anti-oppression approach to community organizing try to put into practice the vision of an anti-oppression theoretical framework. I have highlighted lessons I have learned about the importance of understanding one's positionality in order to better inform one's practice, the necessity of working with and not for communities and of being aware of power dynamics, as well as the value of linking our own struggle to the struggles of others. Guiding our implementation of these principles is the need to shift our vision of people with disabilities as incapable and passive recipients of care to active participants in issues and practices that affect them. Starting from this point, we can begin to see people with disabilities as resources and leaders in change initiatives as opposed to "burdens of care," whether this perception is held in Southern or Northern contexts.

In closing, staying true to my suggestion about needing to constantly reflect on our practice, I leave you with a set of questions to further guide your reflections. If you practise from an anti-oppression perspective with people with disabilities, which of the four principles discussed in this chapter would be the most challenging for you? Which principle do you feel you have learned already? What principles would you find important to add? Which lessons can you learn and which can you teach about being an ally, working with people with disabilities or community practice? Continuing to reflect and to put into practice the principles we value will not only enhance our everyday practice but will also guide us to creating a more solid foundation on which to build long-term change.

Chapter 9

Evidence-Based Practice and Anti-Oppressive Practice

Michelle Bates

Reflecting on my own personal experience and a practical case example, this chapter explores how rational decision-making and reliance on the "evidence" ignores important contextual information and limits available decisions. Evidence-based practice (EBP) in many ways disrupts and constrains social workers' ways of knowing, thinking, and acting; it results in limited attention for social justice issues and limits the capacity to change individual and collective social work identity. While EBP has altered the practice of social work, numerous opportunities to remain anti-oppressive through reflexivity exist and are offered as suggestions to social workers.

As you read this chapter ask yourself the following:
1.   What new activities and ways of thinking are valued within EBP? What activities and ways of thinking are constrained and devalued within EBP?
2.   When social workers focus only on the "evidence" and are distanced from tacit knowledge and contextualized information, what are the implications for social justice concerns?
3.   How can social workers maintain their commitment to social justice and resist the narrowness of practice in the current evidence-based environment?

Not long ago I was an enthusiastic supporter of evidence-based practice (EBP). But further inquiry into and investigation of this newest mode of practice in social work left me feeling troubled and unsettled. Weaving together my own experiences and a practice situation, I argue that EBP broadens and narrows the practice of social work. Amidst pressures for accountability and effectiveness, EBP encourages the push towards a particular kind of "scientific" professionalism influencing the formation of professional identity and undermining our personal and collective ability for social justice-oriented practice. Yet, there are still opportunities for social workers to be anti-oppressive while being evidence-informed.

What is EBP?

EBP was initiated by a group of clinical epidemiologists from McMaster University in the early 1980s (Mykhalovskiy and Weir 2004; Witkin and Harrison 2001) and quickly spread to other allied health professions. EBP argued that physicians were not making use of the best and most recent research findings, that they were relying instead on practice knowledge, intuition, relationships of trust with patients, and old research. EBP aimed to remedy this problem by requiring that physicians remain up-to-date on research findings and integrate them into practice. Rather than integrating multiple sources of research, EBP argues that some research is more credible than others, prompting the group at McMaster and elsewhere to develop systems in which research was rated. Random clinical trials and experimental methods are at the top of the rating hierarchy, while case, qualitative, and participatory research studies, which are very common in social work research, are largely discounted as unscientific and not objective. Practice and tacit knowledge — the intuitive, shared, reflexive knowledge learned on the front lines of social work practice — is almost entirely ignored in this system. Rather than questioning this erasure of a large part of social work knowledge, a number of authors, such as Gibbs and Gambrill (2002: 452), jumped on the EBP bandwagon to argue that "evidence-based practice is the conscientious, explicit, and judicious use of current best evidence in making decisions about the care of clients" (452).

Growing scepticism about the welfare state has created a certain amount of doubt about social work (Harris 2008) in circles that include social workers themselves, service users, politicians, other professionals, and the broader public. The ensuing erosion of trust in the profession and the larger social welfare system left the field vulnerable to claims that social work could benefit from the adoption of unbiased, objective, and scientific approaches. With its emphasis on science, EBP is not dependent upon practitioner judgment and offers the public and others a new objective system of trust that claims to provide certainty and predictability (Trinder as cited in Webb 2002).

The embrace of EBP was enhanced by neoliberal policies of financial con-

Random Clinical Trials

Random clinical trials (RCT) are a form of scientific experiment in which research participants, generally referred to as subjects, are randomly assigned to a treatment group (in which they receive a drug, treatment, or intervention) or a control group (in which subjects receive a placebo or no intervention). Sometimes multiple treatment groups are compared. The randomized aspect of RCTs is thought to provide an effective way to reduce erroneous findings resulting from differences among subjects rather than produced by the intervention.

Positivism

Positivism is a philosophical perspective asserting that the only authentic knowledge is that which is based on sense experience and positive verification. A form of positivism known as scientism dominates EBP. Scientism argues that the methods of the physical sciences should be applied to all kinds of research including philosophical, social scientific, or the arts. Its proponents argue further that knowledge should and can be value-free and testable, and that researchers should ensure that common-sense understandings do not cloud or influence their understandings.

straints and cutbacks in government funding. New and/or continued funding often depended on proving that the agency, and by extension the social workers, were providing effective services. With fewer dollars and increasing demands for accountability and effectiveness, EBP provided a system of rationalization and accountability (Larner 2004) within managed care environments (Gossett and Weinman 2007).

Situated within positivism, EBP emphasizes formal research and objective knowing (Kowalski 2009). It is also connected to the rational choice movement whose supporters argue that people base their everyday choices on what will maximize their individual profit or benefit them most. In order to make the most rational choices, people require full knowledge. In EBP and the rational choice movement, the goal is to reduce subjective/"biased" judgment amongst practitioners (see van de Luitgaarden 2009). Though omitting several types of knowledge that have historically been central to social work, EBP allegedly provides social workers with full knowledge.

Fortunately, some versions of EBP included such contextual considerations as the social worker's knowledge and experience, client preferences and perspectives, existing resources and policies, and moral/political dimensions (see Gilgun 2005; Mullen 2002; Mullen, Bledsoe, and Bellamy 2007; Briggs and McBeath 2009). However, all definitions of EBP direct social work practitioners to access formal research findings, preferably findings generated by random clinical trials (defined earlier in this chapter), and to make clinical decisions based upon them. As stated by Hoagwood et al. (2001: 1182), evidence-based practice is "a shorthand term that denotes the quality, robustness, or validity of scientific evidence as it is brought to bear on (practice) issues" (1182).

Clinical Decisions

Within an evidence-based framework, clinical decision refers to a rational decision-making process regarding the interventions chosen by a social worker in a given practice situation. The process relies heavily on research literature.

The Promises of EBP

Advocates cite numerous benefits of being an evidence-based social worker or agency. Drawing on very little in the way of scientific evidence, EBP supporters suggest that agencies that are evidence-based will enjoy increased or sustained funding (Wheeler and Parchment 2009), demonstrate accountability, and provide effective services. Social workers who are evidence-based are expected to experience the following: increased competence, confidence, and professionalism (Howard et al. 2003); enhanced professional status and credibility (Witkin and Harrison 2001); job security; protection from lawsuits; and the ability to provide ethical services (Gossett and Weinman 2007). For service users, EBP claims to ensure better, less harmful, and more effective services (Zlotnick et al. 2002), and to invite service users into an egalitarian position with the social worker as a result of transparency and collaboration in decision-making (Gambrill 2001).

It is true that in practice, some of these promises are being realized. In a study of EBP, I interviewed school social workers who claimed that using evidence-based practices had provided them with more certainty about their practice, informed them about "what works," and enhanced their individual and collective professional credibility (Bates 2006). However, these social workers also experienced serious tensions in their application and use of EBPs.

Instructions to Social Workers on How to Be Evidence-Based

While I was eagerly reading about and attempting to implement evidence-based practices six years ago, some of my colleagues were openly resisting these new approaches. I felt surprised and confused; "Who wouldn't want to implement an EBP and provide better, more effective services to their clients?" Seeking answers in the literature, I found many articles lamenting the fact that social workers were not incorporating "evidence" into their practice (McNeill 2006; Barwick et al. 2005; Franklin and Kelly 2009; Pignotti and Thyer 2009). Authors noted that social workers lacked the time and resources to read research studies (Gira et al. 2004; Mufson et al. 2004), and that most social workers were not able to read and interpret statistical data (Mullen 2002; Franklin 1999; Gibbs and Gambrill 2002). Social workers were also presented as not interested in or capable of conducting research; it was argued that they tended to remain loyal to their initial training rather than undertaking or using research. They purportedly remained dependent upon supervisors and colleagues for information (Jackson 1997), were reluctant to change in general, and were resistant to EBP in particular (Rubin 2002; Jackson 1997; Barwick et al. 2005; Hemsley-Brown 2004). To me, these descriptions seemed to be an unfair and inaccurate depiction of those of us who were struggling to provide quality services in difficult circumstances. Equally disturbing was the absence of the perspective of frontline social workers in the EBP literature.

With the goal of moving social work practitioners to become evidence-based, initial attempts had centred on disseminating information and identifying preferred interventions. Many of these efforts attended to the provision, accessibility, and readability of high quality research findings (Mullen, Bledsoe, and Bellamy 2007). This perspective reflects a producer-user relationship wherein researchers produce the research and users/practitioners read and apply the findings. This positions social workers as passive consumers of research, applying technical solutions to clients' problems, rather than as those who have and generate knowledge in their own right.

McNeill (2006) suggests that social workers are "uncertain" about how to implement EBP. To remedy this, a variety of authors have laid out detailed steps that social workers should follow when practicing in an evidence-based manner (Rosen 2003; Mullen et al. 2007; Polio 2006; Gossett and Weinman 2007; Briggs and McBeath 2009). For example, Gossett and Weinman (2007) identify the following five steps of evidence-based practice:

1. converting client needs into answerable questions... that lead to an effective electronic search;
2. searching and locating the best external evidence to answer the question;
3. critically evaluating the evidence ... for validity and usefulness to the client;
4. applying the results of the evaluation to policy or practice decisions;
5. taking appropriate action.

Rather than an easy, multi-step approach, I encountered critical challenges in my efforts to implement an evidence-based approach (see also Franklin and Kelly 2009).

EBP in Practice

As a school social worker, I am responsible to investigate and make recommendations in situations when students are absent from school. In the Province of Ontario, school attendance is currently compulsory for registered students up until the student is eighteen years of age. While there is an enforcement component to this part of my job, I consciously seek to maintain my "social work focus." I regularly inquire about students' and parents' experiences with and within the school system (past and present), what they need, and what changes they would recommend for school to be a better experience.

I noticed that in some situations, students re-engaged in school quickly and began attending classes, yet in others, students continued to be absent from school. I had my "tool kit" of strategies and would indiscriminately try them all, hoping that one or two might make a difference. Attendance work had a kind of drudgery about it and I often found it to be stressful and unrewarding. I never quite felt competent — sometimes what I did would work, yet there were other times when nothing I did seemed to help. Concern for the student's future and a sense of responsibility to have them back in school was omnipresent. I also worried about how my performance would look to my employer. Drudgery was short-form for feeling disempowered, de-skilled, and unsure. I was eager to look at the literature and find answers as to how I could help all students successfully attend school.

The literature included a lot of material relating to student non-attendance. Concern over student absenteeism had been written about for at least 100 years! A variety of studies and policy papers identified intrapersonal, interpersonal, familial, school-based, and community/social concerns in an attempt to explain why students did not attend school. They discussed numerous approaches, based upon different conceptualizations of student non-attendance. However, the literature, like my own thinking, was disjointed and conflicted.

Then I encountered one author's research (Kearney 2007) that offered an exciting new way to think about student non-attendance; it validated my clinical intuition and experience, and it provided a conceptual framework and prescriptive treatment approach that offered the hope of improving my effectiveness. Implementing this evidence-based approach changed my ways of thinking, talking, and acting in situations of student non-attendance.

Using this framework shaped the way that I conceptualized a student's situation by drawing my attention to certain details and encouraging me to ignore other "miscellaneous" information. I began to say, "there are four different reasons why students don't attend school. Two are basically 'push' factors — there are things happening at school that push students away from being at school, and there are two reasons that are 'pull' factors: things that are happening outside of school that pull students away from attending school."

The standardized assessment scale that I used in conjunction with this framework helped to determine the main motivation or "type" of school refusal behaviour exhibited by students. Within 15-20 minutes with students and/or their parents I could "get the answer" to what in traditional assessment would have taken me an hour or two. I was also assured that all the "important" areas had been covered in the standardized tool. I did not have to worry about remembering whether or not I had already asked a certain question or if the assessment was failing to produce the information needed to help the student resolve his or her absenteeism problem. Interestingly, I found that students were more likely to answer questions as part of the questionnaire than they were in face-to-face interactions. The framework and assessment tool served as a shortcut, enabling me to arrive at an assessment faster.

The framework tied each "type" of school refusal behaviour to a prescriptive treatment approach. Some of the prescribed activities I was familiar with and had used in my practice, while some of the strategies represented new activities. In addition to learning and using new strategies, I also followed a prescribed intervention plan that identified goals, activities, and number of sessions for each "type."

Being evidence-based altered the relationships I had with others (parents and colleagues) and with myself. I liked the certainty and focus that the prescriptive approach provided. I did not have to sit and ponder what actions I should take or the sequencing of interventions — the prescriptive approach provided a clear step-by-step set of directions. Having the knowledge of experts behind me increased my feelings of confidence and competence as a practitioner. I began to say to students, parents, and staff, "the research says." There was an inherent authority attached to saying this. Moreover, because what I was saying represented "the research," its validity was assumed as well. I had the impression that staff and parents were taking the information quite seriously.

There also seemed to be some reassurance in knowing that this issue had been studied, and that I was obviously current and knowledgeable. Allied professionals seemed impressed when I could use the descriptive titles that referred to the different subtypes in the framework. In addition to feeling more professional, I also believed that I was *seen* by colleagues, students, and families as more professional, with increased credibility and integrity. I also saw myself as more efficient and effective.

This does not mean, however, that I actually *was* more efficient, effective, or helpful. As the practice scenario below shows, EBP narrows social work practice, removing or reducing opportunities to be holistic or to pursue social justice.

Sam

Sam was a fifteen-year-old student in Grade 10. Since the start of the school year, her attendance had become increasingly sporadic. During our meeting, Sam shared with me that she felt very nervous and uncomfortable when she attended school.

According to the "best external evidence," the most effective approach for helping a student whose school refusal behaviour is due to anxiety is to provide individual cognitive-behavioural therapy (CBT), to encourage the development of social skills, and to enhance the student's social support. Assisting the family in improving their problem-solving and communication skills is also required.

I invited Sam to participate in individual CBT sessions, and while initially she was reluctant — the sessions were offered during class time and she already felt far behind in her school work — Sam did meet with me individually. Group CBT sessions are helpful, but there are not always enough students to offer a group, especially when attendance is made more difficult by teachers who are not generally supportive of the idea of students missing class time. In order to avoid making Sam miss more classes, I encouraged her teacher to provide social skills training to the whole class, emphasizing that all the students would benefit. While supportive of Sam and the other students in the class and interested in social skills training, her teacher was unsure about taking time away from the curriculum. In the current environment, with its emphasis on achievement rates and test scores, teachers experience tremendous pressure to deliver only the curriculum and little more. Even teachers who are supportive of social skills programs find little or no budget money for training and curriculum materials. While some teachers would like to have support from me in delivering this new curriculum, rather than doing it all on their own, I am not always able to afford the time to assist.

Engaging Sam's family was a bit challenging. Her mom was a single parent who worked two jobs and was very worried about their financial situation. While concerned and supportive of Sam, she was not allowed to receive non-urgent phone calls at work and could not afford to miss work to attend sessions during my work day. In other client situations, it can be even more challenging to engage families. Sometimes young people are Crown wards and do not have a definable family that can engage in counselling. Other families are hard to get a hold of — they don't have a phone or they can only receive calls after 6 p.m. when I am no longer at work. The EBP literature had little or nothing to say about working class and poor families or those involved in the child welfare system, though these students are often referred to school social workers for absenteeism and other issues.

Curiously, the best evidence approach I was using was silent on some of the areas of a student's life that I have come to appreciate as most important. For example, I wanted to understand the relationships that Sam had with her teachers. Were her teachers a source of support for Sam? Did they ensure that she was emotionally safe in the class, and did they intervene when other students gossiped about or treated Sam poorly? Were her teachers ensuring that she was not left out of group work activities? Were the relationships Sam had with her teachers and her classroom experiences sources of support and strength for her or difficult experiences of stress?

Sam's course subjects, how she felt about them, and how she learned best were also important factors in her school success. Was Sam in the right level of course? Was she entitled to additional school supports, and were they being provided? Were Sam's courses being appropriately modified for her in areas where she might need this? Was the teacher willing to allow Sam other ways of doing class presentations if oral work proved difficult?

I wondered if it would be helpful to encourage Sam to join a club or sport team, though it turned out that she did not want to do so. This may have been due to her feelings about herself or her relationships with peers. For example, I wonder if Sam was feeling uncomfortable or anxious about her body shape and size. Was she questioning her gender identity or sexual orientation? What messages was she hearing at school about this? Maybe she was not refusing school so much as refusing transphobia or homophobia. I also wonder about other forms of violence and oppression. Was Sam experiencing violence in her relationships, or was her mother or a friend being abused? What about other stressful concerns? Was Sam worried about someone she loves — someone who was drinking a lot of alcohol, very ill, or aging? Was Sam feeling guilty or worried about her family's finances? Had her pet recently died, had a friend moved away, or was she experiencing other losses? Though seemingly key in a full assessment of Sam's situation, the recommended EBP intervention was silent about all these potential concerns.

Other issues could also prove important, though unacknowledged by either the framework or the prescribed intervention. For example, was Sam "refusing" school because she was self-conscious about her clothes, her hair, or her teeth? If so, I could have linked Sam with the nutrition program and let her know about the Clothes Closet, a place where she could get second-hand clothes for free. I could also have inquired about washing facilities at the school and arranged for an appointment with the hairdresser. For free dental care I could refer students to the Health Bus. All these issues link to low income, but the EBP intervention did not recognize low or no income as a factor in school absenteeism or in the preferred interventions.

This practice situation highlights one of the main complexities when implementing an evidence-based practice — namely the absence of attention to those social concerns and unique circumstances that social workers know through their practice experience to be important in clients' lives. In my study (Bates 2006), school social workers reported four significant tensions that they encountered when using evidence-based practices. Appreciating the importance of applying the EBP as prescribed while ensuring that the intervention fit each individual client and the practice environment, school social workers balanced the tension of *rigidity versus flexibility*. Sensitive to the necessity of proving the effectiveness of their services, school social workers identified a tension between *measuring the outcomes valued by their organizations and providing changes and improvements found meaningful by clients*. A third tension surrounded the debate between *technique and relationship*. Aware that most EBPs specify particular techniques, the school social workers involved in my study felt pressure to adopt specific techniques, but not at the expense of their relationships with clients. Lastly, they highlighted the tension between *formal and practice knowledge*. While attuned to the higher value placed on formal knowledge, school social workers enthusiastically valued their practice knowledge. As one social worker observed, "So I use both (practice knowledge and formal knowledge), and I'm not apologetic that I use both." (Bates 2006).

Reconstructing and Reconstituting
the Professional Self within EBP

Learning more about EBP and reflecting upon my own experiences with it, I became acutely aware that when I (and other social workers) practice in an evidence-based manner, our previous ways of knowing and practicing become interrupted, disrupted, and constrained. Research knowledge is privileged within EBP: social workers (and all evidence-based practitioners) are told to make explicit use of it. Yet while using certain kinds of research knowledge broadens activities, skills, and thinking are broadened through the use of certain kinds of research knowledge, it also narrows and constains social work practice. Parton (2008) believes that evidence-based practitioners use research knowledge for the purposes of gathering information so that workers can determine risk, classify "needs," and determine resources. This approach to social work separates social workers from some of the core values that have informed our work in the past. Previously, the goal of knowledge-building was to develop a comprehensive and holistic sense of each client, his or her challenges, strengths, and contexts. Workers sought to understand their clients' lived experiences, asking in an open-ended way about their situations, struggles, perspectives, and hopes. Using an evidence-based practice means that social workers ask questions related only to a particular assessment and/or framework; other information is not collected or sought. Webb (2001) calls this "constructed knowledge" as it constructs problems and solutions in the way it asks certain questions and does not ask others. Constructed knowledge is not about knowing or understanding in a holistic sense; rather, knowledge is narrowed, transformed into information that then facilitates or directs "rationalized action." With this reductionist evidence-based approach, knowledge is truncated to information, workers become "information gatherers," and practice becomes mechanistic (Webb 2001). As Parton (2008) states, rather cryptically, "Knowledge and information are quite different."

Another consequence of the information-gathering function within EBP is that practice becomes deterministic — that is, assessments are undertaken and information collected with the unrealistic expectation that social workers will be able to objectively know and accurately predict client situations. Determinism suggests a simplified and straightforward view of practice that removes subjectivity and relativity, eliminating tensions and debates as well as the need or space for reflexivity (Webb 2001).

When social workers look only for certain information, the risk of compartmentalizing clients' experiences (or worse yet, objectifying them) is very real. The shift to information-gathering also suggests that workers are beginning with research, not "where the client is at." This suggests an alliance with science and a weakening of an alliance with clients, as a result jeopardizing our capacity to build trusting relationships with them.

Iedema and Scheeres (2003) have observed that research evidence serves an "assimilating function" through the production of similarities and commonalities between social work and other professions. Shared culture, beliefs, and approaches are linked with both organizational and professional identity (Baruch and Cohen 2007). And while social workers may enjoy this expanded sense of professional identity and/or professional affiliation — for instance with physicians and nurses — within an EBP practice environment social work's unique and vital practice contribution, particularly related to social justice and larger structural interventions, becomes restricted or removed. Instead of identifying with clients and oppressed communities, social work practitioners are bound to other professionals by their shared "talk of EBP" and agreed-upon, evidence-based approach to assessment and intervention (Iedema and Scheeres 2003). As an evidence-based social worker, I run the risk of having my "social work" diluted, particularly if I want to ask larger questions, focus on systemic inequity, or challenge oppression. Pignotti and Thyer's (2009) assertion that novel, unsupported, and/or "unproven" approaches to practice are a threat to social work's professionalism is a clarion signal that these kinds of approaches are in danger of being censored and/or marginalized.

Workers have traditionally been accountable to their employers and to their clients through a number of mechanisms. In an evidence-based environment, co-workers are co-opted into a management role, providing support, giving feedback, monitoring and/or sanctioning one another in the effort to be evidence-based. Questions such as "Is that evidence-based?" and "What evidence do you have for that approach?" are regularly posed in social work workplaces by managers and co-workers alike. Caught between disparate worlds, social workers can experience conflict within themselves and in their relationships because they are neither the ideal evidence-based practitioner nor the ideal social worker.

Another consequence of relying exclusively on formalized research as a source of knowledge is the suppression of social workers' tacit knowledge. Tacit — i.e., experiential knowledge — is the kind of knowledge that practitioners develop through experience in practice (Sheppard, Newstead, DiCaccavo, and Ryan 2001). While studies indicate that poverty has a negative effect on student achievement, it is only through listening to students like Sam that I have come to appreciate the ways in which poverty directly impacts their lives and to take this information into account when working together. In evidence-based practice environments today, tacit knowledge is undervalued, considered weak evidence (Hamilton 2005), and excluded from the rational decision-making model required within EBP. For example, explaining a student's non-attendance in accordance with a standardized assessment scale is considered to be more reliable than saying "in my opinion." In addition to being discredited externally, tacit knowledge is at risk of being squeezed out as a way of knowing as social workers themselves begin to question and devalue this kind of knowledge.

Distancing social workers from tacit knowledge has profound implications. A long-held tradition in social work, tacit knowledge is a strong source of practice guidance valued for its ability to appreciate multiple voices and ways of knowing. Sam's situation showed how the inclusion of perspectives from Sam, her mother, her teachers, and my own practice experience provided an in-depth and robust understanding of Sam's experience. Without these multiple voices and ways of knowing, I would have focused on Sam alone as the point of intervention and excluded other people and other systems. In practice, this pluralistic approach helps practitioners to be responsive to individual client situations in their context and leaves space for interventions that raise critical consciousness or link oppressed people in shared struggles. As noted by many authors, practice that is stripped of political, moral, and ethical considerations becomes objectified, sanitized, and depoliticized (Parton 2008; Baines 2007a; Webb 2001).

Van de Luitgaarden (2009), in his discussion of social work decision-making processes, claims that the type of decision-making consistent with EBP, concerned as it is with cost-benefit effectiveness, is inappropriate for the concerns taken up by social work. Holding firmly to the EBP framework, practitioners narrow both the issues they consider (Webb 2001) and the information they gather to quantifiable, measureable units. Going back to the practice situation I described earlier, strictly adhering to the EBP would have meant focusing on and measuring Sam's feelings of anxiety, while ignoring school, peer, familial, and social factors.

Closely linked to intuitive decision-making and tacit knowledge is the notion of professional judgment. Even though EBP considers professional judgment or professional discretion important, within its framework, intervention "choices" are restricted to those deemed evidence-based and opportunities for worker autonomy are thus severely constrained (van de Luitgaarden 2009; Kowalski 2009). Given that cognitive-behavioural therapy (CBT) is considered an EBP for anxiety, I as a social worker would be taking a professional risk to offer any intervention other than CBT to a client with anxiety. Professional judgment is replaced by practice guidelines, standardized assessment tools, and a technical-rational approach to practice. Within these current confines, Staller (2006) observed that professional judgment is devalued and suppressed, and Webb (2001) worried that workers will substitute "decisionism" for professional judgment.

In a confusing way, EBP social workers are increasingly held accountable for the decisions they make while being constrained in their decision-making processes. While they are expected to act like professionals with expertise, social workers cannot be expert in EBP terms because their claims to tacit knowledge, professional judgment, and the relevance of social theory/broader political analyses are invalidated within positivist frameworks.

Changing the role of professional judgment in social work has also changed the understanding that social workers have of themselves as professionals. Instead of a knowledge-producing self (as is the case in building tacit knowledge), the social worker is reconstituted as a knowledge-using self (Nerland and Jensen 2007). Rather than being lifelong learners who manage knowledge and make good helping choices, as has always been expected in social practice, social workers find the professional self constructed within the EBP framework according to the narrow "rules" of knowledge use and production of EBP framework (Nerland and Jensen 2007; Iedema and Scheeres 2003).

Social Work and Professionalism

Responding to questions about its legitimacy and effectiveness, the field of social work has been heavily influenced by the trend towards professionalization. In this discourse, the "use of scientific or expert knowledge in dealing with everyday problems" is central to the definition of a profession (Fargion 2006: 256; Parton 2008). Others add that professional competence is equated with technical competence (Hugman 2008). Because those who are evidence-based can lay claim to both technical competence and expert knowledge, EBP has become a convenient and highly effective instrument of professionalism. Pignotti and Thyer (2009), in their study of interventions used by social workers, worried that the use of non-evidence-based interventions could "reflect poorly on the social work profession," while Gossett and Weinman (2007) suggest that the use of evidence-based interventions helps social workers "defend their domain" against other disciplines, always a concern during times of underfunding and restructuring.

Over the past century, social work practice has been organized around either structural or individualistic discourses (Strean 1974; Harris 2008; Johnsson and Svensson 2005). At both a collective and interpersonal level, Hugman (2008) suggests, there is a consensus within the field that views micro (individualistic) approaches as "authentic" and macro level (structural) interventions as "not really social work." Choosing to favour individualistic approaches over structural understandings and interventions, as exemplified in EBP, impacts a social worker's capacity to pay attention to or formulate interventions around social justice concerns. Constructing someone's difficulties as a personal responsibility stands in stark contrast to understanding his or her personal troubles as linked to bigger picture issues of oppression cloaked as poverty, homelessness, violence, etc. An individualistic focus, such as that found in EBP, combined with an unwillingness to examine or challenge the bigger picture, results in social work's turning its attention away from clients and social justice, aligning itself with authority, and concerning itself with issues of professionalism (Baines 2007a).

Many authors note that the growth of professionalism in social work has come at a cost. Hugman (2008) believes that social work has been "unable to pursue social justice," while Webb (2001) laments that professionalism has devalued social work's traditional commitment to social justice, and unwittingly supported managerialist ideals. A result of neoliberal forces, managerialist ideals in social service agencies are evidenced through budget constraints and through operations reorganized and restructured for maximum efficiency and accountability. These authors signal an important and troubling shift away from a traditional social justice orientation and set of values in professional social work. Others suggest that it may not be professionalism itself that distracts from social justice pursuits but the particular type of highly competitive, narrow professionalism promoted in the context of neoliberal constraint and restructuring (Baines 2004b, 2007).

How to Be Anti-Oppressive while Being Evidence-Informed

While some might suggest an outright rejection of EBP, there are others who advocate modifications (Stepney 2009). Arguably, EBP's alterations to the practice of social work have created both concerns and opportunities, and EBP has generated important discussions and debates. More research is being conducted on social work issues than in previous eras, and frontline social workers are increasingly involved in the design and implementation of research projects. Some softening is evident in the new incarnation of evidence-informed practice so that other kinds of research (qualitative, participatory, etc.) and knowledge (tacit, practice) may be considered valid at some point in the future. Evidence-based practices can be helpful in a number of straightforward practice situations. However, what is definitely unhelpful is the uncritical and enthusiastic embrace of EBP that would erase other approaches to social work practice and knowledge-building.

While not easy, I think it is possible to maintain a commitment to social justice in an evidence-based practice environment. To do so requires a critical stance to practice and the space for reflexivity. The suggestions below are designed to challenge the dominance of EBP in ways that invite inclusivity, ambiguity, and multiple voices with a structural focus:

1. Seek out and create your own safe spaces for reflexivity. D'Cruz, Gillingham, and Melendez (2007) assert that reflexivity is critical to generating knowledge because reflexivity invites uncertainty into practice, thereby challenging the certainty imposed by managerialism and embedded in EBP (Horwath 2007). Social workers can create opportunities for reflexivity by meeting with colleagues, reading critical literature, acting as field instructors, aligning themselves with clients, and always asking questions (out loud and silently).
2. Advocate for a "range" of evidence, and include various types of evidence as ways of knowing (Sinding 2009). Multiple authors such as Plath (2006) encourage a broad definition of evidence devoid of a hierarchical and evalu-

ative rating scale based upon empiricism. Briggs and McBeath (2009), van de Luitgaarden (2009), and Lymbery (2003) advocate an inclusive approach wherein choice from a variety of types of evidence is guided by the complexity of the situation.

3. Remember the *social* of social work (Sinding 2009; Parton 2008). Maintain an appreciation for your client's social location, and the uniqueness of his or her life, as well as the way that the problems she or he experiences are inextricably linked to larger systems of power, dominance, and inequity.

4. Resist individualistic explanations and interpretations of clients' troubles. Yes, they may be experiencing anxiety, but look for the connection between anxiety and issues of oppression. If you didn't feel like you were accepted or understood at school, would you feel comfortable attending? If you were completely preoccupied by problems at home or in the community, would attending school feel like it held any value?

5. Engage in structural work, even when working with individual clients. For example, link clients' individual experiences with dominant discourse and help clients develop a capacity for social analysis and critique.

6. Advocate. Advise employers, government, and other groups with power of the limiting or harmful effects of policy and practices.

7. Collaborate with clients. Fully explain different interventions and ask for their preferences, determine clients' measures of success, and ask for feed-back about standardized tools — was this helpful?

8. Read literature with a social justice lens. Be alert to what's assumed, what's left out, and whose agenda is supported.

9. Value your tacit knowledge and professional judgment. Tacit knowledge has been built within a field in which a goodly portion of the workers are dedicated to empowerment and social justice. Tacit knowledge should not be excluded from our tool box of interventions and solutions; instead, it should be used in conjunction with other forms of knowledge to best meet the needs of our clients and their communities.

10. Value the adaptations to local context made when implementing evidence-based practices and document them — this is an important source of developing knowledge. EBP cannot be applied in exactly the same way to every situation. Every situation is unique, and our interventions, even when research-based, need to reflect this.

11. Support and conduct research in practice settings. Social workers are in a unique position to influence research questions, methodology, measurement tools, and process of analysis.

12. When you hear "doing what works," ask yourself, "For whom does this work? And for what does this work?"

13. Remember your ethical stance — clients first. Ask yourself who or what is directing your practice.

14. Question things that you are comfortable with or have become routine in your practice. Oppressive discourse can masquerade as common sense.

15. Apply evidence-based practices alongside your own analysis of the situation (Polio 2006).

16. Embrace ambiguity and uncertainty — it's a signal that you're engaging in good social work.

Chapter 10

Research as Practice

The Community-Based Research Practicum as Anti-Oppressive Social Work Education

Saara Greene and Lori Chambers

This chapter presents a personal and professional reflection on how research can be used as a tool to encourage anti-oppressive practices. By illustrating some of the main differences between community-based and traditional research (e.g., differences in how research questions are developed and the degree to which the community is involved in the research process), the authors highlight the ways in which research *is* practice and can be used to address social justice issues. This chapter also provides important information for practitioners who are committed to applying an anti-oppressive practice framework to community-based research — information about issues related to facilitating and supporting community involvement; about the need to provide research capacity-building opportunities for the individuals who will be affected by the research; and about how the research findings will be used to address the needs of the community.

As you read this chapter, ask yourself the following questions:
1. Community-based researchers are guided by a number of anti-oppressive practice principles. Which of these principles are reflected in community-based research? How do community-based researchers apply these principles throughout the research process?
2. In what ways can social work and allied human service professionals integrate community-based research principles into their practices with individuals, groups, and communities?
3. Community-based researchers strive to support community-based leadership, power, and control over the research process. What are some of the important issues that social workers and allied social service workers need to consider to support this process?

This chapter was co-written by an academic (Saara) and a social work researcher/ practitioner (Lori) who have worked together in a number of capacities, particularly within the realm of community-based research. In this chapter, we present some of the things we have learned during our individual work with community-based research and in our work together.

We were each drawn to community-based research (CBR) for a variety of reasons. For Saara, it was a natural transition as she moved from years of community-based practice to an academic career. Saara's initial engagement with CBR came as she worked toward her Ph.D., well before she met Lori. In her community development practice, Saara was strongly committed to community leadership. She worked to identify service needs and opportunities to address these needs in ways that reflected the community's wishes and desires. Within the context of doing research for her Ph.D., this meant developing collaborative research partnerships with the community, supporting community involvement at all stages of the research process, and ensuring that the results of the research reflected the community's vision of social change within both the social policy and practice arenas (Israel et al. 1998; Ruetter et al. 2005; Etowa et al. 2007).

For Lori, CBR was an opportunity to engage in research that could benefit her community. As a Black woman, Lori's early experiences of traditional research were of marginalized communities as the objects of research rather than engaged in the research process. Even research that tried to reflect participants' experiences often lacked the collaborative voice of researcher and participant. Furthermore, she found that traditional research seemed to perpetuate social hierarchies: those in a position of social power chose the research topics rather than inviting the community to choose or help choose.

As Saara and Lori each came to realize through their own work, CBR and anti-oppressive frameworks are based on many of the same principles, making CBR a valuable tool for anti-oppressive practice (AOP) social workers. Like AOP, CBR is a collaborative approach that involves all partners equitably throughout the research process, and like AOP it recognizes the unique strengths that each partner brings to the endeavour. By definition, community-based research is an anti-oppressive practice that emphasizes processes and outcomes based on social justice (Greene et al. 2009). Like AOP, CBR involves service users at every stage of the research project, from identifying research questions to disseminating the research findings.

Objects of Research
In traditional research, participants are often treated as objects of research, on which the research is conducted. This has the effect of excluding the thoughts, feelings, and experiences of the individuals who will be affected most by the research process and results.

Table 10.1 Community-Based Research Principles

Community partners should be involved at the earliest stages of the project, helping to define research objectives and providing input about how the project will be organized, including the original goals, mission, and methods of the project.
Research processes and outcomes should benefit the community. Community members should be hired and trained whenever possible and appropriate, and the research should help build and enhance community assets.
Community members should be part of the data analysis and interpretation and should provide input into how the results will be distributed. This does not imply censorship of data or publication, but rather ensures that the community has the opportunity to voice its opinions about the interpretation before the final publication.
Productive partnerships between researchers and community members should be sustained beyond the life of the project. This will increase the likelihood of research findings being incorporated into ongoing community programs and thus provide maximum possible benefit to the community.
Community members should be empowered to initiate their own research projects to address the needs they have identified (Israel et al. 1998; Israel 2003).

Putting CBR into Practice: Obstacles to Engagement

Saara's initial research plan for her thesis drew on the principles of CBR, which, like those of other action-oriented research frameworks (such as action research and participatory action research; see Bradbury and Reason 2003; Cornwall and Jewkes 1995) are "based on a philosophy of partnership and principles of self-determination, equity and social justice" (Maiter et al. 2008). Saara hoped her Ph.D. thesis research would reflect her commitment to community involvement; she wanted to develop an advisory board of community members before beginning her research to ensure the research outcomes would be meaningful for the community and be useful in the development of social policies and practices. However, she faced a number of obstacles in her attempt to use a CBR framework; according to the university, the thesis had to be *her* research, and including the community in the process would make it a community rather than an individual effort, and therefore unacceptable as a Ph.D. thesis. Saara had to modify her approach in order to meet the requirements.

In her current role as an academic, Saara is now free to engage in CBR in her practice. She continues to believe that engaging in CBR is an effective way for social workers to bridge anti-oppressive practice and research because CBR requires researchers to address issues of power, voice, and interpretation within the research process by engaging with community partners. It also makes researchers accountable to the communities that will be most affected by the research process and its outcomes. This kind of research focuses on the daily realities of the people most affected by the research process and outcomes, and generates opportunities for community members to ensure that these processes and outcomes reflect their needs and interest.

Lori has experienced a different set of challenges. She first participated in CBR while working at a community-based AIDS service organization, first as a volunteer, then as a social work placement student (under Saara's supervision). Lori hopes that her research experiences both as a community member and as a research practitioner will enable her to work with ethno-racial communities to produce not only knowledge that is meaningful to these communities but also social change. However, as a result of her simultaneous roles as a community member and a practitioner ally engaged in front-line work and supporting the community's needs, she has experienced challenges.

Although the CBR framework recognizes the contributions of both community members and allies, Lori has found that these roles are often perceived as mutually exclusive, making it difficult to navigate them. She has tried to integrate her theoretical and experiential knowledge with her research practice, and to work within academic institutions as a researcher while "keeping it real" and being authentic to her cultural roots. These tensions highlight the importance of constant reflection about our practice as critical, anti-oppressive social workers and researchers so that we do not engage in practices reflective of traditional social science research (something we discuss in detail next). Researchers from marginalized communities can address these tensions by integrating their experiences as community members and allies into their reflections and practice, as well as by fostering the participation and research capacity of other community members.

Differences between CBR and Traditional Research

Researchers have many different ideas about how research about or for marginalized communities should be carried out, but traditional research and community-based research projects differ in obvious ways. Because of her university's opposition to the principles of CBR, Saara's actual experiences with social science research as she worked on her Ph.D. reflected traditional social science research methods rather than those of CBR. In this next section, we walk through the differences between traditional and community-based research using Saara's Ph.D. as an example.

As is generally the case with traditional research, the first stage of Saara's research process was choosing a research topic that she found compelling, important, and interesting, and that was related to her experience as a social work practitioner. This resulted in a Ph.D. study that centred on the experiences and needs of young mothers living in one of the most socially and economically deprived communities in Scotland. Once the research topic was determined, Saara followed a number of steps that are often involved in traditional social science research: becoming familiar with the research that had already been done

> ## Qualitative Research
> This kind of research emphasizes the need to understand the experiences of individuals, groups, and communities through careful observation of their words and actions. Qualitative research examines patterns of meaning that emerge from the data; these patterns are often presented in the participants' own words but can also be presented through arts, photography, drama, and other forms of expression. This kind of research differs from "objective research," in which researchers claim that the findings are based on so-called observable scientific facts and are not influenced by the researcher's experiences, beliefs, or assumptions.

in the area; considering the gaps in her chosen field of research; and refining her research questions based on this information.

The second stage of the research process involved determining what methodology to use. This required Saara to think about a number of important questions related to collecting and analyzing the research data: how to gather and record information about the young mothers' experiences; how to analyze the information she received from them; how to ensure that the voices of participants would be included in the research findings and conclusions; and how to share the findings with other researchers, social workers, and policy makers. Since Saara was unable to develop a CBR project, she ultimately settled on a qualitative research design and chose to use in-depth interviews and participant observation to collect the research data.

Saara requested and received permission from a local young parents' community-based organization to meet young mothers, and she attended drop-ins and regularly scheduled programs. She recruited twenty young mothers for in-depth interviews about their experiences. These data collection methods were intended to show Saara how the young mothers talked about and understood their experiences of pregnancy and motherhood, and Saara was able to use direct quotes from these interactions and interviews as part of the process of highlighting participants' experiences and needs. Saara hoped that her data collection and analysis methods would help her develop some generalized statements about the young mothers' experiences that could later be used to develop practice and policy recommendations to address their needs and the needs of other young mothers in similar communities.

Like many other social science researchers, Ph.D. candidates are often the sole owners of the data generated by their studies. Traditional researchers make all or most of the decisions about what questions are important, what methods of data collection and analysis should be used, and how to disseminate or share that data. In addition, most academic researchers maintain complete control over the research results and decide how and where the results will be communicated. Study results are usually circulated through articles in peer-reviewed

Generalizable
Objective data (facts) are sometimes used to form general ideas or conclusions about the experiences of the participants in a research study; the findings are considered generalizable if they can be used to say something about other individuals who have had similar experiences but who did not participate in the actual study.

journals and presented at academic conferences. This means that only a very small, privileged group sees the results and the research usually has few, if any, effects outside universities and other highly-educated spheres. Saara's Ph.D. research experience reflected this process. It serves to exemplify how social science research has traditionally been conducted.

If the study had been based on CBR, Saara would have done a number of things differently. She would have incorporated all the above steps, but community members would have been involved from the very beginning of the process (Reid and Brief 2009). CBR practitioners recognize the importance of community involvement in developing research questions that reflect community needs and experiences, as well as community involvement in determining the tools used to collect and analyze data to address community need. Through this process, community-based researchers ensure that community knowledge and experience is valued and understood as an integral part of developing and doing research projects.

Saara developed her interview questions after attending the young parents' organization and getting to know the young mothers. However, the process would have been even more clear and concrete if the project had been community-based: she would have worked in partnership with a community advisory board made up of community members who represented the needs and experiences of the broader community, and these members would have helped to refine and develop important research questions and themes related to their experiences and needs as young mothers. For example, Saara used interviews to ask about the circumstances surrounding the young mothers' pregnancies and about their reactions to and feelings about being pregnant and becoming and being young mothers. Saara also asked questions about their access to support and services and their experiences with social work and allied health profes-

Community Member
A person in the community who is committed to addressing the needs of the population being researched. This includes the people who are being studied, community-based professionals, community-based politicians, and community-based researchers who have a personal and political stake in the research process and outcomes.

sionals. However, based on some of the young mothers' stories, Saara realized that she had failed to incorporate some important topics into her interview guide. According to CBR, it is vital to include community members in a formal capacity, both as community advisors and as members of the research team, to ensure that important issues are not neglected and that interview questions reflect the community's needs and experiences.

Although community-based researchers ensure that the community is involved in determining how the research will be carried out and what research methods will be applied, the key element here is that CBR is not a research method; rather, *it is a framework for conducting research* that includes the community in the process of choosing the methods that will be used to collect and analyze research data. CBR requires that the community be involved in the following processes: choice of methods; use of these methods; development of data collection tools (e.g., interview questions, surveys, questionnaires); and analysis and interpretation of all research findings. In these ways, CBR differs greatly from traditional methods (and most critical methods) of data collection (Reid and Brief 2009).

Many less-traditional social science researchers try to ensure that their research findings are shared with participants and other relevant stakeholders, including practitioners and policy-makers. They may try to make the results accessible to the community by writing final reports using accessible language(s) and often hold community meetings where the data can be shared and the community can raise questions or brainstorm ways to use the results. One unique feature of CBR is that it ensures the community has equal ownership of the data. This means that community members can use the data for their own purposes, e.g., to publish additional articles or to apply for agency-based or government grants. In some cases, data are stored at a community-based organization rather than an academic institution. Members of a community-based research team must negotiate and agree how and where the results will be shared. In this way, CBR can protect the best interests of the community.

Research has not always been used to help communities: the Aboriginal HIV community, for example, is particularly sensitive to the fact that traditional research on and about this group has been used to hurt and further stigmatize Aboriginal people. Today, most of this research is conducted in partnership with, or led by, the Aboriginal community, and research and publication of results must adhere to the principles of Ownership, Control, Access, and Possession (OCAP), principles that also underlie CBR.

Another unique aspect of CBR is the role that community capacity-building plays throughout the research process. In this context, community capacity-building refers to improving and developing research skills within the community; this is often achieved by including community members as researchers on the investigator team and by hiring community members as peer researchers. These community members are trained in data collection, analysis, and presentation to academic and local audiences. The goal is to enable the community to lead future research studies that can reflect and respond to the community's issues. The community also provides important capacity-building opportunities for researchers, who often have limited knowledge, experience, and understanding of the community with which they are working (Greene et al. 2009). The awareness that all members of the research team contribute to the process of capacity-building is another important and unique aspect of CBR.

Fife House: CBR that Worked

In this section, we describe our shared experience of CBR undertaken in conjunction with the Fife House transitional housing program, where Lori was a BSW placement student and Saara was her Social Work Placement Faculty Advisor. Many researchers do not consider research to be frontline social work practice, but we considered this project to be an extension of our practice as anti-oppressive social service workers. We hoped that it could help change housing

Table 10.2. Summary of Differences Between CBR and Traditional Research

Guiding Principles	Community-Based Research	Traditional Academic Research
What is the purpose of the research?	To provide the community with the tools and information necessary to enact change	To contribute to the body of knowledge on a given topic
Who is the research intended to serve?	The local community and the academic community	The academic community
Whose knowledge counts?	Community members and academic experts	Academic experts
Who determines what topics are researched?	Members of the local community	Funders, academics, professionals, and researchers
What is the rationale for choosing the research methodology?	Community empowerment and mutual learning	Academic conventions; the pursuit of "truth" and "objectivity"
Who controls the research process?	Community members and the researcher	The researcher
Who has ownership over the results of the research?	Community members and the researcher	The researcher
What aspect of research is emphasized?	Process	Outcomes

Source: University of Maryland Edward Ginsberg Center

policies and practices affecting people living with HIV. In fact, we found that while CBR shares the same basic tenets as anti-oppressive practice, the process of engaging in research, even community-based research, can inadvertently reproduce power inequities and marginalization.

Social work practicums, also known as field placements, provide students with experiential education and research opportunities that address social issues and community needs. Rosner-Salazar (2003) argues that social work practicums that integrate CBR can promote social justice and increase students' knowledge and understanding of the effects of stigma, discrimination, and systemic forms of oppression. Potential learning outcomes include teaching the students about the value and importance of research and program or policy evaluations to marginalized communities. Students can also learn about how social, economic, and political factors sustain social problems and affect the functioning of community programs (Rosner-Salazar 2003). Other benefits to students include skill development in the areas of social change and community empowerment; development of a deeper systemic and contextual understanding of how communities are oppressed; an understanding of the organizational factors that facilitate or hinder community engagement; and opportunities to reflect on the positioning of their own communities (Rosner-Salazar 2003). The effectiveness of anti-oppressive social work education depends on a number of factors, especially the skills and knowledge students develop through practice-based education and learning. Community-based research placements can give students the opportunity to work with diverse and often marginalized communities to develop new knowledge that can be applied to community issues and problems.

With the above issues in mind, and her belief that anti-oppressive research equals anti-oppressive practice, Saara supported the development of CBR placement opportunities for social work students in community-based AIDS service organizations (ASOs). ASOs are particularly good sites for CBR, at least in Ontario, because they have a strong culture of supporting and funding CBR initiatives. This culture developed as a result of years of community mobilization by individuals living with HIV and their allies. People living with HIV/AIDS (PHAs) in Canada have been a highly-researched population, but they have had only minimal involvement in the actual research process. Traditional methods of HIV research have contributed to the marginalization of people living with HIV by ignoring their voices, concerns, and issues. Activism by individuals with AIDS and their allies helped CBR became an officially-recognized tool for research within the HIV community (Israel et al. 1998, 2003). Researchers are now asked to work within a framework that ensures a "Greater Involvement of People Living with HIV/AIDS" at all stages of the research process (Travers et al. 2008), and CBR is one way to achieve this goal.

These principles were applied during the CBR project carried out with Fife House. The project explicitly supported Fife House's leadership of the study and the participation of people living with HIV. The experience taught Lori that in contrast to being "outside" social work practice, research (in particular CBR) can be an important way to engage in anti-oppressive practice.

The Fife House Transitional Housing Research Study

This study evaluated Fife House's transitional housing program to identify the strengths and weaknesses of the program and to develop a more effective service. The primary goal was to improve the agency's ability to address the supportive housing needs of people living with HIV. To this end, the project evaluated residents' views and experiences of the transitional housing program, through interviews with twenty-five program staff and residents who were former and/ or current residents of the transitional housing program. The main research question was, "How do HIV+ people view the impact of transitional, supportive housing on their overall health?" The evaluation was community-based in that it was community-driven: Fife House acted as the principal organization with the support of academic researchers. The study was designed and conducted by a Fife House staff member who had a long history with and knowledge of the community and Lori, who, as a social work practicum student, participated as a student community-based researcher during all aspects of the evaluation.

In the early stages of the project, the process also involved service users; the research questions were designed by drawing on the experiential knowledge of the residents. The CBR evaluation process was achieved by inviting service users to meetings at Fife House to develop and finalize the interview questions for the study. Once these questions were agreed upon and finalized, Fife House staff and Lori trained people living with HIV/AIDS so they could act as "peer" research assistants on the project. The main responsibility of these peer researchers was to carry out the in-depth interviews with research participants. This served two main goals: it ensured that community interests were reflected in the overall evaluation; and it improved the research capacity of PHAs. After all interviews had been completed, taped, and transcribed, Fife House staff analyzed the findings, which were then shared with Fife House staff and residents and used to formulate programming changes within the agency. Changes included expanding the transitional housing program, developing alternative models of supportive housing, and initiating more research on the housing needs of people living with HIV.

Peer Research Assistant

A community member who, because of his/her personal experience and/or identification with the issues being studied, is trained and hired to engage in research activities such as data collection, analysis, and dissemination.

One of the best ways to incorporate AOP within the context of a CBR project is to keep thinking about whether research activities are inclusive, collaborative, and centred in the community, whether power imbalances might appear or be intensified during the research process, how immediate and longer-term agency-based changes could be incorporated, and when results will be shared with other groups and researchers. Saara and Lori were strongly committed to ensuring that their research work and decisions were based on the principles of equity, access, and respect for diversity. Although we adhered to these policies explicitly, we did not anticipate how engaging the community in the research process might set some community members up for disappointment and might exclude others.

Principles of Beneficence in CBR

The principle of "beneficence" states that we should do no harm. This principle is embedded within human research ethics, but it takes on additional meaning within a community-based context. The CBR principle of beneficence is based on the assumption that the community under research, research participants, and research team members should all benefit from the project. However, needs vary among individuals and groups, and by class, race, gender, etc. We discovered that many individuals participated in the research in the hopes of individual or immediate benefit, such as stable housing or social services. As researchers who were also social service practitioners, we had to think about how we could ethically involve individuals who might be precariously housed while not acting to address their immediate need for secure and stable housing.

Research ethics required us to inform participants that their involvement in the project would not guarantee service, but we decided that as AOP practitioners, we were obligated to ensure that participants had access to information that might provide them with the services they needed. We provided participants with information about social support services, emergency shelter services, and supportive housing providers. We also referred them to community social workers and other service providers, liaisons to other support services, or information specific to people living with HIV. We felt that "to do no harm" meant that we should give something definite back to many participants; and that failure to do so might be classified as "doing harm," especially given that the goal of the research was to improve housing and social service outcomes for this community.

> ### Beneficence
> All forms of action intended to benefit or promote the good of other persons, based on a moral obligation to act for the benefit of others, helping them to further their important and legitimate interests, often by preventing or removing possible harm.

Power, Exclusion, and Marginalization and the CBR Placement

In our roles of social work educator and social work placement student, we have spent most of our academic and professional careers critically analyzing and deconstructing the concepts of social hierarchy and social exclusion, power, and marginalization. Still, it took eight months of a CBR placement for us to understand the subtleties of power within and among the research team members, research participants, students, and faculty involved in our project.

Communicating with Individuals Lacking a Phone, Email, or Address

During our research, we learned that the process of communication was disempowering for some participants. We realized that our methods of communicating with participants contained a social bias based on class and accessibility: like most middle-class individuals, we assumed that all participants had or could get access to a consistent address, phone number, or voice mail. This was not possible for many participants, especially those who had difficulties securing or maintaining permanent housing. Therefore, some potential participants left several messages on the project's voice mail but were unable to leave a contact number because they did not have a home or cell phone or any other number to leave; some could only make sporadic contact with us when they had access to a free phone at another social agency. Ironically, the process of contacting us exemplified their social marginalization and lack of resources. We immediately rethought our communication process and decided to provide a number of different contact methods: phone, letter, advertising at other ASOs, and old-fashioned word-of-mouth. We let potential participants know when Lori would definitely be at her desk so they could communicate with her directly rather than through voice mail. We also worked closely with a transitional house employee who was on our research team; if Lori was unavailable, calls from potential participants were forwarded to this staff member, who would set up a convenient time for them to contact Lori.

Tensions and Struggles in CBR

Like anti-oppressive social work practice, CBR is based on an ideology grounded in equality, self and social determination, and social justice for individuals, communities, and society. At many points during the research project, we thought about social privilege and how we could integrate our values into practice. Perhaps ironically, we did not develop a strategy for redressing Lori's experience of marginalization as a Black person during the research process and her experiences of racism and racialization. For example, one participant requested that Lori not administer his interview, based on his past experiences of homophobia from persons of colour. We accommodated his request because we did not want to further his experience of prejudice. However, we did not address how his comments were prejudicial towards Lori, or how our accommodation of his request created an environment that valued his gay identity but devalued Lori as a Black person. Neither Lori nor Saara knew how to discuss this devaluation, so we missed a valuable learning opportunity. We were not prepared to deal with the complexity of oppression and were unable to address immediately the issue of how this research participant could simultaneously hold a position of white privilege and a position of marginalization due to his sexual orientation and HIV status. Lori had previously experienced a different, but still complex, situation by being in a position of privilege as a post-secondary student while still being marginalized as a Black woman. Within this context, Lori often felt uncomfortable discussing her feelings of racist devaluation because of her relative social privilege as a university student. Ironically, while her education and social class appeared to offer some protection from racism, they actually prevented her from discussing or resolving her experience of racism. Unfortunately, in the CBR scenario outlined above, we also disempowered and silenced Lori, shutting down what could have been an empowering conversation about multiple forms of racism, oppression, and privilege.

In hindsight, we wish we had integrated some of these issues into Lori's learning and into the research activities. As the faculty advisor, Saara could have worked with Lori to find a way to discuss these issues with the research team and to determine how to address these issues in ways that did not leave Lori feeling silenced and disempowered. One possible solution would be to ask research participants during the interview screening process about research preferences and concerns. With this information in hand, we would be able to discuss our ability to address concerns in ways that did not subject any participants, Lori, or other interviewers to a potential experience of prejudice.

Peer Research

Another situation that challenged our view of community-based research involved the concepts of "community" and "peer." In this context, we defined a peer researcher as an individual living with HIV, but we both encountered participants who considered many individuals who were not HIV-positive to be peers. The understanding of "peer" is connected to identity categories that are very important to particular individuals and their community, such as race, ethnicity, and gender. For example, after co-facilitating an interview with a Black female participant, we noticed that the participant would look to Lori for validation and request her insight into the issue on the basis of their shared racial background. This was particularly apparent when the conversation turned to the participant's racial identity and experience of racism and sexism within the supportive housing residence. We speculated that the experience of having a cultural peer present may have positively shaped the interaction and helped us uncover new and important information.

In some instances we found that the term "peer researcher" was considered to be disempowering. Calling someone a "peer researcher" rather than simply a "researcher" can subtly undermine what he or she brings to the team, highlighting his or her identity rather than the valuable experience and knowledge. We realized that it is important to explore new forms of peer membership that validate all researchers, rather than unintentionally reinstituting a hierarchy of various kinds of differently-valued researchers, and to analyze how we label and facilitate the roles of community members within CBR.

CBR: Potential and Shortcomings

After discussion and reflection, we agreed that community-based research is, or at least has the potential to contribute to, anti-oppressive practice and that community-based research in particular demands that researchers incorporate anti-oppressive social work practice skills at all stages of the research process. We also realized that community-based research can be a politically and socially challenging process, given the range of social positionings and experiences of each stakeholder in the community-based research process. This can be a particularly complex issue for social work students as they navigate the multiple positionings in a community-based research placement.

From Lori's perspective as a social work student, participation in this process strengthened her critical analysis of power and empowerment, and it highlighted the complexity of these issues in any helping endeavour. It also improved her ability to understand how marginalization and social disparity can operate through the research process and within the results of community-based research. She also found it particularly valuable to try to address and support the multiple realities and social positions of the research participants in situations where, as the only Black person on the research team, she was exposed to situations of racism and racialization.

Together, we recognize that anti-oppressive teachers and students must critically reflect on what we are doing, thinking, and feeling at all stages of the research process, and use these reflections to improve our practice and the lives of those with whom we are working.

Chapter 11

Business as Usual

Doing Anti-Oppressive Organizational Change

Lisa Barnoff

This chapter is based on research that explored the strategies AOP practitioners used as they worked to integrate anti-oppression principles into their everyday practices. Twenty women who worked in five different feminist agencies in Toronto participated in individual interviews and focus groups. More specifically, the chapter focuses on the strategies used to institute AOP at an organizational level (i.e., in an agency's systems, processes, and policies). The chapter addresses the question, "What mechanisms need to be put in place at an organizational level, so that 'business as usual' in an agency will promote AOP?"

As you read this chapter, ask yourself the following questions:
1. Why is it important to institute AOP at an organizational level within a social work agency?
2. A number of organizational level AOP strategies are discussed in this chapter. Can you think of additional organizational level AOP strategies that are not mentioned here?
3. Is AOP embedded at an organizational level in the agencies with which you are familiar? If so, how? How could these agencies improve in this area?
4. Why is it that integrating AOP in a social work agency is always a "work in progress?"

In the first edition of this book, I wrote a chapter with Brienne Coleman, exploring how feminist practitioners engage in AOP at a direct service level (Barnoff and Coleman 2007). In contrast, this chapter focuses on organizational change, specifically strategies used by practitioners in feminist agencies to institute AOP at an organizational level (i.e., in an agency's systems, processes, and policies). This chapter addresses the question, "What mechanisms need to be put in place at an organizational level, so that 'business as usual' in the agency will promote

> ### Organizational Change
> Organizational change is a planned, systemic, ongoing, organizational intervention in order to implement and solidify a particular kind of change at an agency-wide level.

AOP?" As Baines (2007a: 4) argues, while "it is possible to practice social justice oriented social work in any organization," it is more difficult to do so in certain organizations. She goes on to suggest that organizations "closer to state power and coercion such as the correctional system, welfare provision and child welfare services" are particularly challenging for AOP practitioners. I concur, but in this chapter I argue that it is also hard to practice anti-oppression in an organization that is not structurally set up to support it. This is true even if staff members are supportive of AOP. Without AOP-oriented organizational systems, structures, processes, and policies in place, the implementation of AOP in direct services is hindered. When AOP-oriented organizational systems, structures, processes, and policies are established, the everyday operations of the agency can maintain, foster, and promote an AOP approach systemically — i.e., AOP can become part of the agency's "business as usual."

Much of the discussion in this chapter is based on findings from a larger study exploring the strategies used by those in feminist social service agencies as they worked to integrate anti-oppression principles into everyday practices. Those feminist agencies I approached had been identified by multiple people in the feminist service community to be the "most advanced" in terms of their AOP. I interviewed fourteen front-line workers and six managers, working in five different agencies. They were diverse in terms of age, racial identity, place of birth, sexual orientation, and disability status, but all these women are experts on AOP. My job was to listen carefully to their ideas, so that I could learn from them.

Organizational Level AOP Strategies

AOP organizational level strategies can be grouped into five themes: (1) increasing diversity; (2) developing and implementing anti-oppression policies; (3) engaging in effective anti-oppression education and training; (4) fostering an organizational culture conducive to AOP; and (5) ensuring the agency engages in social action.

Increasing Diversity
From an anti-oppression perspective, lack of diversity in an organization is a problem. Why? For one, if the diversity of a community is not represented in an agency, there are probably institutional barriers preventing certain groups from accessing the agency, or perhaps even worse, making them not *want* to

> ### Institutional Barriers
> Institutional barriers are organizational policies, procedures, or practices that act (intentionally or non-intentionally) to prevent certain groups of people from fully participating in the organization and/or from receiving equitable treatment. Examples include buildings that are not accessible to people who use wheelchairs, programs that are only available in English, personnel policies that do not allow provisions for Jewish staff members to be away from work on Jewish holidays, or support groups for women that are designed based on the assumption that all participants are heterosexual.

access the agency. Equity and inclusion for all groups in terms of access, decision making, and service delivery systems is important in AOP agencies. For example, Maud[1] said,

> If we know that there is an influx and a growth in the numbers of immigrant families who are experiencing poverty and the only families we are seeing are all Canadian born, then we know that there is something that is amiss in what we are doing and/or something that we need to do proactively.

A commonly mentioned set of strategies involve those that seek to increase diversity in the agency — diversity in the Board of Directors, management and staff, volunteers, and service users. Agencies take many different approaches to do so. To help us think about these various approaches, Hyde and Hopkins (2004) provide an "organizational diversity climate continuum" from organizations that have "mild" or "weak" diversity climates on one end, to those with "robust" diversity climates on the other. In a robust diversity climate, "an organization has considerable demographic diversity, integrated throughout the organization, and ... the benefits of diversity are supported or nourished through various organizational practices embedded in the organization's culture" (Hyde and Hopkins 2004: 27). Diversity in the decision-making body of an organization is especially important. Without diversity, decisions will likely be best suited to the experience only of the few groups represented — in spite of their best intentions to think inclusively (San Martin and Barnoff 2004). Ensuring diversity means including multiple voices, ideas, and perspectives in every aspect of an agency's work.

Increasing diversity is one of the ways an agency demonstrates its commitment to AOP and builds services that are more likely to meet the needs of multiple groups (Barnoff 2001; Doyle and George 2008; Hyde 2003; Mederos and Woldeguiorguis 2003). In the agencies studied, women used a variety of strategies to achieve this goal. For example, they told me that they use an "AOP lens" when it comes to hiring practices. They are deliberate about promoting vacancies in diverse contexts and soliciting potential applicants from multiple groups. This is a strategy that may be more difficult to implement in unionized agencies, because of the ways their collective agreements outline hiring processes (for example, where seniority clauses exist, they generally provide priority to those with the most seniority). However, in the agencies involved in this study, management was able to work with their unions to find suitable ways to achieve the goal of diversity in hiring.

> We have an agreement with our union that there are times in our staffing [when] we just want certain groups [and] to reflect diversity means that we go over the seniority [process] to hire [new] people. (Stella)

Participants told me that when agencies are "increasing diversity" they need to ensure new organizational members are not just "diverse" but are also supportive of the agency's AOP approach. Maud, for example, highlighted this commitment in the process of recruiting a diverse group of board members:

> It's important in the recruitment process to gather board members who have an understanding or who believe in this thing called anti-oppression practice. They may not know the details of how it works out in the service, but who at least come with that commitment about that and its connection to social change.

In an AOP agency, the ultimate goal of strategies to increase diversity moves far beyond simple representation. Achieving diversity is just one step in an overall organizational agenda to challenge oppressions and promote social justice. Having a diverse group of organizational members is a necessary component of that goal, but should not be seen as the goal itself.

Agencies must think not only about recruitment, but also about retention. In other words, what does the agency have to do in order to ensure that new

---

An AOP Agency

An AOP agency is one that operates in accordance with an anti-oppression theoretical framework and in ways that promote anti-oppression principles. AOP agencies have a social justice-oriented mission and constantly work toward all of the following: the eradication of all oppressions and discriminatory practices; continual reflection on and evaluation of their organizational processes and outcomes; wide participation and inclusion in the organization; responsiveness to and reflection of the communities in which they are situated; the fostering of alliances across diverse groups; and engagement in social justice-oriented activities "beyond the walls" of the agency.

> ### Accommodations
> Accommodations refer to organizational changes to ensure that people with disabilities have equal opportunities and are able to participate fully in every aspect of the organization. Accommodations alter the processes by which people with disabilities engage in their work so that they can be successful in performing their job duties. Some examples of accommodations include changes in the physical environment (e.g., ramps and automatic entry doors for people who use wheelchairs), the equipment used (e.g., TTY telephone systems for people with hearing impairments), and the technology used (e.g., computer software like "Zoom text" to enlarge text for people with visual impairments).

members will want to stay? AOP agencies need to create "welcoming environments" that support diversity (Hyde 2003). Stella told me that when her agency was actively seeking to increase the numbers of women with disabilities on staff, they had to do a lot of work to ensure that their physical space was supportive of this effort, and that any required technology or other types of necessary accommodations were in place.

Hyde (2003) suggests mentoring programs as a useful way to increase retention for people of colour in social service agencies. Mederos and Woldeguiorguis (2003: 137) argue that "staff diversity cannot be maintained (and will not become self-perpetuating) by hiring a few individuals who end up feeling isolated. Managers should work with existing employees to ensure that they welcome and integrate new staff." Talking about the challenges of implementing an equity hiring processes, Stella observed that she often has to work with her staff to deal with the tensions that can arise between old and new staff members. Her strategy is to discuss the issues openly with members of the staff and remind them of the organizational commitment to AOP in general and to increasing diversity in particular.

In order to increase diversity among service users, outreach strategies that enable an agency to connect with diverse groups are important (Hyde 2003). In this study, agencies used various approaches to achieve this goal. For example, they promote their services at community events that are oriented toward diverse groups. They also ensure their promotional materials are translated into multiple languages:

> We've noticed there's thirteen languages that [use our services] the most [and it's into those languages that] we're translating. It's a long process. We've gotten an external agency to translate our one from English into the different languages, and now we're working on focus groups to make sure that what they interpreted makes sense and is [worded in such a way that it's] understandable and accessible. (Zoe)

> ## Equity Hiring
> In an equity hiring situation, the organization implements a process to specifically seek out members of groups that are not well represented in the agency. Every aspect of the hiring process will be examined to ensure there are no barriers preventing certain groups of people from knowing about the position or being successful in obtaining it; and beyond this, the organization will engage in outreach and recruitment to members of specific groups. As in every hiring, the organization is looking to find the best-qualified candidate.

Participants argued that in AOP agencies, services need to be provided in multiple languages. In order to accomplish this, these agencies hire from multiple language groups and make constant use of translators and interpreters. These strategies are an important component of increasing access to services and creating a welcoming environment (Hyde 2003).

In order to reflect the constantly changing demographics world-wide, strategies to "increase diversity" should be never-ending, and the composition of a board or a staff or a group of service users needs to be always changing. AOP agencies should reflect on who they are seeing on the board and among the staff and who is missing. Strategies to address these gaps have to be constantly re-evaluated, changed, re-implemented, and monitored (Hyde 2003; Hyde and Hopkins 2004).

Developing and Implementing Anti-Oppression Policies
Participants argued that a crucial aspect of AOP in social work agencies is the development and utilization of anti-oppression policies. What are "anti-oppression policies?" Participants talked about anti-oppression policies in two ways: agency policies developed using an "AOP lens," and specific stand-alone policies that focus on anti-oppression.

Viewing agency policy through an "AOP lens" means that every organizational policy (or procedure) should reflect a commitment to AOP. As the policy is implemented, AOP should be enabled and extended. To take one example, women spoke about policies that guide staff performance appraisals. While this might not seem to be related to AOP, it is. For if the ability to practice in congruence with an anti-oppression framework is important, agencies need to develop mechanisms to ensure staff's daily performance in this area is monitored and evaluated:

> On our new performance evaluation form, the first area [is about] anti-oppression work. [It is] the first area that we look at. And there is a whole bunch of questions [about this]. (Bebot)

Through the design of their performance appraisal form, Bebot's agency has developed an organizational mechanism to monitor the implementation of AOP in direct service work. If staff are not doing this work, or if they are not doing it well, this will be duly noted in evaluations, expectations for change will be outlined, and supports for change will be offered.

An AOP lens should be used from the outset in developing new policy. Agencies need to ask critical questions about how each new policy reflects anti-oppression principles and how its enactment will support AOP in the agency. Every organizational policy or procedure, even those that might not at first seem to be directly related to AOP, should reflect a commitment to AOP. Agencies need to ensure there is congruence between the guiding values and key principles of an anti-oppression approach (such as inclusion, equity, democracy, diversity, and access), the manner in which the agency goes about doing its work, and the outcomes of that work. For example, an AOP agency would explore its governance policies, including the terms of reference of all its board committees, to ensure that they support and uphold the agency's commitment to AOP. The agency would ensure that AOP work is not relegated to only one board committee, but instead, would find ways to ensure that every board committee supports and enhances — in some way — the agency's commitment to AOP.

A second set of strategies involves the development and implementation of specific stand-alone anti-oppression policies (Barnoff 2002; Thomas 1987). Participants gave the following examples: (1) a policy that clearly defines what "anti-oppression" means in the context of this agency; (2) a policy that clearly delineates the kinds of actions that are considered to be oppressive and therefore not acceptable; and (3) a policy that clearly outlines how the agency will respond when (1) and (2) are not upheld — that is, when oppressive actions are (knowingly or unknowingly) perpetuated.

Participants told me that because different people have different understandings of anti-oppression it is important to clearly define its meaning in the context of each agency.

> As management, I can't sit here expecting people to have anti-oppression principles and know how to work within an anti-oppression framework without us, the organization, defining what that means for all of us, right? Because I have this belief that every time that something is unclear, it is always the marginalized who get burned. So let's be clear about what we mean by anti-oppression principles. Let's be clear about what we are expecting people to deliver. (Bebot)

When policies are clear, there is a better chance they will be fully understood and upheld. In particular, it is vital that anti-oppression policies outline *expectations* very clearly.

> [Our policy states] if you witness it, if something happens within the agency that is oppressive and you don't do anything, you are guilty

of it as well. So we make it very clear that this is to be expected ... That is an expectation [we have], that if you don't do anything you are guilty. (Stella)

What has to be equally clear are the *consequences* if the policies are not upheld:

What happens if we have a board member who is not following the anti-racism, anti-oppression policy? How do you get rid of that person? How do you practically hold them to account? Really making sure that for every piece that you're looking to make change, that there is some kind of mechanism organizationally in each of those places that you can say, "This is the tool that you hold to account." (Annie)

For example, an agency should have a clear, written procedure that board members can utilize in instances where one board member is engaging in a pattern of behaviour that does not support the agency's anti-oppression approach. Issues related to implementing anti-oppression policies and holding people accountable to them continue to be a challenge in these agencies. Participants' narratives made clear that having written policies is necessary but not sufficient. More important, and much more difficult, is the daily struggle to ensure they are actively used. In spite of this challenge, participants had no doubt about how staff and board should be held accountable — adhere to the policy or be terminated. As Stella put it, "With the staff, if their behaviour doesn't change, then we say, 'Make sure you change your behaviour or you're out of here.'"

Opinions differed when it came to the question of accountability for service users. Participants agreed that service users who engage in behaviours that promote oppressions should be held accountable. The issue was with how this should occur. Some agencies have an explicit "ban of service policy" which they can use when a service user repeatedly engages in oppressive behaviours without attempting to change. Service users can be asked to leave the agency for a period of time. Across agency settings, however, there was no agreement on whether this type of policy was appropriate. Even the staff who were generally in support of a "ban of service" policy had some difficulties with it, as Adrian noted:

We have women that come in, that it is a pattern, a pattern for them to make these [oppressive] comments. And you're torn, because you wanna provide service to them, but you also don't want to hear the abuse all the time ...

Most managers felt a "ban of service" policy was too harsh. They argued that given service users' differential social positions in relation to staff, their often highly complex needs, and their reasons for engaging with the service in the first place, the nature of the accountability processes for them must be different than for staff and board. These managers note that agencies have a responsibility to assist service users in developing the skills they need to uphold anti-oppression policies.

Engaging in Effective Anti-Oppression Education and Training

Due to its focus on multiple intersecting oppressions, anti-oppression is a complex model to think about, never mind to implement in practice (Barnoff and Moffatt 2007; Dominelli 2002; Mullaly 2007). Few people are able to develop expertise in AOP on their own. Indeed, we all require ongoing education and frequent repeated attempts to practice new approaches. Education and training is an important aspect of any organizational change effort (Galambos, Dulmus and Wodarski 2005). Not surprisingly, then, participants in this study argue that some of the most important organizational-level AOP strategies are those which enhance opportunities for anti-oppression education and training. This training should be mandatory, ongoing, and understood as one component of an agency's AOP work, not the "be-all and end-all" of that work (Hyde 2003; Hyde and Hopkins 2004; Martinez, Green, and Sanudo 2004; Mederos and Woldeguiorguis 2003).

What should anti-oppression training look like? Participants told me it is useful to begin by doing some anti-oppression training with everyone together, to set the stage for future work by attempting to get everyone "on the same page." This first phase should focus on developing a shared basic understanding of what anti-oppression is all about and what it means, in a general way, to be an anti-oppressive agency — that is, it should present key concepts, principles, and language. Giving organizational members a shared language and a foundational set of ideas will help them work together. Later, the content of anti-oppression training can expand. For example, agencies could then begin to explore the needs and issues facing particular marginalized groups, such as Aboriginal women or women with disabilities. But how does an agency know which groups it should focus on? Participants argued that the focus should emerge from the practice realities in each agency's specific context. For example, Zoe described the process her agency uses to make these decisions:

> We get feedback from the counsellors to hear what's gone on [in the service] and what sort of understanding they have ... So a lot of it comes from what we hear about what's going on, current trends about what's going on [in our service] right now. We do a needs assessment to see specifically what they are asking for. Then we have a strategic planning meeting every year. So management will sit down and talk about, "OK, what trainings do we think we need for this year? What current trends have we noticed [in the service]?"

In other words, the content of the training is dependent on what is happening within the agency's services. If staff find there is an increase in the number of transgendered women or of immigrant women accessing the service, or if they notice that a particular group of women is not accessing service, those would be the groups to prioritize in their training. Because issues change, these agencies plan their anti-oppression training program yearly.

It is not enough simply to develop knowledge in an abstract way; there must be an action piece built into this training (Bernard and Hamilton-Hinch 2006). Anti-oppression training should teach agency staff how to translate new knowledge into service delivery methods:

> We tell the facilitators [when they are planning for the training], the information that you're sharing with us, knowledge that you're giving us, [make sure to include a component related to] how's that going to translate in [our service]? How can we do that work specifically [in our service]? (Andrea)

The following questions need to be asked: "At a program level, how does our service provision need to change, in light of this new knowledge we have gained today?" and "How will I practise differently, given this new information?"

Another suggested area for anti-oppression training was teaching the skills needed to confront oppressive behaviours in the agency. Even though AOP policies require staff to engage in dialogue and address oppressive incidents, participants told me that doing so remains a challenge in most agencies. As difficult as these types of conversations can be, however, they are extremely important. There will be negative consequences for organizations that do not find ways to enable them to occur (Moffatt, Barnoff George, and Coleman 2009; Miller, Donner, and Fraser 2004). Training that helps people learn the skills required to communicate difficult issues and to challenge each other respectfully will assist them in becoming better communicators and will go a long way toward facilitating AOP agency-wide (Hyde 2003).

Conflict resolution skills are important to AOP. In every agency, staff members have disagreements with one another, particularly when resources are tight and service needs are high. In the context of diversity, and in agencies which encourage people to engage in dialogue about privileges and oppressions, disagreements are bound to be even more pronounced. Yet conflict is not necessarily a bad thing. It is an inevitable, integral, and important aspect of any process of change in a social justice-oriented organization; indeed, it is only through the processing of conflict that change is possible (Barnoff 2002; Dobbie and Richards-Schuster 2008; Dominelli 2002; Nybell and Gray 2004; Sakamoto and Pitner 2005). In diverse organizations, conflicts also occur among service users. AOP practitioners need to be able to help service users process and resolve these conflicts.

In shelter or residential environments there are very difficult issues that come up with women in crisis in communal living situations that come from very different places, very different cultures, trying to co-exist. And so [we have] to also create a culture of learning where staff can facilitate the kind of discussions, the kind of problem solving, the kinds of things that need to happen so that things don't blow up and somebody says, 'Fuck you, I am going to kill you' and takes a knife, you know? It can get there really easily and the fact is it didn't necessarily have to. (Annie)

Agencies need to help staff and service users develop the skills required to communicate well and to resolve conflicts in ways that are consistent with AOP values and strategies. They can provide these opportunities as part of their anti-oppression training (Hyde 1998).

Agencies often hire outside facilitators to assist them with anti-oppression training. Participants said that this can be a very good idea, but that at the same time, agencies need to be cautious about whom they bring in to do this work. A bad facilitator can be extremely damaging to an agency's efforts to integrate AOP. In a conversation about the importance of allocating sufficient resources for anti-oppression training, Maud offered this analysis:

[It's problematic when] you have the commitment to do the work, but you don't put any resources behind it. So you go out and you get these freebie trainers, who come in and wreak havoc with an organization's culture, breed distrust, because they don't understand the issues [and] they mismanage the conflicts at the table. That makes staff never want to come to another forum to do any other anti-oppression training. Because who is going to cry, who is going to be angry, who is going to storm out of the room? And who is going to be accused and silenced by the facilitator, who is supposed to be a mediator, a broker, somebody who is supposed to facilitate conversation, [not] somebody who just comes with their own personal agenda and just wants to dictate how it should be done and why you aren't doing it right.

The idea that a problematic facilitator can undermine and derail an agency's AOP work is supported by Hyde's (2004: 12) research. She argues that an AOP trainer needs not only to be knowledgeable about the "curriculum" of the training, but to be equally skilled in "assessing and working with group dynamics [and]… in handling difficult moments." In other words, facilitators must be selected with care. In some cases, no training at all is preferable to training with a problematic facilitator.

There is also a more informal and ongoing kind of education that is vital to AOP (Dobbie and Richards-Schuster 2008). In the agencies studied, informal anti-oppression "training" was integrated into multiple venues. An ongoing commitment to constant dialogue and critical questioning was built into the foundation of the agency's operations rather than occurring only within the context of periodic formal training sessions:

> It's almost like the forums where staff naturally come together as staff, like staff meetings or team meetings become a venue for training and for kind of ongoing development, versus bringing in a consultant and having that happen once every ten years and having it only again when there is a crisis. (Maud)

Managers told me that this kind of informal education also takes place within the context of staff supervision and is an important way to reinforce skills and foster a culture of ongoing learning.

Anti-oppression training can develop and enhance a number of specific skills required for engaging in AOP. Participants in this study identified critical self-reflection as one such skill. Critical self-reflection involves thinking critically about our practice and taking action based on our reflection (Suarez, Newman, and Reed 2008). Through this process of reflection "we become aware of our own oppression and privilege — recognizing how our multiple social positions shape our lives and our relationships and how these, in turn, have been shaped by societal systems — and we also act to challenge and change patterns of oppression (Suarez et al. 2008: 408).

> Part of the anti-oppression practice has to be that all of us, whether it be privileged groups or marginalized groups or whatever, that we all need to go through that, so that we also kind of take care of our own territories where there is internalized stuff around being a woman, a woman of colour, a lesbian, whatever. (Bebot)

> I think it's easy to acknowledge where you are oppressed in terms of what is your oppression. It's there. It's in your face. You know it. You see it. So it's kind of hard not to deal with how you're oppressed as a woman, or for me, as a lesbian, blah, blah, blah. But for me, it's around the work [of] learning how to recognize your power and the privilege that you carry. (Sam)

The ability to engage in this ongoing process of reflection, analysis, and learning is a fundamental AOP skill (Baldwin 2008; Burke and Harrison 2002; Dalrymple and Burke 1995a; Fook 1999b; Heron 2005; Issitt 1999; Moffatt 1996; Morley 2008; Sakamoto and Pitner 2005). It is "a necessity, not an option" (Danso 2009: 543) in AOP. As a result, agencies that utilize part of their anti-oppression training curriculum to help staff further develop this skill will be in a good position to move their AOP work forward.

Fostering an Organizational Culture Conducive to AOP

The concept of "organizational culture" refers to the overall climate, tone, or atmosphere within an agency (Galambos et al. 2005). It has to do with the largely unspoken, unseen sets of norms or rules that guide how everyday things happen in the agency: for example, how people interact with and relate to each other, the communication processes and styles used in the agency, and in general how it "feels" in an agency (Glisson 2007). Interventions that have an impact on an organization's culture are a critical component of any agency's efforts to integrate AOP (Hyde 2003).

Participants told me that an organizational culture which values learning helps facilitate AOP. This type of organizational culture would position AOP as a continual, never-ending process, a process that necessitates ongoing learning. Talking about her agency's AOP journey, Andrea made the following observations:

> We've had lots of bumps along the way [in our efforts to integrate AOP], but we're getting there. I wish I could see a clear picture of how I think we would be there at some point. [But] we'd always be learning anyways, because that's the whole thing about an anti-oppression framework. You've got something to learn all the time.

It is essential, then, to create an organizational culture in which efforts to engage in ongoing learning are esteemed and in which multiple opportunities for learning exist (Baldwin 2008; Busch and Hostetter 2009; Doyle and George 2008). In an agency with a high degree of support for engaging in learning processes (rather than expecting people to already always know everything) various mechanisms will be established to ensure staff and board continually support each other's learning. For example, a board might decide to begin each board meeting by discussing a current issue relevant to the agency's work so they can learn from each other's perspectives. Alternatively, a staff team might decide to set aside the first twenty minutes of every staff meeting to share knowledge about their cultural differences or upcoming religious holidays. The staff team might also spend this time in other ways: for example, practising their skills in giving and receiving feedback in respectful ways, or discussing a social policy of relevance to service users so they can all be better informed. The opportunities for engaging in ongoing learning are endless.

Innovation in organizations requires a "risk-taking" rather than a "risk-averse" approach (Baldwin 2008). In order to continue to work at implementing AOP, agency members need to have the freedom to try out new things and to engage service users and colleagues in new ways. To this end, another important aspect of organizational culture in AOP organizations is fostering risk-taking and allowing people to make mistakes (Nybell and Gray 2004).

I always tell people, "It's OK to make mistakes, but if you don't learn from your mistakes, that is where the problems arise." I mean you may say the wrong thing, you may perpetrate a behaviour that is inappropriate, that is oppressive, and it's not OK. But it's fine if you hear the challenge, you hear other people saying why it's oppressive, and you learn from it. You truly learn from it. (Stella)

Not only is it important for staff and service users to be allowed to make mistakes, they should also be able to turn to others in the organization for guidance and support in these situations. Maud noted that AOP is fostered when,

there is an organizational culture that says that we will make mistakes but we want to learn from them so that we don't do them again. Clearly, if the person continues to make the same mistake then you will have a different response, but you don't begin from, 'If this ever happens then you are out!' and then everyone is working from the basis of fear, right? And then there's this really bad behind-the-scenes organizational culture that happens.

Benjamin (2007) suggests that fear, including fear of risk-taking, is a common barrier to AOP which must be overcome. Rather than creating an atmosphere in which people operate from a basis of fear, an agency's culture can be one that fosters and enables open dialogue, risk-taking, and the ongoing effort to implement change, even if the results of those efforts are not always perfect. When people feel silenced because they are afraid to make a mistake, AOP work will be stifled. A willingness to take risks, on the other hand, promotes AOP. Indeed it is often only through engaging in a dialogue or taking some kind of action that people come to even realize their own positions on issues, or the ways they have been thinking about certain groups of people, or the ideas they hold that might be based in stereotypes or problematic learning. When these reactions are allowed to come to the fore, they can be challenged, reflected upon, and ultimately changed. An organizational culture conducive to AOP is one which encourages honest communication, one whose norms around communication value critical questioning and enable people to engage in difficult conversations. By fostering a culture in which every voice is valued and speaking out is expected, such organizations participate in AOP's emphasis on participation and shared empowerment (Bess, Prilleltensky, Perkins, and Collins 2009; Danso 2009; Larson 2008; Karabanow 2004).

According to these participants, a participatory and inclusive team approach demonstrates anti-oppression principles in action. When I asked a group of frontline workers to reflect on the organizational processes that distinguish an agency operating with an AOP approach from an agency using a more mainstream approach, one of the very first responses was about their agency's use of teams:

The thing that strikes me about our organization is the team approach … I mean, it really is more collaborative than I've recently seen in other organizations. Here we build [ideas] together … I think that's something that's distinct about our organization … in terms of planning, putting more than one perspective together, you know, trying to do something as holistically as we can. (Nicole)

Bess et al. (2009) argue that participatory approaches among employees are linked to increased organizational learning. Baldwin (2008) suggests that a collaborative team approach facilitates organizational innovation. In an organizational culture where team work is highly valued, and where collaboration, collegiality, and mutuality are encouraged, then, AOP will be easier to implement.

Ensuring the Agency Engages in Social Action

In feminist analysis, connections have always been made between women's "personal" issues and larger "political" systems (Adams 2008; Hyde 2000; Kravetz 2004; Weeks 1994). Feminist practitioners recognize that the issues women bring to social service agencies are rooted in systems of social oppression. From this perspective, agency interventions need to focus not just on individuals, but on a social level as well. In this way, a feminist approach and an anti-oppression approach meld perfectly, for activist work is an important component of "service" work from an AOP perspective (Barnoff, George, and Coleman 2006; Benjamin 2007; Danso 2009, Dominelli 2002, George, Barnoff, and Coleman 2007; Karabanow 2004; Morley 2008; Massaquoi 2007; Mullaly 2002, 2007; Pollack 2004; Sakamoto 2007). As Baines (2007a: 4) argues, "anti-oppressive practice attempts to integrate the search and struggle for social change directly into the social work experience."

Participants in this study were clear about the need to engage in social action as a part of agency AOP work. For example, talking about her work with immigrant and refugee women who have experienced domestic violence, Vera said,

Women come here without any status, but if they experience any kind of oppression, whether it's racism or sexism or even domestic violence, they don't come forward because of fear of being deported. And me, as a worker I don't have that much confidence to empower the woman to come forward and report it in some cases because I don't know if there is any system that will back her up. So I don't want to take the responsibility to jeopardize her life by being deported! So there are all these things that we really have to look at when we think, talk, about anti-oppression policy. For me, it's not only an agency thing. It shouldn't only be an agency thing. It's more like, it should take a larger, be on a larger scale.

Without transformative change in oppressive systems, women's issues will not be adequately resolved and the need for services will persist. While providing direct service is an important short-term goal, the ultimate goal of any AOP agency is to eliminate the need for its continued existence (Adams 2008).

In this way, anti-oppression social work is political work (Benjamin 2007; Danso 2009). Participants argued that AOP agencies must continually find ways to ensure that staff (and board) are participating in social justice initiatives along with their direct service work.

> Given that we know racism and oppression is systemic, it's political, and to be "anti" is a political piece, one of the things that is important to doing the work is having the connect outside of the organization to the larger political piece. (Annie)

Annie argued that staff who are not encouraged to engage in activist work as part of their agency work may sacrifice their political (feminist, anti-oppression) perspective:

> Staff who have been in the work for a long time get impacted. [They] start to see the clients as being the problem as opposed to a shitty Ontario Works system, lack of affordable housing, and to really be able to see the systemic pieces and who is most marginalized within those pieces. So some kind of links out to political [actions], to the community, I think are things that are important to keep focus on what we are trying to do. Because we aren't just trying to provide to 200 women each year. We are trying to change the huge system in lots of different ways on lots of different levels.

The message is clear: maintaining an organizational commitment to social action and finding ways to ensure organizational members engage in this work as a part of their jobs is fundamental to AOP — perhaps especially so in feminist agencies (Adams 2008).

AOP Involves Everyone, All the Time

In this study women revealed some of their AOP strategies, but were also candid in sharing some of their ongoing struggles. We can learn from both. We see that institutionalizing anti-oppression in an agency context is a complex process, often infused with challenge, difficulty, and uncertainty. At the same time, these women make clear that integrating an anti-oppression framework is indeed an attainable goal.

These practitioners described five important areas in establishing organizational level mechanisms that institutionalize AOP in an agency context:

1. They engage in strategies to increase the diversity of their board and staff teams as well as their service user populations.
2. They bring an AOP lens to bear on all of their organizational policies and procedures, asking critical questions in order to ensure that AOP is supported as each process unfolds. They also establish stand-alone AOP policies which make clear their definition of AOP, the behavioural expectations of organizational members, and the consequences in the event that AOP policies are not upheld.
3. They engage in ongoing AOP education and training, both formally and informally.
4. They work to create an organizational culture conducive to AOP — one in which ongoing learning and risk-taking are valued, mistakes are allowed, a collaborative, supportive environment is fostered, and multiple voices are expected and encouraged.
5. They ensure that the agency continues to engage in social action to bring about transformative change in the oppressive systems that create the issues that women bring to services.

The strategies outlined in this chapter represent only part of what these organizations are doing when it comes to implementing AOP. However, these five areas do help us understand some of what might be important when it comes to integrating AOP in a social work agency.

Integrating AOP in an agency context is perhaps best considered as a work in progress. At every phase, new issues emerge. As anti-oppression work continues, the issues, struggles, questions, and controversies can often become even more complex. These agencies have been engaged in the effort to implement AOP for many years, yet they continue to discover new complications and dilemmas on their paths toward change. Clearly, the work of AOP organizational change is never-ending (Amodeo et al. 2007; Hyde and Hopkins 2004; Moffatt et al. 2009). As AOP work deepens in agencies, the issues and challenges involved do not disappear. They are transformed rather than resolved. Agencies need to expect and plan for this.

If the journey to become an "AOP agency" is expected to be ongoing, then agencies know to be always on the lookout for the next potential "bump in the road" — the next piece of anti-oppression work their organization is going to need to do. Agencies also need to know that experiencing these "bumps" is a normal part of the process. Practitioners do not need to worry they are doing something wrong when they encounter a new challenge. This should be expected. This work is hard. It is messy. It is complex.

Anti-oppression social work can be thought of as based in "uncertainty" and should be "premised on being uncomfortable" (Jeffery 2007: 138). Sakamoto and Pitner (2005) argue that it is important in AOP work to maintain a sense of "discomfort." because this reminds us there is always more work to do. It does not mean that the situation is hopeless and we should throw up our hands. In fact, quite the opposite. It means that we must always be passionately engaged, for there is always another challenge headed our way that we can find ways to creatively confront.

For AOP organizational change to be successful, it has to be systemic, integrated into every aspect of an agency's functioning. It has to involve everyone. It has to incorporate multiple strategies for change (Amodeo et al. 2007). Practitioners make AOP systemic in an agency context by inserting it into every agency process, every procedure, and every policy — even those that might not necessarily appear to be related to AOP (as we saw with performance appraisals for example). AOP is integrated into an agency when it becomes "a central component of agency functioning" (Hyde 2003: 50). A comprehensive, organization-wide, multi-systems approach is what is needed (Martinez et al. 2004; Mederos and Woldeguiorguis 2003).

Focusing attention on organizational-level strategies is important because this is how practitioners make AOP systemic and build it into the foundation of the agency. To come back to the question posed at the outset of this chapter, this is precisely how AOP becomes part of the agency's "business as usual." When an anti-oppression component is built into every aspect of an organization's processes and procedures, it becomes irremovable. Once this condition takes hold, it ensures that regardless of which particular individuals might be working in an agency at any given moment, the routine operations of the agency will promote and uphold AOP. For sure, individuals in the agency still have their work to do, and they can still derail the agency's commitment to AOP if they try hard enough. However, their efforts to do so will be much more difficult if the organizational context itself supports, promotes, and champions AOP at every turn.

Note

1. Names are pseudonyms, chosen by participants themselves.

Section Two

REFLEXIVITY

Introduction

Donna Baines

Reflexivity is an important anti-oppressive practice. It involves reflecting not only on one's own practice, social location, and power but also on the practice, social location, and power of others and on larger social processes and dynamics, in order to strengthen one's anti-oppressive capacity, social analysis and critique, and overall social work practice. Too often, social workers are so pressed for time in their jobs that they cannot find the time to think through what they are doing, whose interests are being met by their practice, and whose needs and interests are being minimized, patronized, or ignored. Social workers need time to think about how things in their everyday practice could be strengthened or improved, even a little bit. As Habermas (1973) notes, reflection is a process of self-determination in which individuals can critically analyze what they are doing and try to move towards mutual liberation and social justice. Hence, it is not surprising that the opportunity for and skills to undertake critical reflexivity are not part of most social work training or workplaces.

The authors in this section use moments in their social work practice when they felt frustrated, hurt, or perplexed to reflect closely on what they were doing and how their social work practice reproduced oppressive relations in unintended, seemingly innocent ways. These authors took their reflections further — reading and thinking about theory or research that might be helpful — and they eventually developed critical new insights into both their own practices and those of the institutions to which they were attached.

Chapter 12

Occupied Spaces

Unmapping Standardized Assessments in Health and Social Service Organizations

Kristin Smith

This chapter explores how the seemingly harmless as-sessment tool known as the Patient Health Questionnaire (PHQ-9) is part of the increasing occupation of health and social service workplaces by corporate interests. The analysis "unmaps" how use of standardized assessments in care work changes what we do with service users. The discussion consid-ers links between local care practices and questionable health research practices occurring beyond the reach of regulatory bodies. The chapter highlights how Western social workers can become implicated in forms of injustice that are often hidden. It concludes with suggestions for resistance.

As you read through this chapter, ask yourself the following questions:
1. How does the introduction of standardized assessment tools affect your own care practices with service users?
2. How can you use critical analysis to unmap links between your local care work and corporate interests both within and beyond your workplace?
3. In what ways can you engage in active resistance against the erosion of public interests?

In this chapter I describe how I use "unmapping" as an approach to critically analyse the emergence of a standardized assessment tool within my work set-ting, a primary health care clinic in Hamilton. In recent years, social workers have faced growing pressure to adopt standardized assessment tools in health and social services, especially where there is an emphasis on decreasing "waste" and "inefficiencies." These tools replace open-ended conversations and in-depth assessments with check-list forms and smaller allotments of service for users. More than just an annoyance, the move towards standardized forms of care has even more sinister implications.

> ### Unmapping
> Borrowed from social geography, this term refers to showing how spaces and places are socially organized in ways that hide hierarchies of power. Razack (2002a) explains that just as mapping helped White European settlers to imagine and make claims that they discovered and therefore owned lands, unmapping reveals the ideologies and practices of domination that continue to shape the spaces in which we live and work today.

At the outset I should note that I am not an "expert" on assessment tools, nor do I have extensive knowledge about the pharmaceutical industry, which as it turns out, is highly relevant to this unfolding story. However, by unmapping the impact of assessment tools on my practice, I have been able to make some important connections between the local and the global; that is, I have begun to see the connections among what I do every day at the medical clinic where I work, the negative effects of government restructuring of public services, and questionable research practices undertaken globally by pharmaceutical corporations. When I unmap standardized assessment tools, I find a form of logic that requires people to become "self-managing" and "self-sufficient" (N. Rose 1999: 27).

This logic lets governments retreat from social welfare obligations while simultaneously opening the door to the creeping advances of corporate interests and the imposition of new bottom-line calculations of what it means to care for others. At first, some of these connections seemed abstract to me. Nevertheless, unmapping revealed how the appearance of a seemingly benign assessment tool signalled the fact that an intersection of government and private corporate interests — whose common objective is the marketization of human life — increasingly occupied this zone of public care. Working in this occupied space has deep implications for who I am and what I do as an anti-oppressive social worker. Once these connections have been revealed, how then, will we as social workers act in order to avoid professional complicity?

> ### Corporate Interests
> This phrase refers to the interests of those who profit from the transfer of public wealth into private hands and from the widening gap between rich and poor; sometimes referred to as the interests of "Big Business" in order to distinguish between the interests of small, locally owned businesses and those of multi-national corporations who gain power by buying up and taking over their competitors. Large multi-national corporations are able to wield power and influence over national governments because of the ever-present threat to take their plants, jobs, and economic investments elsewhere.

> ### Market
> The system of commercial activity, including institutions, proce-
> dures, laws, infrastructures and social relations whereby goods
> and services are bought and sold to form part of the economy.

> ### Marketization
> A process that entails submitting every action and policy decision
> to considerations of profitability. It assumes that all aspects of
> social, cultural, and political life can be reduced to a calculation
> based on market principles, including organizing things based
> on supply and demand, turning everything into a commodity to
> be bought and sold.

Social Safety Net Unravels in Ontario

The story behind this chapter began early in 2008 when my project manager invited me to attend a workplace training session to learn more about
"measurement-based care" (Duffy et al. 2008: 1148) — another name for
standardized assessment tools — that was becoming an increasingly popular
"best practice" in the field of health care. At the time, I was working at a medical
clinic providing direct mental health services to residents of a large inner-city
neighbourhood. People came to the clinic with problems that were wide-ranging
and interconnected: grief and loss, addictions, family issues, abuse and violence,
unemployment and work-related stress, inadequate or dangerous housing, and
poverty, to name a few. The mental health "patients" were mainly women,
and often they were members of marginalized communities, such as first- and
second-generation immigrant settlers, Indigenous women, and other racialized
women. They usually struggled with poverty, and many were raising kids on
their own or with the help of their extended family. I also came in contact with
many people with disabilities, providing assistance, advocating for their rights
to benefits, or acting as a mediator for their care arrangements with different
health professionals.

Throughout the late 1990s and early 2000s, my job as a mental health
counsellor in primary care became increasingly fraught with difficulties and
impossibilities. Funding cuts by successive right-wing governments in Ontario
intensified pressures to provide more with less to people staggering under the
weight of mounting personal and social problems. Growing wait lists left clinic
workers feeling constantly overwhelmed, while many service users simply fell
through the cracks left in the province's shattered social safety net. Squeezed
between funding cuts and the increasing numbers of desperate service users,
many social workers simply ducked for cover. Within this context, spaces for
social activism and advocacy within social and health services diminished and

> ## Social Safety Net
> This term refers to government programs that were intended to prevent the poor or those vulnerable to shocks in the economy from falling below a certain level of material well-being. Examples include income maintenance, social housing, and subsidies for public transportation.

risked drying up altogether. For example, after the cuts I no longer had the time nor did I receive organizational support to sit on community committees or engage in social action events aimed at broader social change as part of my paid work. Instead, I spent my workdays at break-neck speed, meeting face-to-face with an unending number of individual patients.

To the relief of many beleaguered social workers, Dalton McGuinty's Liberal Party, when it came to power in 2005, made a welcome announcement that it would "renew" primary health care services across Ontario. Since then, millions of dollars have been injected into the system with the goal of creating new and expanded comprehensive health services. However, the sense of relief was short-lived. My wait list for services continued to overwhelm me. Other community services to which I referred people for additional help continued to struggle with the effects of previous funding cuts. But instead of validating these concerns and strategizing to deal with the impact of gutted services and long wait-lists, my managers began to suggest that clinic social workers learn new ways of working, using the latest specialized interventions known as "measurement-based care approaches." It was believed that these approaches would speed up our work in order to serve greater numbers of people. The training session on measurement-based care which I was required to attend prompted this chapter; in particular, my introduction to one specific tool - the Patient Health Questionnaire — Nine (PHQ-9).

PHQ-9: Measurement-Based Care

The training meeting that I was asked to attend in spring 2008 included a manager and my frontline service colleagues, mostly social workers and some nurses. The purpose of the meeting was to familiarize us with a new assessment tool which was being introduced as part of a province-wide policy in health care settings. At the meeting we were told that all direct service staff would be expected to start incorporating the PHQ-9 into our practice during our first encounter with new patients. The PHQ-9 is a brief, self-administered (that is, completed by the patient), nine-question survey of a patient's mood with items that correspond to the nine depressive symptoms listed in the Diagnostic and Statistical Manual of Mental Disorders, Fourth Edition (DSM-IV) (Kroenke et al. 2001). Easy to read and seemingly effortless to use,

> ### DSM-IV
> The Diagnostic and Statistical Manual of Mental Disorders cur-
> rently published in its fourth edition. This manual, published by
> the American Psychiatric Association, provides diagnostic criteria
> for mental disorders. It is used around the world by clinicians,
> researchers, health insurance companies, pharmaceutical compa-
> nies, and policy makers to determine and communicate a patient's
> diagnosis through the identification of categories of symptoms.

the PHQ-9 form was described as a series of "simple" questions about the last two weeks of a person's life. For example, question Number Four asks: "Have you been feeling tired or having little energy?" The person's response is scored from "0" (meaning "not at all") to "3" (meaning "I'm tired and have little energy nearly every day"). The maximum overall score is 27. The PHQ-9 measures the severity of depression symptoms with the following thresholds: 0–4 (none); 5–9 (mild); 10–14 (moderate); 15–19 (moderately severe); and 20--27 (severe).[1] What remains hidden amongst all the claims about its usefulness is the way PHQ-9 shortens and narrows assessments and consequently diminishes opportunities to build relationships and communication between helpers and service users.

During the PHQ-9 training, the project manager was careful to explain that this new measuring device was intended merely as one item in a "toolbox" of care practices. I observed many of my colleagues reacting favourably to this new tool, yet I was unsettled by nagging questions. Why was the PHQ-9 being introduced at a time of so-called massive renewal by a health ministry anxious to correct bloated wait-lists and lengthy wait-times? How would the introduction of this new "tool" shape our social work practices? Who would we become as care workers practising in the fast-paced, high-pressured world of restructured health care? Toiling under the weight of heavy caseloads and endless wait-lists certainly made the "quick fix" simplicity of this questionnaire desirable. I worried, though, that the tool would simplify and narrow my margins of practice rather than expanding and enriching the quality of services available to patients. The PHQ-9's seductiveness was further enhanced because it is rooted in the authoritative expertise of the DSM-IV. This aspect had a particular appeal to "secondary" care providers, since using the PHQ-9 potentially elevated our status and aligned our skills with those of physicians and psychiatrists who were considered more "prestigious" within the hierarchy of the health care field. As the training concluded, there was little room to express doubts about the "validity" or to discuss the limitations of this so-called tool. Shrouded in the aura of "scientific evidence," the PHQ-9 was about to be rolled out in primary health care settings across the province, a new "best practice" for frontline service providers. Un-mapping was the counter-tool that I used to critically analyse the questions that surrounded the emergence of PHQ-9 in my place of work, and the impact it would have on who I was becoming and how I would now practice social work.

Unmapping Our Spaces of Work

"Mapping" is an old concept originating in the field of geography and reworked by poststructural and feminist scholars in order to understand the social production of spaces (Lefebvre 1991; Soja 1989; Rose, G. 1999). To state that space is socially produced implies that the places we occupy, those in which we live and work, are never neutral (Lefebvre 1991). For instance, my workplace is never just a building that contains offices in which my colleagues and I deliver mental health care. Something more is happening. Razack (2002a: 9) explains that it is through the recital of everyday routines that "space comes to perform something in the social order, permitting certain actions and prohibiting others." She argues that it is possible to "unmap" spaces — to "denaturalize" them - in order to see the raced, gendered, and classed social hierarchies that are protected and hidden when we accept that such orderings occur naturally (Razack 2002b: 128). I use unmapping in this chapter in part as a metaphor, but also as an exercise in critical reflection, enabling me to uncover and make visible the various discourses and processes that shape me into becoming a specific kind of social work subject within my particular place of work (Razack 2002c; Ng and Mirchandani 2008). If "global processes are embedded in local experiences," (Ng and Mirchandani 2008: 39) then unmapping also enables me to track how my local social work practice is inseparable from the global context.

The actual practices I used for unmapping felt like what I imagined to be detective work. I read critical literature on my topic. I corresponded and met with critical scholars and activists who monitor the pharmaceutical industry. I used web-based search engines to dig for information — that is, I searched for stories covered in the non-mainstream press, and tried to gain access to knowledge about corporate structures and merger activities. Through unmapping the PHQ-9, many processes that were previously hidden from me became more visible. Perhaps the most important lesson I learned through unmapping is this: in a world that is increasingly shaped by globalized capitalism, there is never such a thing as "innocent space" for social work in our local places of work (Rossiter 2005: 201). The growing mobility of global capital involves circulations of knowledge and market-driven expertise that form grim connections between what we do "here" in the West in the name of "renewal" and what gets done elsewhere in the name of "research."

Unmapping the PHQ-9

Designed to be brief and easy to use, measurement-based care and standardized assessment tools are promoted as capable of efficiently providing useful information for problem determination and case planning purposes (Gilgun 2004). Proponents of the PHQ-9 cite its brevity and its ease of administration and interpretation, along with the capability of assessing DSM-IV criteria and symptoms, to argue that the PHQ-9 is a crucial link between "evidence-based practice" (EBP) and routine mental health care (Duffy et al. 2008: 1148-49). Advocates of such EBP interventions contend that they offer improved accountability and transparency along with strengthened effectiveness (Reid 2001; Gilgun 2005). It has been suggested that such interventions will "weed out ineffective therapies" by providing specific guidelines to interventions that are "logically related to predetermined changes" (Witkin and Harrison 2001: 293). Decision-making, within this paradigm, is seen to be made by "rational" social workers who can draw on "logical" consequences of particular findings and apply these to clients' problems with the reasonable expectation of particular outcomes. Promoters note that by integrating scientific methods into their practice, social workers will insert themselves into the mainstream of scientifically oriented disciplines, paralleling themselves with more prestigious professions like doctors (Witkin and Harrison 2001).

A more critical assessment of the PHQ-9 becomes possible when we begin to un-map how its use intersects with the effects of neoliberal funding cuts to Canadian health and social services. Despite claims that social workers will experience greater "prestige" and "effectiveness," recent studies detail alarming trends in the field. For example, in their study of social work practitioners in health and child welfare settings, Aronson and Sammon (2000) found accumulating constraints and tensions at the frontline of service delivery. Respondents in their research reported that their work had both intensified and accelerated, so that they were constantly pressed for time and rushed in their encounters with service users. The standardized processing of service users and narrowed practice boundaries resulted in oversimplified approaches that fragmented care practices. Aronson and Sammon conclude: "Constrained by time pressure, by ill-fitting organizational forms, and by the fragmenting effects of divided labour, workers identified how crucial aspects of what they deemed good practice were effectively squeezed out of their jobs" (2000: 173). By "the fragmenting effects of divided labour," Aronson and Sammon refer to managerial attempts to cut costs by breaking down labour processes into standardized work units that can be delegated to less skilled workers, such as support workers. The resulting services are often disjointed, discontinuous, and characterized by gaps. Similar themes emerge in Baines' (2004c) research, which describes changing work worlds typified by part-time and temporary jobs and dominated by heavy workloads and demanding paperwork. Standardized tasks translate into tightly-monitored work boundaries and diminished space for professional discretion. Workers in Baines' study reported racking up unpaid overtime by working through lunch hours and during coffee breaks, in the evening and on weekends. They described making work-related phone calls from cell-phones while driving, and scrambling to finish case notes late at night. Baines points out that the undocumented nature of this unpaid work means that service organizations can create the illusion of "leanness" for funders while the excessive amount of labour that is really required remains unaccounted for and officially invisible. As Baines notes pointedly, "What gets produced is social services and workplace stress; what is lost is worker control and integrity" (2004c: 3).

These examples from the critical literature on neoliberal restructuring in social and health services reveal sharp contradictions between the realities of new organizational forms and the claims made by advocates of standardized assessment tools. Indeed, the very idea that "best practices" can emerge under such circumstances is highly questionable. How is it, then, that within our health and social service workplaces the wide-spread adoption of these tools continues unabated?

A key to further unmapping the emergence of brief assessments in primary health care settings involves recognizing how these tools are embedded within the "social register of neoliberalism" (Davies 2005; Brown 2005). Important to this discussion is an understanding of neoliberalism as more than simply a set of economic policies. Neoliberalism goes far beyond dismantling social welfare, reducing government regulations, and maximizing corporate profit-taking — although it certainly does all these things. Brown (2005: 40) explains that beyond economic policy, neoliberalism also entails "extending and dis-seminating market values to all institutions and social action." In other words, the market becomes the organizing principle for everything in our daily lives, the norm against which every decision and action is to be measured. What does it mean when all aspects of human life are calculated in terms of the market? According to Bronwyn Davies (2005: 9), the ascendancy of the marketplace in all aspects of our lives represents a major cultural shift in which people take up survival as an individual responsibility, and any form of dependence on the larger social fabric is removed. The rewards of "success" await each person who "gets it right." For Davies as for Brown (2005), neoliberalism is "inserted into our consciousness, into our conscience," (Davies 2005: 4) and in doing so, it becomes a register for everyday life. However, neoliberalism is not simply imposed on us. Rather, neoliberalism requires the active, ongoing participation of individuals. As Davies (2005: 6) explains:

> It is at work here, busily containing what we can do, what we can un-derstand. It is the language in which the auditor is king. It is a language that destroys social responsibility and critique, that invites mindless, consumer-oriented individualism to flourish, and kills off conscience.

Nikolas Rose (1999: 27–28) explains that in the West, neoliberalism involves "governing through freedom": a free-market logic requires that people become "self-managing" and "self-enterprising" individuals making fewer demands on the state. In other words, as the state retreats from expenditures on social spending and responsibilities, techniques are broadly introduced that re-shape how people see themselves and others and how they frame social problems. Drawing on these critical analyses of neoliberalism, it becomes possible to unmap the claims of those who support the use of standardized assessment tools by social workers. Rather than "best practices," standardized assessment tools can be seen as a technology that draws on "specialized knowledge" to produce "experts" who can induce "self-governing" so that citizens can efficiently optimize their individual health choices, especially during times that are characterized by economic constraint (Ong 2006).

Doreen

Doreen,[2] a 27-year-old Mohawk woman, was referred to me for an assessment after her family physician noted concerns about her flat mood and problems with sleep. It did not take long to realize that Doreen has had a very hard life. Despite a college diploma in a skilled trade, stable employment has eluded her. For the last six months she and her young daughter have been living with her parents — who are also struggling to make ends meet — on First Nations land. Her family's home lacks direct access to clean water due to ongoing problems with contaminated well systems and a government bureaucracy that refuses to deal with the problem. Though racism has always been something that Doreen has had to contend with, she observes that a growing land claims movement in her community has made visible the more blatant forms of discrimination and racism in the wider community around her reserve. As a result, Doreen has been unable to find any kind of work in the nearby town. Despondent, she feels stuck in her life, very down on herself, and is quietly losing hope for her future.

As part of our assessment, Doreen completed the PHQ-9. I calculated the results and submitted them to her doctor for review. Not surprisingly, given the high stress levels in her life, Doreen's score on the scale was 20, meaning that her doctor would likely diagnose her with severe depression. Though I made every effort to document and draw attention to the context of Doreen's difficulties, these notes were buried under the PHQ-9 form in her chart. It was not that the doctor dismissed these factors outright; in fact, he was genuinely sympathetic to her situation. However, the presence of the PHQ-9 in her medical file insinuated a particular frame of reference into how the doctor viewed Doreen's life. From the physician's perspective, there was little time in our fast-paced clinic to reflect on or respond to the socio-political context of Doreen's life problems. Instead, after reviewing the assessment findings with her doctor, Doreen left the clinic with a prescription for Zoloft, an anti-depressant medication that happens to be manufactured by the same pharmaceutical company that designed the PHQ-9 and continues to claim ongoing copyright ownership of this tool.

Doreen's case exemplifies the lack of neutrality in my workplace. The health care clinic where I practice social work has become, through the health team's use of the PHQ-9, a place where Doreen's problems are framed as a "sickness" needing to be "cured" with medication. The PHQ-9 produces and demarcates a way of seeing and thinking that leads to forms of "efficient care practices," effectively hiding the social context and relations that are making Doreen so "ill" in the first place. Doreen's life is seen through a lens that decontextualizes, individualizes, and pathologizes the social problems she experiences. The PHQ-9 in this instance works to transform *social* problems into problems of "self-care" in that Doreen, the doctor, and I are effectively recruited into an individualized form of self-governing associated with neoliberalism (Lemke 2001: 201). Doreen's case demonstrates how even "renewed" publicly funded primary health care spaces can be made places where health care workers do the job of cost-containment, enabling the state to further retreat from social responsibilities. In Doreen's case, necessities such as clean water, child care, fair land claims settlements, and access to employment are eclipsed by the power of the PHQ-9 and a pharmaceutical solution: medication. By adopting these efficient care frameworks for the alleviation of social problems, social workers become implicated in a "style of thought" (Rose 2007: 05) in which only certain ways of thinking, seeing, and practicing are made legible and credible. Social workers assign themselves a role in health care that supports and furthers processes intersecting with a neoliberal agenda to dismantle public welfare entitlements and obligations.

Intersections between the Local and the Global: Unmapping Ethical Conflicts of Interest in Health Research

Every time I passed the PHQ-9 form on to a service user, I could not help but notice that on the bottom of the page, in small print, there was a copyright note: Pfizer Incorporated™. Startled to realize that the creator and owner of the PHQ-9 assessment tool was a pharmaceutical company, I began to talk with people who critically study the company whose presence had suddenly become so looming in my workplace.[3] I learned that Pfizer is a major American pharmaceutical company that ranked number one in the world in sales and profits as of 2005, posting $46 billion in earnings (N. Gray 2005: 84). That same year, the anti-depressant Zoloft was listed as one of Pfizer's top selling drugs, with sales of more than $3.3 billion (2005: 85). Drug companies like Pfizer produce many important medications that save lives and help a lot of people. However, emerging evidence points to some deeply troubling research practices undertaken by drug companies including Pfizer as they go about the "big business" of developing their products.

Since the massive cuts to public funding for health research in Canada and the U.S. during the 1990s, pharmaceutical companies have increasingly stepped in to fill this financial void. The industry's enormous financial resources have enabled pharmaceutical companies to assume influential roles in the areas of clinical research and education. In 2007, an American Psychological Association (APA) study reported that pharmaceutical industry money had become so crucial to the funding of American university medical centres that no additional pressure or inducements were required for a pharmaceutical company to exert influence on the practice of medicine (CSPI 2003, cited in Pachter et al. 2007: 1007). In Canada, the private sector, including pharmaceutical companies, is the greatest source of funding for university research, particularly medical studies (Tibbetts 2007). Critics worry that drug companies use their substantial influence in legitimate centres of scientific research to advance their business interests at the expense of credible science. The APA task force on external funding noted that in 2001 alone, the pharmaceutical industry spent approximately $35 billion on what their report referred to as "marketing masquerading as education" and "marketing masquerading as research" (Angell 2004, cited in Pachter et al. 2007: 1008). In an effort to curb such abuse, American federal prosecutors recently fined Pfizer a record $2.3 billion penalty for the illegal marketing of thirteen different drugs including Zoloft (Barrett 2009). However, the industry generally recognizes settlements as part of the cost of doing business; in the absence of effective regulations, companies like Pfizer will continue to violate ethics while in pursuit of larger profits.

Concerns have been raised about other practices of major drug makers — for instance, their releasing selective information about clinical trials, blaming competitive pressures from other companies. In 2005, an article in *The New York Times* (Berenson 2005) cited independent scientists and disclosed that companies, including Pfizer, have been able to hide negative trial results by refusing to publish outcomes of certain studies or by "cherry-picking" only the most favourable data from the studies that do get published. An example of these practices can be found in a Canadian study conducted in the late 1990s by Dr. Nancy Olivieri, a researcher with the University of Toronto (for a detailed report see Thompson, Baird, and Downie 2001). In this case, Apotex, the pharmaceutical company sponsoring Olivieri's research on an experimental drug, abruptly ended the research after she raised concerns about unfavourable findings that the drug could pose risks to patients (Tibbetts 2007). In the much-publicized events, Apotex threatened to sue Olivieri if she informed patients or published the negative findings. Taking a stand against such corporate bullying tactics, Dr. Oliviera released and published them anyway.

The problem of hiding negative research findings relates to the way that the pharmaceutical industry is allowed to create their own guidelines and to self-regulate in terms of compliance. Currently, there is an absence of oversight, including laws that would ensure full disclosure (Berenson 2005). Another example that highlights the pitfalls of self-regulation can be found in ongoing use of "ghostwriters" to publish "scientific papers" in medical journals. A report by Singer (2009) claims that the pharmaceutical company Wyeth paid ghost-writers to produce and publish 26 papers backing the use of hormone replacement therapy in women between 1998 and 2005, suggesting that the hidden corporate influence on medical literature is more widespread than previously thought. Apparently, as Wyeth's sales of hormone drugs soared to nearly $2 billion in 2001, a federal study the following year was stopped abruptly when it was found that women taking the drugs had an increased risk of breast cancer, heart disease, and stroke (ibid). I was interested to see that although Pfizer is not cited directly in recent news reports on "ghostwriting," as a company they seem unconcerned about the practice: Wyeth's recent quarterly financial report notes plans for a corporate merger with Pfizer by the end of 2009 (Wyeth 2009).

Examples of questionable research practices on the part of Pfizer and the pharmaceutical industry in general raise unsettling questions about the validity and credibility of research supported by vested interests. Given the profit-seeking aims of those interests, it could be argued that a standardized assessment tool devised by Pfizer is merely an attempt to gain a larger slice of the market in anti-depressant medication. This thought may seem chilling to a lot of people.

Unmapping the Global Reach of Pfizer
— Copyright Owners of the PHQ-9

The rapid growth of pharmaceutical markets combined with high financial stakes has led to unprecedented demands for human subjects for drug research. It is estimated that a new drug costs an average of $900 million to bring to market, with the majority of costs associated with testing on human subjects for safety and effectiveness (Lustgarten 2005). In order to manage their bottom lines, large Western drug companies are increasingly performing their research trials in "emerging markets" — those geographic areas of political and economic instability where there are frequent health care crises and large, easily accessible populations of desperate subjects. Lustgarten (2005) reports that in the U.S., the cost of running a trial can be about $30,000 per patient — ten times the cost per patient in a less developed context. The Western demand for human subjects in developing countries has roots in the early 1970s when the practice of using prison subjects in the United States was exposed (Petryna 2005: 185). Subsequent legislation curtailed this practice. In response to new regulations, pharmaceutical companies turned to more "regulatory friendly environments" in the so-called Third World (Petryna 2005: 186). Petryna (2005: 187) observes a particularly chilling trend in the search for populations that are "treatment naïve." To be "treatment naïve" means that there is a widespread absence of treatment for common ailments and therefore the populations have not consumed any background medications that "might confuse the results of the trial." Shifting drug trials to developing contexts — where people have lost state protection in the form of access to health care — allows pharmaceutical companies the freedom to use cheap, easily accessible research subjects while avoiding the scrutiny of federal regulators in the West. It is precisely because these research subjects are poor and without access to protections that they become valuable to researchers in the West. These circumstances have made people in developing countries increasingly vulnerable to abuse and exploitation. One particularly disturbing example involves shocking allegations made against the copyright owners of the PHQ-9: Pfizer Incorporated.

In 1996, in the city of Kano, Nigeria, Africa, a meningitis outbreak affected scores of children. Seeing this as an opportunity for researching new uses for their antibiotic drug Trovan, Pfizer sent a team of medical staff to Kano. The international humanitarian group, *Doctors Without Borders,* was already present in Kano's main hospital distributing a cheaper antibiotic with a proven track record for effectiveness against this strain of meningitis. It is alleged that the Pfizer team went to the local hospital and approached over two hundred children and their parents who were waiting in line for treatment (Petryna 2005: 190). It is further alleged that the Pfizer team did not explain the experimental nature of Trovan, leading parents to believe that their children were being offered a proven treatment (ibid). In 2001, the parents filed a legal complaint in New York. They claimed that in order to make Trovan seem more effective, the Pfizer team purposefully under-dosed children in a control group that would have otherwise received the already proven medication (ibid). It is claimed that this action caused the deaths of at least five children and the impairment of two hundred others (Lustgarten 2005). For the record in this case, Pfizer denies any wrongdoing. A company spokesperson insists that Pfizer worked with the full knowledge and approval of the Nigerian government, with the consent of the participants, and within the bounds of Nigerian laws (This Day 2008, 2009). However, it should also be noted that the Nigerian government to which Pfizer refers is the military dictatorship of General Sani Abacha — a brutal regime known for many human rights abuses, including the state-sanctioned execution of nine political opposition activists including Ken Saro-Wiwa in 1995 (BBC News 2009). After dragging the case through the courts for over a decade, in May 2009 Pfizer agreed to a $75 million settlement to be divided amongst the victims, the state government, and the lawyers (This Day 2008, 2009). Meanwhile, Pfizer continues to insist that the children died from meningitis, not the drug trial. Pfizer portrays their actions in Kano as a "humanitarian effort" aimed at "saving" the lives of children (Perlroth 2009).

Resisting the Occupation

Unmapping the PHQ-9 form allowed me to explore the processes whereby a company like Pfizer comes to occupy such a big space in my social work practice, the life of Doreen and her family, and the lives of so many grief-stricken

> *Occupied Space*
> There are two meanings conveyed through the use of this term:
> on one hand, it refers to how social workers' thoughts and atten-
> tion can become engaged or filled up with a particular framework
> for seeing the world, one that fits well with free market policies
> encouraging privatization of social problems and personal re-
> sponsibility. On the other hand, the term builds on the idea that
> a specific place, such as a health or social service workplace, can
> become possessed and controlled by outside forces, in this case,
> the interests of private pharmaceutical corporations.

families in Kano, Nigeria. This unmapping exercise exposes the way that commercial interests in profits increasingly intersect with government interests in
cost containment to dramatically alter different spaces of health care. I have
come to see these places as "occupied spaces" where the values and practices of
neoliberalism are ever-present and increasingly dominant.

It has been pointed out that the ideal neoliberal citizen carries the responsibilities for the consequences of his or her actions no matter how severe
the structural constraints on this action (Brown 2005: 42). Of course some
people, through wilfulness or social barriers, cannot or will not ever manage
to "get it right" in terms of success under neoliberal forms of self-governing.
As a result, neoliberalism is associated with growing numbers of those who are
unable to manage and are therefore deemed disposable, since there is no longer
any obligation to care about them. Aihwa Ong (2006: 23–24) argues that this
is especially true for the "globally excluded" — the millions of marginalized
people who are often hidden from view because they live in "failed states" or
are effectively stripped of rights due to war, famine, and sickness. An emerging
neoliberal logic in these circumstances means that for basic survival, people
cannot turn to the state for assistance but instead, out of desperation, look for
"help" from the very corporations that are driven by the interests of markets. It
could perhaps be argued that my use of the Pfizer product known as the phq-9
is not directly connected to the tragic circumstances that unfolded in Kano in
1996. Yet unmapping this tool does make it possible to see its embeddedness
in the intersections of interests that led the Pfizer research team to Kano. As
a result, I can no longer ignore my professional implication in those interests.
I have learned through this process of unmapping that the spaces of Western
social work are never neutral and never innocent.

It is my hope that the discussion of standardized assessment tools can be
situated at the intersection of the globally excluded and the "responsibilized
selves" that are emerging as the subjects of Western social work organizations.
As Doreen Massey (2004: 98) explains, what we do in a particular place is not
somehow a product of only what goes on there, but results too from the "jux-
taposition and intermixing there of flows, relations, connections from 'beyond.'

Flows, relations and connections which may indeed, go round the world." I am interested in exploring how social workers can achieve "a global sense of place" (Massey 2004: 98) — a better understanding of how our changing practices here in the West implicate us in the marketization of all aspects of human life, both in our local communities and in places that are farther away. This involves learning to unmap our places of work and our care practices in order to more fully understand how it is that these spaces are occupied and saturated with the hidden interests of globalized neoliberalism. Unmapping can show us how we are implicated in these interests, and how we come to invest ourselves in the terms neoliberalism provides. This exercise can also help us to imagine alternative ways to care about each other, both locally and globally, as human beings rather than as marketable commodities.

Massey (2004: 100-101) argues that having a global sense of place implies a "global responsibility" for building awareness of the ramifications of our local daily lives. For me, unmapping reveals at least four fronts for analysis and action towards these ends. The first area that requires our attention is the urgent necessity to confront the ongoing cuts and refashioning of public services where the downsizing of social provisions results in narrowed, so-called efficient forms of care that demarcate only individualized conceptions of problems. Unmapping "efficient care practices" reveals knowledge with which to challenge notions that "renewed" health care is actually expanding our health care system. Social workers drawing on this critical knowledge can engage in productive dialogue with colleagues and managers, and also use information gained for the purposes of lobbying government representatives. A second front for analysis and action involves finding ways to resist the growing privatization and the conversion of publicly funded services into sources of profit-making for companies like Pfizer and others. At the local organizational level, social workers can use unmapping to highlight the importance of providing people access to unbiased information on health- related issues and pharmaceutical drugs. Patients simply have a right to know about any potential conflicts of interest when it comes to their care. Social workers are well-positioned to provide this information. At the broader level, unmapping provides valuable information for provincial and national professional associations as they lobby for a well-funded, universal system of health care throughout Canada. At the international level, these same professional associations can advocate on behalf of their members for universal access to safe primary health care services for everyone, globally. The third target for learning and action involves processes of deregulation; unmapping can provide information that supports a demand for government and regulatory protections that would keep people safe from the negative effects of market forces. Doreen's situation provides many examples, including the need for access to clean water, access to safe and affordable childcare supports for families, access to stable, well-paying full-time jobs with benefits, along with fair resolutions to disputes over land claims. Other possible sites for intervention would be university and hospital review boards for ethics in research practices. Social workers armed with critical knowledge gained through unmapping can make valuable contributions to review boards by ensuring that drug research within mainstream institutions is transparent, safe, and responsible. By working for increased public accountability, social workers can make sure that the systematic review of evidence about potential interventions is carried out by independent people who do not profit from those interventions. Social workers can also organize independent review panels in their own workplaces for the purposes of critically analysing research literature to ensure the integrity of so-called "evidence" upon which social workers are increasingly relying for their clinical practice. The final area for action involves learning about how our workplaces are producing social workers to be new kinds of subjects — practitioners of efficient care. This last target is about me: coming to know how I participate in the day-to-day reshaping of myself so that I am seen to perform "innovation" while calculating for "efficiencies." Unmapping provides an accessible model for critical reflection which encourages a social justice orientation for our day-to-day care practices. This process involves coming to know how it is that I can resist, even in small ways, the corporate occupation of my workplace. Examples of everyday resistance may include finding ways of "fiddling" with standardized assessment tools in order to make them more reflective of the context of people's lives. Additionally, team-based peer supervision models can offer ideal sites for critical analysis and dialogue in order to begin questioning the everyday assumptions that underly the use of standardized tools. Information can be shared with colleagues, managers, and service users, in order to help them make informed choices about how to best make use of standardized assessments in our care work.

As corporate interests increasingly occupy the local and global spaces of health and social services, it becomes more imperative that I learn how to de-mystify and unmap these processes. Unmapping allows me to see where and how I am implicated in the often-hidden production of unequal social relations. Unmapping gives me critical knowledge for speaking out. It motivates me to resist the corporate occupation of my profession. It brings home the urgency of building solidarities with social justice movements both locally and globally, here and elsewhere, places that I previously would have assumed to have little in common with my practice of social work in primary health care in Hamilton, Ontario, Canada.

Notes

*   I offer warm thanks and recognition for contributions made by Dr. Jane Aronson, Dr. Kari Dehli, and Vilma Rossi to earlier drafts of this chapter. Parts of this paper were originally presented at a CASE/CASW forum on May 24, 2008, called "Occupied spaces: Exploring the historical and social significance of the spaces where we live

and work," Canadian Association of Schools of Social Work, Toronto.

1. A copy of the PHQ-9 is available for viewing online at <www.depression-primarycare. org/clinicians/toolkits/materials/forms/phq9/questionnaire_sample/>.

2. Doreen is a pseudonym and the case example provided here represents a compilation of events and circumstances from different patients' lives.

3. I am grateful for the critical knowledge and commentary shared by Dr. Linda Muzzin and Linda Green during the development stage of this chapter.

Chapter 13

Crossing Boundaries to Radicalize Social Work Practice and Education

Notisha Massaquoi

This chapter discusses three experiences in which AOP theorizing required further development. The author argues
that close analysis of moments, such as those she describes
in this chapter, provide rich opportunities to expand practice
and theory. The author uses the image of border crossings to
explore and explain the ways that people resist being "kept
in their place" and the role resistance should play in everyday
social work practice, theory, and education.

As you read through this chapter, ask yourself the following
questions:
1. How does the author describe the concept of a transformative moment?
2. Why does the author believe that transformative moments
   can be used to develop theory, practice, and knowledge?
3. What kinds of borders does the author encounter in the
   three examples, and how does she tie these to issues of
   oppression and resistance?

Within the field of Canadian social work, the term "anti-oppressive practice"
(AOP) is generally understood as a framework or perspective that embraces social
justice initiatives. AOP can also be defined as an umbrella term for liberatory
frameworks such as structural, radical, and critical social work practice as well
as anti-racist and feminist practices (Dominelli 1994; Leonard 2001; Moreau
1993; Carniol 2000; Chambon 1994). AOP seeks to transform existing forms
of social work knowledge into alternative ways of knowing and engaging in
practice. The term "transform" indicates a change-oriented practice that engages
with the specific political agenda of far-reaching social liberation. The goals of
this agenda are to disrupt, overturn, and reconstruct oppressive values, definitions, policies, institutions, and relationships.

The project of transforming social work needs to focus on change at three
levels: knowledge and theory; education; and practice. This chapter will discuss

> **Practice Knowledge**
> This type of knowledge is generated by people in the frontlines of social activity undertaking a particular activity or endeavour. In the case of social work, practice knowledge is generated by those working in frontline social work practice. Practice knowledge is influenced by theory, but it is also the testing ground for the relevance and usefulness of theory. Practice knowledge also generates its own beginning theorizations and critical questions.

overlapping changes in these areas in the context of three moments or scenarios in which it was clear that my AOP theorizing required further refinement and development. I will argue that moments in which AOP theory and practice are found to be inadequate are some of the most important opportunities we have for developing and refining practice.

Indeed, if we never put our theories into practice, we can rest content that they address every practice situation. However, if we actually engage in the struggle of using AOP in our practice, we risk discovering that some of our theories and practices are problematic. Rather than moments of abject failure, these are moments in which practice knowledge emerges, highlighting changes that need to be made and opening possibilities for new and more transformative ways of understanding oppression and liberation. In this process, theory and practice development are interlocked — one feeds directly into the other. As Figure 13.1 shows and as I will discuss throughout this chapter, making the link back to social work education and knowledge building completes the circle.

When we look at transforming social work education, for example, we often talk about exclusion, forced inclusion, and the disconnection between theory and practice. Transforming social work education involves changes not only

Figure 13.1 The Circle of AOP Practice and Theory

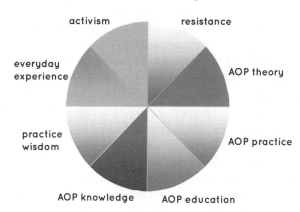

in the structure of the educational process and the institutions within which education takes place, but also in how social work and social workers function in the field. It involves acts of resistance at multiple levels on the part of social workers, educators, and students. Resistance requires us to act and live in opposition to oppressive forces. Resistance sometimes means that we will have to challenge ourselves and others in ways that may make us uncomfortable; it also requires us to redistribute the power and privileges many of us enjoy on the backs of marginalized groups. Resistance also means that we have to use our lives, our experiences, and our struggles to develop strategies to withstand and eliminate oppression.

Acts of resistance and the development of alternative ways of knowing can empower social workers to develop practices that help people overcome their marginalized status within the larger oppressive society. Practitioners can be considered to be "doing" AOP not only when they include resistance into their social work practice but also when they interrogate how dominant forms of knowledge affect service users and frontline workers and when they question how such knowledge is passed on to students. With respect to individual transformation, AOP makes many connections. For example, between the self; its ability to endure, reflect, and be a catalyst for change; the ability of the transformative experience to inform practice, teaching, and empowerment with others; and the capacity to question existing knowledge with the end goal of building better knowledge, theory, and practice. In short, in order to reach its liberatory potential, AOP must link education, practice, and theory, and it must use frontline experience as an important source of practice wisdom and resistance.

Throughout this chapter I use the image of border crossing to explore and explain aspects of the experience of resisting social roles, structures, identities, and expectations that limit marginalized people and keep them "in their place." Moving beyond restrictive relations involves breaking boundaries or crossing real and symbolic borders. The image of a border crossing helps me to understand the emotional, organizational, and political impacts of these crossings. For Carol Boyce Davies (1994), borders are places where different cultures, identities, sexualities, classes, geographies, races, and genders collide or interchange. As Gloria Anzaldua's (1999) work reveals, the concept of borders generates a complex knowledge of subtle identities that should not be generalized. Canadians saw this play out in May 2009 when Suaad Hagi Mohamud, a Somali Canadian woman, tried to board her flight home to Canada after a three-week visit with her ailing mother in Kenya. She was denied access to the flight because airline officials did not think that she resembled her four-year-old passport photo closely enough, an opinion later shared by Canadian officials. When Mohamud sought assistance from the Canadian High Commission in Kenya she was branded an imposter and was turned over to the Kenyan authorities, who jailed her for a week and voided her passport. After being detained for three months in Kenya, she was finally exonerated by DNA testing and allowed to return to Canada. This story highlights how borders reproduce particular meanings assigned to certain people's bodies (in Mohmaud's case, meanings associated with Islamophobia, racism, and illegal immigration were imposed by authorities); borders are also places where such tensions can be examined in their full complexity.

Shifting Paradigms and Transformative Moments

Mainstream social work has historically focused on assisting, integrating, and reconstructing those living in the margins (Howe 1987; Figueira-McDonough et al 2002; Alperin et al 2001). Through the mainstream social work "helping" process, oppressed people were often objectified and repeatedly scrutinized so that they could be understood and assisted within existing systems. In contrast, anti-oppressive social work practice recognizes that world reality is defined through daily experiences of systemic oppression, including racism, sexism, homophobia, ageism, ableism, classism, and so forth, as they interact in the structural levels of society. These experiences are at the centre of my existence and my analysis, both professionally and personally. I try to use them to challenge oppressive dominant culture and oppressive forces that aim to negate my existence. Since oppression shapes everyone's reality in this society, we can often use our own lives as evidence that the dominant view is flawed. By using our own lives, experiences, and self definitions we can validate our existence and experience, while claiming the right to interpret our reality (Kondrat 1999). For example, by living and existing contrary to the negative portrayals of members of Black communities created by white society, we undermine the legitimacy of such claims. This process of self-definition is an effective tool for social change (Campbell and Ungar 2003).

Replacing the dominant culture's images with our own is an essential component in the struggle to resist knowledge systems that create race, gender, sexuality, and class oppression. We need to understand not only how power is held over oppressed groups, but also how to empower others to seek alternative strategies that challenge the status quo. Self exploration is key to doing this. I find that understanding, focusing on, and sharing my experiences with others is at times difficult, but also empowering. Self exploration highlights for me the fact that the most effective means of resistance can come from my own identity and from struggles, opportunities, and barriers that society puts in front of me because of my identity.

Objectification

Objectification refers to a process in which a group or individual is treated like an object or a thing without regard to the complexity of the person's or group's lived experiences in the world and the context in which they occur.

> ### Transformative Disruptions
> This term refers to identity-based experiences in which the individual experiences high tension, confusion, frustration, emotional pain, and/or self doubt. These moments can either stall or halt the learning process, or alternatively provide the opportunity for intense, vivid learning, pushing practice knowledge to a new, critical, and important level.

The following personal accounts explore the concept of using individual experiences, as well as the often painstaking exploration and analysis of those experiences, as sources of knowledge and insight. These experiences often reveal fledgling practice that can be nurtured and applied to other situations. This is an important source of knowledge, known as "practice knowledge," or the wisdom that practitioners develop from their experiences in everyday practice. These accounts also examine the relationship between AOP practice, identity-based experience, and the new knowledge that can result from moments of tension or intense learning that I call "transformative disruptions." In my years as a social work practitioner and educator I have experienced many moments of intense emotional pain, frustration, and self-doubt.

That this type of experience seems to be part of the process of working from AOP and other radical perspectives has been confirmed by other social workers. Transformative disruptions are moments in which one's world threatens to come crashing down, but they simultaneously hold the promise of vivid learning, pushing practice knowledge to a new level. I present three such moments in the hope that they will encourage us to step beyond existing borders around knowledge and practice in order to continue to build AOP's liberatory capacity.

Transformative Disruption #1: We Are Africans First

I was a new M.S.W. graduate working for an African AIDS organization in a large Canadian metropolitan city. It was the mid-1990s and we were grossly under-resourced, under-staffed, and overworked. African communities in Canada had the highest rates of new HIV infections in the country, and the AIDS epidemic within these communities was accelerating rapidly (Tharao et al. 2002). Most clients reached us when they were diagnosed with full-blown AIDS, and most died within eight months of accessing services. Black community members comprised only 4 percent of the population of Ontario, but they comprised 20 percent of the AIDS diagnoses in 2001 and 70 percent of the Mother to Child HIV transmission between 1994 and 1996 (Tharao et al 2006). This was partly because community members had limited and inaccurate knowledge about HIV/AIDS modes of transmission and prevention, as well as limited access to HIV/AIDS information and related services. Compounding this was their frequent experience of racism and cultural discrimination at the hands of service providers, which led to mistrust of the system. Stress caused by the immigration process (accessing housing, education, employment, and language training) reduced people's capacity to pursue their healthcare needs. Further barriers were created by cultural and religious stigma and discrimination related to HIV/AIDS, cultural taboos about homosexuality, and limited discussion about sexuality and the use of condoms (Tharao et al. 2002 and 2006).

I decided to use my newly acquired social work tools to "save" my community by initiating an HIV/AIDS education and outreach campaign targeting African communities in the city. These campaigns had been effective with other high-risk groups such as the white gay male population; I hoped that they would be easily transferable to the larger African community. I arranged to launch this campaign at the largest African cultural event in Canada held yearly in Toronto. A booth was set up early in the morning on day one of the two-day event where we made available brochures and pamphlets in many African languages and we displayed condoms, posters, t-shirts, and other resources. The volunteers assisting me at the event were all female since I could not convince any men to volunteer. This was possibly a sign of things to come.

The day started out slowly but we were extremely committed to the issue and very excited and energetic. We felt that things would improve by the afternoon. However, people avoided our booth; they refused to look at us. People would not take the condoms. We tried talking to people, but we were ignored. People called us whores and a disgrace to the community. Someone shouted "lesbians"; another person spit on the ground in front of us as he passed by. Day two of the event was more of the same. I and several volunteers took the full force of shame, stigma, denial, ageism, sexism, homophobia, and internalized racism. It was one of the most humiliating experiences in my career as a social worker. I realized in that moment that my newly acquired social work skills were useless for me as an African working in a diasporic African context. It was a transformative disruption.

A transformative disruption is so powerful that it freezes you with overwhelming emotion. It can either shatter you or transform you. It is that moment where there is no theory to save you. It is that moment when you have to decide whether this experience will move you forward and transform your practice or silence you. As anti-oppressive practitioners we must learn to address our failures to create adequate models for radical change in everyday life. Indeed, as I learned from this experience, it is easier than one would think to bump into scenarios in which we do not have interventions or strategies that have meaning and significance to other people. Until we construct such models, the anti-oppressive movement will not have the revolutionary impact to transform self and society (hooks 1995). Instead, it will remain a set of practices that reinforce oppressive ways of understanding and acting upon social and individual problems.

I am not telling this story to open a discussion on effective ways to work with African communities. Nor am I claiming that I simply forgot that African people remain culturally African, with all their socio-cultural practices and beliefs, even after they immigrate to Canada, and that African-based social work strategies are therefore needed to reach diasporic communities. As I noted elsewhere,

> [T]he African Diaspora is an environment that fosters the invention of tradition, ethnicity, kinship and other identity markers. It is a place where multiple African communities become a monolithic entity and ethnic differences are replaced with national pride. It is the place where it becomes more advantageous to identify with the homogenous group ... as opposed to ethnic or national identities; and regional differences become less important than our shared experience of immigration, racism and search for belonging in Canadian society. (Massaquoi 2004: 4)

Major western cities are becoming extensions of other home communities and are increasingly less exclusively Western; thus AOP grounded solely in Western social work practices is less useful. Incorporating elements of transnationalism into practice frameworks requires a critical engagement with a "global-local" binary. In this discussion I am not just grappling with a critique of a universal African subjectivity or the African resistance to Western sexual politics in the traditional sense of Amadiume (1997). Instead, I am addressing the emergence of new forms of cultural regulatory practices and strategies that control community members' sexuality within a specific location based on power and definitions of sexuality within that location.

Historically, "local" and "community" were thought to be synonymous. Communities were seen as defining the local and were formed in place (Massey 1994). With the rise of transnationalism, however, communities are on the move, and it is no longer accurate to consider place to be central to their formation. To engage with the notion of an African identity is, according to Cooper (2001), to engage with and appreciate the long-term impact of power across space, the relevance of links between old (colonial) and new (global), and the importance and boundedness of long-distance connections. In a transnational framework of movement and exchange, cultural identities are nonetheless imbued with power relations.

Transnationalism is theoretically significant to the discussion of AOP since oppression is intimately experienced but constructed and constrained within geographic boundaries. I am interrogating the notion that the search for identity, community, and security in Canada by African people is shaped by resistance to oppression within the host country and country of origin. It is also shaped through the act of navigating between two cultures, effecting change in two

Eurocentric Theories

Eurocentric theories refer to theories and knowledge based on and, generally, advantaging the peoples and societies emerging from Europe. Eurocentric theories tend to operate in a hegemonic manner so that it is believed they represent "truth" and the best knowledge, rather than one particular form of knowledge that, often, disadvantages, marginalizes or excludes knowledges from other places and perspectives.

cultures and supporting systems and structures in two often divergent cultural contexts. We need to consider not only how we, as social workers, facilitate acceptance and belonging, but also the larger narrative of how African subjects negotiate their identities and politics across diasporas.

I am primarily arguing that experience and practice should push theory to explain our everyday life and experiences. Prior to my experience with the HIV/AIDS outreach campaign I had no need to push AOP theory to explore how to work with diasporic African communities or to develop practice approaches specific to HIV in African diasporic communities. Suddenly, my need for theory and practice methods was extreme. My first reaction was to denounce social work theory as inherently Western and colonial, flawed in its inability to provide adequate tools for those working in non-western cultures and an impediment to social care and activism. Many have critiqued Eurocentric theories for the way they erase and marginalize the experiences of communities of colour (Razack 1998; Essed 1990; hooks 1990; Dei 1996). However, such critiques were insufficient to explain my experiences. Instead my critique began to focus on the following points:

1. The importance of activist practices is central to AOP and we need to theorize them as a central part of an AOP agenda. This includes activist practices associated with public education and consciousness raising, such as those I was trying to use at the African cultural event.
2. In order for the field of social work to address the needs of people in the African diaspora, AOP needs to draw on the rich tradition of Indigenous practice knowledge and theory that has assisted in the survival of African communities under a range of experiences of colonialism, neo-colonialism and the current HIV/AIDS epidemic (Wane, 2002).
3. As people of colour in the Western and non-Western world, we have contributed significantly to theorizing not only by writing theory but also by pushing for these theories to be integrated into social work practice. In terms of the intersections of race, class, gender and other oppressions, we have also participated in activism that has challenged these multiple oppressions. In some sense, sites of activism can be seen as a crucial stage in the development of theories as it is often where we and how we test our

theories. A closer integration of intersectional approaches and testing theory in activism would strengthen this radical social work model.

In other words, just as diasporic people have crossed borders to build new lives, so, too, must AOP cross knowledge and practice borders to decolonize and expand its liberatory potential.

The separation of reason and emotion in most mainstream theorizing makes it difficult to incorporate experiences or examples of activism that are full of emotion. Indeed, in mainstream social work practice, emotion is often pitted against reason while the experiential is pitted against theory. From a mainstream perspective one cannot be emotional and reasonable at the same time. However, oppression and matters of the oppressed are emotionally charged and cannot be understood in their fullness if emotion is removed. One of AOP's challenges is to develop ways to use intensely emotional experiences as opportunities for reflection, self criticism, and extending theory and practice. Otherwise, moments like the one above will remain as painful memories rather than the starting point for important thinking about the changing realities of urban practice and the role that practice experience, theory, and knowledge from the Global South must play in the development of AOP.

As I recall this transformative disruption, I realize that the recounting of a story has the potential to empower the writer and may also impact readers who have similar realities and experiences. This story highlights the personal risk and sacrifices we have to make in order to secure social change. Readers may be able to relate to the feelings of emotional upheaval, isolation, lack of understanding on the part of peers, and the enormous amount of energy required to critically analyze transformative disruptions. Those of us in positions of privilege and opportunity in the social work world must responsibly create spaces in which transformative disruptions can be debriefed, analyzed, and incorporated into teaching, practice, and theory. In this way, we create a voice not only for our own experience but also for the voiceless, such as those who may need services but cannot access them for fear of social isolation and further marginalization.

Separation of Reason and Emotion

Western knowledge assumes that reason and emotion are very different and can be completely separated from each other. Western scientific thought claims to be objective, free of emotion, and superior, in most ways, to emotion and processes incorporating or acknowledging emotion. Alternative perspectives assert that emotion can never be entirely separated from reason. Moreover, emotion offers an important buffer to reason, while the unity of emotion and reason provides an excellent testing ground for new knowledge and an area in which new knowledge is constantly generated.

Transformative Disruption #2:
So You Think You Are a Professor?

In this encounter, I was teaching for the first time in a faculty of social work, and ironically the course was anti-oppressive social work practice. As far as I could tell, the students had no problem accepting me as their professor, despite the advice I received from seasoned colleagues who warned me about difficulties I may encounter as a Black professor teaching a predominantly white student body. It was, on the contrary, an extremely positive experience for me and the students. My transformative disruption came in both incremental and sudden moments from the wider university community outside my department and classroom. First, there were numerous incidents of what I would call "non-acceptance" as a faculty member. For example, when trying to obtain a faculty identification card during the first week of classes I was asked to step out of the staff and faculty line and join the student line on the other side of the room. Attempting to put books on reserve in the library, booking audio visual equipment, and borrowing resources were extremely difficult because the university staff found it hard to conceive of me as a professor. Despite having the proper faculty identification, I was often required to produce pieces of identification in addition to my faculty card. I was often informed that only the professor could do this or that and I was repeatedly asked who my professor was. There were countless experiences of non-acceptance, of marking me, disciplining me, keeping me in a place historically defined for Black women and out of a place historically not defined for, or by, Black women.

Then, close to the end of the term, the classroom door opened and an older white woman, clearly another professor, first peeked in and than boldly walked to the front of the room as I was in mid-sentence. She asked, "Where is the professor?" I replied, "That would be me, can I help you?" Her expression did not hide her shock. She rudely stated, "Oh, I just needed to borrow some chalk." I fought off the personal feelings of humiliation that racism brought up (or was it ageism, or an intersection of the two?). I decided that I would deal with it when I stepped across the border of the classroom back into my personal life. I continued teaching, picking up where I left off, despite the distress I saw in many of the students' eyes. I was caught off guard, and I was unable to address the incident in the moment. That would have to wait until next week.

Using a process of self-exploration, rather than simply rage against the marginalization I felt within the university, I used this incident to think about the messages I was receiving. Although hired to fill the position of professor, I felt that various levels of the institution were telling me not to cross the borders marking university life from the non-academic life Black women are often relegated to in Canada. When I crossed that border, I was constantly reminded that I was in the wrong place, playing the wrong role. At the risk of sounding clichéd, the "personal is political" in an AOP framework. When I look at myself as a Black Queer African Immigrant Woman, I find numerous times in my life when I encountered borders of acceptable and unacceptable ways of being in the world. This was just one more of many, but it was nonetheless painful. Borders create arbitrary dividing lines that are social, cultural, and psychic. As in my example, borders are often patrolled in order to make sure we keep certain people out — those whom we construct as outsiders and "others" (Brah 1996). Borders are also places where claims of ownership and belonging are staked out, contested, defended, and fought over.

According to Chandra Mohanty (1998), as women of color we need to reflect on the process of moving between different "configurations of meaning and power," which prompt different modes of knowing. The politics of border crossings as Black women brings forward a whole host of identifications and associations around concepts of displacement, dis-location, dismemberment, alienness, boundaries, barriers, and peripheries (Davies 1994). AOP needs to address our geographic, historical, social, economic and educational positions as well as societal positions based on class, gender sexuality, age, and income. AOP also needs to be about emotional reactions and how we are able or not able to access, mediate, or reposition ourselves, or pass into other spaces given oppressive circumstances. Although it is very difficult at times, by recounting deeply personal experiences I can define myself while at the same time challenge the dichotomous nature of the dominant culture. Knowledge in that sphere is hierarchical and value-laden. It is, as I suggested earlier, a sphere in which emotion is pitted against reason and the experiential against the theoretical (Massaquoi 2000). From this perspective one cannot be emotional and reasonable at the same time. But racism and matters of race are emotionally charged, meaning that what I and many other Black women in academia face is the negation of our personal accounts of gendered racism, which are considered to be without merit or reason. An AOP practitioner should question how experiences can be understood if the emotional component of the story is removed: Would this not render it useless in the construction of knowledge by those who experience discrimination daily (Essed 1990)? If I, as a Black woman, in the context of my vignette cannot be conceived as a credible speaker by my colleagues, then how will my writing or theorizing about anti-oppression be taken up by these same colleagues?

As AOP practitioners we need to question how academic borders are regulated or policed, including those in schools of social work. Who is kept out and why? What are the realities for those stigmatized as undesirable border-crossers, and what happens to those bold enough to cross? Some of these realities include the experience of being anti-oppressive practitioners in a white, patriarchal institution or individuals proclaiming a gay or lesbian identity in a social context saturated with homophobia and heterosexism. Borders are those places where different cultures, identities, sexualities, classes, geographies, races, and genders collide or interchange — like a classroom where a young, Black woman teaching a social work course to relatively satisfied white students is repeatedly challenged by white professors, support staff, and administrators. These representatives of the university repeatedly reflect disbelief — sometimes mild, sometimes major — about the fact that she is filling the role of professor. The experiences described above highlight that people from marginalized groups can be re-marginalized and delegitimized even when filling relatively privileged roles, even in relatively progressive institutions. Practitioners and clients from marginalized groups report similar experiences within the relatively progressive borders of social service agencies. An understanding of borders and other mechanisms regulating the distribution of power can help us to trace how people displaying certain characteristics (also known as aspects of identity) must fight for the access, respect, dignity, and power that dominant groups can simply expect.

Foucault (1995) argues that the concept of discipline requires enclosure in a protected place. Classrooms and academic institutions can be viewed as spaces enclosed by protected borders. These borders are created and maintained with unwritten policies. Discipline, in part, works by dividing people vis-a-vis space, rank, or power. These kinds of divisions limited my movement as a visibly Black woman in the academic institution and disciplined me through repeated messages that I could not be a professor. I came to know myself as a Black woman in academia when I encountered these academic borders and had difficulty crossing them. I also became aware of myself as an outsider through my continued experience of non-acceptance, even when it appeared that I had successfully crossed the borders and taught a well-received course on AOP. While disturbing, this experience caused me to rethink the way that various kinds of borders and barriers restrict service users and communities while privileging others. It also helped me think about how to use such moments to teach students about everyday racism and oppression.

Transformative Disruption #3: The Name Game

In this scenario, I had returned to Sierra Leone after a fifteen-year separation from family and from the country of my birth during a civil war. "What is your name?" a teller asked me as I attempted to make a bank transaction. "M-A-S-S-A-Q-U-O-I," I replied. "I can spell," the bank teller snapped. I was very embarrassed. Of course she could spell Massaquoi. It is a common name in Sierra Leone. I insulted her with what was probably perceived as my Western arrogance. However, I had spent most of my life in Canada having to spell my name, spell out my identity, so that now when asked, I don't even say it — I just automatically spell it letter by letter in order to end this kind of interaction as quickly as possible. Otherwise, I tend to end up listening to poor attempts at pronunciation and misspelling, as well as answering questions such as "very unusual, where are you from?" Usually, if the conversation gets this far, I end

> ### Pluralism
> Pluralism refers to the notion that society consists of various ethnic, political, and religious groups with equal access to power, resources, and affirming identities. The role of government is to adjudicate their competing claims. This framework ignores differences that are woven into our social, economic, cultural, and political systems and that are shaped by and reproduced by race, gender, class, disability, and so forth.

up explaining where Sierra Leone — not Surinam, not Senegal, not Sri Lanka — is in the world. This is often followed by a fifteen-minute discussion of how and when I got here and why. The last five minutes of the interaction is routinely spent with me being praised for my wonderful English. Learning to navigate these very diasporic transactions creates tension within my adopted home. In the scenario above, it also created distance and disconnection from my original home country and made me wonder how to cope with these kinds of multiple realities.

In recounting this moment, I realized that crossing national borders from my adopted home to my home of birth meant my sense of who I was and how I had to defend and define myself to others had shifted. I no longer had to assume that I was the "other." Instead, I was surrounded by people who were very familiar with my last name. I no longer stood out as one of the few people of colour in any crowd and could expect a certain level of acceptance for my appearance and achievements. However, having lived most of my life in Canada also meant that I no longer completely fit in with my old life in my country of birth; in fact, I may have seemed like a western snob when I spelled my name out for the teller. The ability to reflect and theorize these complex and disruptive moments helps me to understand who I understand myself to be, how I understand my social work practice, and how I can use self and practice to develop anti-oppressive theory. Indeed, moments like these helped me to begin to theorize identity and its centrality in disruptive and transformative moments.

Anyone who has immersed themselves in a culture other than their own will be confronted, at some point, with fundamental questions regarding their own identity. Identity is a central component of resistance. Affirming identities give energy for resistance, while negative messages about aspects of identities can deplete one's capacity for struggle. A critical sense of one's identity can be attained through an ongoing process of self exploration as well as a sense of one's social position vis-à-vis others. In the ongoing task of building a critical identity, the AOP social worker might ask, who are we as anti-oppressive practitioners? How do we articulate the forces that shape our lives? What are the spaces we can shape and occupy? And how do our identities shift and transform as we cross borders from activism and work in the community and go into the classroom?

Table 13-1 Transformative Moments Challenge AOP

Vignette	Transformative Moment	Challenge to AOP
HIV education for a diasporic community	My social work skills prove useless	Draw on non-western knowledge and practices; attune to non-western realities
Legitimacy as a professor challenged	I am undermined by a fellow professor; my privileges fail to protect me from oppression	Develop practices and theory that challenge exclusions, even among those who appear "safe" from oppression
Spelling out my last name	My identity shifts as I cross international borders	Help people to negotiate situations where identities and the oppressions associated with them suddenly change

Given the global context of migration and increasing levels of international work and travel, anti-oppressive theory and practice needs to explore how anti-oppressive practitioners negotiate their identities and politics across changing places, times, and spaces. Exploring identity in a critical way that connects to social struggles and change rather than a pluralist manner is difficult work. We must foster practices that attempt to carry out the intensely difficult and emotional anti-oppressive interrogation of one's own and other's experiences and interventions. The very act of theorizing about the identity and resistance strategies of oneself as an anti-oppressive practitioner, whether we are ourselves members of oppressed groups or allies in our daily actions, can create alternative spaces which empower us as individuals and as members of communities (Bishop 1994).

Rethinking AOP

These vignettes were moments that offered me the opportunity to rethink AOP. They also emphasized the continuous link between practice moments, practice knowledge, formal knowledge, theory, and critical social work education. This relationship needs to continuously feed into itself if AOP is to be socially grounded in the struggles and challenges of the communities we serve, as well as link our critical and shared understanding of the current situations to transformative and socially just social work practice. In many ways, this is a process of breaking down the borders that separate knowledge, practice, everyday experience, and theory. This involves a rewriting of the traditional split between reason and emotion so that highly charged emotional moments become the spark for analysis, theorizing, and practice methods. This approach ensures that the experience of marginalized people and their communities finds its way into AOP and remains central to its endeavours.

My aim in engaging in this discussion is to kick-start critical thought into taking seriously the issues posed to anti-oppressive practitioners by changing social conditions globally and in Canada. Part of this challenge involves ways of recognizing the importance of transformative disruptions and the self-exploration that needs to go on after pivotal incidents in order to push theory and practice forward in ways that are linked to the constantly changing realities of social life. It also means creating a space within anti-oppressive practice to articulate and act and end our silence and speak our truths about oppression as we know them. The goal of this work is to provide us with the power to remove structures that threaten our potential for human growth and to remove the barriers that blind us from understanding the possibility of a life free from oppression.

Chapter 14

A Resettlement Story of Unsettlement

Transformative Practices of Taking It Personally

Martha Kuwee Kumsa

This chapter reflects the resettlement experiences of Oromo refugee women in Toronto. More than a story of resettlement, however, it is a story of profound unsettlement. It presents the transformative disruption of settled beliefs, ideas, and identities. It also suggests ways for anti-oppressive practitioners to use moments of disappointment as a jumping-off point for new theorizing and critical practice.

As you read through this chapter, ask yourself the following questions:
1. How were multiple oppressions and privilege operating within the scenario discussed in this chapter?
2. Can "taking it personally" help us to identify ways to improve practice and theory?
3. What does the author mean by essentialist AOP, and how does she think it can be avoided?

Historical Background

In this chapter, I will share with you an incident that marks a sharp turning point in my life as an anti-oppressive community practitioner. My discovery of anti-oppressive practice (AOP) in social work came later in life. I know that, in time, AOP will become second nature, a settled way of life for some practitioners. For many of us, however, it is a process of ongoing struggle and discovery. AOP is interpreted and practiced differently by different people across time and space. Here I will share with you the evolution of my AOP — that is, AOP as *I* understand and practice it. I am an Oromo, and my AOP is deeply rooted in the Oromo people's struggle for national liberation. I have been an activist in this struggle all my politically conscious life.

Oromos are a people in the Horn of Africa, spreading beyond colonial

> ## Oromo
> Oromos are a people in the Horn of Africa, spreading beyond colonial boundaries and inhabiting Ethiopia, Kenya, and Somalia. Our ancestors were renowned for their *gada*, an egalitarian socio-political system (Baxter and Almagor 1978; Knutsson 1967; Legesse 1973 and 2000). Oromos live in the most fertile and mineral-rich parts of the Horn of Africa. While they are considered minority ethnic groups in Kenya and Somalia, Oromos constitute more than half of Ethiopia's approximately eighty-five million people.

boundaries and inhabiting Ethiopia, Kenya, and Somalia. Our ancestors were renowned for their *gada,* an egalitarian socio-political system (Baxter and Almagor 1978; Knutsson 1967; Legesse 1973 and 2000). Oromos live in the most fertile and mineral-rich parts of the Horn of Africa. While they are considered minority ethnic groups in Kenya and Somalia, Oromos constitute more than half of Ethiopia's current population of approximately eighty-five million.

This is more than the present population of Canada! However, despite their numerical majority, their *gada* egalitarian culture, and their wealth of resources, in terms of power Oromos are relegated to a politically dominated, culturally degraded, and economically exploited minority status in Ethiopia. This dehumanizing situation can be traced back to European colonization of Africa, a process that empowered the Amhara minority ethnic group and created a dependent colonial state in Ethiopia. Most of the Oromo population was incorporated into the Ethiopian empire through colonial aggression in the latter half of the nineteenth century (Hassen 1990; Holcomb and Ibssa 1990; Jalata 1993; Melba 1988). A century of resistance to colonial oppression led to the birth of the Oromo national liberation struggle. We are presently in the process of reclaiming our egalitarian *gada* and rewriting our history through the macro-level AOP of our national liberation struggle.

The Oromo struggle was launched as part and parcel of the global upheaval of the 1960s. This was a revolutionary period: civil rights, anti-war, women's liberation, gay-lesbian liberation, black power, and red power movements flourished in many western countries at the same time as anti-colonial and anti-imperial national liberation movements flourished in Africa, Asia, and South America. Coming of age in Ethiopia in the late 1960s, I experienced

> ## Diaspora
> Diaspora refers to the breaking up and scattering of people far from their ancestral homes. The term is generally used to describe groups that have been forcibly moved, such as the Black diaspora, which was facilitated by the slave trade and later colonialization of Africa.

> ### Totalitarian Repression
> Totalitarian oppression refers to complete oppression perpetrated on a group of people or area. Democratic participation and dissent are not permitted under totalitarian rule or regimes, although resistance, carried out at great risk, is always present in one form or another.

revolution in the air I breathed. To my youthful revolutionary eyes, the global world was divided into two mutually-exclusive camps, the East and the West. The West was capitalist, colonialist, and imperialist. It was the enemy camp. The East was socialist, anti-colonialist, and anti-imperialist. It was a friendly camp. My local world was similarly divided into two mutually exclusive camps, oppressors and oppressed. I was unequivocally on the side of the oppressed. As the great East/West divide of the Cold War collapsed on me in 1989, however, my little oppressed/oppressor world turned upside down, turning my friend/enemy camp inside out. I found myself in the heart of the enemy camp, running away from friends who had become enemies. I came to the West as a resettled refugee, eventually making Canada my newest home.

Oromo refugees started trickling into Canada in the latter half of the 1980s, when Ethiopia's military regime intensified its totalitarian repression of the Oromo liberation struggle, resulting in a huge exodus of Oromo refugees. Those who survived the atrocities and fled the country joined the Oromo diaspora (Bulcha 1988 and 2002), a group of people who live in exile, hoping to return home one day. Oromos who were resettled in Canada formed Oromo-Canadian community associations. Like many diasporic groups, they tackled issues of adjustment and resettlement on the one hand and long-distance national liberation struggle on the other. I continued my AOP in this now-transnational community, focusing mainly on gender issues and facilitating Oromo women's groups in the diaspora. The Oromo struggle for liberation continues in this era of heightened globalization (Lata 1998, 1999, and 2004). The terms colonialism and imperialism turned stale on my tongue, replaced and euphemized by "globalization." Yet, I continued to situate myself firmly on the side of the downtrodden and the struggle for equity and social justice. Wherever I lived, I thought I always fought for the liberation of the oppressed masses — until, one day, an incident utterly disrupted my very notion of oppression and liberation.

Facing the Oppressor

In the early 1990s, though normally under-resourced, Toronto's Oromo-Canadian Community Association received a bit more government funding for programs, enabling us to run workshops about such issues as violence against women and basic skills training for Oromo women. Many women started get-

> ### Women's Multiple Jeopardy
> Women's multiple jeopardy refers to the double or triple day that most women assume when they take on paid work outside the home; unpaid care work in the home; and unpaid, often unrecognized, advocacy, volunteer or activist work in the community. This compounded and often invisible workload can leave women feeling exhausted and exploited.

ting jobs that were considered menial and were unacceptable to some men. No amount of employment counselling could produce the decent jobs some men sought, but many Oromo women took whatever jobs were available. A reversal of gender roles thus started in the Oromo community. Back in the homeland, it was mostly women who stayed at home, while those who worked outside the home had several helpers for care work. Here, many women became the breadwinners for their families while many men stayed at home. However, their breadwinner status did not save the women from the multiple jeopardy that plagued other poor working women — working full time outside the home only to plunge headfirst into full-time care work at home. Most men did not readily cross the gender taboo line to care for children or cook for their families. Those who stayed at home spent their days watching TV; frustrated by the lack of access to decent jobs, some vented their anger on women. Others went back to school to upgrade their skills while women's efforts to go to school were constantly interrupted. Taking the brunt of society's violence, many women were trapped in abusive homes, burning their candles at both ends to provide for their families.

Without the liberation of women there is no liberation for the nation. That was the AOP motto of the Oromo liberation struggle back in the homeland. Indeed the AOP goal of Oromo liberation was to end *all* forms of oppression. The leaders —all men — paid lip service to women's liberation, although I had to challenge them to practice what they preached.[1] Community elders in the Oromo diaspora repeated this dictum, placing women's emancipation at the heart of Oromo liberation, but this too remained a largely empty rhetoric. Despite this, Oromo women actively organized in their countries of resettlement as they had in their homeland and in refugee camps. Toronto's Oromo-Canadian Women's Organization was the result of our movement to end gender oppression and bring about our own emancipation together with the liberation of our people. I continued to hone my AOP skills in exile through my active participation in this process. As a transnational community, we live in the margins of one country with our deeper longings firmly rooted in another. When I say living in the margins, I mean being excluded from the mainstream centre and squeezed into the periphery. Inhabiting the margins of both countries, then, Oromo women mobilized scant resources to deal with issues of adjustment and resettlement here in Canada and to support the liberation of our people back in the homeland. We looked to each other for solidarity. The commitment to liberation and social justice became our deepest spiritual bond. We met regularly to maintain our tight bonds and to discuss issues from here and from afar that continued to impact our mundane lives so deeply. In these meetings, we found space to vent our frustrations and to support each other emotionally and materially. The issue of women's multiple jeopardy and how to deal with it came up at almost every meeting until one day it exploded in our faces.

The Incident

For several years, women complained about being utterly overworked and about men who were not helping with the care work at home. However, this issue was regularly pushed to the back burner by other issues of survival, such as learning English and making new social ties. "But this *is* an issue of survival!" I remember protesting that day. "Until when shall we stay quiet and watch our sisters die?" said another woman, thrusting the issue of violence into the forefront. "Maybe some of us have bruised faces and broken arms! Maybe we're just too ashamed to come and face the rest of us!" said a second woman. "Just look how many of us are here today!" said a third woman, getting up and counting us. "Less than half of us!" she said, throwing herself down on the chair. "And look how many of us are leaving already," said a fourth woman, getting up and summoning others to leave with her. Several more women left because they had urgent chores to finish before they went to their night-shift jobs. We had been waiting to start the "real" meeting for over an hour, not an unusual event. It was hard to judge the best time for optimum attendance, since women had varying work schedules and came and left at different times. Sometimes husbands would not let women come to the meetings at all. At other times, husbands refused to stay home with sick children. However, waiting was never an empty time. It was a valued time when a lot of informal venting and support work took place. Some women came just for that precious moment of comforting care.

That day, a few more women joined us at the end of the commotion and the meeting went on as scheduled. We shelved the agenda, however, and continued the spontaneous discussion on women's multiple jeopardy. Women vented their frustration with men who evoked "culture" and refused to "help" with housework. They analyzed the ways in which reclaiming Oromo culture became a cover for continuing gender oppression. We agreed to embrace our culture only when it was emancipatory and vowed to reject it when it was oppressive. Ours was a liberation struggle after all! "One way of dealing with this is to teach men how to cook and give them a new culture," a woman said. "They will mess up the entire place!" cried another one sarcastically. "They must want to learn in the first place!" said another. "They will never! Why should they learn when we are always there to slave for them?" said yet another. "Then stop slaving for them!

Refuse to cook!" I said. Heated discussion continued, and we vowed to strengthen our group and speak out on this issue with one voice. Everyone agreed and the mood shifted to sarcasm as though to celebrate the pact.

A week before this meeting, we had asked our men to participate in a workshop on violence against women. One man had utterly denied that there was any violence in our community. Now, a woman mimicked his facial gestures and his language. "You know what? His woman beats him up! That man is ashamed to admit his own violence," said another woman, making us all laugh. "That woman is poisoned with white women's feminism," said yet another woman, continuing the mockery. A woman started singing a poem that had been circulating in the broader community. It was written by a man to ridicule Oromo women who called 911 when their husbands chastised them. We all joined in and sang together, clapping, laughing, twisting the words, and ridiculing the poet. "An Oromo woman should not tell on another Oromo to a Canadian police," teased one woman. "Unless she is a traitor," another added sarcastically. "Is he not a traitor when he beats her? Isn't she Oromo too?" said yet another one. "Men are fools, you know," a woman remarked angrily. "If we refuse to call the police, they think it's because we're afraid of our men! We know what abuse is like and we just don't want the police to abuse our men; that's all!" "That's right! They know the law is on our side. They know we can call 911 anytime. They're just so dumb!" "They're in denial!"

Women opened up and poured out the issues they had bottled up for years. Our talk was highly emotional, even when we were sarcastic. It was the most intimate meeting we'd ever had. We ridiculed men; we tried them in absentia and condemned them all to a life sentence of housework and child care. Ridiculing is a deeply-ingrained means of social control in Oromo culture. Oromos used to maintain the checks and balances of their egalitarian *gada* by shaming and ridiculing abusers of power (Kumsa 1997; Legesse 1973 and 2000). This strategy was also consistent with my AOP. I see venting and gossiping as forms of resistance. The women were fully engaged in resistance and resolving to speak in *one* loud voice was one of our strategies. All we needed now was to generate action plans. This was my treasured moment of revolutionary ecstasy. These strong women did not need anybody for consciousness-raising. As a result of our liberation struggle, they were *more* than conscious! I felt a deep egoistic urge to factor in decades of my own consciousness-raising work: the articles I wrote, the speeches and presentations I made, the radio programs I produced, the women's column I edited, and the formal and informal teachings I conducted. I felt so good!

We were still savoring our wonderful solidarity over some good laughs when several community elders requested five minutes of our time. When we agreed, three men followed the rituals of greetings and blessings with the usual praise for the women's organization. They reminded us that we all needed to work hard to keep our communities together in these trying times of our suffering nation. Then their real motives emerged. They were planning a community function and were requesting that, as usual, women cook for the event. Several of us looked at each other and exchanged smiles. We had just unanimously resolved not to do this any more. I almost burst out laughing, wanting to continue the spirit of resistance that the men had interrupted upon their entry. The meeting room went quiet for a bit. I looked around. Women were not saying anything. The men were now demanding our commitment. I heard one of them say, "Would you help us out?" Silence echoed in the room, as women still refused to speak. I raised my hand and said, "No, we will not cook for your event but we're happy to come and show you how to cook." It must have felt like a bomb, for the men's jaws dropped in disbelief.

But I too had my moment of utter disbelief. Women pounced on me from all sides. "No! Ms. Kuwee! That's not our culture!" I heard one shout. "Since when have you seen our men cook?" chastised another. "I don't believe this! This must be a terrible joke," I told myself. "No! Men don't cook in our culture!" I heard another woman say. Feeling betrayed, I realized that the women seemed more scared of me than they were of the men, who left us to resolve the conflict ourselves.

"Look there!" I pointed towards the door that was closing behind the men. "Those are the oppressors! Don't stare at me like that! I'm not an enemy! I'm not an oppressor!" I said at the top of my lungs. To my chagrin, the woman I thought was the most revolutionary of us all said, "You are oppressor too! You don't speak for us!"

I couldn't believe my ears. Who is "us" and who is "them" here? Her voice came down like thunder and struck me like lightning. It passed right down through my body and shook the ground from under me. Me? Kuwee, an oppressor? There seemed to be a resounding agreement, as not a single woman spoke up in my defense. Now it was my turn to drop my jaw.

What did I do to trigger this complete reversal? What code of conduct did I trample on? One minute we were all laughing together and ridiculing men. The next minute I was alienated, left completely outside the group. I may have goofed and made dangerous mistakes, okay. But how could they call me oppressor when I gave up every semblance of privilege and paid a huge sacrifice for our liberation, when I was jailed and tortured for our struggle? How could they do this to me after I was dragged through hell for them? Being called an *oppressor* hurt more than anything else in the world, and I fled that place feeling utterly betrayed.

That must have been how the male leaders of Oromo liberation felt, I realized, when I called them oppressors. That must have been how white women felt when women of color confronted them with the oppressive privilege of whiteness. As I ran away, I put up all sorts of defences in order to avoid calling myself an oppressor. All sorts of stereotypes raced through my mind — surely these subservient Third World women must love oppression dearly. Surely they were ignorant, not conscious after all. Maybe they were trapped by what Paulo Freire (2003) calls fear of liberation. I wanted to place the entire fault on those women. Of course I was not an oppressor; I had fought against oppression all my life! I was a *liberated* woman!

This incident fractured the solidarity of our Oromo women's group. Suddenly there was a crack in that big "we" and the cohesive group to which I felt I belonged wholly and fully was divided into "us" and "them" camps. I began asking myself: What is oppression anyway? What is community? What holds it together and what pulls it apart? Nothing seemed to make sense. Even through my moments of confusion, however, one thing remained clear to me: the goal of community AOP is both personal liberation and social transformation. My questioning then focused on the role of self in AOP and the conduct of AOP practitioners who wish to achieve these goals.

Interrogating AOP: Don't Take it Personally?

In the ten years since this incident, so much has changed. Those "ignorant" and "subservient" women are now my highly esteemed mentors. What did I (un)learn in the meantime? This painful experience opened my eyes to the inadequacy of the false binaries in my AOP, rigid "us" and "them" camps that are mutually exclusive and oppositional. The binaries through which I understood the world and conducted myself started dissolving on me once again. Since I trust that you will develop your own unique AOP style in the context of your own practice, I do not intend to make this a recipe. I share it in the spirit of an Oromo proverb: *haxxeen halaalatti; dawween of jalatti* [smart ones from afar; fools from underneath them]. It means that smart ones learn from others' follies; fools wait for their own doom. I share my follies so you may learn from them. I use a critically relational perspective to explore some of my underlying assumptions and move my AOP beyond itself.

The Fallacy of Community/Difference

At the time of the incident, I was a social work student —gobbling up everything about cultural competence and AOP. Even when they were written by members of "minority" groups, however, readings were usually meant for mainstream students who needed to learn about "minority" cultures. Desperately seeking some practice tips, I turned to my favourite professor, who pointed me to the notion of "learning from discomfort" in Barb Thomas' anti-racist work (1987). Thomas was an outsider to my community, though, and my pain hurt too much to call it a discomfort. Over a decade later, Bob Mullaly (2002) recommended that these kinds of hurts not be taken personally. How could I not? My hurt was disruptive to my very sense of self! I rejected this advice that came from an outsider to my community who would know little about the experiences of insiders. In fact, some AOP readings affirmed my assumption that a rigid boundary around community sharply separated insiders from outsiders. To my great comfort, not only did the readings unveil a gap in knowledge between outsiders and insiders; they also validated insiders' knowledge and experience as more authentic.[2]

Essentialism and AOP

I felt that readings about insiders/outsiders provided the ultimate AOP since they went *against* the grain, reversing dominant relations of power. They refused the imposition of dominant values on minority groups. Indeed they honoured my insider's experiences as "privileged understanding" and "intimate knowledge" of my community. Later, however, I learned that these readings were informed by essentialism and realized that they resonated with me so deeply because my own AOP was similarly informed. By essentialism, I mean the view that assumes groups and individuals have fixed, predetermined, and unchanging qualities. The essentialist view takes community as given and natural; it assumes that harmony and homogeneity exist within a given boundary — especially that of ethnic communities within pluralistic liberal democratic states like Canada. Essentialists embrace notions of multiculturalism in which cultures are enclosed in their own natural boundaries and rarely, if ever, overlap, reinforce or change each other. This mindset starts from the fundamental assumption that ethnic communities are held together by shared cultural values and norms. It views commonality as the fixed essence of community, minimizing or erasing difference among community members. Since difference evokes conflict and conflict is viewed as dysfunctional, the state is promoted as a neutral arbiter that resolves conflicts between groups and creates harmony and social cohesion. From this perspective, oppression and inequalities of power are played down while harmony and cohesion are played up, even at the price of social justice.

To be fair, essentialist AOP is more than just essentialism. It disrupts the illusion of order and harmony described above, cracking the harmonious "we" of liberal essentialism and viewing conflict as the source of change and social transformation. Far from being a neutral arbiter, the state is viewed as machinery of oppression by which the dominant groups coerce subordinate groups into submission. The glue that holds societies together, then, is oppression and coercion, not cohesion and shared norms. Essentialist AOP starts from the fundamental assumptions that societies are riddled with conflict and our mundane practices are embedded in unequal relations of power. Often, however, these conflicts are restricted to those *between* "mainstream" and "minority" communities, whereas *within* groups solidarity is emphasized, thus creating homogeneous categories and false binaries — that is, false unity within a group and false opposition between groups. If differences within a cultural group are acknowledged at all, they are restricted to gender, class, and sometimes sexuality.

My essentialist AOP enabled me to draw a rigid gender boundary between Oromo women and men. Women were oppressed and men were oppressors. I emphasized commonality within each gender and opposition between them. What I assumed when I stood up and confronted the male community elders was complete commonality and oneness among Oromo women. What I discovered were differences among and between the women. While essentialist AOP suited my rigid insider/outsider binary perfectly, it did not address or soothe the pain that resulted from this discovery; nor did it quench my thirst for liberation. Essentialist AOP creates rigid boundaries between the oppressor and the oppressed and carves out monolithic communities with solid boundaries. Opposition is inherent in this AOP. The term *anti*-oppression itself defines an oppositional strategy of struggle in which the oppressed "us" are set against the oppressive "them." To be transformative, however, it seems to me that AOP needs to move beyond simple binary oppositions and start disrupting the boundaries separating groups. With this in mind, I turn to a close examination of boundaries.

Boundaries and Identities

My own transformative disruptions started with the Oromo women's meeting I described above. Gender is a boundary that defines Oromo women against Oromo men, a boundary of inclusion/exclusion that defines membership and belonging, community, and difference. In our women's meeting, the gender boundary defined a singular (monolithic) identity that held us together in that cohesive moment of solidarity and resistance. But this seemingly solid boundary dissolved the minute the male community elders walked into the room, throwing our differences into sharp relief. The context had shifted as of that moment. With the entry of the men, the women were no longer bound together by a singular notion of gender. Other boundaries had come into play automatically and our multiple identities were realigning around these newer boundaries. However, my assumption of a rigid gender boundary blinded me to this realignment.

I learned the bitter way that identities are multiple and fluid. By this I mean that there are many identities within a single individual, that these identities are flexible and changing, and that identities shift when the contexts and boundaries that created them shift. I learned that community is neither natural nor given. Indeed community is so fluid that it can dissolve or spring to life any time the context is ripe for it. By the time I started questioning the naturalness of boundaries and the singularity of the identities they define, I had already begun to doubt my essentialist AOP and to embrace radical social constructionism. If essentialist AOP is preoccupied with the construction of boundaries, constructionist AOP is preoccupied with the deconstruction of such boundaries.

Social Constructionism

Social constructionism is a school of thought introduced into sociology by Peter L. Berger and Thomas Luckmann (1966). Social constructionism argues that individuals construct their realities collectively and individually. This concept includes social institutions such as governments, religions, nations, genders, races, and so forth. It implies that these institutions can be changed. However, with its focus on deconstructing reality, social constructionism ultimately takes everything apart including the process of taking things apart leading nowhere except, most importantly, to inaction and reluctance to take action, given the near-inevitability of constructing something oppressive. To counterbalance this vacuum, *critical* social constructionists use concepts such as fairness, equity, and social justice strategically as ballast points in their attempts to deconstruct and understand social phenomena.

In constructionist perspectives, communities are socially constructed and held together by narratives and stories (Anderson 1983; Bhabha 1994; Chambon et al 1999; Gergen 2009; Foucault 1980c; Hall 1996; Saleebey 1994; Somers 1994). Focusing on the social construction of gender (Wise and Zimmerman 1987), I learned that our community of Oromo women was defined not by the natural boundary of anatomy/biology (sex) but by the social/historical processes through which society attaches meanings to it (gender).

To say that gender divides people into two mutually exclusive monolithic binaries of men and women is misleading, as it hides the rich multiplicities of gender between the two opposing poles. Even with all its complexity, gender is only one of our multiple identities. We are all women, of course, but we are also Oromos, refugees, liberators, and so forth. And we share most of these identities with most Oromo men. When men entered our women's space, not only the differences among women but also their commonalities with men were highlighted. For example, western education, religion, and region of birth emerged as very important boundaries of identity. Almost all of the women in our group were born into Muslim families in the same predominantly Islamic region of our homeland. I was born into a Christian family in a different and predominantly Christian region. They were educated primarily in Qur'anic schools and I went to schools providing western education. While these experiences set me apart from the other women, they created strong bonds of identification between the women and the male community elders. Privilege is often so deeply hidden (McIntosh 1990) that it was hard for me to realize that in Canada, a country that privileges Christian values and western education, these boundaries marked me as part of a dominant group or an oppressor. And why not? Didn't I reap the benefits of this privilege? What if we were all in an Islamic country? Would it be the same?

The interactions I described above caused me to I realize that we need both intimate knowledge of the insider and distant knowledge of the outsider to fully engage in transformative disruptions of boundaries and in liberatory struggles. I realized that commonality is not the sole basis for understanding. We can gain insights from our differences too. We don't have to be refugees to understand refugee experiences, or be women to empathize with women, or be gays or lesbians to identify with gay and lesbian communities. This is hopeful and helpful in many ways as it shows that we can work across differences and boundaries by drawing on both our insider and outsider knowledge. AOP has come a long way in social work towards better understandings of such identity boundaries.[3] Yet, these changes and insights prompt more questions. If we are all simultaneously oppressed and oppressors and if everybody can work and empathize with everybody, doesn't this erode the very notion of solidarity, the notion that we can find a common cause based on shared interests against known oppressors? For me, solidarity is the very soul of the struggle for liberation. If we can't mobilize and organize as women on the basis of gender, for example, then how can there be liberation from gender-based oppression? Patriarchy will not just drop and die of its own free will.

The Fallacy of Oppression/Liberation

Through the lens of my essentialist AOP, oppression and liberation formed a mutually exclusive dualism. I learned about the dynamics of oppression and liberation from revolutionary thinkers and anti-colonial national liberation leaders from around the world: Baro Tumsa in the Oromo Voice against Tyranny (Gidada et al. 1974), Amilcar Cabral (1979), Frantz Fanon (1967), Che Guevara (1969), Ho Chi Minh (1969), Mao Zedong (1962), and later on Paulo Freire (2003). Ironically, all men! I learned that the violence of oppression, although initiated by the oppressor, is also internalized and lateralized by the oppressed. That is, violence that comes vertically down from the oppressor is deflected sideways and erupts among the oppressed rather than rebounding

Internalized and Lateralized Oppression
Oppression is a dehumanizing process that robs both the oppressed and the oppressor of the capacity to be human and replaces it with false consciousness. These terms refer to processes in which the oppressed internalize the oppressor's distorted view of themselves. When oppressive ideas come vertically down from the oppressor, they are deflected sideways among the oppressed rather than rebounding back up. The oppressed move into self-doubt and self-hatred (internalized oppression) and fight against each other (lateralized oppression), rather than uniting and fighting oppression.

back upwards to the oppressor. Thus, rather than unite and fight against the oppressor, the oppressed often internalize a distorted view of themselves, plunge into self-hatred, and fight against one another. Oppression is a dehumanizing process that robs both the oppressed and the oppressor of the capacity to be human and replaces it with false consciousness. Liberation, on the other hand, is the opposite process of re-humanization that gets rid of false consciousness and gives us back our capacity to be fully human and social. Consciousness-raising is the path to both personal liberation and social transformation. It liberates the oppressed from the oppressor they house in their souls. It also liberates oppressors from their false consciousness and their distorted images of the oppressed so they can have faith in the oppressed, renounce their privileges, and come to the side of the oppressed to fight against oppression.

Subjects and Objects

In the process of Oromo women's self-organizing, I saw myself as the liberated liberator. Why not? Loathing the oppression of my people, I went through an intensive process of consciousness-raising, turned my back on my privileges, and gave up my comfortable social status to fight on the side of the oppressed. I exorcised the national oppressor I housed within myself. With enormous faith in Oromo women to stand by their side and fight against gender oppression, I challenged Oromo men in the liberation struggle to do the same in terms of gender. In my mind, I was liberated without a shadow of doubt; I was a convert unequivocally located on the side of oppressed women, a catalyst to effect radical change and social transformation. I did not realize that I was treating my sisters as objects of my consciousness-raising project. This went against the grain of my own learning that the oppressed should not enter the struggle as objects in order to later become subjects; they must enter as subjects and active participants in the struggle from the outset (Bishop 2002; Freire 2003; hooks 1984). I had refused to be objectified by male "liberators" in the wider Oromo national liberation struggle, but I did not realize that I was, in turn, objectifying Oromo women. When the women refused my objectification, I felt betrayed, hurt and excluded. But who excluded whom? Who hurt whom? Who was the renegade who wreaked all the havoc?

Silence and Power

To address these questions, I needed to go back to and closely examine that moment of tension and silence in our meeting just before I got up and confronted the community elders. I knew something had changed the moment the men walked in, but I did not stop to reflect at the time. When the men demanded women's consent and the women refused to speak, I knew that silence meant something, but I read only my own meaning into it. True to my essentialist

AOP, I believed that silence was just the absence of speech — the poor women were tongue-tied because oppression had damaged their humanity and silenced their authentic voice. This seemed an example of what Freire (2003) calls a "culture of silence." I was the liberated, articulate one who could confront the oppressor. By chastising me the moment I spoke out, I thought the women were kowtowing in loyalty to the oppressor. I interpreted this as a lateralization of violence due to internalized oppression. I didn't completely blame the women. I nevertheless felt deeply hurt and betrayed. I did not recognize the possibility that I was the one who betrayed and hurt those women until I moved beyond my essentialist AOP. There are more meanings to both the silence and the lashing out than I initially knew.

To grasp some of the multiple meanings, I needed to relearn how power works. Power is not just the top-down force that oppresses; it is also the bottom-up and sideways resistance that liberates. More importantly, power and resistance are not mutually exclusive but interwoven and embedded in each other and they emerge in various forms (Abu-Lughod 1990; Foucault 1980c). At the time, I was unable to move beyond a culture of silence to read the women's silence as a culture of resistance (Blackburn 2000). For the women in our meeting, silence, not speech, was the stiffest form of resistance. Later, I learned that silence was women's strategy of everyday resistance even within their homes. The silence in our meeting room meant refusal on the part of the women and the men knew that. I was the one left out of that pattern of communication because I related to men differently and had been educated in the western tradition. For me, naming an issue was important; words signified the most effective resistance. If men spoke in sexist ways I could overpower them by speaking more, and if they wrote I overpowered them by writing more. I felt quite competent to tell men off when needed! Instead of trusting the women and working with their form of resistance, I broke the subtle code of conduct and turned their silence into speech. I attempted to impose my own form of verbal resistance instead of flowing with their richer ways of exercising women's power through silence, unintentionally betraying the eloquence of Oromo women's silence. I failed to hear the powerful language of silence. Silence is not the empty gap between words; it is eloquence Othered by words (Derrida 1997). No amount of training in cultural competence prepared me for this complex meaning that existed, ironically, within my own culture.

Even so, I wondered why the women lashed out at me. If silence is their resistance, why didn't they keep their wonderful quiet at least until the men left? Weren't they embracing oppressive Oromo culture when they said, "No! Ms. Kuwee! This is not our culture!" and "Men don't cook in our culture!"? Weren't they undermining their own resistance?

Multiple Oppressions

The notions of multiplicity and intersectionality of oppression (Collins 2000 and 2001; Lee 1985; Sudbury 1998) were helpful in answering these questions. I realized that I could be both oppressed and oppressor at the same time when gender intersected with others of our multiple identities. It had not occurred to me that I could be oppressive to some men. My assumption that I related to *all* men the same way also crumbled as I realized that I did not talk down to white male professors, for example, the way I did to the male Oromo community elders. But nothing prepared me for the spontaneity and fluidity of the women's contradictory positions. I needed the lens of constructionist AOP to realize that people embrace oppression and resistance simultaneously without feeling any sense of contradiction. Indeed, the spontaneity with which the women shifted their position shows that contradiction is a very ordinary way of navigating the complex world of unequal power relations. The women did not think of it as a contradiction at all.

In this light, then, even the lashing out that hurt me so much can be understood very differently. I can now see that the women lashed out in response to my own attack. I initiated the oppressor's violence. When I confronted the men, I inadvertently but simultaneously confronted the women who intimately identified with the men. What enabled me to lash out against the men was not the gender I shared with the women but the power vested in my other identities. By lashing out and telling the men off, I was exercising this power, setting my self apart from the rest of the people at the meeting — both women and men — as different and more educated, privileged and western. The women responded by excluding me and by lashing out after I used the power they could not access. In yet another incredible reversal, I thought I was the one betrayed.

This analysis makes visible the fallacy of the oppression/liberation dualism. Oppression and liberation are *relational processes*, not a dualism (Gergen 2009). People can be oppressed/oppressors and liberated at the same time. No one is inherently oppressed or oppressor. Nor are we inherently liberators or liberated. The Oromo women and I were in the process of liberating one another through our interactions. Paulo Freire's (2003) insistence on mutuality in the process of liberation deeply resonates with the critically relational perspective I'm presenting in this analysis. Liberation from multiple and complex forms of oppressive relations is a lifelong process. Indeed, as Freire argues so eloquently, liberation is neither a gift nor a self-achievement but a mutual process. I cannot deliver gender liberation to Oromo women on a silver platter as a precious gift. My insistence on being a liberated liberator does not make me any more of a liberator of Oromo women than George Bush is the liberator of Iraqis.

Throughout this section of self-critical analysis, I have been tacitly engaging Mullaly (2002) in a dialogue on his "don't take it personally" advice, without actually naming it so. Even though I deeply appreciate his contribution to my own personal liberation, I have also been thinking with Mullaly against Mullaly — to borrow Pierre Bourdieu's phrase (1977 and 1998). For the longest time, I refused to take it personally. For the longest time, I dug in and entrenched myself in that position: "No, it's not my problem!" I would not take it personally. It was much easier and more comfortable to race to innocence (Fellows and Razack 1998) and point fingers at Others — away from Self. To be fair, Mullaly did not advise us to point to Others; he just asked us to develop a sufficiently tough skin to not take it personally. However, not taking it personally prompted me to dump the fault on the Oromo women at our meeting. It was their problem, not mine. It was their ignorance, their subservience, their fear of liberation. I realized later that, in part, it was my privilege that hurt. My denial, my race to innocence, and my pointing to Others were all defensive strategies that masked my hurt privilege. However, these strong emotions are both concealing and revealing at the same time. They conceal privilege at the same time as they open up space for transformation. They hold up mirrors to the Self to examine its relations of oppression.

Implications for Practitioners of AOP

In conclusion, I would like to share some fears and concerns that I believe constitute important implications for AOP practitioners. There are several risks in sharing an analysis in the first-person voice. First, I fear that these narratives remain confessions without leading to transformative actions. Confession and self-examination may be important steps in the process of transformation — many feminists have used similar processes in the past — but confession alone has not resulted in the end of oppression (Friedman 1998), personal liberation, or social transformation. Pointing to the Self and beating one's chest is no more transformative than pointing to and assigning blame to the Other. We need to unplug ourselves from dug-in positions and move beyond binaries to examine oppression and liberation as relational processes. I hope that, as AOP practitioners, you will be enticed to move beyond confession and self-reflection into the world of transformative actions.

Second, I worry that my reflections will be Othered in the sense that AOP practitioners might direct these follies back to me and away from themselves. I fear that they will refuse to take this analysis personally and, by doing so, they will miss an important opportunity to learn. As I tried to show, we need to distinguish between the righteous pain of the oppressed, which reveals oppression, and the pain of hurt privilege, which conceals it. I hope that when AOP practitioners feel hurt, they will stop and examine the privilege that might be hiding under those feelings. It is very easy, indeed very seductive, to dig in and retreat to the position of not taking it personally, to believe that it is "their" problem, not yours. I hope AOP practitioners drop out of that "race to innocence" and instead pursue the more difficult transformative route of challenging themselves and considering whether they inhabit an oppressive dimension of social relations.

Third, I fear that AOP practitioners will find a way to toughen up and refuse to feel hurt. I hope they do feel hurt and, when they feel hurt, they will be enticed to take it personally and ask why it hurts so much. As I attempted to demonstrate, our sense of Self is woven from our social relations. Of course it hurts when that very fabric from which we are woven is frayed. But I do hope AOP practitioners stay with the pain and work through it. I hope taking it personally will help them reach beyond binaries and experience the fascinating world of multiple identities. Oppressive systems are held in place and defended by powerful emotions. The common response to these powerful emotions is to deny them, to fly away from them, and/or to project them onto Others. Taking it personally spares us from all these pitfalls. Taking it personally means owning up to the relations of our oppressive Self instead of denying them. It means embracing those hurts and staying with those powerful emotions instead of flying away from them. It means examining the structures of oppression that these powerful emotions defend and hold in place. It means pointing to and examining the oppressive relations between Self and Other instead of pointing to and faulting an Other or the Self.

Fourth, I fear that the lessons of my confession might be diluted and oppression might be taken as the norm. I fear that some mainstream AOP practitioners might point to minority communities and say, "If even *they* do it to one another, there is no escape from oppression!" On the other hand, minority AOP practitioners might also feel that if we oppress one another, then there really is no escape from oppression. Oppression is the norm. Oppressive relations are indeed the fabric of social life since we are embedded in a web of unequal relationships of power. Our very sense of Self is woven from such inequities. But I hope that AOP practitioners also realize that oppressive relations are learned, and so they can be unlearned. I hope that my stories have left students with an understanding that oppression is a relational process and that taking it personally and examining the social fabric from which we are woven will facilitate the process of personal liberation and social transformation.

Postscript

So much has changed since the time of the incident I have written about here. The Oromo women's organization does not exist now in that same form and with that same group of women. Like the phoenix rising from its ashes, however, many new women's groups have emerged from the original one, unencumbered by a single politics of liberation. Our organizations now come in many genres, and our liberation comes in many forms and happens in multiple places and at many levels. Now women reach out beyond the Oromo community to link with their sisters in other communities as well. Now our spaces of gathering are not limited to the confining rooms of the local Oromo community: We gather in our homes and other public spaces, and in virtual spaces afforded by the Internet for global connections. Now even those "ignorant and illiterate" women who cannot read or write or use the keyboard can sit in the comfort of their local homes and conduct eloquent meetings with their sisters from around the world. The Internet feature of *paltalk* has opened up a whole new world. All women do is have their children or grandchildren set up a computer in the kitchen and gather around it for coffee — just like in the good days back home, but here they also connect the local and the global as they chat with their sisters in Africa, Australia, Europe, and North America. In fact they have created a *paltalk* space called *Mana Bunaa* [Coffee House] just for women's gathering. Here Oromo women's voices of ageless wisdom and infinite knowledge boom through the global space unhindered by the limits of modern knowledge.

The virtual space, however, is not a replacement for the local space but an enhancement of it. Women still gather locally in Toronto. Several small groups have come and gone and more are in the making. While some forms of organizing have become transient, others still hold their ground and stay put. An example is a new local group reconstituted from our old one and held together by older and wiser women who needed a women's space primarily for connection and comfort. Casting the politics of national liberation aside, they have made a very effective use of the comfort and care that women's space offers. I am not a member of the new group, but we seek each other out with the women when we need each other; nor am I a member of *Mana Bunaa*, but I am often invited for coffee chats.

Moments of tension over differences still exist, but we have learned how to reach out to each other beyond the tensions. But even as we have sought each other out, silence has prevailed over the incident itself. As much as I would have liked for us to put it to words, to work with it, and to make our peace, I have also learned the infinite wisdom of letting it slide without words and to enjoy the depth of the new understanding that emerged. After all, in words or in silence, we have all processed and worked through it in our own ways from our own places. More importantly, we have come back together and healed each other, not through denying our differences but through acknowledging and honouring them. Our Oromo identity has not been demolished by the incident; it has only been opened up for questioning and reworking. Nor is our Oromoness critically reshaped and put back together as a single whole with a single centre and a single origin. On the contrary, it is now open-ended, multi-faceted, multi-centred, and in constant motion.

These wise women are now my highly regarded mentors. The very women who I profoundly believed "hurt" and "betrayed" me now embrace me. When they see me approach and smile, I know in the depth of my soul that theirs are tender loving smiles. When I feel the warmth of their embrace deep in my bones, I know that we have healed each other. It took us years to come to this place, though. At first, when I was still sorting through my hurt feelings and making sense of the incident, occasional encounters at community functions, weddings, and wakes were extremely tense. My wound was still sore and I held on to my pains for as long as I pointed to the women and blamed them, for as long as I refused to take it personally and pointed my finger away from my Self towards the Other. Many dramatic things have happened in the Oromo communities and in the larger world since then, including 9/11 and the rise of Islamophobia. However, for me, an epiphany happened when one of the women in our original group was injured in an accident; I rushed to her bedside and we embraced and cried together. The genuine innocence in her eyes told me that she had no sense of hurting me at all. It occurred to me then that my hurt could actually be my own perception. As my index finger pointed *Otherways*, I started seeing my three Othered fingers pointing back to me and my Self. That was when my defences started crumbling one by one.

This "aha" moment constituted a fundamental shift in my own thinking and being in the world. I realized that Self and Other are mutually constitutive and mutually transformative. Our wounding of each other was as mutual as our healing of each other. I realized that reaching out to my Othered sister was reaching out to my Othered Self; touching her was touching my estranged Self. The betrayal I felt was my own betrayal of my potential Self waiting to happen. Indeed, caring for the Other is ultimately caring for the Self, and, for me, this sits at the heart of personal liberation. Looking back on this incident now with a hindsight humbled by age and maturity, I cherish the painful moment as I do the moment of intense pleasure and ecstasy. Both have taught me unforgettable lessons. The pain would not have been possible without the pleasure and vice versa. Pain and pleasure, wounding and healing, are intimately intertwined. In that moment of intense pleasure, I felt a profoundly spiritual connection with the women. Experiencing the depth of that bond shows me that such a wonderfully soul-nurturing human possibility can be realized in the larger society. The moment of pain and anguish taught me that, for oppression to give way to liberation, such a profound disruption may have to happen and the practitioner may have to come to terms with their own privilege. Instead of looking for commonalities to develop empathy, I learned that profound empathy actually comes out of differences by becoming the Other (Kumsa 2008) in a world where everything points to the fundamental separateness and differentness of the Other.

Notes

1. For example, see Kumsa 1992, 1993, 1994, 1997, 1998, and 2000.
2. For example, see Baskin 2003; Cruikshank 1990; Dumbrill and Maiter 1996; Erlich and Rivera 1995; Lee et al. 2002; Lockhart 1994; Narayan 1988; Sue and

Sue 1990; Van Soest 1995.
3. For example, see Baines 2003; Bishop 2002; Chambon et al. 1999; Fook 1999b; Katz 1995; Leonard 1997; Mullaly 2002; Rossiter 1995a; Sands and Nuccio 1992; Thompson 1997.

Section Three

RESISTANCE

Introduction

Donna Baines

As noted earlier, social workers are employed to work with vulnerable populations at the intersection of the state, private markets, and human pain. The fact that we work within this complex web means that we often find ourselves at odds with practices and policies, whether informal or formal. Some authors have written about how workers undertake small acts of resistance to keep their own sense of integrity in this context and quietly promote the rights of service users (Carniol 2010; Smith 2007; Baines 2000). These forms of resistance include bending rules to get clients everything they are entitled to and more; referring service users to activist groups; putting up posters and artwork in agencies that encourage and affirm social justice and fairness; and helping clients to politicize their problems by sharing social analysis and critical insights. Though still very present, Smith (2007) argues that in many cases resistance practices have had to "go underground" in order to avoid detection and direct confrontation with the new rules and regulations associated with managerialism. Despite the constraints of neoliberalism, larger scale and more collective forms of resistance can also be found in social service agencies and among social workers in every kind of job. Collective forms of resistance vary: using unions as vehicles of social change; joining coalitions to fight cutbacks in funding; developing new services and taking on larger social issues (such as demanding an increase in minimum wage or other measures to address poverty); building opposition to war; standing up to violence against queer people; defending the rights of immigrants and refugees. While acknowledging that "only one in a hundred" clients will follow through on political action, workers regularly make referrals to social action groups, often those in which they themselves are active, in order to link clients with others in the same situation and increase the potential for collective solutions.

Drawing on research and practice experience, this section looks at resistance in social work in its larger and smaller formats, analyzing the skills required and encouraging social workers to live their ethics and expand the space for social justice-directed practice.

Chapter 15

Social Work Activism Amidst Neoliberalism

A Big, Broad Tent of Activism

Meaghan Ross

In this chapter, I argue that current constructs that see frontline and structural level practice not as a continuum of ways to engage in social change but as separate and distinct spheres of action serve only to label our allies as inadequate. I suggest that in order to deepen our anti-oppressive practice, we must first develop more inclusive and dynamic definitions of activism. We live in important and shifting times, and we need to find multiple ways to build radical, transformative change in order to resist the radical dismantling of social welfare.

As you read this chapter, ask yourself the following questions:
1. Why is it important to adopt a broad understanding of what constitutes activism?
2. What are the advantages and disadvantages of structural level activism and direct service level activism?

Though much of social work practice seems very local, politicized, and trans-formative, social work is concerned with people and *their total life worlds*. As such, social work practice cannot be extricated from the impacts of globalization. Social work in western countries is characterized by ongoing restructuring and reorganizing in our workplaces and an increase in precarious work, including contract, part time, self–employment, and temporary positions (Aronson and Sammon 2000; Baines 2004a and 2004b; Silver et al. 2005). This restructuring and increased precariousness amounts to a *flexibilization* of labour that is part of globalization, and it results in diminished job security for workers. It also places greater strain on workers, forcing them to do more with fewer resources, often in isolation from other workers. This global trend, known as welfare state retrenchment, includes changes in the role of the state as governments privatize, deregulate, and downsize public services (see Brodie 1999; Rice and Prince 2000; Garrett 2002; and Rempel 2008). Connected to this shift is an infusion of market values into social work settings (termed "managerialism" or

> ### Retrenchment
> Social welfare retrenchment is a shift away from being an inclusive, universalistic welfare state to becoming one that provides only minimal assistance to very few people. It involves cuts to social spending of all types, privatization of public resources, and a heightened focus on business and corporate solutions to all social problems and challenges.

"marketization") whereby workers must prove their worth by demonstrating productivity and economic efficiency rather than by the ways they build relationships with individuals and communities and promote social justice. Grounded in the increasingly global principles of risk management, social work practice has become tightly regulated and standardized, not in order to advance social fairness or equity but to ensure cost saving.

Neoliberal globalization also presents serious challenges for social workers seeking to engage in anti–oppressive activism. As Baines (2007a: 10) states, "anti–oppressive social work has become harder to do because of the increasingly aggressive nature of globalization and neoliberal governments' response to the processes of global integration." Under neoliberalism, people have become *consumers* of service, rather than *citizens* with entitlements and rights to care and support. As the world becomes more global and the labour force is restructured, migration and immigration have increased, resulting in service users with new and often more complex kinds of needs that existing, under-resourced services have difficulty meeting. More importantly, there are real consequences for workers engaging in activist practice, including the potential loss of employment. Workers may find themselves in a bind, caught between a desire to advance radical social work and a need not to jeopardize their jobs. In short, social justice-oriented social work is increasingly harder to sustain due to the lack of space for advocacy and preventive interventions within our practice settings.

Though problems associated with globalization have been discussed at length in the social work literature, there is less discussion within our field of the ways in which advocacy and social justice have been and continue to be facilitated by social workers. We know that social workers use many strategies to sustain social justice activism despite the context of global neoliberal economic and political policies. Yet the concrete skills and actions used to maintain client advocacy are often absent from social work education. After speaking with workers in the field,[1] I have come to realize that the actual social justice strategies themselves might be less important than *how these practices are conceptualized* in discussions of activist practice. We live in important and shifting times, and we need to find multiple ways to build radical, transformative change in order to combat the radical dismantling of social welfare. In this chapter, I suggest that a fundamental alteration of the concept of politicized social work is needed so that we can recognize and validate activist practice in all its forms.

The Traditional Binary Approach to Social Work Activism: Direct Service versus Structural Action

Generally, references to social work activism are grounded in the notion that to engage in activism is "to take action in pursuit of social justice" (Baines 2007a). Yet there has been wide variance regarding what kinds of actions constitute activism. Some authors, such as Smith (2007) and Fook (1993), focus on the strategies comprising the more immediate, organizational, or localized level of practice. I call this the direct service or frontline realm of resisting social injustice. In this kind of practice, social workers' activism is aimed at changing the immediate environments and institutions harming the individuals and community with whom we work. All of the social workers I talked to, including those in community development and research roles, spoke of their participation in this type of activism as a central component of their politicized practice. For example, Alannah[2] described "helping people navigate service systems that have power over them," and Cheryl discussed doing "practical, functional, problem solving," while Pearl spoke of her research and policy analysis work as "diminishing the exclusion [that] those interacting with services experience with respect to access."

In contrast, other social workers tended to advocate for a conceptualization of activism centred on actions targeted at the more "structural" (or macro/global) level. This reflects the work of authors such as Lundy (2004), Mullaly (2002), and Healy (2000), who argue for workers to integrate their efforts into larger collective strategies aimed at systemic transformation. They think we need to address how globalization changes the structural divisions in society (for example, who is poor, who is marginalized, who has power) and how it shapes human needs, as well as how it affects the provision of welfare and services. As Alannah cautions,

> We can't get stuck in the little picture, because for the one person you see in front of you that is starving, there is a hundred and fifty more; we need to connect the dots to something else that has happened, to look at the systems.

This kind of activism is often understood to be comprised of the mobilization of, and alliance-building between, grassroots movements of marginalized populations.

Unfortunately, these two spheres of action — frontline and structural — are often thought to come from completely opposite positions, rather than be understood as a continuum of ways to engage in and define activism.

This binary perspective is further reinforced by our definitions of social work practice. For example, Hare (2004) notes that there are two components to social work officially acknowledged by the International Federation of Social Work; these are the direct services, aimed at enhancing people's well being, and community development work, aimed at facilitating broad-based changes within the socio-cultural, economic, and political environments shaping service users' lives.

Understanding what activism means within a social work context is also complicated by the narrow way in which the term has been traditionally represented. Often the media use it to invoke notions of radical and potentially violent demonstrations and protests, conveying the notion that activism refers only to very public, overt, and militant forms of social action. An example is the recent G8/G20 protests in Toronto, Ontario, at which all of the actions taken against the summit meetings were attributed to so-called "anarchists who wanted to smash windows," regardless of the thousands of politically diverse views presented via a varied set of marches, events, discussions, and activities. It has been my experience that this misrepresentation leads to a tendency for both social workers and scholars to shy away from using the term activism to describe their work, preferring terms such as "advocacy," "social change," or "progressive." Unfortunately, these factors can also limit our sense of what constitutes social justice-oriented social work practice.

Redefining Activism

Rather than uphold existing binaries related to the definition of the term, and rather than refer to only the stereotypical understandings of activism, I argue that many anti-oppressive and other progressive social workers already engage in a broad spectrum or a "big tent" (as termed by Kristin) of activist activities that centre around the organization, education, and mobilization of oppressed populations and their allies. These big tent activities are not exclusively direct service or structural level, but an amalgam of the two. In reality the "direct service" and "structural level"[3] realms of intervention are not mutually exclusive and do not operate in an opposing binary; rather, they are highly integrated, and need to be, especially in the current context of globalization. Perhaps one of the most important actions social workers can take in the pursuit of anti-oppressive practice is to reframe and broaden the ways in which activism is conceptualized, validated, documented, and undertaken.

This sentiment was well articulated by Kristin, who was employed in a direct service agency and had a long history of social activism within and outside her workplace. Commenting on the new strategies required by globalization within (apparent in the form of service cuts and managerialism) and outside the workplace (existing in the form of increased global insecurity, poverty, and environmental degradation), she noted:

I began to think about this idea that activism needs to be broader, it needs to be a big tent that we are constructing; not just this "who's in and who is out?" It needs to be a big, broad tent.

Many of the workers emphasized the need to re-evaluate our understandings of activism so that both the direct service and structural realms of action were recognized in terms of their benefits and limitations, and with regards to how they are interrelated to each other. As Leah commented:

> I have come to see activism in this globalized, managerialized world of ours in social work as a range of things that we can do, from the more public to the more individual, small group, committee work, in more conventional settings.

Both direct- and structural-level actions play an important role in building social justice as they both improve the quality and quantity of political, social, and civil rights to which marginalized populations have access, and they mitigate the harmful impacts of neoliberal welfare retrenchment. Hence, our strategies and the way we think about, participate in, and teach activism need to reflect a broad, inclusive array of tactics and activities. We need to embrace the notion that all levels of activism are equally valid and important.

Direct Service Level Activism

In order to properly value the range of activist actions that can and should be part of anti-oppressive social work practice, we must understand the benefits and limitations gained from working within each realm. At the direct service level, Smith (2007: 149) reminds us that often the best way to resist the challenges of neoliberalism is to engage in more individual action, for "the usual forums for democratic opposition have been effectively shut down, leaving very few forums to directly contest either management or government from within service agency settings." Leah agreed, stating, "we got our message loud and clear: that kind of advocacy [what she termed more 'public' actions] is not going to work. So you do it in different ways because they weren't hearing us." Pearl also agreed with these reflections, noting that restrictive "institutional mandates mean that we need to alter our methods." Discussing "everyday forms of resistance," Scott (2002 [1985]: 93) reminds us that "open insubordination in almost any context will provoke a more rapid and ferocious response than an insubordination that may be as pervasive, but never ventures to contest the formal definitions of hierarchy and power."

Direct Service Activism is Important

Direct service actions are often the most viable forms of activism that workers in conventional settings can engage in, and they are simultaneously extremely important for meeting the immediate needs of those accessing services. Though most people involved in social services do not know it, frontline workers occupy the intersections between clients and the macro-forces shaping their lives, such as neoliberal economic globalization: "workers are engaged at crucial intersections between people and the various faces of the state, between institutions and community, between medical and social, market and government, pubic and private spheres" (Aronson 2008). Alannah demonstrated a clear understanding of this idea, arguing that an important benefit of her work is that for "people whose voice doesn't get heard, we become part of the voice in the ... world to bring resources to them." Both these workers and our field of literature suggest that it is in these spaces that social workers negotiate resources and *widen the gates* limiting access to social welfare for the most marginalized of society. Without this work, many people's needs and issues would remain unaddressed.

Also, it is within these spaces that social workers connect the populations with whom they work to larger forces shaping their lives through discussion, debate, and information exchange. In other words, by raising consciousness we can create the foundation required for widespread change. Sheena explained that she and a young Iraqi woman residing at the group home in which she worked created an anti-war poster that Sheena took with her on a demonstration. Sheena saw this as an "an opportunity while doing really individualized work to connect it to something bigger." Similarly, reflecting on her work, Kristin said that "activism can happen, even in this really constraining, conservative doctor's office. That we are going to sit ... and do a political analysis of health and people's conditions — there is activist critique everywhere."

Moreover, this activism redefines the radical possibilities existing for social change. The number of social workers who continue to be committed to "organizational tinkering" (Aronson and Sammon 2000) and "stealth social work practices" (Smith 2007) despite globalization and its restructuring shows that a commitment to social justice has survived pro-market restructuring (Baines 2004a). For example, Leah confirmed this when she noted that she knows many social workers who persist in social justice practice even in this difficult era.

Organizational Tinkering

This is a concept developed by Aronson and Sammon (2000), who describe how workers bend organizational rules and cultivate personal contacts with other service providers in order to gain access to social welfare for people with whom they work. This resistance also involves the strategic repackaging of organizational discourses and mandates. For example, Leah described how workers she knew replaced words like "activism" with "public education" on funding proposals in order to continue their progressive work when the government no longer agreed to fund explicit activist activities.

> ### Stealth Social Work Practices
> As Smith (2007) describes in her work, the precarious climate of neoliberal reform creates situations in which workers are not able to openly challenge organizational rules, and as such their activism becomes quieter and more hidden. One example of such covert action came from Leah, who discussed how she experienced hostility from her supervisors when trying to initiate more public actions on the college campus; yet there remains space within her own classroom to implement progressive change, because it is difficult for supervisors to control her actions as they are not immediately present.

Many workers were doing "very creative actions in very conventional settings" even though "sometimes they are the only ones doing it, they are very isolated, and they keep going at it." As long as this kind of commitment survives, the potential exists to shift the politics of organizations to the left and to build support for activism within organizations. As Scott (2002 [1985]: 95) argues, "thousands upon thousands of individual acts of insubordination and evasion create a political or economic barrier reef" that wears down the power of the powerful and acts as a rehearsal for broader acts of resistance.

The Limitations of Direct Service Activism
Though there are many benefits to these types of tactics, it is important we recognize that, like all interventions, there are also limitations to this kind of politicized work. Firstly, as these tactics are usually undertaken individually by social workers, they are less able to cultivate a widespread or trans-generational understanding of how to operate effectively within and against neoliberal policies. The covert nature of direct service tactics makes it difficult for radical social workers to initiate system-wide anti-oppressive practice amongst their colleagues or newer workers, as broad-based activism cannot develop in a sustainable way from covert and little-known actions. Additionally, this work depends on the experience and political orientation of individual workers. Hence, some service users will get better and more politicized care, while others will not.

Many workers will also experience negative health impacts while sustaining these types of resistance practices. For example, Pearl observed: "I find when I do more clinical based work, I experience compassion fatigue quite easily." Similarly, Cheryl mentioned not having any energy left after her paid work to become involved in other community events or actions, and as Kristin noted,

> The impact on people's personal lives is so big: every social worker in my office has talked about feeling stressed out, and there are ways of coping that are starting to undermine our abilities to be well and to be there for each other.

In the current context, social workers cannot expect support from managers or co-workers for their activism, though they can work carefully to build this support. In the absence of this solidarity and in agencies that are increasingly focused on narrow services rather than broad, holistic, community-based interventions, social workers are "responsibilized" to become managers not only of their own workloads, but also of social change. The overtime and stress they accrue under this responsibility are neither adequately acknowledged nor addressed. Baines (2004b) notes that social workers are increasingly working overtime to mediate the demands of neoliberalism and that this work is largely unreported, unrecognized, and unpaid. Ironically, workers actively participate in their own exploitation in an attempt to eradicate the exploitation experienced by service users.

Though very important, strategies undertaken at the direct service level of the activist spectrum are not sufficient, in and of themselves, to build the breadth and depth of transformation required to ensure everyone's socio-political economic entitlements. This is because this work does not necessarily "expose or challenge the insufficiencies in resources or reframe front line tensions as systemic rather than individual issues" (Aronson and Sammon 2000: 176), nor does it suggest viable alternatives. While direct-service practices can help sustain individuals and foster hope and dignity, the tactics described above do not directly engage in the larger actions integral to anti-oppressive practice — i.e., broad-based actions that proactively transform systems such as capitalism, neoliberalism, patriarchy, colonialism, and imperialism, which structure inequalities into the fabric of society.

Structural Level Activism

For the reasons noted above, it is important that when we discuss transformative practice we recognize the value of activism centred on building broader coalitions across geographic and social locations. Mullaly (2002: 193) argues that "anti-oppressive social work practice aimed at the structural level attempts to change those institutional arrangements, social processes, and social practices that work together to benefit the dominant group at the expense of subordinate groups."

Structural Activism Is Important

Clearly, actions such as building international alliances and mobilizing community capacity do not provide immediate solutions to the major disruptions, dislocations, and hardships prompted by cuts to service and increased social work case loads. More macro-level social activism does not do much to relieve the pain of the person standing in front of you needing services and support right now. Yet these tactics can and should be viewed as meaningful actions that connect social work with a more emancipatory praxis. As Garrett (2002: 202) notes, macro-activist strategies "seek to reaffirm a social work commitment to civil and human rights and to promot[e] a more just society." In addition, structural-level practices also combat the individualizing nature of social welfare changes that seek to make people "fit" into their environments, structures, and institutions, rather than making environments, structures, and institutions fit people. For example, Alannah described how her workplace uses "an ecological model when looking at community development to see families as a collective, so we are not out to punish people, but to figure out how we can lessen some of the effects on people and improve their lives."

Perhaps the most essential aspect of broader action is that it creates the possibility or foundation for the development of alternatives to the current structures of society. Westhues (2003) argues that the framework of our vision must move away from reactive measures and towards more proactive actions. Alternative service delivery structures, such as the feminist collectives of which Leah spoke and Indigenous community work, constitute a resistance to the mainstream ideology that is reinforced by conventional agency structures (Carniol 2005). They also create alternative movements outside the current system, decreasing our reliance on traditional structures and invoking systems of participatory democracy. Social, economic, and environmental justice demands a transformation of power, including the democratization of society's structures. It is in broad collective action that we begin to build alternatives and transform the current context created by globalization.

Limitations of Structural Activism

However, it is also important to be clear about the limitations of structural-level action in order to understand how to advance social justice most effectively. It is crucial for us to consistently connect with the individual people with whom we work because these connections serve as a significant motivator, sustaining our macro-level social justice activism. However, immediate connections are not always possible to find within structural practice. Though vitally important, activist strategies such as international coalition-building or comparative policy critique aimed at achieving systemic change have the potential to become disconnected from the local or community context as they spread over wider geographic areas, become more powerful, and need to draw increasingly on those with high-level expertise and experience. Unfortunately, they can unintentionally begin to exclude the marginalized populations for whose benefit they claim to work, inadvertently reproducing systems of oppression.

In addition, the current climate presents very real limitations in terms of enacting broader-based activism. Systemic action is not always an option. Like Alannah, a number of workers emphasized that the "silos and protection of funding promotes fragmentation within communities, and while you hear lots about volunteerism and collaboration, it takes people who are paid to support and build that framework."

Though the space for alternative practice becomes increasingly constrained, careful and consistent work can still build opportunities to advance social justice. Leah, Alannah, and Sheena all noted that once they had "earned the room to do advocacy work" within their communities and workplaces, they were simultaneously seen to have a voice of authority in the social services community and were given more space to advance change. Sheena said, "we've gained sort of a legitimate voice, and we've played the careful political game well, so people trust us now. And I think now is the moment to seize." Ironically, those working at the direct-service level often have more power, space, and resources to advance change than those involved in broader-based community initiatives, who can be easily typecast as "radicals" or "troublemakers."

Transcending the Division:
Building a Broader Conceptualization of Activism

An alternative understanding of activism is one of a broad, big tent that includes both direct service and structural activism. Within this tent we must recognize, validate, and strategically utilize the wide variety of actions available. As social workers we are not just blank slates upon which managerialism or standardization is enacted; rather, we can contest, manipulate and change systems that are exploitive. We must also work to support and engage in building a globalization from below in conjunction with social movements and broader community activism to transform the current systems of competitive and destructive globalization and alter the balance of power away from those who occupy dominant space.

Connected to this is the need to nurture broader and more inclusive understandings of what activist practice looks like. Alannah said it well:

> I'm not a marcher, I've never been, but I think that's so cool that it happens. To me what is problematic is that I might not talk to the marcher. I should talk to them — how do we connect the dots between people, and value different types of work people do.

Globalization from Below
Globalization from below refers to the opportunities created by global integration to expand direct democracy, equitable resource distribution, and sustainable development, as opposed to the current forms of corporate globalization driven by the financial interests of the world's richest people, which is aimed at ensuring their profits regardless of the social or environmental costs. In practice, this refers to the social movements and grassroots organizations that are developing alliances across international borders in order to stop corporate globalization, such the Zapatista movement in Mexico, which has mobilized international allies to resist the destruction of their indigenous culture and lands.

By exploring and embracing the diversity of direct-service and structural-activist strategies in which social workers are engaged, we can hopefully move to a place where we understand that they are not mutually exclusive; rather, each realm enables the other. In discussing some of her work with the Justice for Women campaign, Kristin noted that "some of the other agencies were really able to be emboldened around some things because we were such pains in the asses and they looked like the 'good girls' then," demonstrating that often the more public forms of activism provide space for more conventional organizations to develop new and more progressive practices.

In order to achieve this we must shift our understanding of activism to be more inclusive. In Kristin's words, "it's about saying those activities are necessary and important and the people that can do them should be doing them. But there needs to not be this exclusive thinking that says that's the only game in town." Or as Leah advocated, we "need to support activism where we find it, and recognize that people are finding very creative ways to do activist work." For some workers, focusing their activism on building networks of global alliances is not going to be immediately viable, but we should keep an eye out for opportunities to connect with others who are pursuing these strategies and continuously educate ourselves on the links between direct-service issues and global trends and forces. The conventional contexts in which most workers are employed means they need to pursue more covert radical politics within their organizations. Yet for the six social workers with whom I spoke, this did not mean they focused exclusively on direct-service intervention; rather, they watched for opportunities to build links with outside groups or causes and remained interested in struggles in the larger community. Though different groups of social justice-oriented social workers differ in their activist strategies, it does not mean that we cannot be united in our pursuit of overall social justice.

It means, rather, that we have developed a keen sense of what type of resistance work is viable given the context in which we each operate. Kristin noted that "context is everything and being able to shift gears and being constantly fluid — that's something that working in restructured environments has taught me: you have to be very nuanced and sense your terrain and make the necessary shifts." These workers also emphasized that "making these necessary shifts" to understand and navigate our contexts of practice is dependent upon several factors. One is the political climate that influences the type of work that can be done within the parameters of the ideologies of state leaders and the larger society. For example, Leah mentioned that with "Mike Harris, we got shut down pretty severely, but before that we did a lot of work around feminist activism and housing issues, and we developed a model at the centre where we were really connected to the community." Sheena spoke of how "people of all political colours get behind youth because of the youth engagement buzz ...

Mike Harris

Mike Harris was the Premier of Ontario from June 1995 to April 2002. While in power, Harris, a Progressive Conservative, implemented a host of funding cuts (commonly known as the "Common Sense Revolution") to areas of social policy such as health care, education, and social welfare. Under his leadership the government cut social assistance rates by 22 percent, introduced Ontario Works (workfare), laid off hundreds of public sector workers, and privatized public services. This period was characterized by a far-reaching dismantling of the social safety nets developed during the post-war era. In response, large community coalitions came together in the Days of Action to protest the highly negative impacts his policies had on people, especially those with whom social workers traditionally work.

I think if you were talking to someone who worked with adults experiencing homelessness and poverty, it would be different."

Our context of practice and the actions available to us are also shaped by our particular workplace dynamics. Alannah noted that certain organizations enable workers to have more autonomy than others. This seems to depend on the way each agency constructs the roles social workers perform in their work. Both she and Leah also argued that some organizations are more expressly political, enabling workers to engage in more overt tactics. Alannah commented, "this section of my child welfare agency doesn't do community development in secret ... the agency has fought for this, and someone has said that my job can accommodate that." Similarly, Leah observed that because her previous work was organized around feminist and more client-centred principles, it "offered many opportunities for pickets and protests, policy work, making briefs and participating in committee work." In addition, the workers argued that the organizational parameters regarding what kinds of activism were permitted were connected to the personal and political orientations of coworkers and those in management/leadership roles. For example, Cheryl mentioned the women's shelter at which she works has "a very progressive leader ... but that if she resigned things would probably change."

Thus, part of the work involved in uniting social work activists in a shared project of social justice needs to focus on the development of a framework which acknowledges that workers use different strategies based on the context in which they work and the opportunities available to them. It must simultaneously acknowledge that social workers can work to challenge and change these opportunities and make conditions better for their clients and themselves. Shifting towards building transformational social work practice amidst globalization requires that we become keenly aware of our contexts and learn to take advantage of the opportunities present there. Social workers need to develop "a set of knowledge and skills regarding how to navigate their agencies, which can be highly constraining places" (Pearl).

Coming to Grips with Globalization

Dominelli (1999: 21) argues that "unless social workers come to grips with the ramifications of globalization: impoverishment of the people with whom they work; restructuring of their profession; and deteriorations of their conditions of work, the future of social work looks bleak." This chapter demonstrates that some activist social workers have indeed come to grips with globalization, and many have moved beyond an analysis of these processes towards taking action to resist and revolutionize the negative impacts of global integration. It is important that we, as a profession, continue to document our activist activity, particularly when the individual actions in which we engage seem unconnected to each other, and especially as more politicized work is "driven underground" (Smith 2007).

The conversations I had with practising activist social workers helped me develop a new understanding of the integral action required to advance our social justice work. Redefining activism means that we have to recognize and value the multiplicity of actions occurring at all levels of practice. Ongoing reflection and re-evaluation give us the opportunity to transcend the divisions between "direct practice" and "structural intervention," the "local" and the "global," and social work and other sectors committed to social justice. The women I talked to stressed that far too much energy is devoted to maintaining these divisions, to ostracizing and labelling other activists as inadequate or conversely as too radical. The result is that we construct those with whom we could be aligned as problematic or enemies. We run the risk of closing ourselves off from understanding and valuing the activist practice operating across the many sites in which we practice. And we may fail to see how our work is interrelated and builds upon other progressive work. As such, we are less able to revamp our practice methods so that they address the nuances and context of neoliberal globalization.

Hopefully, redefining our activism as broader and more inclusive will permit social workers to move forward in meeting the multiple aspects of social justice required in this globalizing world. We need to understand and locate ourselves in the particular political and historical environments that shape our work, and creatively develop a flexible and constantly evolving set of direct service and macro-activities to address these conditions. In this way, we will begin to develop the necessary knowledge and skills required to transform the monolith of neoliberal globalization in order to build the alternative visions of society we seek to create.

Notes

1. The voices in this chapter come from a study involving six social workers talking with me about their anti-oppressive practice. They were recruited through social service networks within southern Ontario and then interviewed for the project. As anticipated, given the higher proportion of females working within caring professions such as social work, the majority of participants were women. Employment within the field ranged from two years of experience to twenty-five years, with an average of twelve years of practice experience. The participants have a collective history of working within community housing, social work education, child protection and child welfare, policy development, women abuse, queer rights, employee assistance programs, foster care, community mental health, primary health, and youth services. All of them have been frontline workers, and three of the participants have also occupied a director or management role. Each of them self–identified as activists, and thus was able to provide concrete examples of how they have sought to facilitate progressive practice amidst neoliberalism.

2. Any identifying information such as the names of research participants, agencies, and places of work has not been included in this chapter in order to protect confidentiality. Workers interviewed shall be referred to by their assigned pseudonym throughout the chapter.

3. As noted earlier in the chapter, some social work authors and practitioners use the term "macro" to mean the same as structural-level practice.

Chapter 16

Unions: A Vehicle for Anti-Oppressive Resistance

Donna Baines

Drawing on historical evidence and some of my recent studies, this chapter explores the similarities and connections between social justice-oriented social work and unions. A long relationship between the social work profession and unions is revealed by historical and contemporary studies; social workers have sometimes worked for employers who opposed unionization and social programs and have often joined in solidarity with unions to advance fairness and equity. The chapter concludes with some innovative ways anti-oppressive social service workers have creatively used modified union structures and strategies to provide them with the space to pursue progressive social change.

As you read through this chapter, ask yourself the following questions:
1. What are some of the similarities between unions and social justice-oriented social work?
2. What is the difference between social workers who see themselves as *allies* of workers and poor people and working on their behalf and social workers who see themselves *as workers* or members of the working class struggling alongside others in similar situations? Where do you think most AOP social workers today fall in this division?
3. What is social unionism and how have some social workers used this model to resist restructuring and expand social justice?

Social workers frequently report feeling alone and disempowered in the struggle for service users' rights and equity (Carniol 2005; Mullaly 2002). Similarly, social work students often report that their growing awareness of social injustice means that they spend hours at every social gathering and event arguing about anti-oppressive practice with friends and family. Though much of the struggle in social work today is a battle of ideas, it is wrong to suppose that social workers are the only groups working for social change — and feeling isolated and immobilized does not help our clients or our causes. Many other groups and social movements share the same value base as social work and pursue the same or similar goals. The challenge is to find these groups, figure out what we share, and negotiate ways to work together for our mutual benefit.

This chapter explores historical and contemporary similarities between social work and the union movement, one of the oldest movements for rights in the workplace and larger society. Though almost a third of working people and close to 40 percent of social service workers are unionized in Canada (Statistics Canada 2007), many people remain ill-informed about this movement, influenced by ideologies that cast unions as self-serving, undemocratic, and bad for the economy. Drawing on my larger studies of how social services are being restructured globally, this chapter will discuss ways that anti-oppressive social workers can work with and within unions to resist workplace and societal oppression. This chapter also addresses practical considerations for those wanting to work within and with unions and various ways that social justice-oriented social workers can draw hope and sustenance from being part of a bigger movement without losing a focus on our unique concerns and issues.

Unions and AOP Share a Values Base and Social Policy Agenda

Long before the social work profession took hold in Canada, unions were fighting for decent wages and conditions within the workplace and for social programs and benefits outside (Canadian Labour Congress 2010; Carniol 2005). Though unions are often accused of caring only about the wages of their members, there have always been unions that struggled for "progressive social policies that would benefit the community as a whole" (Canadian Labour Congress 2010: 2). As Carniol (2000) notes, Canadian unions were at the forefront of campaigns for social benefits such as old age pension, unemployment insurance, minimum wage, pay equity, and medicare (see also Lundy 2004; Hick 2002). While some of the early unions in Canada and elsewhere prided themselves on working within the larger political and economic system, organizing and representing skilled workers exclusively, and focusing single-mindedly on what they called "bread and butter" issues (that is, their own wages and conditions), as early as 1881 unions such as the Knights of Labour organized both unskilled and skilled workers, demanded an end to child and convict labour, pursued equal pay for women and Black workers, appealed to the government to tax the rich more steeply than the poor, and campaigned for mines and factories to be owned and operated cooperatively (Weir 1996). Highlighting the shared values base between unions and the emerging profession of social work, social workers in settlement houses were at around the same time actively supporting the unionization of immigrants in the garment industry and beyond, providing funds during strikes, urging employers to bargain in good faith, and lobbying for better social and labour legislation (Rosenburg and Rosenburg 2006; Pennell 1987).

As is true today, however, not all social workers in those earlier times supported labour activism (Haynes 1975). There was a split between settlement-house workers and those working for charities and the private sector, with the former supporting unions and social activism and the latter distancing themselves (Benjamin 2007; Kurzman 2009; Pennell 1987). Much of the reason for this lies in the fact that most early social workers were employed in private charities who received much of their funding from the very businesses and companies fighting to stop unionization. Private companies were also major employers of social workers in the role of "welfare secretaries" who were charged with keeping unionization out of their employers' factories and mines by providing minimal supports for workers (Kurzman 2009). Social workers in these jobs were encouraged to identify with the employer and the company rather than with the workers and their organizations.

As legislators slowly responded to calls from unions and other progressive groups to build social programs and supports, social work jobs were created in the newly government-funded, public sector (Abramovitz 1988). Freeing social workers from their direct ties with corporate capitalism opened up a new relationship with unions (Kurzman 2009). By the early 1930s social work organizations such as the Rank and File Movement and settlement houses worked closely with unions in the struggle to reduce poverty, provide quality employment for all, and spread socialist values such as social participation and shared responsibility for social well-being (Rosenburg and Rosenburg 2006; Pennell 1987; Withorn 1984). Echoing themes still reverberating in social justice-oriented social work today, some social workers saw themselves as allies of workers and poor people, while others saw themselves as workers struggling alongside others in similar situations (Haynes 1975). The two philosophies differed considerably, with the former viewing themselves as altruistic professionals working *on behalf* of oppressed others, while the latter saw themselves *as part* of a large class of people known as the working class who have no way to make their living other than their capacity to work. They argued that like factory workers and poor people, social workers' lives were insecure as they regularly faced problems such as wage cuts, unpaid vacations and overtime, and layoffs (Haynes 1975: 90). Like other oppressed groups, social workers' best strategies for change were argued to lie in joining with others to end the power of the wealthy and those benefitting from high unemployment and poverty, and to reorganize society in a completely equitable way. Those favouring a more professionalized approach thought fundamental reorganization of society was unnecessary, believing instead that unions could work with others to introduce reforms aimed at regulating capitalism and reducing its harsh excesses, thus addressing the most pressing problems of poor people and workers.

> ### *Working Class*
> The working class is composed of anyone who has to use his or her intellect and/or bodies to work for a living rather than owning the enterprises in which he or she is employed. The vast majority of Canadians are working class even though they may fill different kinds of jobs, earn very different wages, and receive different levels of prestige and power for the kinds of work they do. Marx and others believed that members of the working class had common political, social, and political interests because of their shared situation of having nothing to sell but their labour power.

As social programs ebbed and flowed, unions continued to be among the first groups in society calling for expanded social welfare and a more equitable distribution of wealth and income. As well, they demanded justice for exploited and oppressed groups including women, people of colour, queer people, people with disabilities, Indigenous people, and others (Mullaly 1997). Often social workers joined with or provided leadership to their unions on these initiatives, sometimes adopting the philosophy that social workers share a common concern with all others in the working and poor classes, sometimes adopting a more altruistic, professional commitment to struggle alongside those who are oppressed. Interestingly, many social justice-oriented social workers embraced a somewhat contradictory but fairly functional amalgam of both perspectives, pressing ahead for equity and fairness using a variety of tactics, strategies, and ideologies.

Social work professional organizations have been known to join with unions and other groups in these demands though they are often much more cautious than unions and grassroots organizations (Lundy 2004), aligning their responses, and *de facto* their interests, with other professional and corporate groups.

Unions — Strengths and Limitations

One of the strengths of unions is their capacity to increase the wages and working conditions of those they represent. For example, overall, unionized workers in Canada make $25.20 an hour compared to $20.61 for non-unionized workers (Statistics Canada 2007), a difference of $4.59 per hour or 22.3 percent, and this gap continues to grow. The gap increases for women in unionized jobs, who make $24.46 an hour versus $18.22 for non-union women, a difference of 34.2 percent. Women are more likely than men to be employed part-time and here we see the gap widen again. Part-time workers in unionized jobs make $20.79 per hour versus $13.16 for non-union, a difference of 58 percent (Statistics Canada 2010). This makes unionization a very effective strategy for addressing poverty, as well as for improving the quality of life for marginalized groups. Improving wage levels also transfers money from employers to those they employ, representing an important way to redistribute wealth in society.

Currently around 39 percent of social service workers in Canada are un-ionized (Statistics Canada 2007), largely with unions such as the Canadian Union of Public Employees (CUPE), provincial public sector unions such as the Ontario Public Sector Employees' Union (OPSEU) or the Nova Scotia Union of Government Employees' Union (NSGEU), amalgamated unions such as the Canadian Auto Workers (CAW), or American-based unions such as UNITE-HERE or the Services Employees' International Union (SEIU).

As noted above, unions have also been at the forefront, or at least part of, struggles to extend rights for systemically marginalized groups. This included early efforts to introduce equal pay and benefits for all groups, extend pensions and workplace benefits to same-sex partners, demand accessibility for people with disabilities, and so forth. Though effective at achieving major reforms in the workplace and larger society, unions operate within a distinct legal climate that limits the way they address social issues. Much of this is the result of historical developments.

Though people formed unions in Canada as early as 1812, employers could use various parts of the Criminal Code and common law to lay serious charges against unionists. They could also fire union members with impunity, hire private police to harass and attack those at union events, and replace striking workers with substitute employees. Responding to union agitation and jumping at the chance to embarrass the opposition, in 1872 Sir John A. MacDonald introduced legislation making unions and union activities lawful. However, it continued to be very difficult to get employers to agree to bargain (negotiate the terms of wages and working conditions) with unions, agree or adhere to contracts, collect union dues, or treat unionists fairly. The 1945 sit-down strike at Ford Motor Company in Windsor prompted the introduction of the famous "Rand Formula" whereby employers agreed to recognize unions, abide by recognized rules for bargaining and dispute resolution, and collect dues on behalf of the union. In return for union security, labour had to agree that the employer had the exclusive right to manage the workplace and organize the work. For those wanting to use unionization as a way to reform as well as for those wanting to fundamentally change society, the Rand Formula represented a historic step forward, giving unions formal standing in society and a stable financial base from which to grow. For those seeking a fundamental reorganization of capitalism and democratic or collective power within the workplace, the Rand Formula also represented a significant compromise, as it legally confirmed the right of employers to dominate the labour process.

For anti-oppressive social workers, the legal context in which Canadian unions operate means that while they can be used to improve working con-ditions for poorly paid groups in society and for social workers themselves, as well as to work in solidarity on an endless array of justice-seeking causes, unions do not have the right to run the workplace or even challenge the way management understands the agency's mission or how programs are planned and delivered. Nor do they have the right to insist on the reorganization of ineffective and harmful social programs or approaches. This poses many problems for anti-oppressive social workers who value participation at all levels of social service delivery and who, along with service users, are often the best-positioned to see that the services they are delivering are part of the problem, requiring fundamental change. Though unions and unionized workers do not have the formalized right to demand a role in the operation of social service agencies, many workers and their unions have developed formal and informal strategies to increase workplace participation in decision-making and evaluation around a myriad of issues.

Managerialism: Restructuring in the Social Services

From the anti-oppressive perspective, social services in the western world — though arguably meeting many social needs and reducing poverty — have been consistently seen to need ongoing improvement. However, the beginning of neoliberalism in the mid-1980s marked a dramatic change in social service organization, entitlement, and delivery (McDonald 2006; Cohen 1997). Globally, governments cut funds to public services and encouraged citizens to rely on themselves, their families, and the private market (that is, to buy services from private companies or individuals) to meet their human service needs (Teeple 2000). At the level of the social service agency, services were often cut back and programs redesigned. Most of the remaining services were targeted at specific problems rather than being universal (available to everyone) and holistic (multi-integrated services) (Lightman 2003; Dominelli and Hoogvelt 1996; Carniol 2000). Ongoing waves of funding cuts meant that services were underresourced and overstretched. While in the past it was seen as appropriate to offer a choice of services to clients, this pluralism was seen as duplication, resulting in the merging or shutting down of entire programs, and sometimes agencies (Baines 2004a). These and other reductions in services meant that many more people sought assistance, often presenting themselves at social service agencies in much more serious distress than they would have in the past, when services were less restrictive and more available; now, facing increased demand, agencies had fewer services and social workers available to assist them (Dominelli 2004; Carniol 2000).

The neoliberal era in social services, often referred to as "managerialism," ushered in standardization in two overlapping forms (Baines 2004a; Cunningham 2008). The first was in management models, the second in service delivery. Drawing on management models popular in retail sales, social service agencies began to adopt a version of performance management known as New Public Management (NPM). The goal of this model was "remove waste," "reduce inefficiencies," and "improve accountability" through meeting performance targets and outcome measures (McDonald 2006; Dominelli 2004). Outcome measures and best practices metrics are processes in which a concrete number or numbers are assigned to social work processes, such as number of people who request service (Baines 2006b). These metrics are thought to work well when complex social work practices can be broken down into measurable, bite-sized pieces such as number of cases opened or closed, number of days or hours each case was open, number of referrals completed, or number of meetings attended. These kinds of measures represent a fraction of what social workers actually do on a case, and the kinds of creativity and individual attention required to provide high-quality social justice-oriented care and service provision (Baines 2006b). It is almost impossible for outcome measures to capture the open-ended, collaborative, relationship-building, social change-oriented practices that characterize anti-oppressive social work. For example, the goals of social and individual empowerment underlie most anti-oppressive social work interactions. Empowerment involves complicated processes that can occur very quickly and/or over a long period of time. It is hard to conceptualize what sort of measures might be applied to prove that empowerment occurred and to avoid making empowerment that takes longer seem less valuable than empowerment that happens immediately.

Hence, performance indicators and outcome measure generally narrow and standardize social work to practices that can be easily measured (McDonald 2006). They also remove social workers' capacity to use their own discretion, knowledge, and practice skills to individualize care plans to the needs of the service user rather than provide the most cost-efficient, easily measureable interventions (Smith 2007; Baines 2006b). Many social justice-oriented practices fall outside the standardized outcome measures, making it hard for anti-oppressive social workers to find the space for the kind of work they want to undertake (Baines 2006a). It is ironic that in an era in which people are encouraged to "think outside the box" and innovate, workplace management models provide little, if any, positive recognition for practices that do not contribute to cost saving and efficiency.

In British Columbia, for example, workers experienced what was then a new model of management, New Public Management (NPM), as a loss of practice skills, heavier workloads, standardized work, a lack of resources, and little or no voice for workers and service users (Baines 2006a). They also felt that these changes contributed to a loss of vision and sense of direction for social workers, as well as a growing social meanness in which individuals are encouraged to look out for themselves and their families, rather than for the larger social good (Baines 2006a). Interestingly, though they felt hemmed in and limited in how they could practice or even envision practicing social justice-oriented social work, these same workers suggested far-reaching measures that should be taken to build a more equitable and fair society. These measures included turning the whole system "on its head" so that most of the funding would be used in holistic, comprehensive, community-based preventive and proactive services emphasizing public care and non-exclusion (Baines 2006a: 23). Some of the workers argued that governments and social service agencies should implement processes of participatory democracy in which planning and policy-setting would start with the grassroots, including service users, their communities, and services providers in as many mass meetings and consultations as necessary to involve "dispossessed people" in solving their own complicated, deeply rooted social problems and collectively build strong, inclusive communities (Baines 2006a: 25). On a final note, one long-term child welfare advocate argued that any jobs attached to these initiatives should be unionized.

Social workers in non-profit social services in Australia and Canada are often drawn to the work because of the opportunity to work in tandem with their values. However, managerialism, work speed-up, and standardization meant that they were just as often required to work contrary to their values, contributing to a deep sense of frustration and burn-out (Baines 2010b).

I am very interested in how social workers cope in response to restructuring — why some workers continue with their lives as if nothing has changed while others resist and organize and make social change. Experience in Australia shows that in order to feel ethical and to believe that they are still changing the world for the better, many social justice-oriented social workers undertake activist work outside their workplaces (Baines 2010b). In Canada, some social workers are undertaking strategies similar to those used by Australian social workers while others are turning to their unions as vehicles for social change, in the process developing new forms of activism and changing their unions to meet their unique set of needs and demands (Baines 2010a).

Social Workers and Unions: Building New Forms of Resistance

Social Work Union Activism

For historical reasons, American unions have legal standing to operate in Canada and used to dominate the Canadian labour movement. Dovetailing with the introduction of neoliberalism in the mid-1980s, a number of Canadian units began to split off from their U.S. parent unions. In contrast to American unions, generally thought of as "business unions" that focus primarily on "bread and butter" issues such as their members' wages and benefits, the new Canadian unions promoted themselves as "social unions" — representing members at the bargaining table while simultaneously campaigning for social justice "in every aspect of the economic, social and political life of Canadians" (Canadian Labour Congress 2010).

Though laudable, social unionism in Canada operates largely as the official ideology of the union movement: union officials and staff promote social reform

> ### Business Unionism
> A system in which unions defend the workplace and human rights, wages, and benefits of their members.

> ### Social Unionism
> A system in which unions see the struggles of communities as inseparable from union struggles for expanded rights, decent standards of living for all, improved social policy, and increased opportunities for full social participation.

ideals, involve members in policy decisions and formal mobilizations (such as mass rallies), but rarely undertake sustained, grassroots organizing or activism (Black 2005). However, some Canadian social service workers use their unions in strategic ways to promote the kinds of social justice values and activities that have been structured out of their workplaces. For example, when asked why they unionized or became union activists, some social workers say that they had "lost their voice." This included their voice in the workplace on policy issues, advocacy, community development, service delivery, planning and evaluation, and most importantly, client needs. Having a voice on social justice issues provided one of the most meaningful aspects of many social workers' jobs and as one young female worker for Canadian immigration services put it, "If you haven't got meaning in these jobs, what else have you got?" (Baines 2010a).

For most activists, "bread and butter" union issues, though important, were closely linked to social justice initiatives within and beyond the workplace. As the local president in a mid-sized, multi-service agency noted:

> Wages and working conditions are always important to our members, but people really want a voice in how decisions get made. We have expertise in our program areas, we know our clients and communities and we want some say in how things get done.

Social work union activists drew their union locals, set up largely to bargain the conditions of work and wages, into a wide variety of causes including homelessness, poverty, racism, homophobia, violence, public and non-profit sector funding cuts, refugee and immigration issues, and the war in Iraq. Rather than providing a boundary on what type of activities the local union should take on, the workplace acted as a springboard for contact with community organizations, advocacy groups, and other union locals.

Rather than accept the parameters dictated in labour law, the president of a large union local reported that they "don't operate within the confines of our collective agreement. We challenge layoffs and cuts whenever they occur, in our agency or in others." This particular local became involved in a number

> ### Union Local
> The basic building block of the union. A union local is usually comprised of the people who work in a given workplace. The local elects an executive who keep the union local running on a day-to-day basis. Shop Stewards are also elected to represent different areas in an agency and to provide feedback from the front lines to the executive. The local is affiliated to city (or municipal), provincial, and national bodies in the union as well as to city or municipal labour councils, provincial federations of labour, and national labour bodies such as the Canadian Labour Congress in English Canada.

of multi-group, multi-union, multi-agency coalitions, including the left-liberal Toronto Disaster Relief Committee; the more radical Ontario Coalition Against Poverty; community actions aimed at stopping deportations and addressing immigrant issues; and a mass campaign against homophobic violence in the downtown core. In all these examples, social justice-oriented social workers used their unions as a way to extend care for clients and communities, explicitly linking agency and larger social change. In these and other examples, the union local and the resources it could draw on from the national and provincial union bodies became an additional means through which social care (in the form of community mobilization and advocacy for policy change) could be extended to and with the community (Baines 2010a).

On the other hand, when union structures prove too bureaucratic or cumbersome to meet the needs of the members, social work activists often initiate new ones. In one union local the social service workers initiated a "buddy system" in which newer activists were twinned with experienced ones to share skills and knowledge, drawing more people into "the life of the local" (Baines 2010a). One union president noted that she drew on her experience in social work and community activism to build a union local that was formally hierarchical (to meet the requirements of the parent union's constitution) but operated more or less on a consensus basis, providing opportunities for all members to have a voice and influence priorities and activities. Another union president told me that she and a core of activists in the union worked very hard to maintain a spirit that was "creative, effective, and very positive, not negative and draggy." Their goal was to create "an oasis for the members," a comfortable space to counteract the frequently negative feelings associated with working in an increasingly stressed and frustrating workplace.

Social Workers as Workers: A Child Welfare Worker Strike

Though child welfare is not often thought of as a hotbed of community activism, Tara La Rose (2009) writes convincingly about the lessons learned during a struggle in a social work local of the Canadian Union of Public Employees.

Neoliberal restructuring has resulted in highly standardized and circumscribed work practices in child welfare, with open-ended, interactive processes such as intake assessments and case planning replaced by computerized tick-box assessment tools and closely monitored timelines for the completion of pre-set tasks. Funding cuts and public demand for increased vigilance significantly increased the size and intensity of case loads. At the time of the strike, government funding was actually tied to pre-set timelines for completion of tasks, leaving child welfare workers feeling highly stressed and intrusively scrutinized as well as increasingly deskilled and totally exhausted. Prior to the strike — and important to the process of building bonds of support and solidarity among workers — child welfare workers used their union local to rally around a fellow worker facing criminal charges in a tragic case in which a child died (the charges were eventually overturned). Social workers knew that the child's sad death was the result of systemic rather than individual failure, and that managerial restructuring had created the conditions in which it was almost impossible to stay on top of caseloads. Though child welfare workers had tried to raise issues through the regular channels, their concerns were not addressed and new strategies were clearly needed. During contract negotiations, the union asked for caps on caseload sizes and improved wording around workload in the contract. Management refused to agree and the workers finally went out on strike.

Though their strike issues were very serious, workers reported that the strike gave them the opportunity to build relationships across programs and departments, sharing experience and ideas, in effect coming out of their bubbles and understanding the agency in a larger way (La Rose 2009: 240). La Rose reports that each picket line had its own character — one focused on singing, eventually forming a choir and recording a CD, while another emphasized fun and irreverence, featuring a "bring your pet to the picket" day, a pyjama day, and a "make-over on the picket line" day. While some managers were supportive throughout the strike, others gained a new appreciation for the frontline workers through filling their jobs during the six-week strike. The local returned to work having won their issues and set a precedent for child welfare locals

Strike

A legally regulated process in which the members of a union vote to stop working in order to protest management's offer during bargaining. Bargaining is a legally regulated process in which representatives of the union and management meet to work out the wages and conditions of work. When agreement cannot be reached, the parties can choose to continue bargaining or either side can stop work — that is, go on strike. Strikes end when the union members accept an offer from the employer with a majority vote. In rare instances, workers can also be ordered back to work by government.

across the province. Their gains were quickly expanded to other worksites that demanded and won similar caseload caps and workload contract language (La Rose 2009: 241). This wording not only improved social workers' quality of work life through smaller caseloads but also improved care for service users.

Though none of the workers involved would call themselves heroes, and few realized the importance of their strike, this episode in the life of a child welfare union local brought the struggle against neoliberalism down to the frontlines of everyday social work. The workers challenged the logics of managerialism, pointing out the ways that standardization permitted work to be sped up but removed such important aspects of child welfare work as open-ended relationship-building between workers and service users; intensive, shared case planning; and worker discretion. The struggle also challenged the notion that employers and governments should have the exclusive right to set caseloads and determine work practices. In this case, workers and their union won the right to set caps and insist on dispute mechanisms, all of which generated much-needed improvements for clients as well. As one of the participants in La Rose's (2009: 243) study noted, the workers also gained respect, empowering themselves and realizing that they could make significant changes by using their union local as a vehicle for social change.

Practical Considerations

The examples above show that unions can be used to pursue the kinds of social justice causes and issues central to anti-oppressive agendas. They also show that activists can push and stretch unions to adopt new forms and organization structures, such as collective decision-making, that encourage participation and are more in-tune with social work values than are hierarchies, bureaucracies, and formalism. Not all locals are as flexible and creative as those described in the examples above. Many eager activists have been discouraged or deterred by the inaction, disinterest, and bureaucracy of their local union. For example, while studying for my M.S.W. I worked as a summer student for a unionized child welfare agency. Thrilled to bump into the local president, I told him I would be happy to be involved in any union activities while I was working at the agency. He was dismissive, noting that part-time and contract staff come and go and that his primary concerns were the full-time, permanent staff. I was incensed but somewhat confused and a little intimidated. By the time I had sought out advice from others (who were annoyed but not surprised at this particular individual's response and advised me not to take no for an answer), my summer job was almost over and I left without ever attending a single union event. However, I took this experience with me to my next unionized job and immediately got involved, eventually being elected to the executive and taking on the editing of their newsletter (which was huge fun).

It is true that part-time and contract employees are hard to organize and hard to represent, so that many locals focus on the staff more likely to be around for a long time. Social workers employed in precarious forms of employment, however, need union representation as much or more than full-time staff, and it is in the interest of unions to make sure they are included in union activities, particularly bargaining. The advice of my child welfare colleagues remains *apropos*: if you want to be involved in your union local, do not take no for an answer, persist in your inquiries, draw in like-minded colleagues, and present a united front. The local is not likely to ignore concerns and interests coming from even a small group of workers, regardless of whether they are temporary or full-time.

Union activities may be particularly difficult for women to undertake, because of the care responsibilities they face at home, and the social work labour force is overwhelmingly female. Some unions have taken steps to assist members with care obligations, providing on-site childcare or monies for babysitting and adult care. While these measures help, union activists must be aware of the home life obligations most women (and some men) undertake and try to be respectful and supportive of these responsibilities. However, as one union representative in Australia noted, if women do not make their presence felt in a local union, issues such as home-work balance, parental leave, maternity leave top-up, and other benefits central to women are much less likely to get raised with the employer or become a priority in bargaining (Baines and Cunningham, forthcoming). Women need to find ways to make their voices heard within unions and contribute to important debates and issues across the sector.

I started the chapter by noting that many social workers and social work students wish there were other people around who shared their convictions and passion for social justice. Reasonable caseloads, greater discretion and autonomy for social workers, opportunities for ongoing education and training are all benefits that unions have fought for and won. Interestingly, all of these gains benefit workers and clients, and likely the larger community as well, through improved practice and quality of care. Though not perfect — limited by labour law, sometimes drifting into "routinism" and bureaucracy, and like other social justice organizations still struggling with sexism, racism, homophobia, and other forms of oppressive relations — unions, particularly social unions, provide a vehicle that can be used very effectively in struggles for social justice and can link social justice-oriented social workers with others seeking equity and fairness in the workplace and larger society.

Note

Those seeking more information about unions in Canada can go to <www.canadianlabour.ca> or visit the websites of any of the unions mentioned in this chapter.

Chapter 17

Self-Care, Social Work, and Social Justice

Norma Jean Profitt

For years I've felt dissatisfied with the ways that notions of self-care for social workers fail to capture the complexity of social life. In this chapter I discuss four themes integral to self-care in social work practice: the interrelation between the personal and the professional; institutional parameters; the ongoing negotiation of boundaries; and responses to working with victims of violence. Based on the experiences of social workers, I argue that social work needs a critical, collective notion of self-care that expands the individual notion of self-care currently pervading the profession.

As you read this chapter, ask yourself the following questions:
1. How have you thought about self-care in social work practice?
2. How do you understand the relationship between the self-care of social workers and the socio-political, cultural, and economic context in which we work?
3. What do you see as the possible potentials of and barriers to a critical, collective approach to self-care?

Over the years I have heard social workers talk about the need to do self-care or the need to undertake strategies aimed at caring for the self. These declarations generally follow discussions about heavy workloads and demands to do more with less in everyday social work practice. Invariably, self-care is advanced as a means to cope with stressful and under-resourced work environments. Social workers then vehemently affirm the *need* to take care of themselves and proceed to give examples of how they practice self-care, for example, through yoga, bubble baths, or pastimes. Some incorporate self-care into their workday, for instance, by claiming their lunch hours or sitting on a park bench communing with nature. Without a doubt, these practices are indispensable for managing stress levels and averting fatigue.

After listening to these discussions, however, I yearned for a deeper conversation that integrated context and struggles for social justice into self-care.

> ### Self-Care
> Self-care, broadly conceived, consists of an approach, strategies, and practices aimed at caring for oneself by oneself. Situation- and culture-specific, self-care concerns the purposeful use of practices to enhance personal well-being and healthful functioning.

Discussing the ethical-political dimension of social work, Marta Picado Mesén (2004:137) argues that given current neoliberal regimes, social work education must recommit itself to be "on the side of social justice, equity, the universality of access to goods and services, the consolidation of citizenship, and the guarantee of civil, political, and social rights." In the face of neoliberal agendas, political conservatism about the family and women's place in our world, and unrelenting discourse about "the economy" as if it were a god, I pondered how a bubble bath would help with my distress at growing social injustice.

My questioning surfaced again in a research project on gender and family violence.[1] Early in the project, self-care emerged as a significant issue. These social workers situated self-care in the context of sweeping social and economic changes, in this case those which have taken place in Costa Rica. Neoliberal policies and the effects of globalization have further impoverished *el pueblo* (the people), making it very difficult to meet the most basic needs of food, shelter, health, and education, and fostering a deterioration of the fundamental fabric of society, including the quality and rights of citizenship (Picado Mesén 2004). In an effort to address some of the needs of social workers, I organized two popular education workshops on self-care, integrating critical reflection, bodywork, music, and meditation. These helped us name themes, explore the rich, multifaceted aspects of self-care, and develop a *critical, collective notion of self-care*. These conversations deepened my thinking about self-care as a useful concept in social work, as a politicized notion of self-care.

> ### Critical, Collective Notion of Self-Care
> Critical, collective signals the need to think about self-care in ways that go beyond the individual to recognize both the larger social and political context of existing inequalities and the intertwined nature of self and others.

Self-Care in the Social Work Profession

The need for self-care is often associated with ethical social work practice (Neumann and Gamble 1995; Hesse 2002). If our ability to provide competent and adequate services to clients is hampered by psychological distress, mental health, or personal problems, then we must seek appropriate remedies to care for ourselves (Canadian Association of Social Workers 2005a and 2005b). In

> ### The Personal
> The personal usually refers to our unique individual biographies, personalities, internal states, and experiences. In critical social work, the notion of the personal also encompasses an understanding of our multiple social identities and our place in relations of power in social work practice.

the helping professions, self-care is considered essential in maintaining positive energy, enhancing capacity for empathy, and appreciating processes of healing and regeneration (McCann and Pearlman 1990; Neumann and Gamble 1995). In the last two decades, helpers have paid particular attention to self-care and vicarious trauma, which describes the profound effects and changes that some professionals experience due to empathic engagement with people who have suffered traumatic experiences (McCann and Pearlman 1990; Figley 1995; Pearlman and MacIan 1995; Pearlman and Saakvitne 1995; Astin 1997; Regehr and Cadell 1999; Hesse 2002; Bell 2003; Cunningham 2003).

In contemplating the concept of self-care, however, it is important to consider how we conceptualize the spheres of the "personal" and the "professional" in social work theory and practice. Differing assumptions about their relation underlie mainstream and critical social work perspectives, carrying different implications for the practice of self-care.

Mainstream social work exhorts us to be conscious of how our values, beliefs, attitudes, and personal experiences influence practice (Hepworth, Rooney and Larsen 1997) and to bracket them off so they will not influence our practice. This assumes that the personal can be easily left out of the professional equation (Sheppard 2000) and that a position of objectivity, or at least neutrality, can be achieved to avoid contaminating practice with the personal.

In contrast, anti-oppressive social work (feminist, critical, structural, radical, progressive) conceptualizes the relation between the personal and the professional with much more complexity. Personal and professional identities are formed through multiple and multifaceted experiences, including diverse socialization processes traversed by hierarchies of gender and class, among others. Personal identity and professional identity are inseparable and two sides of the same coin; both shape professional practice (Fernández Vargas 2006; Guzmán Stein 2002; Méndez Vega 2003). Social relations of power clearly permeate and influence all intrapersonal and interpersonal phenomena, including interactions between social workers and clients (Rossiter 2000). If we are to understand social work as a political endeavour, then the social cannot be separated from the political (Dudziak 2002).

Four Themes Integral to the Concept of Self-Care

Four themes shape self-care: the interrelation between the personal and the professional; institutional parameters; the ongoing negotiation of boundaries; and responses to working with victims of violence. Drawing on these themes, I argue that a more politicized critical, collective notion of self-care is needed to expand the individualized notion of self-care that currently pervades the profession. Conceptualizations of self-care must move beyond individualized responses to negative stressors in the workplace, discomforting emotions, and difficult micro-relations. An expanded notion must recognize both the life-giving and wearing effects of practice as well as the multiple and diverse processes of "conscientization," growth, and struggle that social workers engage in during the course of our labours. Self-care must take into account our meaning-making activities as we make sense of our practice and our personal and social worlds.

Interrelation between the Personal and Professional

Earlier in this chapter I mentioned a project I worked on in Costa Rica on gender and violence. This section of the chapter draws on that study (see also endnote 1). For the social workers I interviewed, the personal and the professional illuminated each other and led to significant personal/professional growth that expanded and enriched conceptual frameworks and social work practice. Professional practice sparked reflection about personal formation and biography, prompting a reinterpretation of past experience in a critical light. It served as a mirror, reflecting the power dynamics in intimate and familial relations, child-rearing, domestic work, and care arrangements.

As a social worker in family court, Ziomara's[2] practice with victims of woman abuse and aggressors was a catalyst for conscientization about gender.

> For all the professional training that you have ... you have to break down your own worldview, the worldview of your family. I come from a very traditional family with very established patriarchal roles and I say: "Well, the same thing happened to me in my family with me and my brothers," and all that is reflected back to you because you come from the same environment, from the same mechanism of socialization that

Conscientization

Conscientization or *conscientização*, a popular education concept developed by Brazilian Paulo Freire in *Pedagogy of the Oppressed*, entails a process of learning to see and analyze social, political, and economic contradictions in our society, to understand how power operates, and to act against oppressive elements of reality. A key piece of conscientization involves understanding how we are implicated in relations of domination and oppression and using such insight to make change.

> ## Subjectivity
> Subjectivity refers to our individuality, self-awareness, sense of ourselves, conscious and unconscious thoughts and feelings, and understanding of where we fit in the world. Implicit in the notion of subjectivity is understanding how we are socially constructed within social relations of power, privilege, and penalty.

is so deeply rooted. Also, the knowledge that you gain in professional practice helps you, it gives you the option of changing and modifying your personal and familial life. In what sense? I am going to teach my son this and that, the same as with my daughter, and create equality in the home because you know very well the consequences of gender inequality and that is very applicable to our personal life.

Although Ziomara had studied theories of gender in social work training, practice was what sparked a process of conscientization in which she more profoundly questioned the social devaluation of women. It spurred her to make significant changes in her personal life and develop a framework of gender for her practice (Guzmán Stein 1994, 2002, and 2004; Fernández Vargas 2006).

Subjectivity was an invaluable resource for deepening social workers' understanding of social processes, in this case of gendering, in their lives. This learning prompted shifts in their intimate lives, interpersonal expectations, sense of self, and personal and professional identities. Meaning-making informed their professional identities and led to an integration of their personal and professional selves.

Institutional Parameters

As many chapters in this book note, social workers are often unable to work with people as they would like because of restrictions in the workplace. Some Costa Rican social workers spoke at length about their struggles within institutional ideologies, structures, and rules that organized "the problems" of the people as private, individual matters to be dealt with through casework, thus hindering more liberatory, collective ways of working. Their consciences, ethics, and identities as social workers were shaped by working within institutions that trampled on their personal and professional values and created a sense of complicity and shame as provisioners of humiliating and inadequate services.

As a young woman, Cristina experienced an intense process of conscientization, coming to see as "truth that the social making of woman is a power struggle." Highly attuned to women's aspirations and needs, she expressed anger and disgust at the state institution where she worked. Although it provided financial assistance to the poorest of the poor, it offered only institutionalized solutions to women's poverty and woman abuse rather than real alternatives.

This is a vulgar, palliative institution that silences the conscience of poor people in order to demoralize them socially, never will it ever touch a hair of structural poverty unless it develops, under the concept of education for liberation, projects of real knowledge and understanding at the grassroots. Meanwhile what I do is earn a salary with a lot of vulgarity ... it's a professional dissatisfaction because one isn't contributing or learning but rather describing a historical process that is more than well documented; you only have to go to the bank of the International Monetary Fund to see what is the range, the index of poverty in Costa Rica, oh, and then to put faces to it? Rosa, Carolina, it's shameful, it's a shame but that is what gives me the means to eat and what can I do?

Much of her energy was consumed by the contradiction between the act of helping and the act of oppressing. Burdened by the ethical distress that her role raised, she constantly sought a relation with the people "that does not violate the Other" (Cornell 1995: 78).

Unable to develop the political potential of the people they served in the ways they desired, these social workers moved carefully within institutional parameters. To maintain their integrity, they consciously chose to resist in strategic ways, educate and politicize others, including professionals, advocate for service users' rights, capture resources for women and children's support groups and formation, and look for, and sometimes find, alternative spaces in which to foster political potential. Their actions, rooted in personal and professional values, served to quietly and directly protest institutionalism.

Ongoing Negotiation of Boundaries

Social workers worked on a number of fronts to continuously negotiate boundaries between the professional realm and personal space. They struggled with internal conflicts, intense emotions, intrusive images of abused women, and preoccupations about clients and other pressures; and they tried to keep them from spilling into or overtaking the personal and familial domain.

In María Elena's case, an explicit political-ideological vision guided how she lived her life and practiced social work. Although it was impossible for her to establish a definitive boundary between personal life and her commitment to social struggle, she did seek to balance political commitments with personal life:

In my situation at times the desire to advance was so great that I violate even my own rhythm until I sacrifice my own necessities, so the challenge is how do I establish a balance between the personal, the professional, and the political that doesn't absorb me more, how to achieve that equilibrium ... In the personal I believe that I have sacrificed a lot in this struggle ... So for example, when there are formal spaces for self-care (one training offered by Costa Rican Social Insurance), suddenly I am justifying the fact that I have so much work that I don't have time for self-care ... because I learned very well the lesson that I have to be doing for others, but in addition, I learned very well the lesson of always having to do everything with double the effort in order to demonstrate that what I am doing is worthy.

While most of María Elena's colleagues viewed her commitments to women's and popular struggles outside the normal workday as a "personal sacrifice," she was living her vision and values. Like her, social workers in this study identified strongly with the people they served and their critical consciousness about social justice and human rights was a fountain of strength and motivation for practice.

Contrary to popular social work discourse that suggests that the personal and professional are easily held separate, social workers showed that the boundary lines between them were fluid, complex, and overlapping. Cherished values of caring for people and social fairness that infuse personal life also permeate professional practice and cannot simply be separated, repressed, or dismissed in social work practice.

Responses to Working with Victims of Violence

This theme speaks to how social workers were affected, somatically, emotionally, and spiritually, by the work they do. As witnesses to pain and suffering on a daily basis, they felt many things, among them a moral responsibility and desire to help people, a wish to rescue them from suffering, an identification with their anguish, a sense of powerlessness and impotence in helping, a great respect for service users, and a fierce commitment to political struggle. Ana spoke of how images of women's violation came unbidden into her mind after work as she frantically searched for ways to help them escape grave situations.

In her work with women victims, Pilar had to learn to protect her human sensibility from too much hurt by setting limits on the degree to which she empathized with them. Distinct from the notion of maintaining professional distance or objectivity, she carved out a protective space for herself where she could feel for women without absorbing and taking on their feelings and problems.

At times Pilar also found that the sadness of her work invaded her whole person. Immersion in a world of woman abuse that others do not share created both a feeling of isolation and a desire to isolate herself:

> At times it is a chaos for us here, to detach from the experiences that I live here with this turbulence in society and the person, Pilar, arrives home, how is the person Pilar? At times it is very difficult for me to let go of everything, of the sadness of this place ... at times my children come to tell me about some situation to find some solutions and I say:

"Today I don't want to listen to situations," then I close my door and everything else up because I don't want to see anyone and the same thing happens, I feel isolated.

Although Pilar valued her care work, her point of reference of the plight of individual women and the bigger picture of systemic gender oppression sometimes eclipsed other windows on the world.

The above responses to witnessing pain and suffering co-existed with the joy that social workers expressed at women's disposition toward change, the solidarity they demonstrated with the people, their gratitude at contributing to service users' consciousness-raising and healing, and their commitments to social change, whether individual and/or collective.

Doing Self-Care

In contemplating self-care in social work practice, one can make several observations from the experiences of Costa Rican social workers. First, through processes of conscientization, growth, and struggle, they made meaning about experiences that traversed their personal and professional lives, not just about workplace situations that provoked stress, fatigue, or vicarious trauma. Second, in critically analyzing how power works, they took action to resist institutional limitations, conscientize others, meet clients' needs, and engage in social movements. They also directly confronted feelings of complicity and shame in their social work role. Third, they recognized the deep satisfaction derived from their relations with service users and at the same time dealt with internal conflicts, tensions, and feelings in everyday practice. Fourth, they sought to carve out personal spaces of reprieve from concerns about service users and the weight of their knowledge of "social suffering" (Pederson 2002: 187). Their efforts to understand their personal and professional selves in social work practice were dynamic and changing over time, shaped by factors such as political climate, workplace, engagement with particular client populations, and personal biography and circumstances. An important implication of these experiences for doing self-care is that the whole self and meaning-making are situated in a socio-political, cultural, and economic context.

Common conceptualizations of self-care rarely integrate the context of our work as social workers, but instead use frameworks rooted in the language of private feelings, psychology, or individual trauma (Summerfield 1999). Such frameworks individualize the witnessing of social phenomena such as violence against women, hunger, or the structural violence of poverty, and essentially relocate this witnessing to the realm of private injury. However, "suffering arises from, and is resolved in, a social context, shaped by the meanings and understandings applied to events" (Summerfield 1999: 1454). Consequently, self-care and transcendence are not only individual intra-psychic or religious issues but also community, collective ones (Hernández 2000). In the same vein, the interpretive frames we use to understand and analyze self-care shape our strategies for addressing it. If we situate self-care in a framework that values community, advocacy, and social justice, then taking care of ourselves is indivisible from taking care of others.

In the workshops on self-care that I organized with social workers, they articulated a critical, collective approach to self-care that would support social workers in socializing and analyzing the life-giving and exhausting aspects of social work, meaning-making about our personal and professional selves, and our actions for social justice and human rights in practice with individuals, communities, and social movements. In the current political climate, such an approach would support social workers in caring for ourselves while we care for others and engage in social justice activities.

Several possible avenues for a critical, collective approach to self-care, proposed by Costa Rican social workers, can be translated to our Canadian social work context. First, we can create intentional collective spaces, in or outside the workplace, that nourish self-care and growth, clear the mind and emotions, and recharge energies. Activities could include sharing personal-professional struggles, giving mutual feedback on particular situations or challenges, taking stock of one's current state of being in practice, and collective discernment around strategizing to confront organizational and workplace barriers that affect our ability to help service users. For example, such a space could help those struggling with weight of sadness of woman abuse or those experiencing intense frustration and impotence in their role in state institutions and social services agencies that offer inadequate policies and programs to meet social needs.

Second, a critical, collective approach to self-care could break down social isolation among social workers and foster learning from each other's processes of maturation in dealing with particular issues and breaking through fears. If indeed "social workers live their own histories in practice," as María Elena observed, then collective spaces can help us reflect on how pressing or unresolved struggles, or "knots" at which we are snagged, impinge on or limit our practice. For example, social workers who are having difficulty speaking out against unfairness could benefit from others who have developed strategies for doing so in the face of fears of workplace discipline and marginalization and/or the triggering of lived experiences.

Third, in this era of neoliberal restructuring, it is imperative to have spaces that enable social workers to maintain and continue to sharpen critical analyses and political practice at multiple levels, including social action. Such spaces could provide vital support and alliances for social workers who are resisting institutional absorption and co-optation, seeking timely and context-appropriate strategies for making change in organizations and communities, and aligning themselves with community groups and social movements. Both newly graduated and seasoned social workers could also benefit from opportunities to collectively make sense of what is happening in our workplaces and the profession of social work in Canada, such as the increasing managerial control of practice and delimitation of social work's sphere of action, including de-skilling. Without a network of like-minded actors, new social workers who experience the challenges and contradictions of putting anti-oppressive theory into practice can lose energy, hope, and vision. Similarly, collective self-care could help us ground ourselves and regain perspective when we feel worn out and/or disillusioned by growing forms of injustice, repressive workplaces, dominant rhetoric about the "free market" and individual choice, and the shutting down in our society of democratic avenues to express views and dissent. Such collective care could help us remain connected to our compassion for self and others – not "a perspectiveless cofeeling" but an informed passion that leads to outrage, solidarity, and political action for confronting injustice and oppression (Spelman 1997: 85).

Toward a More Politicized, Collective Notion of Self-Care

If self-care is important to us as social workers, how can we move toward a politicized, collective notion of self-care that embraces multiple aspects of our selves and our integrity as human beings? First, we must interrogate professional discourses that assume we can, as compassionate human beings, serve people and witness structural injustice, oppression, and violence without being affected in a multitude of ways, for example, experiencing personal suffering, impotence, outrage or "moral distress" (Weinberg 2009: 141). Indeed, some studies have found that social and political action helps professionals counter feelings of frustration, anger, powerlessness, and vicarious trauma (Comas-Díaz and Padilla 1990; Schauben and Frazier 1995; Iliffe and Steed 2000; Coholic and Blackford 2003; Clemans 2004). Such a discourse pathologizes social workers affected in a variety of ways by their work. Furthermore, expectations that social workers take care of themselves amidst crushing workloads without clearly assigned organizational resources to do so constitute an additional burden of responsibility.

Second, since the very need for self-care is most often generated by our social, political, and economic systems that cause social suffering and then place unrealistic administrative and workload demands on social workers, we must question the assumption of current managerial discourses that individual self-care alone can avert distress or other maladies. Clearly, this is another example of offloading the consequences of structural inequalities, accelerated by "global capitalism" (Baines 2007a) onto the backs of others. Third, we can be alert to how this managerial strategy, in denying the systemic factors that shape social work practice, then allows individual social workers to be blamed for poor coping skills or "burning out," a message that we must resist internalizing. Ironically, at the same time that social workers are being burned out (usually considered to be an individual fault) by insufficient resources and unrealistic demands, social agencies and institutions in, for example, health care tout a discourse of "quality assurance" or "client service." This ruling strategy also permits the muzzling of social workers' discontent and critical analyses of current social arrangements as well as the marginalization and dismissal of those who speak out for compassion, fairness, and social justice. Our professional associations could be taking up these issues on behalf of their memberships and challenging current managerial constructions of self-care.

Finally, we can recognize that self-care is a structural and ethical issue. As social workers who practice anti-oppressively, we can collectivize our struggles and care for each other in ways that are congruent with our visions and values. As a form of resistance, critical, collective self-care, like other forms, is vital in maintaining our integrity. Although self-care is a dimension of ethical practice intended to ensure quality service to clients, we must also claim it for ourselves as a social work practice directed at the well-being and interconnectedness of social workers with our communities and struggles for social justice.

Notes

Some of this material appeared previously in *La Revista Costarricense de Trabajo Social* (Profitt 2008) and the *Canadian Social Work Review* (Profitt 2008).

1. In this research I interviewed five social workers working in government institutions and a women's non-profit organization in San Ramón, Costa Rica for the purpose of exploring the relation between processes of personal, professional, and political growth and social work practice with individuals and communities. The four key themes that shape self-care emerged from interviews and workshops with research participants. As a group, we later held a community meeting to present our research report to sixty social workers, professionals, community members, and social work students; pioneered a workshop on self-care, incorporating bioenergetics, for eighteen local health care and social service professionals; and published an article on our conceptualization of self-care in *La Revista Costarricense de Trabajo Social,* the social work journal of the national College of Social Workers (Profitt 2008). These forums shared our findings with a larger audience and hopefully had wider influence.

2. I have used pseudonyms for the Costa Rican social workers quoted here.

Doing Anti-Oppressive Social Work

The Importance of Resistance, History, and Strategy

Akua Benjamin

This important book takes up the challenge articulated in the mission statement of the Canadian Association of Schools of Social Work:

> to encourag[e] scholarship and debate on social work and social welfare with particular attention to how individual and social problems come to be defined and addressed, and to develop[ing] effective empowering methods of education and research relevant to a diverse society caught up in a rapidly changing economic and social world order.

The book's title and themes definitely focus on the complexities and challenges of "doing" anti-oppressive social work practice as we build a more transformative politicized social work profession. Engaging in transformative and politicized social work, however, is nothing new. There are lessons to be learnt from those who, in the past, have undertaken social work and in so doing have addressed difficult problems individually and socially, thereby resisting and transforming the status quo. I will discuss some of these early leaders of radical social work later in this Afterword. I will also discuss various ways to develop strategies and tactics of resistance, for it is vitally important that we reflect on the processes that often begin and/or accompany transformation, and that is resistance.

First, however, let me explain what I mean by *resistance*. My definition is very broad. It sweeps wide as it takes into account all those acts or actions in which an individual or individuals take a stand in opposition to a belief, an idea, an ideology, a climate, a practice, or an action that is oppressive and damaging to individual and social well being. The individual or individuals who engage in such a challenge often find themselves drawn into more challenges as they encounter overlapping layers of repression and injustice. Indeed, to be involved in transformative processes is to resist, in multiple ways, standard practices and the social normativity that support inequities and oppressions.

There are three points that I will focus on in this discussion of resistance:

1. Reasons for its importance to social work practice and social transformation.
2. How to resist, or ways to resist, and the strategies and tactics of resistance.
3. Critical reflections of some of the dynamics associated with the reluctance to undertake resistance, particularly fear and silence.

Resistance and the Reasons for Its Importance to Social Work Practice and Social Transformation

There are a number of compelling reasons why resistance is importance to social work. We all interface with a world that, according to Noam Chomsky (1991), manufactures consent to ongoing socio, politico, economic, militaristic structures and processes that oppress, kill, decimate, and dehumanize populations around the globe. That is, the pervasive media discourse on war, death, suffering, destruction, poverty, racism, homophobia, and so forth produces a populace, of which we are a part, in which these images create nihilism, an acceptance that these oppressive events and relations are part and parcel of the everyday and there is little or nothing to be done about them. As part of this process of manufacturing consent to the perpetration of atrocities, we learn to expect that every day we will hear of more deaths in Iraq, see more photos of tortured Iraqis and images of starving children, read more stories about the AIDS pandemic in Africa and statistics on genocidal campaigns around the world. Or closer to home, we hear pronouncements on the denial of same-sex marriage promoted self-righteously by officials in many American states and as well as by politicians within our own country. In Canada, we come to expect images of the homeless in our major cities, increases in child poverty across the land, and more reports of shootings in low-income neighborhoods.

We are horrified by these stories and images, and often outraged, but we still go about our jobs and our lives, thinking and talking about these instances but rarely resisting the endless onslaught of such images and discourses or the social conditions and relations that permit them to exist. Perhaps we say to ourselves, "What can I do, as these are historical, structural problems that require concerted organized actions?" We may feel that there is very little that one individual can do to change these major worldwide issues. For many people, there is a sense of helplessness, a feeling of being overwhelmed and unable to tackle such major structural, social, economic, and political problems.

However, it is important that we involve ourselves in daily resistance to the deadening impact of these images and discourses. We cannot afford to see them as just the unfortunate realities of yet another day, the consequences of aggressive government policies, or the unavoidable impact of neo-conservative agendas supporting the rich while penalizing and forgetting the poor. Involvement in the process of social work transformation means that we must resist and struggle against these and other unjust images and the unjust social relations that produce them. Resistance and struggle are not activities that should take place outside of everyday social work practice. They are key social work practices using highly sophisticated social work practice skills. They are also political acts, and as such they are completely consistent with the mission of social work stated above.

Social justice-oriented social work has a long history of multi-level resistance and organizing against oppressive forces. We can draw on these history lessons for ideas and inspiration. For instance, as most social workers know, although part of a larger movement of social reform, Jane Addams is credited with assisting the early formation of the profession of social work in North America. She and other women during the 1890s resisted and addressed problems of industrialization, urbanization, and immigration in the U.S. Addams, Ellen Gates Starr, and other activists founded Hull House and inaugurated an era of social action. Not only did these women establish the settlement houses, they dreamed large, and through initially small measures eventually founded the settlement house movement in North America. From this initial resistance and transformative base, they worked on projects aimed at benefiting children and families, lobbied government to regulate child labour, help set up a juvenile court system, and spearheaded the first U.S. Children's Bureau. They supported birth registration to facilitate compulsory education laws and administered enforcement of the first federal child labour statute in 1916. They also collaborated on the development of social science studies of women, the family and employment.

Jane Addams and her fellow activists also helped to inspire the development of the settlement house movement in Canada. These agencies remain central to the delivery of services to marginalized communities in a number of Canadian cities. While it is certainly not necessary to wait for an outstanding personality or social worker to come along and lead us in building resistance and social movements, it is exciting to remember that these services and this social movement were generated by the initial resistance and social change efforts of a handful of hardworking social work radicals, who were later joined by thousands of other activists to create long-lasting changes.

Unfortunately, this early transformative period of social work moved into the era of scientific philanthropy, and the pace of social justice slowed. The new approach departed from the pre-Jane Addams charitable model, with its moral judgments of deservingness, to one in which the client was seen as having an objective problem and the role of the social worker was to rationally and scientifically help him or her deal with the problem. Earlier forms of resistance and transformation such as advocacy, lobbying, changing policy, and challenging the status quo took a back seat while social work put on the garb of respectability through the adoption of the scientific philanthropy approach.

During a much later era, the 1960s, social work again expressed a method of resistance, advocacy, and transformation through social movements such as the feminist movement, the civil rights movement, and the peace movement. With the early settlement house movement, as well as these later phases, social work has a wonderful history of resistance and transformation. We need to thank these pioneers for their vision, their voices, and their legacy. They provide inspiring examples of social work using radical strategy and tactics to address the major problems of society. These radical social workers were some of the main catalysts for change, laying the foundations of our current anti-oppressive approaches to social work and social transformation. However, let us not forget that while social movements were mobilizing in North America, whole populations were being decimated and systematically marginalized. Populations such as First Nations Peoples faced genocide during Jane Addam's era and again with the continuation of the residential schools in the 1960s. Though acts of resistance and the rise of a militant gay and lesbian rights movements from the 1960s onward won major gains in the last few decades, queer people were forced into the closet during both eras. And during Jane Addams' era and beyond, Blacks were being lynched with the tolerance or participation of the law. Thus, while radical forms of social work resisted oppression in some communities, oppression found expression in the everyday life of many other communities. To address the complexity of all types of oppression, social work and its many forms of resistance and transformation needed to adopt an ever-larger world view and set of strategies that could challenge social oppression and injustices for all. Anti-oppressive practice emerged out of this need for an analysis that could incorporate practices contesting all forms of injustice.

How to Resist or Ways to Resist and the Strategies and Tactics of Resistance

The "how" of how to resist involves strategy and tactics. Indeed, resistance *requires* both strategy and tactics. A strategy is a plan of action, while tactics are the specific procedures and processes for carrying out that plan.

Many strategies for resistance and social change were explored in this book. To recap, a strategy should begin with knowing whom or what you are up against. We need to assess not only the barriers but also the opportunities and potential supports. We need to ask, for instance, Who are our allies? What is to be gained? What is to be lost? Can you afford the trade-off? A plan of action may therefore include processes of assessment, research, building relationships, advocacy, organizing, lobbying, and so forth. Above all, the beginning of any strategy involves the application of critical analysis and critical reflection to determine the steps and considerations needed in resisting and transforming oppressions. I want to emphasize that the process of critical analysis is the key to resistance and transformation of oppression. Without it, our strategies are often short-sighted, while our tactics may never become more than superficial. In social work, it has been said that the strength of anti-oppressive, structural social work begins and ends with analysis.

I make no apologies for emphasizing critical analysis and critical reflection. They are not the only practice skills, but they are critical skills in building strategies of resistance and transformation. I am deliberately challenging the notion that anti-oppressive practice begins and ends with critical analysis. While our strategies should involve critical analysis in all stages, including critical debriefing after the completion of a strategy, anti-oppressive practice also involves a range of practice skills that can and are enacted as resistance to an often uncaring, inhospitable, and alienating world. Many of these important practice skills were discussed in the chapters of this book.

Pivotal to any successful strategy are tactics, including the procedures, actions, and arguments used to advance a strategy. Given the diverse types of problems encountered in social work practice, it is often necessary for each strategy to develop its own actions, arguments, procedures, or processes. This is important for the development of tactics specific to each workplace or social problem. It needs to take into consideration things like context, recent changes within an agency or community, and past processes of resistance that we can continue to rely on or need to change. In other words, we need to know what works and what does not work in any given situation and struggle. Above all, it means knowing ourselves and our readiness to initiate and to follow through on our intended plan of action.

In schools of social work we teach that it is not a good idea to go into an agency and *carte blanche* immediately begin to analyze oppression and de-nounce the many systems that perpetuate oppression. After all, although they may have evolved into professionalized bureaucracies, many agencies began as resistance strategies against the oppression of particular groups. For instance, many women's services began as resistance against the sexism and violence perpetrated against women. Likewise, many youth employment services began as resistance against the joblessness, marginalization, and criminalization faced by high numbers of young people. Keeping this kind of detail in mind is key to shaping one's approach within a given agency on any given problem. It helps us choose which types of arguments are likely to be well-received and which tactics are likely to build consensus. Thus, the formation of a strategy, as well as the plans, processes, and procedures for carrying out that strategy, needs to take into account the historical roots of an agency and social problem. There are many ways to learn from the past. I would go as far as to argue that it is important to begin any strategy with an understanding that many social services — and indeed the social work profession itself — were originally forms of resistance, and, in their time, they were acts of social transformation.

Particularly today, in light of our increasingly global context, strategies of resistance must involve analysis of the overarching and specific forces that must be resisted. The analysis of systems of capitalism, racism, and heterosexism is not an abstract theoretical debate that has little to do with the everyday social work practice and must be left behind as we respond to the immediate, the crisis, the day-to-day work for which we were hired. The application of a critical analysis can move us to clearly understand what we are up against. It helps us understand that this is a long, complex struggle and our solutions will not be immediate. Our strategies of resistance also need to include ally-building (Bishop 1994). We cannot and should not undertake these struggles alone. Our resistance tactics in all areas must work against the compelling tide of pressures that seek to individualize us and to reward us individually for good work. While it is important for individuals to feel recognized and valued in the workplace, think how much more rewarding it will be for a whole group or a whole profession to stand up against oppression with a variety of strategies and tactics. Think of the transformation that can be brought about by such force. Every one of us needs to begin this strategy of ally-building. This takes me to my third and final point.

Individual Responsibility in Resistive Work

Ultimately it is the responsibility of each and every one of us to resist. Using the process of critical reflection, each of us much think through this notion of responsibility for resistance and transformative work. In addition to understanding our individual responsibilities, we need to critically reflect on the context in which we must do this work. I think of the context of any social problem or struggle as the stage that launches us into the process of resistance. Many of us will begin this process of understanding context with an understanding of our own social location, identities, background, and experiences. Many of us got into social work because of some experience or some difficulty that we either wanted to resolve or had resolved and wanted to share with others. Some measure of empowerment allowed us to move from a position of being in struggle to a position of being able to and wanting to contribute and change conditions, not just for ourselves but for a group, a community, or our world. Many of us return to these past struggles, and to the insights and powers they provided, as we interact on a day-to-day basis with our clients, as we enliven our writing, as we invigorate our research work, and as we build stronger ties with communities and activist groups.

In the context of the workplace, many social workers understand that they have a responsibility to resist homophobia, racism, sexism, ableism, and so forth. Fortunately, many social service organizations today have adopted equity and human rights policies that support equity and take a stand against oppressive behaviours or policies, particularly when they are expressed overtly or individually. These policies provide us with tools for grievances and appeals when these policies are violated. In addition, specific programs and services aimed at addressing these injustices have been generated by resistance to inequities at the systemic level and advocacy at the micro-level of social service agencies.

Once again, a basis exists for appealing and grieving instances in which clients are not served in a fair and equitable manner or communities find themselves marginalized and unable to access needed services. The need for new policies aimed at expanding and deepening equity and services aimed at redressing systemic gaps continues to be the subject of lobbying, demonstrating, challenging, banner waving, marching. and radical protest from social workers and other justice-minded groups. Social workers must find themselves among these numbers and continue to adopt and refine the activist skills that place social workers at the forefront of these struggles.

To my mind, however, resistance and transformation, although espoused in principles and implemented to some degree within the policies, collective agreements, and human rights codes within our agencies and organizations, are often very limited in the practice of social work at the micro-level, or within the normative processes of everyday practices. In terms of everyday micro-practice, we might ask how to resist, much less transform, systems and practices of oppression that are part of the everyday normativity of mainstream social work practice.

Let me give a little example of the everyday normativity of oppression and the way that this normativity needs resistance and transformation at the frontlines of social work practice. In many agencies we see the over-representation of certain clients, co-workers, or community members. We must then ask ourselves, do we often see in the same agencies a lack of these voices at the table when decisions are being made? Or how about the way that the provision of services on certain social issues normalizes these issues and marginalizes and pathologizes others? For example, many services for Black youth focus on unemployment, education, and mental health, but not explicitly on racial profiling. Given that racial profiling is one of the most devastating issues impacting the lives of Black youth and their families (including whether or not they will be able to avoid police violence), why is it that racial profiling does not make it onto the list of issues that social workers address? Or finally, what about ignoring oppressive statements made by managers, co-workers, or clients because the issues are too sensitive or controversial, and seem too hard to address?

These kinds of oppressive micro-practices are "normalized" in many workplaces. You may say, "But these are not just micro-issues; they are connected to systemic issues." This is certainly true. However, problems of everyday practice require frontline practice changes as well as systemic redress. Too often, AOP social workers feel overwhelmed and wait for systemic change rather than working on the pieces of these questions that we may be able to change.

The issues listed above are all examples of frontline program delivery, program services, organizational structure, and hiring and retention policies that we can influence from our position as social workers. By the same token, our lack of intervention on these kinds of issues reflects and concretizes norms of injustice and inequity, which require resistance, mobilization, and active responses. The process of resistance and transformation means putting one's self on the line. It means walking the talk. It means risk. While we may be willing to support clients to take risks, we ourselves are too often adverse to risk. I think the reason for this aversion is fear — the fear of being isolated and alone, the fear of reprisals, stated or unstated, when we take a stand, and the fear of the unknown when we resist and take a stand against oppression.

Let me name and explore fear. It includes the fear of finding out that you are the only person in your work unit prepared to take a stand, and deciding that you need to take a stand anyway, although you know you will be alone. This kind of experience is new for many of us. Taking on new experiences means that the individual may have to step outside the norm, step outside the self, go beyond one's current sense of one's limits, without knowing for certain whether he or she has the capacity to stretch far enough to get the job done. Indeed, among the first fears that one encounters are the fears that surround loss — the fear of losing familiar ground; the fear of uncertainty; the fear of asking oneself, and wondering if anyone will answer, who will stand with me?

The complexity of this fear also goes much deeper. While not belittling the personal or micro-level experience of fear, let me put this fear of resistance into a larger systemic frame. At the systemic and societal level, we see a fear of change, of bringing in elements or groups of society that have been excluded, marginalized, or banished. This is a fear of losing power and privilege and having to do things differently, the fear of doing without. This societal fear maintains the status quo, holds things in check, and allows oppression to continue. That systemic fear, at some level, is in all of us, even if we have been trained as anti-oppressive practitioners.

It is most likely this systemic level of fear that we reflect when we do not speak out. It is likely also a form of systemic fear when we forget to raise our voices about a practice that we know is unjust, or when we just happen to forget to ask a critical question or forget to allow other voices to be heard. Is it not systemic fear when we do not dislodge everyday practices that include some while excluding others? Where are our voices when situations call for exploring problems respectfully, sharing our perspectives, listening with care? Where are our voices when situations call for full participation rather than just a passive form of head nodding that silences and recreates oppression? Is it systemic fear that keeps us, after an oppressive meeting or a case conference has ended, from raising our voices, allows us simply to maintain silence, not disturbing the peace?

Just as fear is systemic, so is silence. Silence is valued under the guise of politeness in our society. It is a way to avoid conflict or unpleasantness. A great value, politeness. Many argue that it is at the bottom of respect. However, silence also operates as a norm that allows us not to resist. The only way to address fear is to carefully and thoughtfully face the issues generating the problems. As many of the chapters in this book note, the best way to build social justice is through a collective effort in concert with others. Building allies and strategies is one of the best ways to confront our fears and the social problems generating inequity and injustice. By building strategies and allies, we also break the silence that surrounds most oppression and keeps it politely in place. And so we come full circle. Effective resistance is each individual's responsibility, but it is best undertaken in concert with others, using shared strategies, analysis, and tactics.

This book challenges us to work to resist and transform social work practice and wider society. This resistive process means that we need to take a stand in opposition to certain beliefs, ideologies, practices, and actions that have come to overwhelmingly define our profession of social work — a definition that historically has situated us as do-gooders, bleeding hearts, baby snatchers, and so forth. However, as noted earlier, we also have the inspiring examples, past and present, of many social movement activists and leaders who, like Jane Addams and others, sparked far-reaching change, generations of resistance, and transformative practice. This book invites us to make our own history as social justice advocates and activists, to dialogue, to speak, to give voice, and to lift our voice in a shared space that claims resistance and works toward complete social transformation. Let us do so with respect, care, laughter, and struggle.

References

Abbott, P., and C. Wallace. 1999. "Social Work and Nursing: A History." In P. Abbott and C. Wallace (eds.), *The Sociology of the Caring Professions*. London: Falmer Press.

Abram, F.Y., J.A. Slosar, and R. Wells. 2005. "Reverse Mission: A Model for International Social Work Education and Transformative Intra-National Practice." *International Social Work* 48, 2.

Abramovitz, M. 1988. *Regulating the Lives of Women: Social Policy from Colonial Times to the Present*. Boston: Southend Press.

Absolon, K., and E. Herbert. 1997. "Community Action as a Practice of Freedom: A First Nations Perspective." In B. Wharf and M. Clague (eds.), *Community Organizing: Canadian Experiences*. Don Mills: Oxford University Press.

Abu-Habib, L. (ed.). 1997. *Gender and Disability: Women's Experiences in the Middle East*. London: Oxfam UK and Ireland.

Abu-Lughod, L. 1991. "Writing Against Culture." In R.G. Fox (ed.), *Recapturing Anthropology: Working in the Present*. Santa Fe: School of American Research Press.

_____. 1990. "The Romance of Resistance: Tracing Transformations of Power through Bedouin Women." *American Ethnologist* 17, 1.

Adams, R. 2008. *Glass Houses: Saving Feminist Anti-Violence Agencies from Self Destruction*. Halifax/Winnipeg: Fernwood Publishing.

Adams, R., L. Dominelli, and M. Payne (eds.). 2009. *Practicing Social Work in a Complex World*. Second edition London: Palgrave MacMillan.

Ahmed, S. 2000. *Strange Encounters: Embodied Others in Post-Coloniality*. London: Routledge.

Akin, B.A., and T.K. Gregoire. 1997. "Parents' Views on Child Welfare's Response to Addiction." *Families in Society: The Journal of Contemporary Human Services* 78, 4.

Alcoff, L. 1988. "Cultural Feminism Versus Post-Structuralism: The Identity Crisis in Feminist Theory." *Signs: Journal of Women in Culture and Society* 13, 3.

Alfred, T. 2005. *Wasáse: Indigenous Pathways of Action and Freedo*. Peterborough, ON: Broadview Press.

_____. 1999. *Peace, Power and Righteousness*. Toronto: Oxford University Press.

Alinsky, S. 1972. *Rules for Radicals: A Pragmatic Primer for Realistic Radicals*. New York: Random House.

Allan, J., B. Pease, and L. Briskman. 2003. *Critical Social Work: Theories and Practices"* Sydney: Allen and Unwin.

Altman, J.C. 2008. "Engaging Families in Child Welfare Services: Worker Versus Client Perspectives." *Child Welfare* 87, 3.

Amadiume, I. 1997. "Cycles of Western Imperialism: Feminism, Race, Gender, Class and Power." In I. Amadiume (ed.), *Reinventing Africa: Matriarchy, Religion and Culture*. London: Zed Books.

Amodeo, M., M.A. Ellis, J. Hopwood, and L. Derman. 2007. "A Model for Organizational Change: Using an Employee-Driven, Multilevel Intervention in a Substance Abuse Agency." *Families in Society* 88, 2.

Anderson, B. 1983. *Imagined Communities. Reflections on the Origin and Spread of Nationalism*. London and New York: Verso.

Anthias, F., and N. Yuval-Davis. 1992. *Racialized Boundaries, Race, Nation, Colour, Class and the Anti-Racist Struggle.* London: Routlege.

Aronson, J. 2008. "Institutional Structuring of Practices in Social Work." *McMaster University Seminar.*

Aronson, J., and S. Sammon. 2000. "Practice Amid Social Service Cuts and Restructuring: Working with the Contradictions of Small Victories." *Canadian Social Work Review* 17, 2.

Aronson, J., and K. Smith. 2009. "Managing Restructured Social Services: Expanding the Social?" *British Journal of Social Work* 40, 2.

Askeland, G.A., and M. Payne. 2006. "Social Work Education's Cultural Hegemony." *International Social Work* 49, 6.

Astin, M. 1997. "Traumatic Therapy: How Helping Rape Victims Affects Me as a Therapist." *Women & Therapy* 20, 1.

Bailey, B., and M. Brake. 1975. "Introduction: Social Work in the Welfare State." In B. Bailey and M. Brake (eds.), *Radical Social Work.* New York: Pantheon Books.

Baines, C. 1998. "Caring: Its Impact on the Lives of Women." In C. Baines, P.M. Evans and S.M. Neysmith (eds.), *Women's Caring. Feminist Perspectives on Social Welfare.* Toronto: Oxford Press.

_____. 1991. "The Professions and an Ethic of Care." In. C. Baines, P.M. Evans and S. Neysmith (eds.), *Women's Caring: Feminist Perspectives on Social Welfare.* Toronto: Oxford University Press.

Baines, C, P.M. Evans., and S.M. Neysmith (eds.). 1998. *Women's Caring: Feminist Perspectives on Social Welfare.* Toronto: Oxford University Press.

Baines, D. 2010a. "Neoliberal Restructuring/Activism, Participation and Social Unionism in the Nonprofit Social Services." *Nonprofit and Voluntary Sector Quarterly* 39, 1.

_____. 2010b. "In a Different Way: Social Unionism in the Nonprofit Social Services— An Australian/Canadian Comparison." *Labor Studies Journal* First published on March 30, 2010 as doi:10.1177/0160449X10365543.

_____. 2010c. "'If We Don't Get Back to Where We Were Before': Working in the Restructured NonProfit Social Services." *British Journal of Social Work* 40, 3: 928–45.

_____. 2008. "Race, Resistance and Restructuring: Emerging Skills in the New Social Services." *Social Work* 53, 2.

_____ (ed.). 2007a. *Doing Anti-Oppressive Practice: Building Transformative Politicized Social Work.* Halifax/Winnipeg: Fernwood Publishing.

_____. 2007b. "Anti-Oppressive Social Work Practice: Fighting for Space, Fighting for Change." In. D. Baines (ed.), *Doing Anti-Oppressive Practice: Building Transformative Politicized Social Work.* Halifax/Winnipeg: Fernwood Publishing.

_____. 2007c. "Introduction: Anti-Oppressive Social Work Practice: Fighting for Space, Fighting for Change." In D. Baines (ed.), *Doing Anti-Oppressive Practice, Building Transformative Politicized Social Work 2007.* Halifax/Winnipeg: Fernwood Publishing.

_____. 2007d. "'If You Could Change One Thing': Restructuring, Social Workers and Social Justice Practice." In D. Baines (ed.), *Doing Anti-oppressive Practice: Building Transformative Politicized Social Work.* Halifax/Winnipeg: Fernwood Publishing.

_____. 2006a. "'If You Could Change One Thing': Social Service Workers and

Restructuring." *Australian Social Work* 59, 1.

_____. 2006b. "Whose Needs Are Being Served? Quantitative Metrics and the Reshaping of Social Services." *Studies in Political Economy* 77, (Spring).

_____. 2004a. "Pro-Market, Non-Market: The Dual Nature of Organizational Change in Social Services Delivery." *Critical Social Policy* 24, 1.

_____. 2004b. "Caring for Nothing: Work Organisation and Unwaged Labour in Social Services." *Work, Employment and Society* 18, 2.

_____. 2004c. "Seven Kinds of Work: Only One Paid: Raced, Gendered and Restructured Care Work in the Social Services Sector." *Atlantis. A Women's Studies Journal* 28, 2 (Spring).

_____. 2004d. "Losing the 'Eyes in the Back of Our Heads': Social Service Skills, Lean Caring and Violence." *Journal of Sociology and Social Welfare* 31, 3.

_____. 2003. "Race, Class, and Gender in the Everyday Talk of Social Workers: The Ways We Limit the Possibilities for Radical Practice." In Shera, W. (ed.), *Emerging Perspectives in Anti-Oppressive Practice*. Toronto: Canadian Scholars Press.

_____. 2002. "Radical Social Work: Race, Class, and Gender." *Race, Gender and Class* 9, 1.

_____. 2000. "Everyday Practices of Race, Class, and Gender: Struggles, Skills, and Radical Social Work." *Journal of Progressive Human Services* 11, 2.

_____. 1997. "Feminist Practice in the Inner City: Challenges of Race, Class and Gender." *Affilia, Journal of Social Work and Women* 12, 3.

Baines, D., and Ann-Sylvia Brooker. 2007. "Bullying and Power: Manufacturing Vulnerability in a Small Canadian Town." *Women and Work* November. 21–38.

Baines, D., C. Cunningham, and F. Fraser. 2010. "Constrained by Managerialism: Caring as Participation in the Voluntary Social Services." *Economic and Industrial Democracy*. Published on-line.

Baines, D., and I. Cunningham. Forthcoming. "White Knuckle Care Work: Working on the Edge with the Most Excluded." *Work, Employment and Society*. Published on-line.

Baines, D., and N. Sharma. 2002. "Migrant Workers as Non-Citizens: The Case Against Citizenship as a Social Policy Concept." *Studies in Political Economy* 69, (Autumn).

Baker, M. 2006. *Restructuring Family Policies: Convergences and Divergences*. Toronto: University of Toronto Press.

_____. 2001. *Families, Labour and Love*. Vancouver: University of British Columbia Press.

Baldwin, M. 2008. "Promoting and Managing Innovation: Critical Reflection, Organizational Learning and the Development of Innovative Practice in a National Children's Voluntary Organization." *Qualitative Social Work* 7, 3.

Ball, T.J. 1998. *Prevalence Rates of Full and Partial PTSD and Lifetime Trauma in a Sample of Adult Members of an American Indian Tribe*. Ph.D. dissertation, Ann Arbor, MI: ProQuest Company.

Ballour, M., and N. Gabalac. 1985. *A Feminist Position on Mental Health*. Springfield: Charles C Thomas Publisher.

Barnes, C., and M. Oliver. 1995. "Disability Rights: Rhetoric and Reality in The UK." *Disability & Society* 10, 1.

Barnoff, L. 2005a. "Implementing Anti-oppressive Principles in Everyday Practice: Lessons from Feminist Social Services." Unpublished report, School of Social

Work, Ryerson University.

_____. 2005b. "Implementing Anti-Oppressive Principles in Everyday Practice: Lessons from Feminist Agencies. Final Research Report. Nov. 2005." Toronto: Ryerson University.

_____. 2002. "New Directions for Anti-Oppression Practice in Feminist Social Service Agencies." Unpublished doctoral dissertation, University of Toronto.

_____. 2001. "Moving Beyond Words: Integrating Anti-Oppression Practice into Feminist Social Service Organizations." *Canadian Social Work Review* 18, 1.

Barnoff, L., and B. Coleman. 2007. "Strategies for Integrating Anti-Oppression Principles: Perspectives from Feminist Agencies." In: D. Baines (ed.), *Doing Anti-Oppressive Practice: Building Transformative, Politicized Social Work*. Halifax/ Winnipeg: Fernwood Publishing.

Barnoff, L., P. George, and B. Coleman. 2006. "Operating in 'Survival Mode:' Barriers to Implementing Anti-Oppression Practice within Feminist Social Service Agencies." *Canadian Social Work Review* 23, 1–2.

Barnoff, L., and K. Moffatt. 2007. "Contradictory Tensions in Anti-Oppression Practice in Feminist Social Services." *Affilia: The Journal of Women and Social Work* 22, 1.

Barnoff, L., H. Parada, and P. Grassau. 2005a. "Transforming Social Work: Creating Space for Anti-oppression and Social Justice Practices." Unpublished report, School of Social Work, Ryerson University.

_____. 2005b. "Transforming Social Work: Creating Space for Anti-Oppression and Social Justice Practices. Conference Report." Toronto: School of Social Work, Ryerson University.

Barreiro, J., and C. Cornelius (ed.). 1991. *Knowledge of the Elders: The Iroquois Condolence Cane Tradition*. Ithaca, NY: Cornell University.

Barrett, D. 2009. "Pfizer Hit with Record $2.3-billion Penalty." *Globe and Mail,* September 3.

Barsamian, D., and E.W. Said. 2003. *Culture and Resistance: Conversations With Edward W. Said*. Cambridge: South End Press.

Baruch, Y., and A. Cohen. 2007. "The Dynamics Between Organizational Commitment and Professional Identity Formation at Work." In A. Brown, S. Kirpal, and F. Rauner (eds.), *Identities at Work*. Dordrecht, The Netherlands: Springer.

Barwick, M.A., K.M. Boydell, E. Stasiulis, H.B. Ferguson, and D. Fixsen. 2005. *Knowledge Transfer and Implementation of Evidence-Based Practices in Children's Mental Health*. Toronto, ON: Children's Mental Health Ontario.

Baskin, C. 2003. "Structural Social Work as Seen from an Aboriginal Perspective." In W. Shera (ed.), *Emerging Perspectives in Anti-Oppressive Practice*. Toronto: Canadian Scholars Press.

Batavia, A.I. 2001. "The New Paternalism (Evaluating the Idea of Disabled Persons as Oppressed Minority)." *Journal of Disability Policy Studies* 12, 2.

Bates, M. 2006. "School Social Workers: A Critically Reflective Approach to Evidence-Based Practice." *Canadian Social Work Review* 23, 1/2.

Battle, K. 1998. "Transformation: Canadian Social Policy since 1985." *Social Policy and Administration* 32, 4.

Baxter, P.T.W., and U. Almagor (eds.). 1978. *Age, Generation and Time: Some Features of East African Age Organizations*. London: C. Hurst.

Bayat, A. 2000. "From 'Dangerous Classes' to 'Quiet Rebels': Politics of the Urban

Subaltern in the Global South." *International Sociology* 15, 3.

BBC Monitoring Newsfile. 2008. "New Lebanese President Delivers Inaugural Speech, Notes 'Promising Phase.'" May 26. Accessed May 30, 2008, from ProQuest Newsstand database.

BBC News. 2009. "Timeline: Nigeria: A Chronology of Key Events." Available at <news. bbc.co.uk/2/hi/Africa/country_profiles/1067695.stm>. (Accessed July 27, 2009).

Beck, U. 1997. *The Reinvention of Politics: Rethinking Modernity in the Global Social Order.* Malden: Blackwell.

Beddoe, L. 2010. "Surveillance or Reflection: Professional Supervision in the Risk Society. *British Journal of Social Work* 40.

Bell, H. 2003. "Strengths and Secondary Trauma in Family Violence Work." *Social Work* 48, 4.

Bendana, A. 1995. "A Sandinista Commemoration of the Sandino Centennial." Available at <hartford-hwp.com/archives/47/003.html>.

Benjamin, A. 2007. "Doing Anti-Oppressive Social Work: The Importance of Resistance, History and Strategy." In. D. Baines (ed.), *Doing Anti-Oppressive Practice: Building Transformative Politicized Social Work.* Halifax/Winnipeg: Fernwood Publishing.

Berenson, A. 2005. "Despite Vow, Drug Makers Still Withhold Data." *New York Times,* May 31.

Berger, P., and T. Luckmann. 1966. *The Social Construction of Reality. A Treatise in the Sociology Of Knowledge.* New York: Anchor Books.

Bernard, W.T., and B. Hamilton-Hinch. 2006. "Making Diversity Work: From Awareness to Institutional Change." *Canadian Review of Social Policy* 56.

Bernard, W.T., L. Lucas-White, and D.E. Moore. 1993. "Triple Jeopardy: Assessing Life Experiences of Black Nova Scotian Women from a Social Work Perspective." *Canadian Social Work Review* 10, 2.

Bérubé, M. 2003. "Citizenship and Disability." *Dissent* 50, 2.

Bess, K.D., I. Prilleltensky, D.D. Perkins, and L.V. Collins. 2009. "Participatory Organizational Change in Community-Based Health and Human Services: From Tokenism to Political Engagement." *American Journal of Community Psychology* 43.

Bishop, A. 2005. *Beyond Token Change: Breaking the Cycle of Oppression in Institutions.* Halifax/Winnipeg: Fernwood Publishing.

_____. 2004. *Grassroots leaders building skills: A course in community leadership.* Halifax: Fernwood.

_____. 2002. *Becoming an Ally: Breaking the Cycle of Oppression in People.* Second edition. Halifax/Winnipeg: Fernwood Publishing.

_____. 1994. *Becoming an Ally. Breaking the Cycle of Oppression.* First edition. Halifax/ Winnipeg: Fernwood Publishing.

Black, S. 2005. "Community Unionism: Strategy for Organizing in the New Economy." *New Labor Forum* 14, 3.

Blackburn, J. 2000. "Understanding Paulo Freire: Reflections on the Origins, Concepts, and Possible Pitfalls of His Educational Approach." *Community Development Journal* 35, 1.

Bordo, S. 1993. *Unbearable Weight: Feminism, Western Culture, and the Body.* Berkeley, CA: University of California Press.

_____. 1990. "Feminism, Postmodernism, and Gender Skepticism." In L. Nicholson (ed.), *Feminism/Postmodernism.* New York: Routledge.

Bourdieu, P. 1998. *Practical Reason: On the Theory of Action*. Cambridge, UK: Polity Press.
_____. 1977. *"Outline of a Theory of Practice."* London: Cambridge University Press.
Bowdry, C. 1990. "Toward a Treatment-Relevent Typology of Child Abuse Familes." *Child Welfare* 69, 4.
Bradbury, H., and P. Reason. 2003. "Issues and Choice Points for Improving Quality of Action Research." In M. Minkler and N. Wallerstein (eds.), *Community-Based Participatory Research for Health*. San Francisco: Jossey-Bass.
Braidotti, R. 1989. "The Politics of Ontological Difference." In T. Brennan (ed.), *Between Feminism and Psychoanalysis*. New York: Routledge.
Brake, M., and B. Bailey. 1980. "Contributions to a Radical Practice in Social Work." In M. Brake and B. Bailey (eds.), *Radical Social Work and Practice*. London: Ed Arnold.
Brant, C.C. 1990. "Native Ethics and Rules of Behavior." *Canadian Journal of Psychiatry* 35 (August).
Brave Heart-Jordan, M.Y.H. 1995. "The Return to the Sacred Path: Healing from Historical Trauma and Historical Unresolved Grief Among the Lakota." Ph.D. dissertation, Northhampton, MA: Smith College School for Social Work.
Braverman, H. 1974. *Labour and Monopoly Capital: The Degradation of Work in the Twentieth Century*. New York: Monthly Review Press.
Bricout, J.C., and K.J. Bentley. 2000. "Disability Status and Perception of Employability by Employers." *Social Work Research* 24, 2.
Briggs, H.E., and B. McBeath. 2009. "Evidence-Based Management: Origins, Challenges, and Implications for Social Service Administration." *Administration in Social Work* 33, 3.
Broad, D. 2000. *Hollow Work, Hollow Society? Globalization and the Casual Labour Problem in Canada*. Halifax/Winnipeg: Fernwood Publishing.
Brodie, J. 1999. "The Politics of Social Policy in the Twenty First Century." In D. Broad and W. Antony (eds.), *Citizens or Consumers? Social Policy in a Market Society*. Halifax/Winnipeg: Fernwood Publishing.
Brody, C. 1984. *Women Therapists Working with Women: New Theory and Process of Feminist Therapy*. New York: Springer.
Brook, E., and A. Davis. 1985. *"Women, the Family, and Social Work."* New York: Tavistock.
Brotman, S., and S. Pollack. 1998. "Loss of Context: The Problem of Merging Postmodernism with Feminist Social Work." *Canadian Social Work Review* 14 (Winter).
Broverman, I., D. Broverman, F. Clarkson, P. Rosenkrantz, and S. Vogel. 1970. "Sex Role Stereotypes and Clinical Judgements of Mental Health." *Journal of Consulting and Clinical Psychology* 24, 1.
Brown, C. 2007a. "Situating Knowledge and Power in the Therapeutic Alliance". In C. Brown and T. Augusta-Scott (eds.), Narrative Therapy: Making Meaning, Making Lives. Thousand Oaks, CA: Sage.
_____. 2007b. " Discipline and Desire: Regulating the Body/Self." In C. Brown and T. Augusta-Scott (eds.), Narrative Therapy: Making Meaning, Making Lives. Thousand Oaks, CA: Sage.
_____. 2007c. "Dethroning the Suppressed Voice: Unpacking Experience as Story." In C. Brown and T. Augusta-Scott (eds.), Narrative Therapy: Making Meaning, Making Lives. Thousand Oaks, CA: Sage.

_____. 2007d. "Talking Body Talk. Merging Feminist and Narrative Approaches." In C. Brown and T. Augusta-Scott (eds.), Narrative Therapy: Making Meaning, Making Lives. Thousand Oaks, CA: Sage.

_____. 2006. "Situating Knowledge and Power in the Therapuetic Alliance." In C. Brown and T. Augusta-Scott (eds.), *Narrative Therapy: Making Meaning, Making Lives.* Thousand Oaks, CA: Sage.

_____. 2003. "Narrative Therapy: Reifying or Challenging Dominant Discourse." In W. Shera (ed.), Emerging Perspectives on Anti-oppressive Practice. Toronto: Canadian Scholar's Press.

_____. 1994. "Feminist Postmodernism and the Challenge of Diversity." In A. Chambon and A. Irving (eds.), *Essays on Postmodernism and Social Work.* Toronto: Canadian Scholar's Press.

Brown, C., and T. Augusta-Scott (eds.). 2007a. Narrative Therapy: Making Meaning, Making Lives. Thousand Oaks, CA: Sage.

_____. 2007b. "Introduction: Postmodernism, Reflexivity, and Narrative Therapy." In C. Brown and T. Augusta-Scott (eds.), Narrative Therapy: Making Meaning, Making Lives. Thousand Oaks, CA: Sage.

Brown, C. and K. Jasper (eds.). 1993. *Consuming Passions: Feminist Approaches to Weight Preoccupation and Eating Disorders.* Toronto: Second Story Press.

Brown, L. 2006. "Still Subversive After All These Years: The Relevance of Feminist Therapy in the Age of Evidence-Based Practice." *Pyschology of Women Quarterly* 30, 1.

_____. 1991a. "Ethical Issues in Feminist Therapy." *Psychology of Women Quarterly* 15.

_____. 1991b. "Anti-Racism as an Ethical Imperative: An Example from Feminist Therapy. *Ethics and Behaviour.*

_____. 1990a. "A Feminist Framework for Ethical Therapy." In H. Lerner and N. Porter (eds.), *Feminist Ethics in Psychotherapy.* New York: Springer Publishing.

_____. 1990b. "Confronting Ethically Problematic Behaviours in Feminist Therapist Colleagues." In H. Lerman and N. Porter (eds.), *Feminist Ethics in Psychotherapy.* New York: Springer.

_____. 1990c. "The Meaning of Multicultural Perspective for Theory Development in Feminist Therapy." In L. Brown and M. Root (eds.), *Diversity and Complexity in Feminist Therapy.* New York: Haworth Press.

_____. 1989a. "Fat-Oppressive Attitudes and the Feminist Therapist: Directions for Change." *Women and Therapy* 8, 3.

_____. 1989b. *Beyond Thou Shalt Not: Thinking About Ethics in the Lesbian Therapy Community.* New York: Haworth Press.

_____. 1988a. "From Perplexity to Complexity: Thinking about Ethics in the Lesbian Therapy Community." *Women and Therapy* 8.

_____. 1988b. "Harmful Effects of Posttermination Sexual and Romantic Relationships Between Therapists and Their Former Clients." *Psychotherapy: Theory, Research, Practice, Training* 25, 2.

_____. 1987. "Lesbians, Weight and Eating: New Analyses and Perspectives." In Boston Lesbian Psychologies Collective *Lesbian Psychologies: Explorations and Challenges.* Chicago: University of Illinois Press.

Brown, L., and M. Root (eds.). 1990. *Diversity and Complexity in Feminist Therapy.* New York: Harrington Park Press.

Brown, W. 2005. *Edgework: Critical Essays on Knowledge and Politics.* Princeton: Princeton University Press.

Bruner, E. 1986. "Experience and its Expressions." In V. Turner and E. Bruner (eds.), *The Anthropology of Experience.* Chicago: University of Illinois Press.

Buckner, S. 2005. "Taking the Debate on Reflexivity Further: Psychodynamic Team Analysis of BNIM Interview." *Journal of Social Work Practice* 19, 1.

Bulcha, M. 2002. *The Making of the Oromo Diaspora: A Historical Sociology of Forced Migration.* Minneapolis, MN: Kirk House Publishers.

_____. 1988. *Flight and Integration: Causes of Mass Exodus from Ethiopia and Problems of Integration in the Sudan.* Upsaala: Scandinavian Institute for African Studies.

Burghardt, S. 1982. *The Other Side of Organizing. Resolving the Personal Dilemmas and Political Demands of Daily Practice.* Vermont: Schenkman Books.

Burke, B., and P. Harrison. 2002. "Anti-Oppressive Practice." In R. Adams, L. Dominelli, and M. Payne (eds.), *Social Work: Themes, Issues, and Critical Debates.* Second edition. Houndmills: Palgrave.

Burstow, B. 1992. *Radical Feminist Therapy: Working in the Context of Violence.* Newbury Park, CA: Sage Publications.

Burstow, B., and D. Weitz (eds.). 1988. *Shrink Resistant: The struggle Against Psychiatry in Canada.* Vancouver: New Star Books.

Burtle V. 1985. "Therapeutic Anger in Women." In L. Rosewater and L. Walker (eds.), *Handbook of Feminist Therapy: Women's Issues in Psychotherapy.* New York: Springer.

Burton, M., and C. Kagan. 2006. "Decoding *Valuing People.*" *Disability & Society* 21, 4.

Busch, M., and C. Hostetter. 2009. "Examining Organizational Learning for Application in Human Service Organizations." *Administration in Social Work* 33, 3.

Bush, B. 2006. *Imperialism and Postcolonialism: History: Concepts, Theories and Practice.* Toronto: Pearson Education Limited.

Butler, J. 1993. *Bodies that Matter: On the Discursive Limits of "Sex."* New York: Routledge.

_____. 1992. "Contingent Foundations: Feminism and the Question of Postmodernism." In J. Butler and J. Scott (eds.), Feminists Theorize the Political. New York: Routledge.

Butler, J., and J. Scott (eds.). 1992. *Feminists Theorize the Political.* New York: Routledge.

Butler, M. 1985. "Guidelines for Feminist Therapy." In L. Rosewater and L. Walker (eds.), *Handbook of Feminist Therapy.* New York: Springer Publishing.

Cabral, A. 1979. *Unity and Struggle: Speeches and Writings.* London: Monthly Review Press.

Cameron, C. 2007. "Whose Problem? Disability Narratives and Available Identities." *Community Development Journal* 42, 4.

Cammaert, L., and C. Larsen, C. 1988. "Feminist Frameworks of Psychotherapy." In M. Dutton-Douglas and L. Walker (eds.), *Feminist Psychotherapies: Integration of Therapeutic and Feminist Systems.* New Jersey: Ablex.

Campbell, C. 2002. "The Search for Congruency: Developing Strategies for Anti-Oppressive Social Work Pedagogy." *Canadian Social Work Review* 19, 1.

Campbell, C., and M. Ungar. 2003. "Deconstructing Knowledge Claims: Epistemological Challenges in Social Work Education." *Journal of Progressive Human Services.*

Campbell, I. 2002. "Snatching at the Wind? Unpaid Overtime and Trade Unions in Australia." *International Journal of Employment Studies* 10, 2.

Campbell, I., and P. Brosnan. 1999. "Labour Market Deregulation in Australia: The Slow Combustion Approach to Workplace Change." *International Review of Applied Economics* 13, 3.

Campbell, M., and F. Gregor. 2002. *Mapping Social Relations: A Primer in Doing Institutional Ethnography.* Aurora: Garamond Press.

Canadian Association of Social Workers. 2005a. *Code of Ethics.* Ottawa: CASW.

_____. 2005b. *Guidelines for Ethical Practice.* Ottawa: CASW.

Canadian Labour Congress. 2010. "Canadian Labour History." Ottawa: Canadian Labour Congress.

Canadian Mental Health Association (CMHA). 1987. "Women and Mental Health Committee." *Women and Mental Health in Canada: Strategies for Change.* Toronto: CMHA.

Caplan, P. 1987. "The Name Game: Psychiatry, Misogyny, and Taxonomy." *Women and Therapy* 6, 1/2.

Caragata, L., and M. Sanchez. 2002. "Globalization and Global Need: The New Imperatives for Expanding International Social Work Education in North America." *International Social Work* 45, 2.

Carey, A.C. 2003. "Beyond the Medical Model: A Reconsideration of 'Feeblemindedness,' Citizenship, and Eugenic Restrictions." *Disability & Society* 18, 4.

Carey, M. 2009a. "It's a Bit Like Being a Robot or Working in a Factory: Does Braverman Help Explain the Differences in State Social Work in Britain Since 1971?" *Organization* 16, 4.

_____. 2007. "White Collar Proletariat? Braverman, the Deskilling/Upskilling of Social Work and the Paradoxical Life of the Agency Care Manager." *Journal of Social Work* 7, 1.

_____. 2006. "Selling Social Work by the Pound? The Pros and Cons of Agency Care Management." *Practice* 18, 1.

Carniol, B. 2010. *Case Critical: The Dilemma of Social Work in Canada.* Sixth edition. Toronto: Between the Lines.

_____. 2005. *Case Critical: The Dilemma of Social Work in Canada.* Fifth edition. Toronto: Between the Lines.

_____. 2000. *Case Critical: Challenging Social Services in Canada.* Fourth edition. Toronto: Between the Lines Press.

_____. 1992. "Structural Social Work: Maurice Moreau's Challenge to Social Work Practice." *Journal of Progressive Human Services* 3, 1.

_____. 1987. *Case Critical: The Dilemma of Social Work in Canada.* First edition. Toronto: Between the Lines.

Carniol, B., and V. Del Valle. 2007. "'We Have Voice': Helping Immigrant Women Challenge Abuse." In S. Hicks, H. Corner, and T. London (eds.), *Structural Social Work in Action: Examples from Practice.* Toronto: Canadian Scholar's Press.

Carriere, J. 2005. "Connectedness and Health of First Nations Adoptees." Unpublished doctoral thesis, University of Alberta.

Castles, F.G., and D. Mitchell. 1993. "Three Worlds of Welfare Capitalism or Four?" In F.G. Castles (ed.), *Families of Nations: Public Policy in Western Democracies.* Dartmouth: Brookfield VC.

Chamberlin, J. 1975. "Women's Oppression and Psychiatric Oppression." In D. Smith and S. David (eds.), *I'm Not Mad: I'm Angry.* Vancouver: Press Gang.

Chambon, A. 1994. "Postmodernity and Social Work Discourse(s): Notes on the Changing Language of a Profession." In A. Chambon and A. Irving (eds.), *Essays on Postmodernism and Social Work*. Toronto: Canadian Scholars Press.

Chambon, A., and A. Irving (eds.). 1994. *Essays on Postmodernism and Social Work*. Toronto: Canadian Scholars Press.

Charles, G.. and J.M. White. 2008. "Outcome Research, Best Practices, and the Limits of Evidence." *Canadian Social Work Review* 25, 1.

Chen, X. 2005. *Tending the Gardens of Citizenship: Child Saving in Toronto, 1880s–1920s*. Toronto: University of Toronto Press.

Chesler, P. 1972. *Women and Madness*. New York: Avon Books.

Chimedza, R., and S. Peters. 1999. "Disabled People's Quest for Social Justice in Zimbabwe." In F. Armstrong and L. Barton (eds.), *Disability, Human Rights and Education: Cross Cultural Perspectives*. Philadelphia, PA: Open University Press.

Chodorow, N. 1989. *Feminism and Psychoanalytic Theory*. New Haven: Yale University Press.

Chomsky, N. 1991. "Manufacturing Consent." *Publizistik* 36, 1.

Church, K. 1995. *Forbidden Narratives: Critical Autobiography as Social Science*. Amsterdam: Gordon and Breach.

Churchill, W. 1995. *Since Predator Came: Notes from the Struggle for American Indian Liberation*. Littleton, CO: Aigis Publications.

Clarke, J., S. Gewirtz, and E. McLaughlin (eds.). 2000. *New Managerialism, New Welfare?* London: Sage.

Clemans, S.E. 2004. "Life Changing: The Experience of Rape-Crisis Work." *Affilia* 19, 2.

Coalition for Feminist Mental Health Services. 1992. *Missing the Mark: Women's Services Examine Mental Health Programs for Women in Toronto*. January. Toronto.

Coffman, S. 1990. "Developing a Feminist Model for Clinical Consultation: Combining Diversity and Commonality." In L. Brown and M. Root (eds.), *Diversity and Complexity in Feminist Therapy*. New York: Harrington Park Press.

Cohen, M. 1997. "From Welfare State to Vampire Capitalism." In P. Evans and G. Wekerle (eds.), *Women and the Canadian Welfare State: Challenges and Change*. Toronto: University of Toronto Press.

Cohen, M.B., and D. Wagner. 1982. "Social Work Professionalism: Reality and Illusion." In C. Derber (ed.), *Professionals as Workers: Mental Labour in Advanced Capitalism*. Boston: G.K. Hall.

Coholic, D., and K. Blackford. 2003. "Exploring Secondary Trauma in Sexual Assault Workers in Northern Ontario Locations: The Challenges of Working in the Northern Ontario Context." *Canadian Social Work* 5, 1.

Coleridge, P. 1993. "Lebanon: Rebuilding Civic Consciousness." In *Disability, Liberation, and Development*. Oxford: Oxfam GB.

Collins, B. 1986. "Defining Feminist Social Work." *Social Work* 31, 3.

Collins, P.H. 2004. *Black Sexual Politics, African Americans, Gender and the New Racism*. New York: Routledge.

_____. 2002. "Work, Family, and Black Women's Oppression." In B.R. Hare, (ed.), *Race Odyssey: African Americans and Sociology*. New York: Syracuse University Press.

_____. 2001. "Like One of the Family: Race, Ethnicity, and the Paradox of US National Identity." *Ethnic and Racial Studies* 24, 1.

_____. 2000. *Black Feminist Thought: Knowledge, Consciousness and the Politics of*

Empowerment. Second edition. New York and London: Routledge.

_____. 1997. "How Much Difference Is too Much? Black Feminist Thought and the Politics of Postmodern Social Theory." *Current Perspectives in Social Theory* 17.

_____. 1991. "Knowledge, Consciousness, and the Politics of Empowerment." In P.H. Collins (ed.), *Black Feminist Thought.* New York: Routledge.

_____. 1990. *Black Feminist Thought: Knowledge, Consciousness, and the Politics of Empowerment.* New York: Routledge.

_____. 1989. "The Social Construction of Black Feminist Thought." *Signs* 14, 4 (Summer).

_____. 1986. "Learning from the Outsider Within: The Sociological Significance of Black Feminist Thought." *Social Problems* 33, 6, Special Theory Issue (Oct.– Dec.).

Comas-Díaz, L., and A.M. Padilla. 1990. "Countertransference in Working with Victims of Political Repression." *American Journal of Orthopsychiatry* 60, 1.

Considine, M. 2000. "Competition, Quasi-Markets and the New Welfare State." In I. O'Connor, P. Smyth, and J. Warburton (eds.), *Contemporary Perspectives on Social Work and the Human Services: Challenges and Change.* Surrey Hills: Longman.

Cooper, F. 2001. "What is the Concept of Globalization Good For? An African Historian's Perspective." *African Affairs* 100.

Cooper, M. 1999. "The Australian Disability Rights Movement Lives." *Disability & Society* 14, 2.

Corby, B. 2000. *Child Abuse: Towards a Knowledge Base.* Second edition. Buckingham: Open University Press.

Corcoran, J. 2001. "Solution-Focused Therapy." In Lehman and Coady (ed.), *Theoretical Perspectives for Direct Social Work Practice: A Generalist-Eclectic Approach.* New York: Springer Publishing.

_____. 1999. "Solution-Focused Interviewing with Child Protective Services Clients." *Child Welfare* 78, 4.

Corker, M., and S. French. 2002. "Reclaiming Discourse in Disability Studies." In S. French and M. Corker (eds.), *Disability Discourse.* Philadelphia, A: Open University Press.

Cornell, D. 1995. "What Is Ethical Feminism?" In S. Benhabib, J. Butler, D. Cornell, and N. Fraser (eds.), *Feminist Contentions: A Philosophical Exchange.* New York: Routledge.

Cornwall, A., and R. Jewkes. 1995. "What Is Participatory Research?" *Social Science and Medicine* 41, 12.

Corrigan, P., and P. Leonard. 1978. *Social Work Practice Under Capitalism. A Marxist Approach.* London: Macmillan Press.

Crosby, C. 1992. "Dealing with Difference." In J. Butler and J. Scott (eds.), *Feminists Theorize the Political.* New York: Routledge.

Cruikshank, J. 1990. "The Outsider, an Uneasy Role in Community Development." *Canadian Social Work Review* 7, 2.

Cunningham, I. 2008. *Employment Relations in the Voluntary Sector.* London: Routledge.

Cunningham, M. 2003. "Impact of Trauma on Social Work Clinicians: Empirical Findings." *Social Work* 48, 4.

Dalrymple, J., and B. Burke. 1995a. "Some Essential Elements of Anti-Oppressive Theory." In J. Dalrymple and B. Burke (eds.), *Anti-Oppressive Practice: Social Care and the Law.* Buckingham: Open University Press.

_____ (eds.). 1995b. *Anti-Oppressive Practice: Social Care and the Law.* Buckingham: Open University Press.

Danso, R. 2009. "Emancipating and Empowering De-Valued Skilled Immigrants: What Hope Does Anti-Oppressive Social Work Practice Offer?" *British Journal of Social Work* 39.

Daragahi, B. 2008. "Disabled Activists Helped Prod Lebanon Politicians into Accord." *Los Angeles Times.* May 22. Available at <latimes.com/news/nationworld/world/la-fg-lebanon22- 2008may22,0,3813876.story> (accessed May 27, 2008).

Darrah, C. 1997. "Complicating the Concept of Skill Requirements: Scenes from a Workplace." In G. Hull (ed.), *Changing Work. Changing Workers: Critical Perspectives on Language, Literacy and Skills.* Boulder, CO: Westview Press.

Davies, B. 2005. "The (Im)possibility of Intellectual Work in Neoliberal Regimes." *Discourse: Studies in the Cultural Politics of Education* 26, 1.

Davies, C. 1994. *Black Women, Writing and Identity: Migrations of the Subject.* London: Routledge.

Davis, A.Y. 1981. *Women, Race and Class.* New York: Random House.

Davis, B. 2001. "The Restorative Power of Emotions in Child Protection Services." *Child and Adolescent Social Work Journal* 18, 6.

Davis, L. 1986. "A Feminist Approach to Social Work Research." *Affilia*, Spring.

_____. 1985. "Female and Male Voices in Social Work." *Social Work* 30, 2.

D'Cruz, P., A. Gillingham, and S. Melendez. 2007. "Reflexivity, its Meanings and Relevance for Social Work: A Critical Review of the Literature." *British Journal of Social Work* 27.

de Lauretis, T. 1990. "Upping the Anti(sic) in Feminist Theory." In M. Hirsch and E. Fox Keller (eds.), *Conflicts in Feminism.* New York: Routledge.

_____. 1985. "The Essence of the Triangle or, Taking the Risk of Essentialism Seriously: Feminist Theory in Italy, the U.S., and Britain." *Difference: A Journal of Feminist Cultural Studies* 1.

de Montigny, G. 2005. "A Reflexive Materialist Alternative." In S. Hick, J. Fook, and R. Pozzuto (eds.), *Social Work: A Critical Turn.* Toronto: Thompson Educational Publishing.

Dei, G.J.S. 1996. *Anti-Racism Education: Theory and Practice.* Halifax/Winnipeg: Fernwood Publishing.

Derrida, J. 1997. *Of Grammatology.* Baltimore, MD: Johns Hopkins University Press.

Di Stephano, C. 1990. "Dilemmas of Difference: Feminism, Modernity, and Postmodernism." In L. Nicholson (ed.), *Feminism/Postmodernism.* New York: Routledge.

Dobbie, D., and K. Richards-Schuster. 2008. "Building Solidarity Through Difference: A Practice Model for Critical Multicultural Organizing." *Journal of Community Practice* 16, 3.

Dominelli, L. 2004. *Social Work: Theory and Practice for a Changing Profession.* Cambridge: Polity Press.

_____. 2002. *Anti-Oppressive Social Work Theory and Practice.* Hampshire: Palgrave, Macmillan.

_____. 1999. "Neo-liberalism, Social Exclusion and Welfare Clients in a Global Economy". *International Journal of Social Welfare* 8, 1.

_____. 1998. "Anti-Oppressive Practice in Context." In R. Adams, L. Dominelli, and

M. Payne (eds.), *Social Work: Themes, Issues and Critical Debates*. Houndmills: MacMillan.

_____. 1996. "Deprofessionalizing Social Work: Anti-oppressive Practice, Competencies, Postmodernism." *British Journal of Social Work* 26.

_____. 1994. "Anti-Racist Perspectives in the Social Work Curriculum." In L. Dominelli, N. Patel, and W.T. Bernard (eds.), *Anti-Racist Social Work Education: Models of Practice*. U.K.: SSSU.

_____. 1988. *"Anti-Racist Social Work."* London: MacMillan.

Dominelli, L., and A. Hoogvelt. 1996. "Globalization and the Technocratization of Social Work." *Critical Social Policy* 16.

Dominelli, L., and E. McLeod. 1989. *Feminist Social Work*. London: Macmillan.

Dore, M.M., and L.B. Alexander. 1996. "Preserving Families at Risk of Child Abuse and Neglect: The Role of the Helping Alliance." *Child Abuse and Neglect* 20, 4.

Dossa, P. 2009. *Racialized Bodies, Disabling Worlds. Storied Lives of Immigrant Muslim Women*. Toronto: University of Toronto Press

_____. 2006. "Disability, Marginality and the Nation-State: Negotiating Social Markers of Difference: Fahimeh's Story." *Disability & Society* 21, 4.

Douclos, N. 1990. "Lessons of Difference: Feminist Theory on Cultural Diversity." *Buffalo Law Review* 38, 2.

Doyle, R., and U. George. 2008. "Achieving and Measuring Diversity: An Organizational Change Approach." *Social Work Education* 27, 1.

Drucker, D. 2003. "Whither International Social Work? A Reflection." *International Social Work* 46, 1.

Dudziak, S. 2002. "Educating for Social Justice: Challenges and Openings at the Beginning of a New Century." *Critical Social Work* 2, 2.

Duffy, F.F., H. Chung, M. Trivedi, D.S. Rae, D.A. Regier, D.J. Katzelnick. 2008. "Systemic Use of Patient-Rated Depression Severity Monitoring: Is it Helpful and Feasible in Clinical Psychiatry?" *Psychiatric Services* 59, 10.

Dumbrill, G. 2006. "Ontario's Child Welfare Transformation: Another Swing of the Pendulum?" *The Canadian Social Work Review* 23, 1/2.

_____. 2003. "Child Welfare: AOP's Nemesis?" In W. Shera (ed.), *Emerging Perspectives on Anti-Oppressive Practice*. Toronto: Canadian Scholars Press.

Dumbrill, G.C., and W. Lo. 2009. "What parents Say: Service Users' Theory and Anti-Oppressive Child Welfare Practice." In J. Carriere and S. Strega (eds.), *Walking this Path Together: Anti-Oppressive Child Welfare Practice*. Halifax/Winnipeg: Fernwood Publishing.

Duran, E., and B. Duran. 1995. *"Native American Postcolonial Psychology."* New York, NY: State University of New York.

Duran, E., B. Duran, M.Y.H. Brave Heart, and S.Y. Horse-Davis. 1998. "Healing the American Indian Soul Wound." In Y. Danieli (ed.), *International Handbook of Mulitgenerational Legacies of Trauma*. New York: Plenum Press.

Dutton-Douglas, M., and L. Walker. 1988. *Feminist Psychotherapies: Integration of Therapeutic and Feminist Systems*. New Jersey: Ablex.

Ebert, T. 1991. "Postmodernism's Infinite Variety." *The Women's Review of Books* 8.

Ehrenreich, B. 2003. "Just Another Job? The Commodification of Domestic Labour." In B. Ehrenreich and A. Hochschild (eds.), *Global Women: Nannies, Maids and Sex Workers in the New Economy*. New York: Metropolitan Books (Doubleday).

Ehrenreich, B., and D. English. 1973. *Complaints and Disorders: The Sexual Politics of Sickness*. New York: Feminist Press.

Eichenbaum, L., and S. Orbach. 1984. "Feminist Psychoanalysis: Theory and Practice." In C. Brody (ed.), *Women Therapists Working with Women. New Theory and Process of Feminist Therapy*. New York: Springer.

_____. 1983. *Understanding Women: A Feminist-Psychoanaltyic Approach*. New York: Basic Books.

Elliot, H. 1998. "En-gendering Distinctions: Postmodernism, Feminism, and Narrative Therapy." In S. Madigan and I. Law (eds.), *Praxis: Situating Discourse, Feminism and Politics in Narrative Therapies*. Vancouver: Cardigan Press.

Elsass, P. 1992. *Strategies for Survival: The Psychology of Cultural Resilience in Ethnic Minorities*. New York: New York University Press.

Epstein, L. 1993. "The Therapeutic Idea in Contemporary Society." Unpublished paper presented at University of Toronto, School of Social Work Postmodernism Workshop.

Erlich, F.G., and J.L. Rivera. 1995. *Community Organizing in a Diverse Society*. Second edition. Boston: Allyn & Bacon.

Esping-Andersen, G. 1996. "After the Golden Age? Welfare State Dilemmas in a Global Economy." In G. Esping-Andersen (ed.), *Welfare States in Transition. National Adaptations in Global Economies*. London: Sage Publications.

_____. 1990. *The Three Worlds of Welfare Capitalism*. Princeton: Princeton University Press.

Essed, P. 1990. *Everyday Racism: Reports from Women of Two Cultures*. Alameda: Hunter House.

Etowa, J.B., W.B. Bernard, B. Oyinsari, and B. Clow. 2007. "Participatory Action Research (PAR): An Approach for Improving Black Women's Health in Rural and Remote Communities." *Journal of Transcultural Nursing* 18, 4.

Evans, K., E. Kincade, and A. Marbely. 2005. "Feminism and Feminist Therapy Lessons from the Past and Hope for the Future." *Journal of Counselling and Development* 83, 3.

Fanon, F. 1967. *Black Skin White Masks*. New York: Grove Press.

Faour, M.A. 2007. "Religion, Demography, and Politics in Lebanon." *Middle Eastern Journal* 43, 6.

Fargion, S. 2006. "Thinking Professional Social Work, Expertise and Professional Ideologies in Social Workers' Accounts of Their Practice." *Journal of Social Work* 6, 3.

Fawcett, B. 2000. *Feminist Perspectives on Disability*. New York: Pearson Education.

Fay, J. 1997. "From Welfare Bum to Single Mum: The Political Construction of Single Mothers on Social Asistance in Nova Scotia, 1966–77." Masters thesis, Halifax: Dalhousie University School of Social Work.

Fellows, M.L., and S. Razack. 1998. "The Race to Innocence: Confronting Hierarchical Relations." *Journal of Gender, Race and Justice* 1, 2.

Fernández Vargas, X. 2006. "Género e Identidad Profesional en Trabajo Social." *Revista Costarricense de Trabajo Social* 18.

Figley, C.R. (ed.). 1995. *Compassion Fatigue: Secondary Traumatic Stress Disorder from Treating the Traumatized*. New York: Brunner/Mazel.

Fish, J. 2008. "Invisible No More? Including Lesbian, Gay and Bisexual People in Social Work and Social Care." *Practice: Social Work in Action* 21, 1.

Flax, J. 1990. "Postmodernism and Gender Relations in Feminist Theory." In L. Nicholson (ed.), *Feminism/Postmodernism*. New York: Routledge.

Flower, J., and S. Wirz. 2000. "Rhetoric or Reality? The Participation of Disabled People in NGO Planning." *Health Policy and Planning* 15, 2.

Fook, J. 2002. *Social Work, Critical Theory and Practice*. London: Sage Publications.

_____. 2000. "The Lone Crusader: Constructing Enemies and Allies in the Workplace." In L. Napier and J. Fook (eds.), *Breakthroughs in Practice: Theorizing Critical Moments in Social Work*. London: Whiting and Birch.

_____. 1999a. "Critical Reflectivity in Education and Practice." In B. Pease and J. Fook (eds.), *Transforming Social Work Practice: Postmodern Critical Perspectives*. London: Routledge.

_____. 1999b. "Critical Reflectivity in Education and Practice." In. B. Pease and J. Fook (eds.), *Transforming Social Work Practice: Postmodern Critical Perspectives*. London: Routledge.

_____. 1993. *Radical Casework: A Theory of Practice*. St. Leonards, Australia: Allen & Unwin.

Fook, J., M. Ryan, and L. Hawkins. 2000. *Professional Expertise. Practice, Theory and Education for Working in Uncertainty*. London: Whiting and Birch.

Forrester, D., J. McCambridge, C. Waissbein, and S. Rollnick. 2008. "How Do Child and Family Social Workers Talk to Parents about Child Welfare Concerns?" *Child Abuse Review* 17, 1.

Fortune, A., and E. Proctor. 2001. "Research on Social Work Interventions." *Social Work Research* 25, 2.

Foucault, M. 1995. *Discipline and Punish: The Birth of the Prison*. New York: Random House, Vintage Books.

_____. 1991. "Truth and Power." In C. Gordon (ed.), *Power/Knowledge: Selected Interviews and Other Writings 1972–1977*. New York: Pantheon Books.

_____. 1980a. *The History of Sexuality. Volume 1: An Introduction*. New York: Vintage.

_____. 1980b. "Two Lectures." In C. Gordon (ed.), *Power/Knowledge: Selected Interviews and Other Writings, 1972–1977*. Harlow: Longman.

_____. 1980c. *Power/Knowledge: Selected Interviews and Other Writings 1972–1977*. New York: Pantheon Books.

_____. 1979. *Discipline and Punish: The Birth of the Prison*. New York: Vantage Books.

Franklin, C., and M.S. Kelly. 2009. "Becoming Evidence-Informed in the Real World of School Social Work Practice." *Children and Schools* 31, 1.

Freeman, B. 2004. "Resiliency of a People: A Haudenosaunee Concept of Helping." Unpublished Masters thesis, Hamilton: McMaster University.

Friedman, S.S. 1998. *Mappings: Feminism and the Cultural Geographies of Encounter*. Princeton, NJ: Princeton University Press.

Freire, P. 2003. *Pedagogy of the Oppressed*. Second edition. New York: Continuum.

_____. 1994. *Pedagogy of the Oppressed*. M. Bergman Ramos, Translator. New York: Continuum.

_____. 1974. *Pedagogy of the Oppressed*. New York: Seabury Press.

_____. 1973. *Education for Critical Consciousness*. New York: Seabury Press.

Gagné, M-A. 1996. "The Role of Dependency and Colonialism in Generating Trauma in First Nations Citizens: The James Bay Cree." In A. Marsella, M. Friedman, E. Gerrity, and R. Scurfield (eds.), *Ethnocultural Aspects of Posttraumatic Stress*

Disorder: Issues, Research, and Clinical Applications. Washington, DC: American Psychological Association.

Galambos, C., C.N. Dulmus, and J.S. Wodarski. 2005. "Principles for Organizational Change in Human Service Agencies." *Journal of Human Behaviour in the Social Environment* 11, 1.

Galper, J.H. 1975. *The Politics of Social Services.* New Jersey: Prentice Hall.

Garrett, P. 2009. 'Transforming' Children's Services? Social Work, Neoliberalism and the 'Modern' World." Maidenhead, England: Open University Press.

_____. 2008 "How to be Modern: New Labour's Neoliberal Modernity and the Change for Children Programme." *British Journal of Social Work* 38, 2.

_____. 2002. "Social Work and the Just Society: Diversity, Difference and the Sequestration of Poverty." *Journal of Social Work* 2.

Geertz, C. 1986. "Making Experience, Authoring Selves." In V.W. Turner and E. Bruner (eds.), The Anthropology of Experience. Chicago: University of Illinois Press.

George, P. 2004. "Structural Social Work in Toronto Agencies: Perspectives from Social Service Constituents." Unpublished manuscript.

George, P., L. Barnoff, and B. Coleman. 2007. "Finding Hope in a Hostile Context: Stories of Creative Resistance in Progressive Social Work Agencies." *Canadian Social Work* 9, 1.

George, P., K. Moffatt, L. Barnoff, B. Coleman, and C. Paton. In press. "Image Construction as a Strategy of Resistance by Progressive Community Organizations." *Nouvelles Pratiques Sociales* 21, 2.

George-Kanentiio, D. 1995. "How Much Land Did the Iroquois Posses?" *Akwesasne Notes* 1, 3/4. Kahniakehaka Nation.

_____. 1995. "Iroquois Population in 1995." *Akwesasne Notes* 1, 3/4. Kahniakehaka Nation.

Gergen, K. 2009. *An Invitation to Social Construction.* Second edition. Los Angeles, London: Sage Publications.

_____. 1985. "The Social Constructionism Movement in Modern Psychology." American Psychologist 40, 3.

Ghai, A. 2001. "Disability in The Indian Context: Postcolonial Perspectives." In M. Corker and T. Shakespeare (eds.), *Disability/Postmodernity: Embodying Disability Theory.* New York: Continuum.

Gibbs, L., and E. Gambrill. 2002. "Evidence-Based Practice: Counterarguments to Objections." *Research on Social Work Practice* 12, 3.

Gidada, N., T. Namara, and Y. Noggo. 1974. *The Oromo Voice against Tyranny.* Addis Ababa: Oromo Liberation Front.

Gilgun, J.F. 2005. "The Four Cornerstones of Evidence-Based Practice in Social Work." *Research on Social Work Practice* 15 ,1.

_____. 2004. "Qualitative Methods and the Development of Clinical Assessment Tools." *Qualitative Research* 14, 7.

Gilligan, C. 1982. *In a Different Voice: Psychological Theory and Women's Development.* Cambridge, MA: Harvard University Press.

Gilligan, C., N. Lyons, and T. Hanmer. 1990. *Making Connections: The Relational Worlds of Adolescent Girls at Emma Willard School.* Cambridge, MA: Harvard University Press.

Gilroy, J. 1990. "Social Work and the Women's Movement." In B. Wharf (ed.), *Social*

Work and Social Change in Canada. Toronto: McClelland and Stewart.

Gindin, S., and J. Stanford. 2003. "Canadian Labour and the Political Economy of Transformation." In W. Clement and L. Vosko (eds.), *Changing Canada: Political Economy as Transformation.* Montreal & Kingston: McGill-Queen's University Press.

Gladstein, G.A. 1970. "Is Empathy Important in Counseling?" *Personal and Guidance Journal* 48, 4.

Glisson, C. 2007. "Assessing and Changing Organizational Culture and Climate for Effective Services." *Research on Social Work Practice* 17, 6.

Goffman, E. 1963. *Stigma Notes on the Management of Spoiled Identity.* Englewood Cliffs, NJ: Prentice-Hall.

_____. 1961. *Asylums: Essays on the Social Situation of Mental Patients and Other Inmates.* New York: Anchor Books.

Goldhor Lerner, H. 1989. *Women in Therapy.* New York: Harper & Row.

Gordon, L. 1988. *Heroes of Their Own Lives: The Politics and History of Family Violence.* New York: Penguin.

Gormond, J. 1993. "Postmodernism and the Conduct of Inquiry in Social Work." *Affilia* 8, 3.

Gossett, M., and M.L. Weinman. 2007. "Evidence-Based Practice and Social Work: An Illustration of the Steps Involved." *Health and Social Work* 32, 2.

Gottfried, H. 1994. "Learning the Score: The Duality of Control and Everyday Resistance in the Temporary-Help Service Industry." In J. Jermier, D. Knights, and W. Nord (eds.), *Resistance and Power in Organizations.* London and New York: Routledge.

Gough, P., N. Trocmé, I. Brown, D. Knoke, and C. Blackstock. 2003. "Pathways to the Over-representation of Aboriginal Children in Care." CECW Information Sheet #23E. Montreal: McGill University, School of Social Work. Available at <cecw-cepb.ca/publications/424>.

Gray, M. 2005. "Dilemmas of International Social Work: Paradoxical Processes in Indigenisation, Universalism and Imperialism." *International Journal of Social Welfare* 14, 3.

Gray, N. 2005. "Untying the Gordian Knot." *Pharmaceutical Executive* 25, 5 (May).

Gray, N., and P.S. Nye. 2001. "American Indian and Alaska Native Substance Abuse: Co-Morbidity and Cultural Issues." *Journal of the National Center American Indian and Alaska Native Mental Health Research* 10, 2.

Greene, S., A. Ahluwalia, J. Watson, R. Tucker, S.B. Rourke, J. Koornstra, M. Sobota, L. Monette, and S. Byers. 2009. "Between Scepticism and Empowerment: The Experiences of Peer Research Assistants in HIV/AIDS, Housing and Homelessness Community-Based Research." *International Journal of Social Research Methodology* 12, 4.

Greenspan, M. 1983. *A New Approach to Women and Therapy.* New York: McGraw-Hill.

Gremillion, H. 2001. "Anorexia: A Canary in the Mine. An Anthropological Perspective." In *Working with the Stories of Women's Lives.* Adelaide: Collected by Dulwich Centre Publications.

Guevara, E. 1969. *Che: Selected Works of Ernesto Guevara, 1928–1967.* Cambridge, MA: MIT Press.

Guzmán Stein, L. 2004. "Valores y Enfoques en el Currículo de Trabajo Social: Una Primera Aproximación a la Aplicación del Enfoque de Género en el Currículo de Trabajo Social." En M.L. Molina M. et al., *La Cuestión Social y la Formación*

Profesional en Trabajo Social en el Contexto de las Nuevas Relaciones de Poder y la Diversidad Latinoamericana. Cuidad Autónoma de Buenos Aires, Argentina: Espacio Editorial.

_____. 2002. "Identidad Profesional y Sexismo en la Formación en Trabajo Social." *Revista Costarricense de Trabajo Social* 14.

_____. 1994. "Relaciones de Género y Estructuras Familiares: Reflexiones a Propósito del Año Internacional de la Familia." *Revista Costarricense de Trabajo Social* 4.

Habermas, J. 1973. *Knowledge and Human Interests.* London: Heinemann.

Hall, S. 1996. "Ethnicity: Identity and Difference." In G. Eley and R.G. Suny (eds.), *Becoming National.* New York: Oxford University Press.

Hamilton, J. 2005. "Clinician's Guide to Evidence-Based Practice." *Journal of American Academy of Child and Adolescent Psychiatry* 44, 5.

Hammer, I., and D. Statham. 1989. *Women and Social Work: Toward a Woman-Centered Practice.* Chicago: Lycaim.

Hand, S. (ed.). 1989. *The Levinas Reader.* Oxford: Blackwell.

Haraway, D. 1990. "A Manifesto for Cyborgs: Science, Technology, and Socialist Feminism in the 1980s." In L. Nicholson (ed.), *Feminism/Postmodernism.* New York: Routledge.

_____. 1988. "Situated Knowledges: The Science Question in Feminism and the Privilege of Partial Perspective." *Feminist Studies* 14.

Harding, S. 1997. "Comment on Hekman's Truth and Method: Feminist Standpoint Theory Revisited: Whose Standpoint Needs the Regimes of Truth and Reality." *Signs: Journal of Women in Culture and Society* 22.

_____. 1987. *Feminism and Methodology.* Bloomington, IN: University of Indiana Press.

_____. 1986. *The Science Question in Feminism.* Ithaca, NY: Cornell University Press.

Hare, I. 2004. "Defining Social Work for the Twenty First Century: The International Federation of Social Workers' Revised Definition of Social Work." *International Social Work* 47, 3.

Hare-Mustin, R. 1994. "Discourses in the Mirrored Room: A Postmodern Analysis of Therapy." *Family Processes* 33 (March).

Harris, J. 2008. "State Social Work: Constructing the Present from Moments in the Past." *British Journal of Social Work* 38.

Hartman, H. 1981. "The Unhappy Marriage of Marxism and Feminism. Towards a More Progressive Union." In L. Sargent (ed.), *Women and Revolution.* Boston: South End Press.

Hartsock, N. 1997. "Comment on Hekman's Truth and Method: Feminist Standpoint Theory Revisited: Truth or Justice?" *Signs: Journal of Women in Culture and Society* 22.

_____. 1985. *Money, Sex, and Power: Toward a Feminist Historical Materialism.* Boston: Northeastern University Press.

Harvey, D. 2005. *A Brief History of Neoliberalism.* London: Oxford University Press.

_____. 1990. *The Condition of Postmodernity.* Malden, MA: Blackwell.

Hassen, M. 1990. *The Oromo of Ethiopia.* Cambridge: Cambridge University Press.

Haug, F. 1992. "Learning from Experience: A Feminist Epistemology." Unpublished paper presented at the Ontario Institute for Studies in Education.

Hayashi, R., and M. Okuhira. 2001. "The Disability Rights Movement in Japan: Past, Present and Future." *Disability & Society* 16, 6.

Hayes, D. 2009. "Social Work with Asylum Seekers and Others Subject to Immigrant Control." In R. Adams, L. Dominelli, and M. Payn (eds.). *Practising Social Work in a Complex World*. Second edition. London: Palgrave MacMillan.

Haynes, J. 1975. "The Rank and File Movement in Private Social Work." *Labor History* 16.

Healey, L.M. 2001. *International Social Work: Professional Action in an Interdependent World*. New York: Oxford University Press.

Healy, K. 2005. "Under Reconstruction: Renewing Critical Social Work Practices." In S. Hick, J. Fook, and R. Pozzuto (eds.), *Social Work: A Critical Turn*. Toronto: Thompson Educational Publishing.

_____. 2002. "Managing Human Services in a Market Environment: What Role for Social Workers?" *British Journal of Social Work* 32, 5 (August).

_____. 2001. "Reinventing Critical Social Work: Challenges from Practice, Context and Postmodernism." *Critical Social Work* 2, 1.

_____. 2000. *Social Work Practices: Contemporary Perspectives on Change*. London: Sage Publications.

Healy, K., and P, Leonard. 2000. "Responding to Uncertainty: Critical Social Work Education in the Postmodern Habitat." *Journal of Progressive Human Services* 11, 1.

Hebert Boyd, M. 2007. *Enriched by Catastrophe: Social Work and Social Conflict after the Halifax Explosion*. Halifax/Winnipeg: Fernwood Publishing.

Hefferman, K. 2006. "Social Work, New Public Management and the Language of 'Service User.'" *British Journal of Social Work* 36, 1.

Heinrich, R.K., J.L. Corbine, and K.R. Thomas. 1990. "Counseling Native Americans." *Journal of Counseling & Development* 69 (November/December).

Hekman, S. 1997a. "Truth and Method: Feminist Standpoint Theory Revisited." *Signs: Journal of Women in Culture and Society* 22.

_____. 1997b. "Reply to Hartsock, Collins, Harding, and Smith." *Signs: Journal of Women in Culture and Society 22*.

Hepworth, D.H., R.H. Rooney, and J.A. Larsen. 1997. *Direct Social Work Practice: Theory and Skills*. Fifth edition. Pacific Grove, CA: Brooks/Cole.

Herd, P., and M.H. Meyer. 2002. "Care Work: Invisible Civic Engagement." *Gender and Society* 16, 5.

Hernández, M.P. 2000. "A Personal Dimension of Human Rights Activism: Narratives of Trauma, Resilience and Solidarity." Doctoral dissertation, University of Massachusetts.

Heron, B. 2007. *Desire for Development: Whiteness, Gender, and the Helping Imperative*. Waterloo: Wilfrid Laurier University Press.

_____. 2005. "Self-Reflection in Critical Social Work Practice: Subjectivity and the Possibilities of Resistance." *Reflective Practice* 6, 3.

Herring, R.D. 1992. "Seeking a New Paradigm: Counseling Native Americans." *Journal of Multicultural Counseling & Development* 20, 1.

Hesse, A.R. 2002. "Secondary Trauma: How Working with Trauma Survivors Affects Therapists." *Clinical Social Work Journal* 30, 3.

Hick, S. 2002. *Social Work in Canada. An Introduction*. Toronto: Thompson Educational Publishing.

Hick, S., J. Fook, and R. Pozzuto (eds.). 2005. *Social Work: A Critical Turn*. Toronto: Thompson Educational Publishing.

Hick, S., and R. Puzzuto. 2005. "Towards "Becoming" a Critical Social Worker." In S. Hick, J. Fook, and R. Pozzuto (eds.), *Social Work: A Critical Turn*. Toronto: Thompson Educational Publishing.

Hill, D., B. Antone, and M. Myers. 1980. *The Power Within People: A Community Organizing Perspective*. Deseronto, ON: Peace Tree Technologies.

Hill, M. 1990. "On Creating a Theory of Feminist Therapy." *Women & Therapy* 9, 1.

Hillyer, B. 1993. *Feminism and Disability*. Norman: University of Oklahoma Press.

Ho Chi Minh. 1969. *Ho Chi Minh: Selected Articles and Speeches, 1920–1967*. London: Lawrence & Sichart.

Hoagwood, K., B.J. Burns, L. Kiser, H. Ringeisen, and S.K. Schoenwald. 2001. "Evidence-Based Practice in Child and Adolescent Mental Health Services." *Psychiatric Services* 52.

Holcomb, B.K., and S. Ibssa. 1990. *The Invention of Ethiopia: The Making of a Dependent Colonial State in Northeast Africa*. Trenton, NJ: Red Sea Press.

Holden, C., and P. Beresford. 2002. "Globalization and Disability." In C. Barnes, M. Oliver, and L. Barton (eds.), *Disability Studies Today*. Cambridge, UK: Polity Press.

Hollis, F., and M.E. Woods. 1981. *Casework: A Psychosocial Therapy*. Third edition. New York: Random House.

hooks, b. 1995. "Power, Passion and Pedagogy." *Shambhala Sun* (winter).

_____. 1995. "Postmodern Blackness." In W. Truett Anderson (ed.), *The Truth about the Truth: De-confusing and Re-constructing the Postmodern World*. New York: Penguin Putnam.

_____. 1992. *Black Looks: Race and Representation*. Toronto: Between the Lines.

_____. 1990. *Yearning: Race, Gender and Cultural Politics*. Toronto: Between the Lines.

_____. 1989. *Talking Back: Thinking Feminist, Thinking Black*. Toronto: Between the Lines.

_____. 1984. *Feminist Theory: From Margin to Center*. Boston: South End.

Horvath, A., and L. Greenberg. 1989. "Development and Validation of the Working Alliance Inventory." *Journal of Counseling Psychology* 36, 2.

Horwath, J. 2007. "The Missing Assessment Domain: Personal, Professional and Organizational Factors Influencing Professional Judgments when Identifying and Referring Child Neglect." *British Journal of Social Work* 37.

Hough, G. 1999. "The Organisation of Social Work in the Customer Culture." In B. Pease and J. Fook (eds.), *Transforming Social Work Practice: Postmodern Critical Perspectives*. London: Routledge.

Hough, G., and L. Briskman. 2003. "Responding to the Changing Socio-Political Context of Practice." In J. Allan, B. Pease, and L. Briskman (eds.), *Critical Social Work: An Introduction to Theories and Practices*. Crows Nest, NSW: Allen & Unwin.

Howard, D. (ed.). 1986. *A Guide to Dynamics of Feminist Therapy*. New York: Harrington Park Press.

Howard, M.O., C.J. McMillen, and D.E. Pollio. 2003. "Teaching Evidence-Based Practice: Toward a New Paradigm for Social Work Education." *Research on Social Work Practice* 13,2.

Howe, D. 1987. *An Introduction to Social Work Theory*. Ashgate: Ashgate Publishing.

Hugman, R. 2008. "But Is It Social Work? Some Reflections on Mistaken Identities." *British Journal of Social Work*.

Humphrey, J.C. 1999. "Disabled People and the Politics of Difference." *Disability &*

Society 14, 2.

Hyde, C. 2004. "Multicultural Development in Human Services Agencies: Challenges and Solutions." *Social Work* 49.

_____. 2003. "Multicultural Organizational Development in Nonprofit Human Service Agencies: Views from the Field." *Journal of Community Practice* 11, 1.

_____. 2000. "The Hybrid Nonprofit: An Examination of Feminist Social Movement Organizations." *Journal of Community Practice* 8, 4.

_____. 1998. "A Model for Diversity Training in Human Service Agencies." *Administration in Social Work* 22, 4.

Hyde, C., and K. Hopkins. 2004. "Diversity Climates in Human Service Agencies: An Exploratory Assessment." *Journal of Ethnic and Cultural Diversity in Social Work* 13, 2.

Hyde, C.A., and M. Megan. 2004. "A Collaborative Approach to Service, Learning and Scholarship: A Community-Based Research Course." *Journal of Community Practice* 12, 1/2.

IASSW Website. N.d. Definition of Social Work <http://www.iassw-aiets.org/images/Documents/Download%20Definition%20of%20Social%20Work.pdf>.

Iedema, R., and H. Scheeres. 2003. "From Doing Work to Talking Work: Renegotiating Knowing, Doing and Identity." *Applied Linguistics* 24, 3.

Iliffe, G., and L.G. Steed. 2000. "Exploring the Counselor's Experience of Working with Perpetrators and Survivors of Domestic Violence." *Journal of Interpersonal Violence* 15, 4.

Illich, I. 1981. "Medical Nemesis." In P. Conrad and R. Kern (eds.), *The Sociology of Health and Illness: A Critical Perspective*. New York: St. Martin's Press.

Israel, B.A., A.J. Schulz, E.A. Parker, and A.B. Becker. 1998. "Review of Community-Based Research: Assessing Partnership Approaches to Improve Public Health." *Annual Review of Public Health* 19.

Israel, B., A. Schulz, E. Parker, A. Becker, A. Allen, and J.R. Guzman. 2003. "Critical Issues in Developing and Following Community-Based Participatory Principles." In M. Minkler and N. Wallerstein (eds.), *Community-Based Participatory Research for Health*. San Francisco, CA: Jossey-Bass/Wiley.

Issitt, M. 1999. "Towards the Development of Anti-Oppressive Reflective Practice: The Challenge for Multi-Disciplinary Working." *Journal of Practice Teaching* 2, 2.

Jackson, N. 1997. "Reframing the Discourse of Skill." In J. Kenway, K. Tregenza, and P. Watkins (eds.), *Vocational Education Today: Topical Issues*. Victoria: Deakin University Press.

Jalata, A. 1993. *Oromia and Ethiopia*. Boulder, CO: Lynne Reinner Publishers.

Janack, M. 1997. "Standpoint Epistemology Without the Standpoint? An Examination of Epistemic Privilege And Epistemic Authority." *Hypatia* 12, 2.

Jeffery, D. 2007. "Radical Problems and Liberal Selves: Professional Subjectivity in the Anti-Oppressive Social Work Classroom." *Canadian Social Work Review* 24, 2.

Jenson, J. 1993. "Deconstructing Dualities: Making Rights Claims in Political Institutions." In G. Drover and P. Kerans (eds.), *New Approaches to Welfare Theory*. Brookfield, VT: Edward Elgar.

Johansen, B. 1995. "Dating the Iroquois Confederacy." *Akwesasne Notes* 1, 3/4. Kahniakehaka Nation.

Johnsson, E., and K. Svensson. 2005. "Theory in Social Work: Some Reflections on

Understanding and Explaining Interventions." *European Journal of Social Work* 8, 4.

Jordan, J., A. Kaplan, M. Baker, I. Stiver, and J. Surrey (eds.). 1991. *Women's Growth in Connection: Writings from the Stone Center.* New York: Guilford Press.

Joseph, S. 1993. "Fieldwork and Psychosocial Dynamics of Personhood." *Frontiers: A Journal of Women Studies* 13, 3.

Josefowitz Siegel, R. 1990. "Turning the Things that Divide Us into Strengths that Unite Us." In L. Brown and M. Root (eds.), *Diversity and Complexity in Feminist Therapy.* New York: Harrington Park.

Josefowitz Siegel, R., and C. Larsen, C. 1990. "The Ethics of Power Differentials." In H. Lerman and N. Porter, *Feminist Ethics in Psychotherapy.* New York: Springer.

Karabanow, J. 2004. "Making Organizations Work: Exploring Characteristics of Anti-Oppressive Organizational Structures in Street Youth Shelters." *Journal of Social Work* 4, 1.

Kaschak, E. 1992. *Engendered Lives. A New Psychology of Women's Experience.* New York: Basic Books.

_____. E. 1990. "How to Be a Failure as a Family Therapist: A Feminist Perspective." In H. Lerman and N. Porter (eds.), *Feminist Ethics in Psychotherapy.* New York: Springer.

Katz, I. 1995. "Anti-Racism and Modernism." In M. Yelloly and M. Henkel (eds.), *Learning and Teaching in Social Work: Towards Reflective Practice.* London: Jessica Kingsley.

Keefe, T. 1981. "Empathy Skills and Critical Consciousness." *Social casework* 61, 7.

Kelly, A.E., and K.H. Yuan. 2009. "Clients' Secret Keepng and the Working Alliance in Adult Outpatient Therapy." *Psychotherapy Theory, Research and Practice Training* 46, 2.

Keys, C., A. Horner-Johnson, K. Westlock, B. Hernandez, and L. Vasiliauskas. 1999. "Learning Science for Social Good: Dynamic Tensions in Developing Undergraduate Community Researchers." *Journal of Prevention and Intervention in the Community* 18, 2.

Khor, M. 2001. *Rethinking Globalization: Critical Issues and Policy Choices.* Halifax/ Winnipeg: Fernwood Publishing.

Kjellberg, A. 2002. "Being a Citizen." *Disability & Society* 17, 2.

Knutsson, K.E. 1967. *Authority and Change: A Study of the Kallu Institution among the Matcha Galla of Ethiopia.* Gothenburg: Museum of Ethnography.

Kondrat, M.E. 1999. "Who Is the 'Self' in Self-Aware: Professional Self-Awareness from a Critical Theory Perspective." *Social Service Review* (winter).

Kothari, S., and K.L. Kirschner. 2006. "Abandoning the Golden Rule: The Problem with 'Putting Ourselves in the Patient's Place'." *Topics in Stroke Rehabilitation* 13, 4.

Kowalski, T. 2009. "Need to Address Evidence-Based Practice in Educational Administration." *Educational Administration Quarterly* 45.

Kravetz, D. 2004. *Tales from the Trenches: Politics and Practice in Feminist Service Organizations.* Dallas: University Press of America.

Kroenke, K., R.L. Spitzer, J.B.W. Williams. 2001. "The PHQ-9: Validity of a Brief Depression Severity Measure." *Journal of General Internal Medicine* 16, 9.

Kumsa, M.K. 2008. "Social Working the Dance of Otherness." *Canadian Social Work Review* 25, 1.

_____. 2000. "Discourses on Human Rights and Peoples' Rights in the Oromo Quest for National Liberation." *Journal of Oromo Studies* 7, 1 & 2.

_____. 1998. "Oromo Women and the Oromo National Movement: Dilemmas, Problems and Prospects for True Liberation." In A. Jalata (ed.), *Oromo Nationalism and the Ethiopian Discourse.* Lawrenceville, New Jersey: Red Sea Press.

_____. 1997. "The Siiqqee Institution of Oromo Women." *Journal of Oromo Studies* 4, 1 & 2.

_____. 1994. "The Liberation of Self." *Qunnamtii* 4, 1.

_____. 1993. "Voices of Oromo Women: Woman to Woman." *Qunnamtii* 3, 2.

_____. 1992. "The Voices of Oromo Women: A Whisper into the Souls of Oromo Men." *Qunnamtii* 2, 4.

Kurzman, P. 2009. "Labour-Social Work Collaboration: Current and Historical Perspectives." *Journal of Workplace Behavioral Health* 24.

Kuyek, J. 2009. *Fighting for Hope: Organizing to Realize Our Dreams.* Montreal: Black Rose Books.

Laidlaw, T., and C. Malmo. 1990. *Healing Voices: Feminist Approaches to Therapy.* San Francisco: Jossey-Bass.

Larner, G. 2004. "Family Therapy and the Politics of Evidence." *Journal of Family Therapy* 26.

Larson, G. 2008. "Anti-Oppressive Practice in Mental Health." *Journal of Progressive Human Services* 19, 1.

Lata, L. 2004. *The Horn of Africa as Common Homeland. State and Self-Determination in the Era of Heightened Globalization.* Waterloo, Canada: Wilfrid Laurier University Press.

_____. 1999. *The Ethiopian State at the Crossroads: Decolonization & Democratization or Disintegration?* Lawrenceville, NJ: Red Sea Press.

_____. 1998. "Peculiar Challenges to Oromo Nationalism." In A. Jalata (ed.), *Oromo Nationalism and the Ethiopian Discourse.* Lawrenceville, NJ: Red Sea Press.

Lavia, J. 2007. "Girls and Special Education in the Caribbean." *Support for Learning* 22, 4.

Lee, B., S. McGrath, K. Moffatt, and U. George. 2002. "Exploring the Insider Role in Community Practice." *Critical Social Work* 2, 2.

Lee, C.D., and C. Ayon. 2004. "Is the Client-Worker Relationship Associated with Better Outcomes in Mandated Child Abuse Cases?" *Research on Social Work Practice* 14, 5.

Lee, E. 1985. *Letters to Marcia: Anti-Racist Education in School.* Toronto: Cross Cultural Communication Centre.

Lefebvre, H. 1991 [1974]. *The Production of Space.* Trans. D. Nicholson-Smith. Oxford: Basil Blackwell.

Legesse, A. 2000. *Oromo Democracy. An Indigenous African Political System.* Lawrenceville, NJ: Red Sea Press.

_____. 1973. *Gada: Three Approaches to the Study of African Society.* New York: Free Press.

Lemke, T. 2001. "'The Birth of Bio-Politics': Michel Foucault's Lecture at the College de France on Neo-liberal Governmentality." *Economy and Society* 30, 2.

Leonard, P. 2001. "The Future of Critical Social Work in Uncertain Conditions." *Critical Social Work* 2, 1. Available at <uwindsor.ca/criticalsocialwork/the-future-of-critical-social-work-in-uncertain-conditions>.

_____. 1997. *Postmodern Welfare: Reconstructing an Emancipatory Project.* London: Sage.

_____. 1994. "Knowledge/Power and Postmodernism." *Canadian Social Work Review*

11, 1 (Winter).

Lerner, H., and N. Porter (eds.). 1990. *Feminist Ethics in Psychotherapy*. New York: Springer Publishing.

Leslie, D.R., K. Leslie, and M. Murphy. 2003. "Inclusion by Design: The Challenges of Social Work in Workplace Accommodation for PWDS." In W. Shera (ed.), *Emerging Perspectives on Anti-Oppression Practice*. Toronto: Canadian Scholar's Press.

Levine, H. 1982. "The Personal Is Political: Feminism and the Helping Professions." In G. Finn and A. Miles (eds.), *Feminism from Pressure to Politics*. Montreal: Black Rose Books.

——. 1981. "Feminist Counselling: Approach or Technique?" In J. Turner and L. Emery (eds.), *Perspectives of Women in the 80's*. Winnipeg: University of Manitoba Press.

Lewchuk, W. 2002. *Workload, Work Organization and Health Outcomes: The Ontario Disability Support Program*. Hamilton, ON: Institute for Work in a Global Society.

Lewis Herman, J. 1992. *Trauma and Recovery: The Aftermath of Violence from Domestic Abuse to Political Terror*. New York: Basic Books.

Lightman, E .2003. *Social Policy in Canada*. Toronto: Oxford University Press.

_____. 2002. *Social Policy in Canada*. Toronto: Oxford University Press.

Lightman, E., A. Mitchell, and D. Herd. 2009. "Searching for Local Solutions: Making Welfare Policy on the Ground in Ontario." *Journal of Progressive Human Services* 20, 2.

_____. 2005. "Welfare to What? After Workfare in Toronto." *International Social Security Review* 58, 4.

Lo, W. 2007. "Parents Speak: 'Treat Us with Respect.' A Study of Child Protection Service User Perspectives." MSW thesis, McMaster University: Hamilton, Ontario.

Lockhart, A. 1994. "The Insider-Outsider Dialectic in Native Socioeconomic Development: A Case Study in Process Understanding." In R. Compton and B. Gallaway (eds.), *Social Work Process*. Fifth edition. California: Brooks/Cole Press.

London Edinburgh Weekend Return Group. 1980. *In and Against the State*. London: Pluto Press.

Longino, H. 1993. "Feminist Standpoint Theory and the Problems of Knowledge." *Signs: Journal of Women in Culture and Society* 19, 1.

Lordan, N. 2000. "Finding a Voice: Empowerment of PWDS in Ireland." *Journal of Progressive Human Services* 11, 1.

Lourde, A. 1984. *Sister Outsider*. Freedom: Crossing Press.

Lundy, C. 2004. *Social Work and Social Justice: A Structural Approach to Practice*. Peterborough, ON: Broadview Press.

Lustgarten, A. 2005. "Drug Testing Goes Offshore." *Fortune* 152, 3. (August).

Lymbery, M.E. 2003. "Negotiating the Contradictions between Competence and Creativity in Social Work Education." *Journal of Social Work* 3,1.

Lyons, K., L.K. Manion, and M. Carlsen. 2006. *International Perspectives on Social Work: Global Conditions and Local Practice*. New York: Palgrave Macmillan.

Lyons, O. 1984. "Spirituality, Equality, and Natural Law." In L. Little Bear, J. Menno Bolt, and A. Long (eds.), *Pathways to Self-Determination: Canadian Indians and the Canadian State*. Toronto: University of Toronto Press.

MacDonald, J. 2008. "Anti-Oppressive Practices with Chronic Pain Sufferers." *Social Work and Health Care* 47, 2.

MacDonald, K., and G. MacDonald. 1999. "Empowerment: A Critical View." In W. Shera, (ed.), *Empowerment Practices in Social Work: Developing Richer Conceptual Foundations*. Canadian Scholars Press.

Madigan, S. 1998. "Practice Interpretations of Michel Foucault. Situating Problem Externalizing Discourse." In S. Madigan and I. Law (eds.), *Praxis: Situating Discourse, Feminism and Politics in Narrative Therapies*. Vancouver: Cardigan Press.

Madigan, S., and I. Law (eds.). 1998. *Praxis: Situating Discourse, Feminism and Politics in Narrative Therapies*. Vancouver: Cardigan Press.

Maiter, S., L. Simich, N. Jacobson, and J. Wise. 2008. "Reciprocity: An Ethic for Community-Based Participatory Action Research." *Action Research* 6.

Maluccio, A.N. 1979. *Learning from Clients: Interpersonal Helping as Viewed by Clients and Social Workers*. New York: Free Press.

Manson, S., J. Beals, T. O'Nell, J. Piasecki, D. Bechtold, E. Keane, and M. Jones. 1996. "Wounded Spirits, Ailing Hearts: PTSD and Related Disorders among American Indians." In A. Marsella, M. Friedman, E. Gerrity, and R. Scurfield (eds.), *Ethnocultural Aspects of Posttraumatic Stress Disorder: Issues, Research, and Clinical Applications*. Washington, DC: American Psychological Association.

Manwearing, T., and S. Wood. 1984. "The Ghost in the Machine: Tacit Skills in the Labour Process." *Socialist Review* 14, 2 (March).

Marchant, H., and B. Wearing (eds.). 1986a. *Gender Reclaimed. Women in Social Work*. Sydney: Hale and Iremonger.

_____. 1986b. "Introduction." In H. Marchant and B. Wearing (eds.), *Gender Reclaimed: Women in Social Work*. Sydney: Hale and Iremonger.

Martin, D. 2002. "Demonizing Youth, Marketing Fear: The New Politics of Crime." In J. Hermer and J. Mosher (eds.), *Disorderly People. Law and the Politics of Exclusion in Ontario*. Halifax/Winnipeg: Fernwood Publishing.

Martinez, K.M., C.E. Green, and F.M. Sanudo. 2004. "The CLAS Challenge: Promoting Culturally and Linguistically Appropriate Services in Health Care." *International Journal of Public Administration* 27, 1–2.

Marziali, E. 1988. "The First Session: An Interpersonal Encounter." *Social Casework* 69, 1.

Marziali, E., and L. Alexander. 1991. "The Power of the Therapeutic Relationship." *American Journal of Orthopsychiatry* 61, 3.

Massaquoi, N. 2007. "Crossing Boundaries to Radicalize Social Work Practice and Education." In D. Baines (ed.), *Doing Anti-Oppressive Practice: Building Transformative Politicized Social Work*. Halifax/Winnipeg: Fernwood Publishing.

_____. 2000. "Writing Resistance." In G. Sophie Harding (ed.), *Our Words, Our Revolutions: Diverse Voices of Black Women, First Nations Women and Women of Color in Canada*. Toronto: Inanna Publications and Education.

Massey, D. 2004. "The Responsibilities of Place." *Local Economy* 19, 2.

_____. 1994. "Double Articulation: A Place in the World." In A. Bammer (ed.), *Displacements: Cultural Identities in Question*. Indianapolis: Indiana University Press.

McCann, I.L., and L.A. Pearlman. 1990. "Vicarious Traumatization: A Framework for Understanding the Psychological Effects of Working with Victims." *Journal of Traumatic Stress* 3, 1.

McDonald, C. 2006. *Challenging Social Work: The Institutional Context of Practice*. Palgrave Macmillan, Houndmills: Basingstoke.

McIntosh, P. 1990. "White Privilege: Unpacking the Invisible Knapsack." *Independent*

School 49, 2.

———. 1989. "White Privilege: Unpacking the Invisible Knapsack." *Working Paper #189, Peace and Freedom*, July/August.

———. 1988. "White Privilege and Male Privilege: A Personal Account of Coming to See Correspondences through Work in Women's Studies." In A. Minas (ed.), *Gender Basics: Feminist Perspectives on Women and Men*. Second edition. Canada: Wadsworth.

McLauglin, H. 2009. "What's in a Name: 'Client', 'Patient', 'Customer', 'Consumer', 'Expert by Experience', 'Service User'—What's Next? *British Journal of Social Work* 39, 6.

McNair, L. 1992. "African American Women in Therapy: An Afrocentric and Feminist Synthesis." *Women & Therapy* 12, 1/2.

McNeill, T. 2006 "Evidence-Based Practice in an Age of Relativisim: Toward a Model for Practice." *Social Work* 51, 2.

Mead, G. 1977. *On Social Psychology*. Chicago: University of Chicago Press.

Mederos, F., and I. Woldeguiorguis. 2003. "Beyond Cultural Competence: What Child Protection Managers Need to Know and Do." *Child Welfare* 82, 2.

Meekosha, H., and L. Dowse. 2007. "Integrating Critical Disability Studies into Social Work Education and Practice: An Australian Perspective." *Practice: Social Work in Action* 19, 3.

Melba, G. 1988. *Oromia: An Introduction*. Khartoum, Sudan.

Méndez Vega, N. 2003. "La Atención a Mujeres Víctimas de Violencia Intrafamiliar en Organizaciones o Institutiones." *Revista Costarricense de Trabajo Social* 15.

Miehls, D., and K.J. Moffatt. 2001. "Constructing Social Work Identity Based on the Reflexive Self." *British Journal of Social Work* 30, 3 (June).

Miller, J., S. Donner, and E. Fraser. 2004. "Talking When Talking Is Tough: Taking on Conversations about Race, Sexual Orientation, Gender, Class and Other Aspects of Social Identity." *Smith College Studies in Social Work*. 74, 2.

Miller, J. Baker. 1976. *Toward a New Psychology of Women*. Boston: Beacon Press.

Mitchell, M. 1984. *Traditional Teachings*. Cornwall Island, ON: North American Indian Travelling College.

Moffatt, K. 1996. "Teaching Social Work as a Reflective Process." In N. Gould and I. Taylor (eds.), *Reflective Learning for Social Work*. Aldershot: Arena.

Moffatt, K., L. Barnoff, P. George, and B. Coleman. Forthcoming. 2009. "Process as Labour: Struggles for Anti-Oppressive/Anti-Racist Change in a Feminist Organization." *Canadian Review of Social Policy* 62, 34-54.

Mohanty, C. 1998. "Critical Feminist Genealogies: On the Geography and Politics of Home and Nation." In E. Shohat (ed.), *The Age of Globalization*. Massachusetts: University of Massachusetts Press.

Mohawk, J. 1986. "Prologue." In P. Wallace (ed.), *The White Roots of Peace*. Chauncey Press.

Moore, D. 1997. "Remapping Resistance: 'Ground for Struggle' and the Politics of Place." In S. Pile and M. Keith (eds.), *Geographies of Resistance*. London and New York: Routledge.

Moosa-Mitha, M. 2005. "Situating Anti-Oppressive Theories Within Critical and Difference-Centred Perspectives." In L. Brown and S. Strega (eds.), *Research as Resistance*. Toronto: Canadian Scholars Press.

Moreau, M.J. 1993. *Empowerment II: Snapshots of the Structural Approach in Action.* Ottawa: Carleton University Press.

_____. 1981. "A Comparative Study of the Preferred Helping Networks of Women and Men." Unpublished doctoral thesis, New York: Columbia University.

_____. 1979. "A Structural Approach to Social Work Practice." *Canadian Journal of Social Work Education* 5, 1.

Morley, C. 2008. "Teaching Critical Practice: Resisting Structural Domination through Critical Reflection." *Social Work Education* 27, 4.

Morris, J. 2001. "Social Exclusion and Young Disabled People with High Levels of Support Needs." *Critical Social Policy* 21, 2.

Morrissette, V., B. McKenzie, and L. Morrissette. 1993. "Toward an Aboriginal Model of Social Work Practice: Cultural Knowledge and Traditional Practices." *Canadian Social Work Review* 10, 1 (winter).

Morrow, D.F., and L. Messinger. 2006. *Sexual Orientation and Gender Expression in Social Work Practice: Working with Gay, Lesbian, Bisexual, and Transgender People.* New York: Columbia University Press.

Mosher, J. 2000. "Managing the Disentitlement of Women: Glorified Markets, the Idealized Family, and the Undeserving Other." In S.M. Neysmith (ed.), *Restructuring Caring Labour: Discourse, State Practice, and Everyday Life.* Toronto: Oxford University Press.

Mullaly, B. 2007. *The New Structural Social Work.* Third edition. Toronto: Oxford Press.

_____. 2002. *Challenging Oppression: A Critical Social Work Approach.* Toronto: Oxford University Press.

_____. 2001. "Confronting the Politics of Despair: Toward the Reconstruction of Progressvie Social Work in a Global Economy and Postmodern Age." *Social Work Education* 20, 3.

_____. 1997. *Structural Social Work: Ideology, Theory and Practices.* Second edition. Toronto: Oxford University Press.

_____. 1993. *Structural Social Work. Ideology, Theory and Practice.* Toronto: McClelland and Stewart.

Mullen, E.J. 2002. "Evidence-Based Social Work: Theory and Practice: Historical and Reflective Perspective." 4th International Conference on Evaluation for Practice. July 4–6.

Mullen, E.J., S.E. Bledsoe, and J.L. Bellamy. 2007. "Implementing Evidence-Based Social Work Practice." *Research on Social Work Practice* 18, 4.

Munro, E. 1996. "Avoidable and Unavoidable Mistakes in Child Protection Work." *British Journal of Social Work* 26, 6.

Murdoch, L. 2006. *Imagined Orphans: Poor Families, Child Welfare, and Contested Citizenship in London.* New Brunswick, NJ: Rutgers University Press.

Murphy, B.K. 1999. *Transforming Ourselves, Transforming the World: An Open Conspiracy for Social Change.* Halifax/Winnipeg: Fernwood Publishing.

Mykhalovskiy, E., P. Armonstrong, H. Armstrong, I.L. Bourgeault. J. Choiniere, J. Lexchin, S. Peters, and J. White. 2008. "Qualitative Research and the Politics of Knowledge in an Age of Evidence: Developing a Research-Based Practice of Immanent Critique." *Social Science and Medicine* 67.

Mykhalovskiy, E., and L. Weir. 2004. "The Problem of Evidence-Based Medicine: Directions for Social Science." *Social Science and Medicine* 59.

Narayan, K. 2003. "How Native Is a 'Native' Anthropologist?" In R. Lewis and S. Mills (eds.), *Feminist Postcolonial Theory: A Reader*. New York: Routledge.

Narayan, U. 1988. "Working Together across Difference: Some Considerations on Emotions and Political Practice." *Hypatia* 31, 2.

Navarro, V. 2004. "Introduction." In V. Navarro and C. Muntaner (eds.), *Political and Economic Determinants of Population Health and Well-Being: Controversies and Developments*. New York: Baywood Publishing.

Navarro, V., J. Schmitt, and J. Astudillo. 2004. "Is Globalization Undermining the Welfare State? The Evolution of the Welfare State in Developed Capitalist Countries During the 1990s." *International Journal of Health Services* 34, 2.

Nabigon, H., and A. Mawhiney. 1996. "Aboriginal Theory: A Cree Medicine Wheel Guide for Healing First Nations." In F. Turner (ed.), *Social Work Treament*. Fourth edition. New York: Free Press.

Nerland, M., and K. Jensen. 2007. "The Constitution of a New Professional Self: A Critical Reading of the Curricula for Nurses and Computer Engineers in Norway." In A. Brown, S. Kirpal, and F. Rauner (eds.), *Identities at Work*. New York: Springer.

Neumann, D.A., and S.J. Gamble. 1995. "Issues in the Professional Development of Psychotherapists: Countertransference and Vicarious Traumatization in the New Trauma Therapist." *Psychotherapy* 32, 2.

Neysmith, S.M. 2000. *Restructuring Caring Labour. Discourse, State Practice, and Everyday Life*. Toronto: Oxford University Press.

Ng, R., and K. Mirchandani. 2008. "Linking Global Trends and Local Lives: Mapping the Methodological Dilemmas." In K. Gallagher (ed.), *The Methodological Dilemma: Creative, Critical and Collaborative Approaches to Qualitative Research*. London and New York: Routledge.

Nicholson, L. 1990. Feminism/Postmodernism. New York: Routledge.

Novogrodsky, C. 1996. "The Anti-Racist Cast of Mind." In C.E. James (ed.), *Perspectives on Racism and the Human Services Sector: A Case For Change*. Toronto: University of Toronto Press.

Nybell, L.M., and S.S. Gray. 2004. "Race, Place, Space: Meanings of Cultural Competence in Three Child Welfare Agencies." *Social Work* 49, 1.

O'Brien, C.A. 1994. "The Social Organization of the Treatment of Lesbian, Gay, and Bisexual Youth in Group Homes and Youth Shelters." *Canadian Review of Social Policy* 34 (winter).

O'Leary, V. 1977. *Toward Understanding Women*. Monterey, CA: Brooks/Cole.

Ong, A. 2006. *Neoliberalism as Exception: Mutations in Citizenship and Sovereignty*. Durham and London: Duke University Press.

Ontario Advisory Council on Women's Issues. 1990. "Women and Mental Health in Ontario.".A background paper. Ottawa.

Ontario Assocation of Children's Aid Societies. 2001. "Workload Measurement Report Project." *OACAS Journal* 45(1).

Orbach, S. 1986. *Hunger Strike. The Anorectic's Struggle as a Metaphor for Our Age*. New York: W.W. Norton.

Orlinsky, D.E., K. Grawe, and B.K. Parks. 1994. "Process and Outcome in Psychotherapy." In A.E. Bergin and S.L. Garfield (eds.), *Handbook of Psychotherapy and Behavior Change*. Fourth edition. New York: John Wiley.

Oromo Voice against Tyranny. 1974. Pamphlet. Addis Ababa, Ethiopia.

Osmond, J. 2006. "Knowledge Use in Social Work Practice: Examining its Functional Possibilities." *Journal of Social Work* 6.

Otto, H., A. Polutta, and H. Ziegler. 2009. "Reflexive Professionalism as a Second Generation of Evidence-Based Practice." *Research on Social Work Practice* 19, 4.

Pachter, W.S., R.E. Fox, P. Zimbardo, and D.O. Antonuccio. 2007. "Corporate Funding and Conflict of Interest: A Primer for Psychologists." *American Psychologist* 62, 9.

Paniagua, F.A. 1994. *Assessing and Treating Culturally Diverse Clients: A Practical Guide.* Thousand Oaks: Sage Publishing.

Panitch, L., and C. Leys (eds.). 1999. "Necessary and Unnecessary Utopias." *Socialist Register 2000.* London: Merlin.

Panitch, L., and S. Gindin. 2004. "American Imperialism and EuroCapitalism: The Making of Neoliberal Globalization." *Studies in Political Economy* 71/72 (autumn).

Parada, H. 2004. "Social Work Practices within the Restructured Child Welfare System in Ontario." *Canadian Social Work Review* 21, 1.

Parker, A.C. 1990. *The Code of Handsome Lake, The Seneca Prophet.* Ohsweken, ON: reprinted by Iroqrafts Ltd.

Parrott, L. 2009. "Constructive Marginality: Conflicts and Dilemmas in Cultural Competence and Anti-Oppressive Practice." *Social Work Education* 28, 6.

Parton, N. 2008. "Changes in the Form of Knowledge in Social Work: From the 'Social' to the 'Informational'?" *British Journal of Social Work* 38.

_____. 2004. "Post-Theories for Practice: Challenging the Dogmas." In L. Davies and P. Leonard (eds.), *Social Work in a Corporate Era: Practices of Power and Resistance.* Burlington, VT: Ashgate.

Parvin, R., and M. Biaggi. 1991. "Paradoxes in the Practice of Feminist Therapy." *Women & Therapy* 11, 2.

Payne, M. 1997. *Modern Social Work Theory.* Second edition. Chicago: Lyceum Books.

Pearlman, L.A., and P.S. MacIan. 1995. "Vicarious Traumatization: An Empirical Study of the Effects of Trauma Work on Trauma Therapists." *Professional Psychology: Research and Practice* 26, 6.

Pearlman, L.A., and K.W. Saakvitne. 1995. *Trauma and the Therapist: Countertransference and Vicarious Traumatization in Psychotherapy with Incest Survivors.* New York: W.W. Norton.

Pease, B. 2007. "Critical Social Work Theory Meets Evidence-Based Practice in Australia: Towards Critical Knowledge-Informed Practice in Social Work." In K. Yokota (ed.), *Emancipatory Social Work.* Kyoto: Sekai Shisou-sya.

_____. 1999. "Postmodern Critical Theory and Emanicipatory Social Work." In B. Pease and J. Fook (eds.), *Transforming Social Work Practice: Postmodern Critical Perspectives.* London: Routledge.

Pennell, J. 1987. "Union Participation of Canadian and American Social Workers: Contrasts and Forecasts." *Social Service Review* 61, 1.

Perlroth, N. 2009. "Pfizer Finalizing Settlement in Nigerian Drug Suit." Available at <forbes.com/2009/04/03/Pfizer-kano-trovan-business-healthcare-settlement.html> (accessed July 27, 2009).

Perry, J. 1993. *Counselling for Women.* Bristol: Open University Press.

Peterson, A. 2006. "An African-American Woman with Disabilities: The Intersection of Gender, Race and Disability." *Disability & Society* 21, 7.

Petras, J. 2003. "Argentine Popular Struggle: Full Circle and Beyond. Monthly Review."

An Independent Socialist Magazine 55, 4 (September).

Petruchenia, J., and R. Thorpe (eds.). 1990. *Social Change and Social Welfare Practice.* Sydney: Hale Iremonger.

Petryna, A. 2005. "Ethical Variability: Drug Development and Globalizing Clinical Trials." *American Ethnologist* 32, 2.

Pettifor, J., C. Larsen, and L. Cammaert. 1984. *Therapy and Counselling with Women: A Handbook of Educational Materials.* Ottawa: Canadian Psychological Association.

Phoenix Rising. 1985. "The Voice of the Psychiatrized." Women and psychiatry issue: Fall/Winter 5, 1 (February).

Picado Mesén, M. 2004. "Algunos planteamientos para repensar la formación profesional en Trabajo Social." En M.L. Molina M. et al., *La Cuestión Social y la Formación Profesional en Trabajo Social en el Contexto de las Nuevas Relaciones de Poder y la Diversidad Latinoamericana.* Cuidad Autónoma de Buenos Aires: Espacio Editorial.

Pignotti, M., and B.A. Thyer. 2009. "Use of Novel Unsupported and Empirically Supported Therapies by Licensed Clinical Social Workers: An Exploratory Study." *Social Work Research* 33, 1.

Pilsecker, C. 1994. "Starting Where the Client Is." *Families in Society* 75, 7.

Pincus, A. and A. Minahan. 1973. *Social Work Practice: Model and Method.* Itasca, ILL: F.E. Peacock.

Plath, D. 2006. "Evidence-Based Practice: Current Issues and Future Directions." *Australian Social Work* 59, 1.

Platt, D. 2008. "Care or Control? The Effects of Investigations and Initial Assessments on the Social Worker-Parent Relationship." *Journal of Social Work Practice* 22, 3.

Polanyi, K. 1944. *The Great Transformation.* New York and Toronto: Rinehart.

Polio, D.E. 2006. "The Art of Evidence-Based Practice." *Research on Social Work Practice* 16, 2.

Pollack, S. 2010. "Labelling Clients 'Risky': Social Work and the Neo-liberal Welfare State." *British Journal of Social* Work 40, 4.

_____. 2004. "Anti-Oppressive Social Work Practice with Women in Prison: Discursive Reconstructions and Alternative Practices." *British Journal of Social Work* 34, 5.

Prince, R.M. 1985. "Second Generation Effects of Historical Trauma." *Psychoanalytic Review* 73.

Profitt, N.J. 2008. "¿Quién Nos Cuida a Nosotras? Abriendo Senderos para un Autocuidado Colectivo." *Revista Costarricense de Trabajo Social* 20.

_____. 2008. "Who Cares for Us? Opening Paths Toward a Critical, Collective Notion of Self-Care." *Canadian Social Work Review* 25, 2.

Race, D., K. Boxall, and I. Carson. 2005. "Towards a Dialogue for Practice: Reconciling Social Role Valorization and the Social Model of Disability." *Disability & Society* 20, 5.

Radmilovic, S. 2005. "The Capacity to Change and Child and Youth Care Practice: A Program Example and Framework." *Child and Youth Care Forum* 34, 2.

Ramazanoglu, C., and J. Holland. 2002. *Feminist Methodology: Challenges and Choices.* Thousand Oaks, CA: Sage.

Razack, N. 2002. "A Critical Examination of International Student Exchanges." *International Social Work* 45, 2.

_____. 2000. "North/South Collaborations: Affecting Transnational Perspectives for Social Work." *Journal of Progressive Human Services* 11, 1.

Razack, N., and D. Jeffrey. 2002. "Critical Race Discourse and Tenets for Social Work." *Canadian Social Work Review* 19, 2.

Razack, S. 2002a. "Introduction: When Place Becomes Race." In *Race, Space, and the Law: Unmapping a White Settler Society.* Toronto: Between the Lines.

_____. 2002b. "Gendered Violence and Spatialized Justice: The Murder of Pamela George." In *Race, Space, and the Law: Unmapping a White Settler Society.* Toronto: Between the Lines.

_____. 2002c. *Race, Space and the Law: Unmapping a White Settler Society.* Toronto: Between the Lines.

_____. 1998. *Looking White People in the Eye.* Toronto: University of Toronto Press

Rebick, J. 2000. *Imagine Democracy.* Toronto: Stoddart Publishing Company.

Rees, S. 1992. *Achieving Power. Practice and Policy in Social Welfare.* North Sydney: Allen Unwin.

Regehr, C., and S. Cadell. 1999. "Secondary Trauma in Sexual Assault Crisis Work." *Canadian Social Work* 1, 1.

Reid, C., and E. Brief. 2009. "Confronting Condescending Ethics: How Community-Based Research Challenges Traditional Approaches to Consent, Confidentiality and Capacity." *Journal of Academic Ethics* 7.

Reid, W.J. 2001. "The Role of Science in Social Work: The Perennial Debate." *Journal of Social Work* 1, 3.

Rempel, S. 2008. "Considering the Unthinkable: Post–Structural Challenges to Critical Social Work Field Education." Unpublished, Ontario Institute for Studies in Education of the University of Toronto.

Reynolds, B.C. 1963. *An Uncharted Journey.* New York: Citadel Press.

_____. 1951. *Social Work and Social Living.* New York: Citadel Press.

_____. 1946. *Rethinking Social Casework.* San Diego: Social Service Digest.

Rice, J.J., and M.J. Prince. 2000. *Changing Politics of Canadian Social Policy.* Toronto: University of Toronto Press.

Riemann, G. 2005. "Ethnographies of Practice — Practicing Ethnography: Recourses for Self-Reflective Social Work." *Journal of Social Work Practice* 19, 1.

Riley, D. 1992. "A Short History of Some Preoccupations." In J. Butler and J. Scott (eds.), Feminists Theorize the Political. New York: Routledge.

_____. 1988. *Am I That Name? Feminism and the Category of "Women" in History.* Minneapolis, MN: University of Minnesota Press.

Ristock, J.L., and J. Pennell. 1996. *Community Research as Empowerment: Feminist Links, Postmodern Interruptions.* Toronto: Oxford University Press.

Robbins, J., and R. Siegel. 1985. *Women Changing Therapy: New Assessments, Values and Strategies in Feminist Therapy.* New York: Harrington Park Press.

Robin, R.W., B. Chester, and D. Goldman. 1996. "Cumulative Trauma and PTSD in American Indian Communities." In A. Marsella, M. Friedman, E. Gerrity, and R. Scurfield (eds.), *Ethnocultural Aspects of Posttraumatic Stress Disorder: Issues, Research, and Clinical Applications.* Washington, DC: American Psychological Association.

Rose, G. 1999. "Performing Space." In D. Massey, J. Allen, and P. Sarre (eds.), *Human Geography Today.* Cambridge, UK: Polity Press.

Rose, N. 2007. "Molecular Biopolitics, Somatic Ethics and the Spirit of Biocapital." *Social Theory and Health* 5.

_____. 1999. *Powers of Freedom: Reframing Political Thought.* Cambridge: Cambridge

University Press.

_____. 1996. "Psychiatry as a Political Science: Advanced Liberalism and the Administration of Risk." *History of the Human Sciences* 9, 2.

Rosenberg, J., and S. Rosenberg. 2006. "Do Unions Matter? An Examination of the Historical and Contemporary Role of Labour Unions in the Social Work Profession." *Social Work* 51, 4.

Rosenhan, D. 1973. "On Being Sane in Insane Places." *Science* 179, January.

Rosewater, L. 1985. "Schizophrenic, Borderline, or Battered?" In L. Rosewater and L. Walker (eds.), *Handbook of Feminist Therapy: Women's Issues in Psychotherapy*. New York: Springer.

Rosewater, L., and L. Walker (eds.). 1985. "*Handbook of Feminist Therapy: Women's Issues in Psychotherapy*. New York: Springer.

Rosner-Salazar. 2003. "Multi-Cultural Service Learning and Community-Based Research as a Model Approach to Social Justice." *Social Justice* 30, 4.

Rossiter, A. 2005. "Where in the World Are We? Notes on the Need for a Social Work Response to Global Power." In S. Hick, J. Fook, and R. Pozzuto (eds.), *Social Work: A Critical Turn*. Toronto: Thompson Educational Publishing.

_____. 2000. "The Professional Is Political: An Interpretation of the Problem of the Past in Solution-focused Therapy." *American Journal of Orthopsychiatry* 70, 2.

_____. 1996. "A Perspective on Critical Social Work." *Journal of Progressive Human Services* 7, 2.

_____. 1995. "Entering the Intersection of Identity, Form, and Knowledge: Reflections on Curriculum Transformation." *Canadian Journal of Community Mental Health* 14, 1.

_____. 1995. "Teaching Social Work Skills from a Critical Perspective." *Canadian Social Work Review* 12, 1.

Roth, A., and P. Fonagy. 2005. *What Works for Whom? A Critical Review of Psychotherapy Research*. New York: Guilford Press.

Roy, C., T. Black, N. Trocmé, B. MacLaurin, and B. Fallon. 2005. "Child Neglect in Canada." cecw Information Sheet #27E. Montreal, QC: McGill University, School of Social Work. Available at <cecw-cepb.ca/publications/438>.

Ruch, G. 2007. "Reflective Practice in Contemporary Child-Care Social Work: The Role of Containment." *British Journal of Social Work* 27.

Ruetter, L., M.J. Stewart, D.L. Williamson, N. Letourneau, and S. McFall. 2005. "Partnerships and Participation in Conducting Poverty-Related Health Research." *Primary Health Care Research and Development* 6.

Russell, G., and J. Bohane. 1999. "Clinical Implications." In J. Bohane, G. Russell, et al. *Conversations about Psychology and Sexual Orientation*. New York: New York University Press.

Russell, M. 1989. "Feminist Social Work Skills." *Canadian Social Work Review* 6, 10.

_____. 1984. *Skills in Counselling Women: The Feminist Approach*. Springfield: Charles C Thomas.

Ryan, W. 1971. *Blaming the Victim*. New York: Vintage Books.

Safka, R. 2003. "The Impacts of Management in Commissioned Retail Work." Hamilton, ON: Unpublished manuscript, McMaster University, Hamilton, Ontario.

Said, E. 1997. *Covering Islam*. Second edition. New York: Vintage Books.

_____. 1978. *Orientalism*. New York: Pantheon Books.

Sainsbury, D. 2001. "Welfare State Challenges and Responses: Institutional and Ideological Resilience or Restructuring?" *Acta Sociologica* 44, 3.

Sakamoto, I. 2007. "A Critical Examination of Immigrant Acculturation: Toward an Anti-Oppressive Social Work Model with Immigrant Adults in a Pluralistic Society." *British Journal of Social Work* 37.

Sakamoto, I., and R.O. Pitner. 2005. "Use of Critical Consciousness in Anti-Oppressive Social Work Practice: Disentangling Power Dynamics at Personal and Structural Levels." *British Journal of Social Work* 35, 4.

Saleebey, D. 1994. "Culture, Theory, and Narrative: The Intersection of Meanings in Practice." *Social Work* 39, 4.

Samantrai, R. 2002. *AlterNatives: Black Feminism in the Postimperial Nation.* Stanford, California: Stanford University Press.

Samuelson, L.. and W. Antony (eds.). 2003. *Power and Resistance: Critical Thinking About Canadian Social Issues.* Third edition. Halifax/Winnipeg: Fernwood Publishing.

San Martin, R.M., and L. Barnoff. 2004. "Let Them Howl: The Operations of Imperial Subjectivity and the Politics of Race in One Feminist Organization." *Atlantis: A Women's Studies Journal* 29, 1.

Sanders, C. 1998. "Substance Misuse Dilemmas: A Postmodern Inquiry." In S. Madigan and I. Law (eds.), *Praxis: Situating Discourse, Feminism and Politics in Narrative Therapies.* Vancouver: Cardigan Press.

Sands, R., and R. Nuccio. 1992. "Postmodern Feminist Theory and Social Work." *Social Work* 37, 6.

Sargent, M. 2005. "Disability and Age-Multiple Potential For Discrimination." *International Journal of the Sociology of Law,* 33.

Sassen, S. 2003. "The State and Globalization." *Interventions International Journal of Postcolonial Studies* 5, 2.

_____. 1998. *Globalization and its Discontents.* New York: New York Press.

Schauben, L.J., and P.A. Frazier. 1995. "Vicarious Trauma: The Effects on Female Counselors of Working with Sexual Violence Survivors." *Psychology of Women Quarterly* 19.

Scherer, M.J. 2005. *Living in the State of Stuck: How Assistive Technology Impacts the Lives of People with Disabilities.* Fourth edition. Manchester, NH: Brookline Books.

Schiele, J. 1997. "The Contour and Meaning of Afrocentric Social Work." *Journal of Black Studies* 27, 6.

_____. 1996. "Afrocentricity: An Emerging Paradigm in Social Work Practice." *Social Work* 41, 3.

Schnarch, B. 2003. "Ownership, Control, Access, and Possession (OCAP) or Self-Determination Applied to Research." *Journal of Aboriginal Health* 1, 1.

School of Social Work. 2006. "BSW Alumni Survey." Unpublished report, McMaster University, Hamilton, ON.

Schoolcraft, H.R. 1992. *The Hiawatha Legends: North American Indian Lore.* Au Train, MI: Avery Color Studios.

Schuerman, J., H. Soydan, G. Macdonald, M. Forslund, D. de Moya, and R. Boruch. 2002. "The Campbell Collaboration." *Research on Social Work Practice* 12, 2.

Schwandt, T.A. 1994. "Constructivist, Interpretivist Approaches to Human Inquiry." In N.K. Denzin and Y.S. Lincoln (eds.), *Handbook of Qualitative Research.* Thousand Oaks: Sage.

Scott, J. 1992. "Experience." In J. Butler and J. Scott (eds.). Feminists Theorize the Political. New York: Routledge.

_____. 1988. "Deconstructing Equality-Versus-Difference: Or the Uses of Poststructuralist Theory for Feminism. *Feminist Studies* 14.

_____. 2002 [1985]. "Weapons of the Weak: Everyday Forms of Peasant Resistance. New Haven: Yale University Press." In S. Duncombe (ed.), 2002. *Cultural Resistance Reader* Verso: London

Scourfield, P. 2007. "Social Care and the Modern Citizen: Client, Consumer, Service User, Manager and Entrepreneur." *The British Journal of Social Work* 37, 1.

_____. 2005. "Implementing the Community Care (Direct Payments) Act: Will the Supply of Personal Assistants Meet the Demand and at What Price?" *Journal of Social Policy* 34, 3.

_____. 2003. *Gender and Child Protection*. Houndmills, Basingstoke: Palgrave MacMillan.

Searing, H. 2003. "The Continuing Relevance of Casework Ideas to Long-Term Child Protection Work." *Child and Family Social Work* 8.

Sewpaul, V. 2006. "The Global-Local Dialectic: Challenges for African Scholarship and Social Work in a Postcolonial World." *British Journal of Social Work* 36, 3.

Sheppard, J. 2000. "Learning from Personal Experience: Reflections on Social Work Practice with Mothers in Child and Family Care." *Journal of Social Work Practice* 14, 1.

Sheppard, M., S. Newstead, A. DiCaccavo, and K. Ryan. 2001. "Reflexivity and the Development of Process Knowledge in Social Work: A Classification and Empirical Study." *British Journal of Social Work* 30.

Shera, W. (ed.). 2003. *Emerging Perspectives on Anti-oppressive Practice*. Toronto: Canadian Scholars Press.

Sherman, W.R., and S. Wenocur. 1983. "Empowering Public Welfare Workers Through Mutual Support." *Social Work* (September-October).

Showalter, E. 1985. *The Female Malady: Women, Madness, and English Culture, 1830–1980*. New York: Pantheon.

Shragge, E. 2003. *Activism and Social Change: Lessons for Community and Local Organizing*. Peterborough, ON: Broadview Press.

Silver, S., J. Shields, and S. Wilson. 2005. "Restructuring of Full–time Workers: A Case of Transitional Dislocation or Social Exclusion in Canada? Lessons from the 1990s." *Social Policy & Administration* 39.

Sin, R., and M.C. Yan. 2003. "Margins as Centres: A Theory of Social Inclusion in Anti- Oppression Social Work." In W. Shera (ed.), *Emerging Perspectives on Anti-Oppression Practice*. Toronto: Canadian Scholar's Press.

Sinding, C. 2009 "Evidence-Based Practice." Presentation to the Canadian Association of Schools of Social Work Education. July.

Singer, N. 2009. "Medical Papers by Ghostwriters Pushed Therapy." *New York Times*, August 5.

Smith, D. 1999. *Writing the Social: Critique, Theory, and Investigations*. Toronto: University of Toronto Press.

_____. 1997. "Comment on Hekman's Truth and Method: Feminist Standpoint Theory Revisited." *Signs: Women in Culture and Society* 22.

_____. 1990. *The Conceptual Practices of Power: A Feminist Sociology of Knowledge*.

Toronto: University of Toronto Press.

_____. 1987. *The Everyday World as Problematic: A Feminist Sociology.* Toronto: University of Toronto Press.

_____. 1986. "Institutional Ethnography: A Feminist Method." *Resources for Feminist Research* 15.

Smith, D., and V. Burstyn (eds.). 1985. *Women, Class, Family and the State.* Toronto: Garamond Press.

Smith, D., and S.J. David (eds.). 1975. *Women Look at Psychiatry.* Vancouver: Press Gang Publishers.

_____ (eds.). 1975. *I'm Not Mad: I'm Angry.* Vancouver: Press Gang Publishers.

Smith, K. 2007. "Social Work, Restructuring and Resistance: 'Best Practices' Gone Underground." In D. Baines (ed.), *Doing Anti-Oppressive Practice: Building Transformative, Politicized Social Work.* Halifax/Winnipeg: Fernwood Publishing.

Soja, E. 1989. *Post-Modern Geographies: The Reassertion of Space in Critical Theory.* London: Verso.

Solas, J. 1994. *The (De)construction of Educational Practice in Social Work.* Aldershot, UK: Avebury.

Spelman, E. 1997. "The Heady Political Life of Compassion." In E. Spelman, *Fruits of Sorrow: Framing our Attention to Suffering.* Boston: Beacon Press.

_____. 1988. *Inessential Woman: Problems of Exclusion in Feminist Thought.* Boston: Beacon Books.

Spivak, G.C. 1987. *In Other Worlds: Essays in Cultural Politics.* New York: Methuen.

Stack, C. 1974. *All Our Kin: Strategies for Survival in a Black Community.* New York: Harper and Row.

Staller, K.M. 2006. "Railroads, Runaways, and Researchers: Returning Evidence Rhetoric to Its Practice Base." *Qualitative Inquiry* 12, 3.

Stanford, J. 2004. "The North American Free Trade Agreement: Context, Structure, and Performance." In J. Michie (ed.), *The Handbook of Globalization.* Oxford: Oxford University Press.

Stanley, L., and S. Wise. 1990. "Method, Methodology and Epistemology in Feminist Research Processes." In *Feminist Praxis.* New York: Routledge.

Statistics Canada. 2010. *Survey of Labour and Income Dynamics.* Ottawa: Statistics Canada.

_____. 2007. *Perspectives on Labour and Income.* Ottawa: Statistics Canada.

Stepney, P. 2009. "English Social Work at the Crossroads: A Critical View." *Australian Social Work* 62, 1.

Stoppard, J. 1997. "Depression: Towards a Reconciliation of Material and Discursive Accounts." In J. Ussher (ed.), *Body Talk: The Material and Discursive Regulation of Sexuality, Madness and Reproduction.* New York: Routledge.

Strauss, A.L., and J. Corbin. 1990. *Basics of Qualitative Research: Grounded Theory Procedures and Technique.* Newbury Park, CA: Sage Publications.

Strean, H.S. 1974. "Choosing Among Practice Modalities." *Clinical Social Work Journal* 2,1.

Stubbs, S. 1999. "Engaging with Difference: Soul-Searching for a Methodology in Disability and Development Research." In E. Stone (ed.), *Disability and Development.* Leeds: Disability Press.

Sturdivant, S. 1980. *Therapy with Women: A Feminist Philosophy of Treatment.* New

York: Springer Publishing.

Suarez, Z.E., P.A. Newman, and B.G. Reed. 2008. "Critical Consciousness and Cross-Cultural/Intersectional Social Work Practice: A Case Analysis." *Families in Society: The Journal of Contemporary Social Services* 89, 3.

Sudbury, J. 1998. *Other Kinds of Dreams: Black Women's Organizations and the Politics of Transformation.* London and New York: Routledge.

Sue, D.W., and D. Sue. 1990. *Counseling the Culturally Different: Theory and Practice.* Second edition. New York: Wiley.

Summerfield, D. 1999. "A Critique of Seven Assumptions behind Psychological Trauma Programmes in War-affected Areas." *Social Science & Medicine* 48.

Surrey, J. 1991. "The Self-In-Relation: A Theory of Women's Development." In J. Jordan, A. Kaplan, J. Baker-Miller, I. Stiver, and J. Surrey (eds.), *Women's Growth in Connection: Writings from the Stone Centre.* New York: Guilford.

Swift, K. 2001. "The Case for Opposition: An Examination of Contemporary Child Welfare Policy Directions." *Canadian Review of Social Policy* 47 (Spring).

_____. 1996. "An Outrage to Common Decency: Historical Perspectives on Child Neglect." In E. Smith and Merkel-Holguin (eds.), *A History of Child Welfare.* New Brunswick, NJ: Transaction Publishers.

_____. 1995. *Manufacturing 'Bad Mothers': A Critical Perspective on Child Neglect.* Toronto: University of Toronto Press

_____. 1995. "An Outrage to Common Decency: Historical Perspectives on Child Neglect." *Child Welfare* 74, 1.

Szasz, T. 1974. *The Myth of Mental Illness: Foundations of a Theory of Personal Conduct.* New York: Harper and Row.

_____. 1970a. *Ideology and Insanity: Essays on the Psychiatric Dehumanization of Man.* Garden City, NY: Doubleday.

_____. 1970b. *The Manufacture of Madness.* New York: Dell.

_____. 1968. "The Myth of Mental Illness." In S. Spitzer and N. Denzin (eds.), *The Mental Patient: Studies in the Sociology of Deviance.* New York: McGraw-Hill.

Tanesini, A. 1999. *An Introduction to Feminist Epistemologies.* Malden, MA: Blackwell.

Teeple, G. 2000. *Globalization and the Decline of Social Reform.* Second edition. Toronto: Garamond Press.

Tester, F. 2003. "Anti-Oppressive Theory and Practice as the Organizing Theme for Social Work Education." *Canadian Social Work Review* 20, 1.

Tharao, E., and N. Massaquoi. 2002. "Black Women and HIV/AIDS: Contextualizing Their Realities, Their Silence and Proposing Solutions." *Canadian Women's Studies* 21, 2.

Tharao, E., N. Massaquoi, and S. Teclom. 2006. *Silent Voices of the HIV/AIDS Epidemic: African and Caribbean Women in Toronto 2002–2004.* Toronto: Women's Health in Women's Hands.

This Day. 2008. "FG Ordered to Produce Documents on Approval of Clinical Study." Available at <allafrica.com/stories/printable/200804280884.html> (accessed May 28, 2008).

Thomas, B. 1987. *Multiculturalism at Work: A Guide to Organizational Change.* Toronto: YWCA of Metropolitan Toronto.

Thomas, J. 1994. *Teachings from the Longhouse.* Toronto, ON: Stoddart Publishing.

Thomason, T.C. 1991. "Counseling Native Americans: An Introduction for Non-Native

American Counselors." *Journal of Counseling & Development* 69 (March/April).

Thompson, J., P. Baird, and J. Downie. 2001. "The Olivieri Report: The Complete Text of the Report of the Independent Inquiry Commissioned by the Canadian Association of University Teachers." Toronto: J. Lorimer.

Tibbetts, J. 2007. "Universities Shouldn't Accept Corporate Research Funding." *Ottawa Citizen,* November 04.

Todd, S. 2005. "Unfinished Fictions: Becoming and Unbecoming Feminist Community Organizers." In S. Hick, J. Fook, and R. Pozzuto (eds.), *Social Work: A Critical Turn.* Toronto: Thompson Educational Publishing.

Todd, S., and D. Coholic. 2007. "Christian Fundamentalism and Anti-Oppressive Social Work Pedagogy." *Journal of Teaching in Social Work* 27, ¾.

Travers, R., M.G. Wilson, S. Flicker, A. Guta, T. Bereket, C. McKay, A. Van der Meulen, S. Cleverly, and S.B. Rourke. 2008. "The Greater Involvement of People Living with AIDS Principle: Theory vs. Practice in Ontario's HIV/AIDS Community-Based Research Sector." *AIDS Care* 20, 6.

Trevithick, P. 2003. "Effective Relationship-Based Practice: A Theoretical Exploration." *Journal of Social Work Practice* 17, 2.

Trocmé, N., B. Fallon, B. MacLaurin, J. Daciuk, C. Felstiner, T. Black, et al. 2005. *Canadian Incidence Study of Reported Child Abuse and Neglect.* Ottawa, ON: Minister of Public Works and Government Services Canada.

Trotter, C. 2004. *Helping Abused Children and Their Families.* Thousand Oaks: Sage.

_____. 2002. "Worker Skill and Client Outcome in Child Protection." *Child Abuse Review* 11, 1.

Turney, D. 1999. "Speaking up and Speaking out: A Dialogic Approach to Anti-Oppressive Practice." In A. Jokinen, K. Juhila, and T. Posco (eds.), *Constructing Social Work Practice.* Aldershot, UK: Ashgate.

UNAIDS. 2007. *The Greater Involvement of People Living with HIV (GIPA).* UNAIDS Policy Brief, Joint United Nations Programme on HIV/AIDS, March.

University of Michigan Edward Ginsberg Center for Community Service and Learning, <quod.lib.umich.edu/m/mjcsl>.

van de Luitgaarden, G.M.J. 2009. "Evidence-Based Practice in Social Work: Lessons from Judgment and Decision-Making Theory." *British Journal of Social Work* 39.

Van Den Bergh, N., and L. Cooper (eds.). 1986. *Feminist Visions for Social Work.* Silver Spring, MD: National Association of Social Work.

Van Soest, D. 1995. "Multiculturalism and Social Work Education: The Non-Debate about Competing Perspectives." *Journal of Social Work Education,* 31.

Wade, A. 1995. "Resistance Knowledges: Therapy with Aboriginal Persons Who Have Experienced Violence." In P. Stevenson, S. Elliott, T. Foster, and J. Harris (eds.), *A Persistent Spirit Towards Understanding Aboriginal Health in British Columbia.* Victoria: Department of Geography, University of Victoria.

Wainwright, H. 2003. "Making a People's Budget in Porto Algre." *North American Congress on Latin America Report on the Americas* 36, 5 (Mar/Apr).

Walker, L. 1991. "Post-Traumatic Stress Disorder in Women: Diagnosis and Treatment of Battered Woman Syndrome." *Psychotherapy* 28, 1, Spring.

_____. 1990. "Feminist Ethics with Victims Of Violence." In H. Lerman and N. Porter (eds.), *Feminist Ethics in Psychotherapy.* New York: Springer.

_____. 1985. "Feminist Therapy with Victim/Survivors of Interpersonal Violence." In

L. Rosewater and L. Walker (eds.), *Handbook of Feminist Therapy: Women's Issues in Psychotherapy*. New York: Springer.

_____ (ed.). 1984. *Women and Mental Health Policy*. London: Sage Publications.

Wallace, P.A.W. 1997. *The White Roots of Peace*. Ohsweken, ON: Irocrafts.

Watson, N., L. Mckie, B. Hughes, D. Hopkins, and S. Gregory. 2004. "(Inter) Dependence, Needs and Care: The Potential for Disability and Feminist Theorists to Develop an Emancipatory Model." *Sociology* 38, 2.

Webb, S. 2002. "Evidence-Based Practice and Decision Analysis in Social Work: An Implementation Model." *Journal of Social Work* 2, 1.

_____. 2001. "Some Considerations on the Validity of Evidence-Based Practice in Social Work." *British Journal of Social Work* 31.

Weeks, W. 1994. *Women Working Together: Lessons from Feminist Women's Services*. Melbourne: Longman.

Wehbi, S. 2009. "Deconstructing Motivations: Challenging International Social Work Placements." *International Social Work* 52, 1.

_____. 2008. "Teaching International Social Work: A Guiding Framework." *Canadian Social Work Review* 25, 2.

_____. 2006. "The Challenges of Inclusive Education in Lebanon." *Disability & Society* 21, 4.

_____. 2002. "'Women with Nothing to Lose': Marriageability and Women's Perceptions of Rape and Consent in Contemporary Beirut." *Women's Studies International Forum* 25, 3.

Wehbi, S., and Y. El-Lahib. 2007a. "The Employment Situation of pwds in Lebanon: Challenges and Opportunities." *Disability & Society* 22, 4.

_____. 2007b. "Organizing For the Voting Rights of pwds in Lebanon: Reflections for Activists." *Equal Opportunities International* 26, 5.

Weinberg, M. 2009. "Moral Distress: A Missing but Relevant Concept for Ethics in Social Work." *Canadian Social Work Review* 26, 2.

Weir, R. 1996. *Beyond Labor's Veil. TheCculture of the Knights of Labor*. University Park, PA: Pennsylvania State University Press.

Werbner, P. 1997. "Essentialising Essentialism, Essentialising Silence: Ambivalence and Multiplicity in the Construction of Racism and Ethnicity." In P. Werbner and T. Modood (eds.), *Debating Cultural Hybridity: Multicultural Identities and the Politics of Antiracism*. London: Zed Books.

Wise, C., and D.H. Zimmerman. 1987. "Doing Gender." *Gender and Society* 1, 2.

Westhues, A. 2003. "The Challenges Ahead." In A. Westhues (ed.), *Canadian Social Policy, Issues and Perspectives*. Third edition. Waterloo, ON: Wilfred Laurier University Press.

Westhues, A., S. Cadell, J. Karabanow, L. Maxwell, and M. Sanchez. 1999. "The Creation of Knowledge: Linking Research Paradigms to Practice." *Canadian Social Work Review* 16, 2.

Wetherly, P. 2008. "Can Capitalists Use the State to Serve Their General Interests." In P. Wetherly, C.W. Barrow, and P. Burnham (eds.), *Class, Power and the State in Capitalist Society: Essays on Ralph Miliband*. Basingstoke and New York: Palgrave and Macmillan.

Wexler, S. 1970. "Practicing Law for Poor People." *Yale Law Journal*.

Wharf, B., and M. Clague. 1997. *Community Organizing: Canadian Experiences*. Toronto:

Oxford University Press

Wheeler, D.P., and T.M. Parchment. 2009. "Building Capacity for Evidence We Can Believe In: The Argument for Social Change as an Evidence-Based Practice Agenda." *Health and Social Work* 34, 1.

White, M. 2007. *Maps of Narrative Practice*. New York: W.W. Norton.

_____. 2004. "Narrative Therapy Series: Narrative Therapy — New Modalities of Practice." Workshop notes. Truro, Nova Scotia, March 8–9, 2003.

_____. 2001. "Narrative Practice and the Unpacking of Identity Conclusions." *Gecko: A Journal of Deconstruction and Narrative Ideas in Therapeutic Practice* 1.

_____. 1995. *Re-Authoring Lives: Interviews & Essays*. Adelaide: Dulwich Centre Publications.

_____. 1994. "The Politics of Therapy: Putting to Rest the Illusion of Neutrality." *Dulwich Centre*.

_____. 1991. "Deconstruction and Therapy." *Dulwich Centre Newsletter* 3.

_____. 1989a. "The world of Experience and Meaning." *Dulwich Centre Newsletter* 1–2.

_____. 1989b. "Therapy in the World of Experience." *Dulwich Centre Newsletter* 4–6.

_____. 1989c. "Narrative Therapy: What Sort of Internalizing Conversations?" *Dulwich Centre Newsletter* 1–5.

White, M., and D. Epston. 1990. *Narrative Means to Therapeutic Ends*. New York: W.W. Norton.

Wijeyesinghe, C.L., P. Griffin, and B. Lowe. 1997. "Racism Curriculum Design." In M. Adams, L.A. Bell, and P. Griffin (eds.), *Teaching for Diversity and Social Justice: A Sourcebook*. London: Routledge

Williams, C. 1999. "Connecting Anti-Racist and Anti-Oppressive Theory And Practice: Retrenchment or Reappraisal?" *British Journal of Social Work* 29.

Wiseman, J. 1998. *Global Nation? Australia and the Politics of Globalization*. Cambridge: Cambridge University Press.

_____. 1996. "National Social Policy in an Age of Global Power? Lessons from Canada and Australia." In J. Pulkingham and G. Ternowetsky (eds.), *Remaking Canadian Social Policy: Social Security in the Late 1990s*. Halifax/Winnipeg: Fernwood Publishing.

Withorn, A. 1984. *Serving the People: Social Service and Social Change*. New York: Columbia University Press.

Witkin, S.L., and W.D. Harrison. 2001. "Whose Evidence and For What Purpose?" *Social Work* 46, 4.

Wong, M-K. 2000. "A New Look at Self-Determination." In L. Napier and J. Fook (eds.), *Breakthroughs in Practice: Theorizing Critical Moments in Social Work*. London: Whiting and Birch.

Worell, J., and P. Remer. 1992. *Feminist Perspectives in Therapy. An Empowerment Model*. New York: Wiley.

Wyeth. 2009. "Wyeth Reports Earnings Results for the 2009 Second Quarter and First Half and Raises Full Year 2009 Guidance." Available at <idea.sec.gov/Archives/edgar/data/5187/000119312509153575/dex991.htm>.

Yee, J. 2005. "Critical Anti-Racism Praxis: The Concept of Whiteness Implicated." In S Hook, J Fook and R Pozzuto (eds,), *Social Work: A Critical Turn*. Toronto: Thompson.

Yeo, R., and K. Moore. 2003. "Including Disabled People in Poverty Reduction Work:

'Nothing about Us, without Us'." *World Development* 31, 3.

Zedong, M. 1962. *Mao Tse-Tung: An Anthology of his Writings, 1893–1976*. New York: New American Library.

Zlotnik, J., D. Biegel, and B. Solt. 2002. "The Institute for the Advancement of Social Work Research: Strengthening Social Work Research in Practice and Policy." *Research on Social Work Practice* 12, 2.

Zola, K. 1981. "Medicine as an Institution of Social Control." In P. Conrad and R. Kern, (eds.), *The Sociology of Health and Illness: A Critical Perspective*. New York: St. Martin's Press.

Index

Acknowledgements

As with every political project, this book came to be only because of the work and creativity of many lovely people. I would like to thank all the authors for their hard work, keen analysis, and good humour. Huge gratitude is extended to my research assistant, Evgeny Neiterman, who also worked on the first edition of this book. Linn Clark deserves much applause for her helpful edits and good humour. I also want to thank Dr. Tracy McIntosh, Dr. Bruce Curtis, and the Sociology Department at the University of Auckland for providing me an office in which to spend my research leave and work on this book, as well as top-notch collegiality, great discussions, endless hot beverages in the best tea room in the world, and lots of fun and friendship. Many academics, students, and practitioners provided feedback on the first edition, which strengthened this edition immeasurably. They are too numerous to list but I want to thank them for their insights, commitment to social justice practice, and willingness to engage with this project.

Once again the team at Fernwood has offered unparalleled support and skill, especially Wayne Antony. Special thanks to Wayne for his warmth and compassion in shepherding the book through the final bits of work. Also, thanks to Judith Kearns and Brian Turner for their copy editing of the final manuscript and to the production group at Fernwood. Thanks are also due to three anonymous reviewers for very helpful and constructive feedback and insights. Any errors remain my own....

And oceans of thanks to those in my home life: Jim, Maxine, and Thea. As Che Guevara said, "At the risk of seeming ridiculous, let me say that the true revolutionary is guided by a great feeling of love."